THE UNFINISHED
PALAZZO

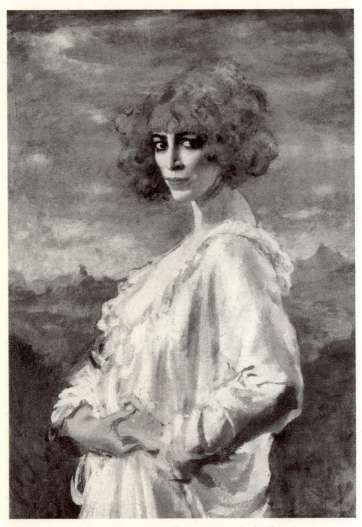
Luisa Casati, painted by Augustus John (1919).

Judith Mackrell

THE
UNFINISHED
PALAZZO

LIFE, LOVE AND ART
IN VENICE

The stories of
Luisa Casati, Doris Castlerosse
and Peggy Guggenheim

With 69 illustrations

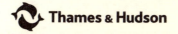
Thames & Hudson

Judith Mackrell is the Guardian's dance critic and a successful author of biographical non-fiction titles including *Bloomsbury Ballerina: Lydia Lopokova, Imperial Dancer and Mrs John Maynard Keynes* and *Flappers: Six Women of a Dangerous Generation*.

First published in the United Kingdom in 2017
by Thames & Hudson Ltd,
181A High Holborn, London WC1V 7QX

This compact paperback edition first published in 2018

The Unfinished Palazzo: Life, Love and Art in Venice
© 2017 and 2018 Thames & Hudson Ltd, London
Text © 2017 and 2018 Judith Mackrell

Page design by Lisa Ifsits

British Library Cataloguing-in-Publication Data
A catalogue record for this book is available from
the British Library

ISBN 978-0-500-29443-7

Printed and bound in the UK by CPI (UK) Ltd

To find out about all our publications, please visit
www.thamesandhudson.com.
There you can subscribe to our e-newsletter,
browse or download our current catalogue,
and buy any titles that are in print.

CONTENTS

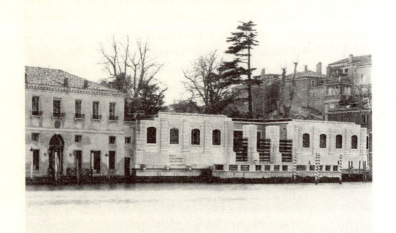

The Palazzo Venier dei Leoni in the late 20th century
– home of the Peggy Guggenheim Collection.

INTRODUCTION

One hot evening in September 1913 a traffic jam formed on the Grand Canal in Venice, as gondolas ferrying elaborately costumed partygoers converged on the eastern stretch of the water, just as it widened out towards the lagoon. Buildings of great distinction lined the canal here, their façades glowing with the light of enormous glass chandeliers that hung from their upper stories, their magnificence reflected back at them from the waters below. Yet in the middle of this classic Venetian scene, one building obtruded like a broken tooth. Only one storey high, the Palazzo Venier dei Leoni appeared to be in a state of near-dereliction, its white stone walls overrun with ivy, its roof gaping with holes.

It was to this building, however, that the gondolas were heading. A halo of golden lights shimmered over its roof, music could be heard from its grounds and on the wide waterfront terrace a spectacular scene of greeting was in progress. Two black men, six feet tall and costumed as Nubian slaves, stood on either side of the landing steps; one of them was striking a ceremonial gong to herald the arriving boats, the other throwing metal filings onto a brazier and sending flares of white light up into the night sky. A little way behind was the party's hostess, a tall, narrow woman dressed like a Persian princess in a gauzy costume of white and gold. She stood in the centre of a wide shallow bowl filled with tuberoses; and as she received her guests she uttered no words of welcome, gave no smile of recognition, but simply bent to hand each one a single flower.

During the three years in which the Marchesa Luisa Casati had been tenant of the Palazzo Venier, she and her parties had become the stuff of local legend. Although she was by nature profoundly and eccentrically shy, she was convinced that she possessed the soul of an artist and that it was her métier to turn herself and her surroundings into works of art. Even in a city famous for its carnivals and masquerades, there was nothing to match the theatre of the Marchesa's entertainments, and all of her guests were expected to play their parts. As she stood silent and grave among the tuberoses, the men and women alighting from their gondolas on that September night were titled socialites in harem trousers, middle-aged painters with turbans and false beards – a colourfully self-conscious assortment of slave girls, pashas and booted corsairs.

Oriental parties were much in vogue during this last summer before the Great War, but few had so apt a setting as this. Once the Marchesa's guests had been ushered through the palazzo's crumbling portico, they found themselves in a scene of improbable fantasy. In place of the gloomy marbled expanse of a typical entrance hall was a gold-coloured salon, shimmering with mirrors and noisy with the chatter of caged monkeys and parrots. Beyond the salon lay an overgrown garden in which white peacocks, pedigree greyhounds and a semi-tame cheetah roamed among gold-painted statues. As waiters in richly dyed brocade served flutes of champagne, as a black jazz band played ragtime and tango, the world Luisa had created in her palazzo that night was as elaborate, as flamboyant a meeting place of east and west as the history of Venice itself.

* * * * *

Luisa's world could not have been more different from the vision that had inspired the Venier family to commission the palazzo in the mid-18th century. The Veniers were one of the great Venetian dynasties, dating their ancestry back to the Emperors Valerian and Gallienus, who'd ruled over 3rd-century Rome; they claimed to be among the earliest settlers in Venice, back in a time when it had been little more than a precarious island outpost salvaged from mud, marsh and sea.*

As the city had expanded into a powerful republic, the Veniers too had risen to prominence. One of the tightly knit caste of families listed in the city's Golden Book of nobility (a register of all those qualified for

---

* The Venier family name first appeared in official documents in the year 1009. Their property holdings were not only extensive in Venice, but also in Dalmatia and the Veronese.

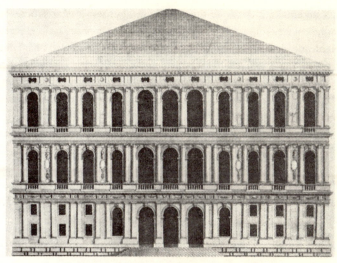

The palazzo as it was envisaged by the Venier family
in the mid-18th century, a monument to dynastic pride.

high office), they had served as doges, procurators, archbishops, admirals and consuls. They had reached the apex of their glory in 1571 when their most distinguished patriarch, the Admiral Sebastiano Venier, had led the Venetian fleet to a historic victory against the Turks. Even though the admiral had been seventy-five years old when he'd fought at the Battle of Lepanto – even though he'd had to wear slippers because his feet were so badly calloused, and had been too weak to load his own crossbow – it had been Sebastiano's fire that claimed the first Turkish victims, and his courage that galvanized the fleet to victory. Afterwards the admiral was lionized by a grateful city. Tintoretto painted his portrait – a sage and silver-haired warrior in shining armour – and he was unanimously elected Doge.

The Veniers were even more successful as traders than they were as politicians, accumulating riches both within the city and beyond. If a whisper of corruption was attached to some of their enterprises, if Venier ships were rumoured to conduct illegal piratical operations on the fringes of the Venetian empire, they had money enough to redeem their reputation. Across Venice an increasing number of monuments, churches, streets and palaces began to boast the Venier name, including the old towered palazzo on the Dorsoduro bank of the Grand Canal that had been the family's principal dwelling since the mid-14th century.

By 1749, that palazzo had been subdivided to accommodate several branches of the family, and Nicolò Venier and his brother were ready to expand onto the vacant plot next door. The architect Lorenzo Boschetti was hired to design a new, modern building that would make the grandest possible statement of Venier pride: a five-storey neoclassical stone palazzo with a ground floor, mezzanine, two *piani nobili* and an attic. It would be not only one of the tallest domestic properties on that stretch of the canal, but also the widest.

The family knew they would have to wait two, maybe three decades to see this vision materialize. There had been a short delay at the start of the project – for some reason Boschetti passed it on to a more junior architect, Domenico Rizzi, and it was not until 1752 that work began on laying the foundations. Given the marshiness of the terrain, this was a complex project in itself: a forest of slender pine pilings had to be driven deep into the Venetian ooze, ready to support the thin wooden platform and brickwork on which the building would rest. Some of the workforce who laboured on site, through the summer mosquitoes, the high autumn tides and dank winter mists, would not expect to see the building's completion. But the family Corner, who lived on the opposite bank of the canal, watched its progress with close and hostile attention. Their own palace, known locally as Ca' Grande, had long dominated the neighbourhood, but as the Venier palazzo slowly rose above ground the Corners realized they were going to be overshadowed by a building of an even more arrogant scale.

The Corner family pride, as well as the Corner views of Venice, were under threat, and they petitioned the city council with demands that the Venier project be scaled down or even stopped. Work continued, however, until the front section of the basement and ground floor were nearly complete. The three pillars that would eventually form the triple-arched portico were in place, and jutting from the base of the building were eight stone lion heads, their eight mouths carved in identically regal snarls.

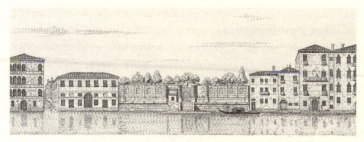

'Il palazzo non finito' – the Veniers' aborted building project,
shown in an 1831 engraving.

But at that point, construction of the Palazzo Venier dei Leoni came to an abrupt halt. Many explanations have been offered, but as is often the way with Venetian folklore, none comes with any hard proof. The scale of the building may finally have attracted official concern and been judged too large, too unstable for that particular site;* it's equally possible that the Veniers had overstretched themselves financially and, because of some bad trade or lost lawsuit, were unable to continue the construction work as planned. There is a suggestion, too, that the family's dynastic ambitions had crumbled with their failure to produce a new generation of sons and heirs. Whatever the reason, when Nicolò Venier died in 1780 the great scheme had been aborted and the building was left at a dwarfish approximation of its original scale – just a single storey high, and two rooms deep. Far from being a monument to the family name, it would soon become known derisively in Venice as *il palazzo non finito*: the Unfinished Palace.

* * * * *

The Veniers were not the only family in Venice to suffer a downturn in their fortunes at the end of the 18th century. For hundreds of years, the Venetian nobility had grown rich on the city's trading links with the

---

* This would be supported by the fact that the façade of the old palazzo next door had cracked during construction, and the whole edifice had been demolished three decades later.

east and on its own superior system of banking. Yet by the 17th century
the Turks, British and Dutch were all taking trade routes and custom
away from Venice; and as the city's economy began to falter, it became
renowned less for its financial acuity than for its gambling, its prostitu-
tion and the excesses of its carnival season. In 1797, when Napoleon's
troops invaded Venice and put an end to its 1,000-year history of independence, there were some who saw it as a necessary punishment for
a city grown decadent and slack.

During Napoleon's occupation, the political power of the Venetian
nobility was broken and many of its families were stripped of their

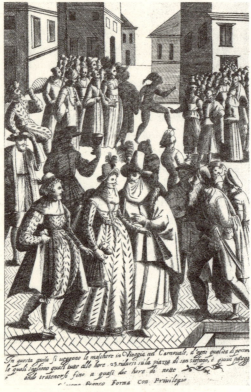

Seventeenth-century Venice
during carnival season.

treasures and homes. If the Veniers had ever hoped to restart the building of their own palazzo, their plans were derailed by the French; and they were doomed entirely when Venice was handed over to Austria in 1815. During the five decades of the Austrian occupation the city went into dismal decline, its economy shackled and its great ship-building industry broken apart. Although it acquired a different kind of melancholic beauty, which appealed to the romantically inclined tourists of the 19th century, the reality of Venetian life was grim, with many of its neighbourhoods sunk into squalor and its population depleted by poverty, unemployment and chronic ill health.

The Unfinished Palazzo, meanwhile, had been inherited in 1780 by Nicolò's cousin Maria – the daughter of Girolamo Venier, a proud patrician and talented amateur composer. Maria had inherited her father's musical gifts; back in 1758, when she'd married into the prominent Contarini family, her wedding had been marked with the publication of a beautifully ornamented collection of poetry and songs. It's possible to imagine that Maria made the palazzo a place of music, conversation and light during her brief occupancy, but after her death, her son Girolamo Contarini seems to have let it fall into decay. Given its unfinished state, the building did not weather well; and while its basement floor was eventually converted to a cheap boarding house, one area of the ground floor became uninhabitable as ivy gained deeper purchase on the crumbling walls, and parts of the roof began to cave.

Every few years, one of the neighbours would petition to have the building torn down, but it was eventually bought and saved by a wealthy French aristocrat, the Comtesse Isabelle de la Baume-Pluvinel. Towards the end of the 19th century the Comtesse had purchased the nearby Ca' Dario, one of the loveliest buildings on that stretch of canal, with its delicate columns, stone latticework, Islamic arches and lustrous marble inlay. The Comtesse may have had plans for the Venier palazzo too, but by 1910 her health was failing and she was seeking a tenant to take the property off her hands. It may have been a mystery to her why the young and extremely rich Marchesa Casati should be so eager to rent such a decrepit property. But while the rest of the world saw the building as a crumbling eyesore, to Luisa it was a place of poetic mystery and potential.

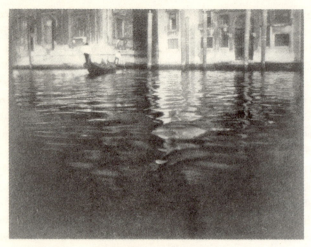

'A city floating in the sea' –
Venice photographed in 1913.

Like so many before and after her, Luisa had been drawn to Venice
by a fantasy. She had seen it as a place of otherwordly beauty – a city
floating in the sea, where solid stone dissolved into water and light –
but she also saw it as place of magical otherness. For centuries, Venice
had been the favoured destination of poets and artists, promising an
escape from the drabness and constraint of ordinary life. When Byron
came to live in the city in 1816, he greeted it as the 'greenest island
of my imagination'; when Proust arrived, he exclaimed that his dream
had become his address. And when Luisa came to Venice, she too was
hoping to find her own 'heterotopia', a parallel world where she could
escape the tedium of her life among the Milanese aristocracy and create
a new, theatrical persona on the stage of the Unfinished Palazzo.

* * * * *

Luisa rented the palazzo for fourteen years, during which she and her
parties came to rank as one of the temporary wonders of the city. After
she moved on, it was that same lure of the Venetian life, with its promise of freedom and fresh beginnings, that drew two other women to the

palazzo. For Doris, Lady Castlerosse, Venice represented the chance to relaunch her social career after her husband had left her and her private life had become the subject of scandal. Doris had risen through the ranks of London society on the strength of her youth, wit and startling sexual charisma, but by the mid-1930s, as her reputation began to tarnish and middle age loomed, she needed to make a new start. Venice was far more forgiving than London; and, funded by one of her wealthy lovers, Doris had the palazzo refurbished into a luxurious summer salon from which she intended to hold court over the city.

The Second World War put an end to Doris's aspirations, however, and the building was again lying empty and neglected when Peggy Guggenheim came to view it in late 1948. After two failed marriages and a string of unhappy love affairs, Peggy was restless and lonely, yet she was also in possession of a remarkable collection of modern art to which she'd dedicated most of her inheritance and her energy. Bruised by her recent experience of the competitive art world of New York, she was in search of a more accommodating and uncritical place to settle. Having purchased the palazzo, she stripped out the remains of Doris's ostentatious decor and turned the building into a showcase for her art. She would remain there until her death, some thirty years later, and today the palazzo lives on as the home of the Peggy Guggenheim Collection.

The lives that Luisa Casati, Doris Castlerosse and Peggy Guggenheim fashioned for themselves in the Palazzo Venier were unlike anything Nicolò Venier could have imagined when he first commissioned it. There is a fine historical irony in the fact that a building designed to glorify a patriarchal dynasty, and one that had been left to rot once that dynasty crumbled, was eventually rescued from obscurity by three independent single women. Luisa made it notorious; Doris made it smart; and Peggy, finally, transformed it not only into one of the world's great museums, but one of the most beloved and most visited buildings in Venice.

LUISA CASATI

THE LIVING
WORK OF ART

CHAPTER 1

The building had looked barely habitable when Luisa Casati first came to view it in 1910. Open sky was visible through sections of the flat stone roof, and rough wooden boarding patched up holes in the exterior walls. The basement was mildewed with damp and the grounds, hedged by a dark line of cypress and lime trees, were overrun with brambles. In Venice's official register of properties, the Palazzo Venier did not even rank as a proper dwelling, merely 'a garden with the fundamentals of a palace'.

Yet if the building was nearly derelict, the sweep of its waterfront terrace was still intact, and with it came one of the most commanding views of Venice. Directly opposite was the still-magnificent Ca' Grande, now converted to the offices of the city's Prefecture. To the left was the Accademia Bridge, and to the right, as the canal widened out towards the lagoon, sky and water met over a tumble of crooked chimneys, domed roofs and the restless weave of Venetian water traffic: gondolas, vaporetti, tradesmen's boats and tall sailing ships.

To possess such a view, to see it flat and enamelled in the midday sun, silvered by moonlight or wreathed in dawn mist, was part of the dream that had gripped Luisa when she'd first come to Venice in 1905 – a rich, nervous, impressionable young woman, travelling by herself. Her imagination had vibrated with expectations of a city that would be magically unlike the bustling, commercial urbanity of her home in Milan, a city that her friend, the celebrated writer Gabriele D'Annunzio, considered to be the 'most wonderful' union of art and life. It was partly through the rapturous prose of D'Annunzio's Venetian novel *Il fuoco* (Fire) that Luisa's first impressions of Venice were filtered: the 'flaming gold' of a sunset over the lagoon; the 'mysterious and fantastic obscurity of the little canals': the drama of a city where every sensual impression of the present was freighted with stories of the past.[1]

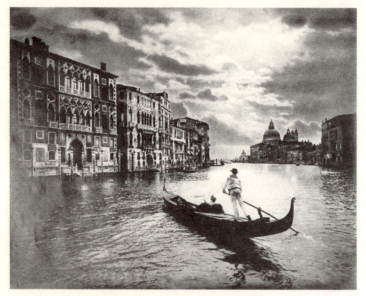

A gondola on the Grand Canal, c. 1900.
The Venier palazzo is on the far right bank.

During that first visit Luisa would have explored the city like any privileged tourist: setting out from her hotel suite for tours of churches and galleries, retaining a pair of gondoliers for daily trips around the canals. Luisa had an educated eye for the buildings that she passed: she could admire the dusky, peeling coloration of pink and umber stucco, the rich patina of gilt, mosaic, marble and old red brick. She could respond to the enchantment of the light as it glanced off the water and made shadow patterns under bridges and steps. But even now, Luisa was aspiring to be more than a tourist. She was only twenty-four; she had left a husband and tiny daughter at home; yet already she was envisaging the city as the backdrop to a life she would lead entirely on her own.

Afterwards Luisa was obliged to return to Milan, but as a promise to the future she took back home a pair of decorative 'negro' statues that seemed to her particularly emblematic of Venice. Many of the city's larger dwellings had their entrance halls adorned with such figures

– naked African women laden with gold necklaces and bangles; spear-carrying warriors in turbans and breastplates; or diminutive slave boys holding out trays for the depositing of cigar butts and calling cards. These statues, both exotic and crass, told a story of the city's chequered racial attitudes, harking back to a period when Venice used former West African slaves as gondoliers, but also to a period when black sailors and merchants were a far more familiar and accepted presence on the streets than they would have been in other European cities. Luisa, however, saw only an arresting novelty and charm in the two black figures that she installed in her Milan townhouse. So blind was she to the possible offence of her 'Venetian blackamoors', as such pieces were widely known, that five years later when she took over the Venier palace she took the tradition to her own theatrical extremes and made a point of having black servants to attend her.

These men may well have been hired from the North African immigrant community in Paris; and if the work Luisa offered was relatively undemanding, it was also demeaning. When she processed around the city she would always have a tall black manservant walking just behind her, holding up a peacock-feathered parasol to shade her from the sun. When she held the largest of her parties in Venice, the black staff who were hired as extra help would be subjected to her artistic caprices, dressed up in 18th-century wigs and frock coats, stripped to the waist and painted gold; or, for one very public event that Luisa held in the Piazza San Marco, roped together with scarlet silk to form a human barrier against the crowds.

* * * * *

Such a degree of entitlement and ostentation would have been impossible to envisage for anyone who'd known Luisa as a small child, when, curled up in a corner with her books, drawings and daydreams, she'd actively flinched from drawing attention to herself. Accounts of Luisa's early life are sketchy, but they indicate that she was an intensely withdrawn little girl. She was deeply attached to her mother Lucia and to her lively older sister Francesca, but in the company of anyone other than her family, she slid into a shell of stubborn silence. Within a less protective household her manner might have been punished as wilful or rude.

But Luisa was born into love and money, and during the first years of her childhood her behaviour was put down to an unfortunate shyness which it was assumed she would eventually grow out of.

The family's wealth had been amassed by Luisa's father, Alberto Amman, a clever, striving man who'd built on the foundations of his father's cotton mill to develop the most streamlined textile plant in Italy. Assisted by his business partner Emilio Wepfer, he'd installed the latest technologies from Britain and instituted efficiently humane conditions for the workforce. Despite the uncertain economy of the newly unified Italy, the two men had prospered, and Alberto's professional star reached its zenith in 1887 when, in recognition of his contribution to industry, he was honoured with the title of Conte.*

Together with his wife Lucia, a pretty, sociable and artistic young woman from Vienna, Alberto established a domestic life to match his professional eminence. The couple had married in 1879, producing Francesca in January 1880 and Luisa Adele Rosa Maria almost exactly a year later on 23 January 1881. Their lives were divided between their several residences: a town house in Milan; a villa further north near the mill in Pordenone; and a country retreat close to the summer residence of King Umberto 1 – whom Alberto was proud to claim as a personal friend. But their principal home, and the main setting of Luisa's privileged childhood, was the magnificently romantic Villa Amalia, nestling in the foothills of the Lombardy Alps.

It was a large neoclassical building, and as the former summer residence of Count Roco Maliani, a leading politician, it had been designed to impress – with columns and pediments strutting along its front façade, and ceilings painted by the Renaissance master Bernardino Luini. Yet the villa's rambling grounds were its special beauty, planted with coppices and scented shrubs, with landscaped walkways that wound through classical statuary, a Grecian 'temple d'amitié', and fountains festooned with nymphs and gods.

---

*   The Amman mill became famous for its standards of safety, its maintenance of basic employment rights and its provision of decent lodgings and schooling for workers and their families. Alberto's other great success was the establishment of a national guild of cotton spinners – the Associazione Cotoniera Italiana.

The Ammans entertained frequently – dinners in the winter, picnics and croquet parties in the summer. But if Lucia was a busy hostess, she seems, by the conventions of the times, to have been an involved and loving mother. Years later Luisa would cling to the memory of Lucia's bedtime kiss, 'her laces jewels and pearls brush[ing] my face and mingling with the scent of her perfume', and would recall the afternoons they had spent together, reading fairy tales and leafing through the pictures in *L'Illustration*, the lavish French periodical that reported on the lives, fashions and houses of the European élite.[2]

Luisa was quietly content within this world of social fantasy and make-believe. With her sister Francesca she played games of dressing up, raiding the family wardrobes for hats, cloaks, dresses. Left to herself she drew in her sketchbooks, or cut out images from magazines that she assembled into fanciful collages. When guests were in the house Luisa could rarely be coaxed into joining their activities, but was happy to draw them, posed into formal groups like the pictures she saw in *L'Illustration* and with Alberto Amman in the centre, as king of his domestic court.

Lucia encouraged her daughter's creative gifts, introducing her to the art treasures in nearby Milan, the old masters at the Brera Museum, Leonardo da Vinci's *Last Supper* at the convent of Santa Maria delle Grazie. Yet when Luisa studied these works or produced her own little pieces there was an intensity to her concentration that suggested these images were more real, more present to her than ordinary life. By the time she approached puberty, Lucia may have begun to worry that her daughter's reclusive nature was more than a childish form of shyness. She was still stubbornly withdrawn, socially farouche, and her confidence was not improved by her newly teenage appearance: her limbs all sharpness and angles, her thin face dominated by her enormous greenish eyes and by her mane of thick, unruly brown hair. Already Lucia may have begun to wonder what kind of future her daughter could look forward to; to worry how she would ever find the confidence to marry and run her own household. And she would have worried far more profoundly if she had known that Luisa would be navigating these adult transitions without her.

Luisa was just thirteen when, in April 1894, Lucia and Alberto left her and Francesca with servants at the Milan town house while they took a short business trip to Florence. Alberto had been working excessively hard since the recent death of his partner, and such trips were not unusual. However, he and Lucia had promised that as soon as they returned they would take the sisters on a short family holiday to Turin. The city was a small, beautifully preserved gem of Renaissance architecture and a popular destination for wealthy Italians; for the teenage Amman girls it promised a rare family outing, and a rare change of scene. But on 11 April, while they were awaiting their parents' return, Luisa and Francesca received the shattering news that their mother had died.

Lucia had been so youthfully pretty, with her creamy skin, black curls and lively dark eyes, that her death must have seemed inconceivable to her daughters, and it's likely that she had fallen victim to the influenza pandemic that was rampant in Europe during the 1890s. The illness struck indiscriminately, killing the young and healthy as well as the sickly and old, and its course could be cruelly rapid, moving from the first symptoms of nausea to the final asphyxiating attack in just a few short hours.

This sudden loss of their mother, followed by the grim ceremony of her interment in the family mausoleum, was traumatic for both girls, yet for Luisa it was particularly hard. She'd depended on Lucia to mediate between her and the outside world, and without her patience and understanding she was in danger of withdrawing entirely into her shell. But if Alberto was worried about the fragile state of his youngest daughter, he was helplessly ill-equipped to deal with her. His own response to his wife's death was to bury his grief in work, and it was work, the family believed, that killed him as well. Just two years after Lucia, Alberto fell ill and died.

Although their father had been a more distant figure, this was yet another tragedy for the sisters. For their uncle Eduardo and his wife Fanny it presented a formidable duty of care. By the ages of fifteen and sixteen Luisa and Francesca had not only been orphaned, they'd been made heirs to a vast fortune, each of them inheriting a half-share of Alberto's cotton business, his several properties and his impressive portfolio of stocks and shares. Although they were still too young to control the money themselves, the sisters would soon be old enough to attract the interest of fortune hunters.

In practical ways, Eduardo and Fanny tried to maintain some continuity in their nieces' lives. The two girls lived part of the time at their uncle's house at Ello – a short carriage ride away – but they also stayed at Villa Amalia, where there was a large staff to care for them. Diversions were arranged: there were trips to the shops and museums in Milan, games of tennis and riding, and their gregarious cousin Bice kept them company. But while Luisa became passionate about horses, learning to ride with a courage that bordered on recklessness, she found it no easier to engage with human society. She'd also developed new and worryingly arcane interests: reading books about magic and the occult, and studying the lives of darkly fated characters like Cristina Trivulzio di Belgiojoso, the Italian princess who was rumoured to conduct esoteric rites with the bodies of her dead lovers, or Mary Vetsera, the young Austrian woman who'd recently died in a lurid suicide pact with the mad Crown Prince Rudolf.

To Eduardo and Fanny, Luisa's interest in death and the supernatural must have seemed like fanciful nonsense; nonsense that would surely be drummed out of her once she'd found a suitable husband. Back then, the Ammans had no language with which to frame the behaviour of their niece, other than to regard it as an unfortunate product of grief and an overdeveloped imagination. Yet with the hindsight of modern medical science, it's possible to speculate that Luisa was not simply a lonely, troubled teenager, but was living with the more complicated and potentially more disabling condition of Asperger's syndrome.

Any posthumous diagnosis of a neurological condition can only ever be guesswork – at best a kind of storytelling. Yet so many wild and improbable stories would later be told about Luisa, once she had constructed her extravagant adult persona, that it's justifiable to float this other alternative narrative, a narrative that might explain how so introverted a child could transform herself into so exhibitionist a legend.

Asperger's is an essentially isolating condition – sometimes described as 'mind blindness' by those who live with it, because of the difficulties they experience when engaging with other people. It is a daily struggle for many of them to decipher the body language through which the rest of the world communicates; to read emotion from a facial expression or intention from a tone of voice. And as disadvantaged as they are in interpreting the feelings of others, many people with Asperger's suffer from the assumption that they themselves are ego-centric or cold. Often they function most effectively when they are able to retreat from social interaction into worlds over which they have more control – a significant number of those diagnosed with the condition are gifted as scientists, mathematicians or musicians.

At a very basic level, this list of symptoms resonates suggestively with accounts of Luisa's own character. Even when she was an adult, and had learned to function quite effectively in the outside world, her behaviour was markedly idiosyncratic: she avoided eye contact, and her conversation tended to veer between distracted silences and sudden rapid monologues. While her dress and demeanour were excessively attention-seeking, few would have described her as a natural extrovert. On the contrary, she was so obsessively meticulous in the orchestration of her public performances, it was as though she were still operating within the solitary fantasy world of her childhood. Throughout her life she formed very few close friends.

To the American writer Natalie Clifford Barney, who met Luisa in 1920, the disparity between her outward theatrics and her shuttered inner life was unsettling to witness. Luisa seemed to Barney to be a woman who was 'ever trying by strange disguisements to escape from the inner strangeness'.[3] Whether that 'inner strangeness' would now be diagnosed as Asperger's is a moot issue: if Luisa did have the condition, it did not prevent her from leading a far more independent existence than most other women of her time, from eliciting admiration for her intelligence and taste, or from being courted by artists and intellectuals. While an astute observer like Barney might ponder the complicated, fragile core of Luisa's personality, many others were beguiled by the elaborate, astonishing edifice of her public self.

This adult Luisa would take over a decade to create, however, and back in 1899, when she'd just turned eighteen and was due to make her formal debut in society, she was still almost entirely undefended and unequipped for the task.

*****

Fanny Amman must have done her best to prepare Luisa for her forthcoming season, yet turning her into a debutant was a dispiriting challenge. She'd acquired no skill in small talk or flirtation, and the extensive wardrobe that had been bought for her could not disguise the fact that her appearance was almost as gauche as her manner. She had grown alarmingly tall – nearly six feet in height – yet her body remained flat and angular as a child's. In a few years' time the most fashionable women of Europe would attempt to starve themselves into a physique like Luisa's, but at the turn of the century her slenderness was still judged to be an egregiously unfeminine flaw.

Within the trading logic of the Italian marriage market, however, money was a far more valuable asset than beauty, and the following year Luisa found herself and her fortune being courted by one of Italy's most eligible bachelors: the handsome, moustachioed and magnificently titled Marchese Camillo Casati Stampa di Soncino. Twenty-two years old, Camillo came from an impeccably aristocratic and patriotic lineage, his family still basking in the glory of Count Gabrio Casati who, back in 1848, had led Milan in its rebellion against the Austrian forces who were then occupying much of Italy. The Casati finances, however, were far shakier than their ancestry, and there's little doubt that Camillo (whose inheritance was valued at a mere 70,000 lire) had been advised by his family to pay careful attention to Luisa and to the millions that she would bring with her as a dowry.[4]

Eduardo and Fanny Amman were equally hopeful of the match. They were anxious to get Luisa settled and into a home of her own, but they were fully aware of the social benefits that would accrue to them from such an alliance. While the cotton business had made the Ammans rich and given Alberto his title, the family still ranked far below the established clans of the Italian nobility – the Casatis, the Sforzas and the Orsinis. They were *arrivistes* – their money was new and they themselves were only second-generation immigrants, Alberto and Eduardo's grandfather having been born in Austria. A union between Luisa and Camillo was thus as desirable to the Ammans as it was to the Casatis; and by the end of the season, when the young couple had danced a suitable number of quadrilles and waltzes and had been seated together at dinners and galas, they were formally engaged.

Luisa's own feelings about the match were unrecorded, but the portrait that was painted to mark her engagement suggests she was an unwilling bride. She'd posed with touching attempt at sophistication, wearing a low-cut evening dress, with a pair of opera glasses resting on her lap. But she was clearly modelling on sufferance. Despite the best efforts of her artist – the society portraitist Vitellini – Luisa's smile was anxiously tight-lipped, and her eyes were fixed in a glassy stare. And while it's not clear why one of her hands was left unfinished, the blurriness of its outline gives the impression that she might have tried to flee the studio before the artist could complete his work.

Possibly Luisa would have liked to run away from the wedding itself, although in Camillo she'd been lucky in finding a relatively benign husband. Despite his aristocratic swagger, he was a mild, rational young man who wouldn't ask much from his new wife other than that she provide him with a dowry and an heir, and accept that his main passions in life would always be horses and hunting. Camillo would not be cruel to Luisa; he wouldn't drink or gamble away her fortune. At worst, he would treat her with casual neglect.

They were married on 22 June 1900 and they honeymooned in Paris, giving Luisa her first taste of foreign travel. The city that summer was crammed with the sights and sounds of the Exposition Universelle, a giant trade fair which had brought the rest of the world to Paris. Moving walkways transported the crowds between technological and cultural marvels: between the Muscovite palace that served as Russia's national pavilion and the perfect replica of a Buddhist temple; between the newly built Eiffel Tower and the small public cinema that screened short, hand-coloured films of celebrated stage performers. Here, in the midst of an entranced crowd, Luisa could gaze at Sarah Bernhardt acting a scene from *Hamlet*, or the comedian Little Tich tripping nimbly over his outsize shoes.

Travelling to Paris, Luisa found a new and purposeful confidence as she immersed herself in the wonders around her; in Paris, too, she discovered the pleasures of shopping. The city was home to the great couture houses of Doucet and Worth, whose names she'd learned to revere from her mother. Now, as a married woman with access to her own money, Luisa was able to leave Camillo to his own devices and concentrate on the planning of her adult wardrobe. As she did so she discovered what an effective social armour clothes could provide. Just as she had found an escape from shyness in her childhood games of fancy dress, so, in her new Parisian couture, she learned to mimic the demeanour of a fashionable bride. That summer, when she posed for the society portraitist Paul César Helleu, she looked very different from the frightened girl who'd sat for Vitellini. It was a blandly conventional likeness, but the black feathered hat perched on Luisa's elegantly coiffed hair presented a new image of her – womanly, composed, and almost knowing.

In late summer, when she and Camillo returned to Italy, it was to the promise of more diversions and change. Their married life was to be divided between two of Camillo's family homes: the immense 16th-century Villa Casati, which lay close to the rural town of Cinisello Balsamo, and the elegant town house in the centre of Milan (whose via Soncino address not only bore one of Camillo's ancestral names, but was dominated by another of the family's stately properties, the Palazzo Stampa). The ten miles that separated the two dwellings represented a longish journey by horse or carriage; yet shortly after they were married, the young Casatis acquired a motor car and chauffeur. They were among the first Italians to do so, and Luisa derived intense pleasure from the speed of their new toy, eventually learning to drive it herself.

During the summer there were to be holidays in the Alpine cool of St Moritz; during autumn and winter there were to be visits to Rome (where Francesca would shortly move with her new husband, Conte Giulio Padulli). There was also extensive fox-hunting in the Lombardy countryside around their home. Riding to hounds was Camillo's passion, the most consuming interest of his life, and this at least was one with which Luisa could identify. She'd developed skill and nerve during the gallops of her teenage years, and even riding sidesaddle and encumbered by long riding skirts, she was able to keep up with Camillo at the head of the hunt, sharing with him the adrenalin of the chase, the pounding hooves and whiplash air.

Other marital duties were a more brutal challenge for her, though. Even later, when Luisa was able to choose her own lovers, she would remain ambivalent about sex, flinching from its raw intimacies, finding orgasm difficult to achieve – and it's unlikely she was able to experience much pleasure with her new husband, since he was much more instinctively attuned to horses than to women. Outside of the bedroom too Camillo expected her to face other ordeals, accompanying him to parties and dinners and hosting soirées of their own. On such occasions, Luisa could not be permitted to remain quietly in the corner as she had done at home, but had to smile, nod and parrot the gossip around her. She must often have felt trapped and flounderingly inept within this world of young married couples; yet there were some nights at least when she was thrown a conversational lifeline, and when she was able to participate with some of Camillo's friends on almost equal terms.

A craze for magic and mysticism had taken hold among these young Italian aristocrats: they hired fortune-tellers to read their palms after dinner; held séances in darkened drawing rooms; showed off their knowledge of witchcraft, diabolism and telepathy; and the most daring of them boasted ownership of the *Calendrier Magique*, a calendar devised by occultist Austin de Croze in which the Christian festivals were replaced with profane celebrations of the dark gods.

Such pursuits were dear to Luisa, and she not only plunged boldly into conversations where they were discussed but participated in the spooky amateur theatricals with which Camillo and his set liked to while away the long winter evenings. One of these performances had been inspired by Luisa's teenage heroine, the Principessa Cristina Trivulzio di Belgiojoso, who had been infamous during her lifetime both for her alleged promiscuity and for the bizarre ways in which she was said to have mourned lovers of hers who had died.

Trivulzio was actually an impressive woman, a feminist of the mid-19th century, a free thinker, writer and political activist; yet all that concerned Camillo and his set were the necrophiliac rumours surrounding her sexual life, including the story that she had embalmed the heart of one lover in oil and secreted the corpse of another away in her wardrobe.

As they acted out these ghoulish episodes, Camillo's younger brother Alessandro was given the role of the stashed corpse and Luisa was chosen to play Trivulzio. She bore a passing physical resemblance to the Principessa, but she could also bring to the role her passionate

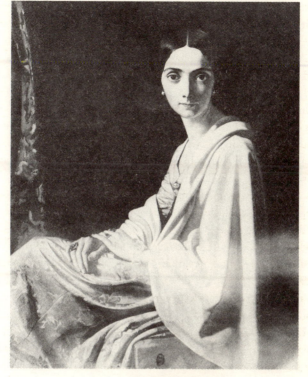

Luisa's teenage heroine, the Principessa
Cristina Trivulzio di Belgiojoso, painted in 1843.

knowledge of Trivulzio's life, and so earnestly did she identify with her
material that she seems to have both unnerved and impressed her audience. It's possible that the success of this drawing-room playlet laid the
seeds for Luisa's subsequent and lifelong dedication to performance.
But at the time, Camillo may well have regretted encouraging his wife
to take part; for after that night Luisa developed the morbid belief that
she and the Principessa were kindred souls.

There were certain similarities between their lives that seemed to
her beyond coincidence. Like Luisa, Trivulzio had been an introverted
child, who would burst into tears if required to converse in public; like

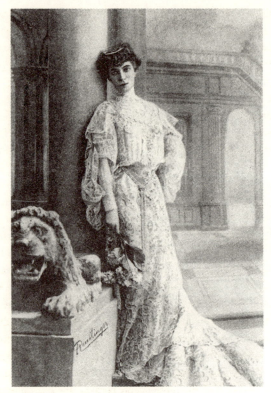

A society photograph of Luisa
taken in the early years of her marriage.

Luisa, she had inherited a fortune but had felt at odds with the fashionable society to which she was expected to conform. Luisa seized on these connections as signs of a deep psychic kinship, and she became obsessed by the idea of contacting Trivulzio's spirit through séances. When she discovered that she was pregnant, a few months into the marriage, she insisted to Camillo that if the baby was a girl it must be called Cristina.

The baby *was* a girl, born on 15 July 1901, and Camillo was apparently happy to indulge Luisa over her name. Perhaps he assumed that once she became a mother she would abandon her stranger fancies and settle into more orthodox routines. Yet having got her way over the naming of the child, Luisa struggled to form any closer bond with her. Notions of maternal love were of course pragmatic then, especially among the upper classes, and there was nothing unusual in the fact that Luisa immediately handed her baby over to the care of wet nurses and nannies. Yet a photograph taken of mother and daughter in 1902 suggests that even by the standards of the time, Luisa lacked some instinct for maternal warmth. Staring fixedly at the camera in front of her, she seems entirely oblivious of Cristina seated in the infant chair beside her, and far more connected to the dog by her feet, whom she is reaching down to stroke.

Immature and insecure as she still was at twenty-one, Luisa may not have been ready to take responsibility for a tiny, unformed life. But as the years passed, she did not grow into motherhood. Intimacy was most difficult for her when she felt coerced into it and Luisa's happiest adult relationships were always those in which she felt free to come and go, without any sense of obligation. Some of those who knew her best would be convinced that her deepest attachments were never to people, but to the large menagerie of pets she accumulated over the years. As for Cristina, who spent most of her childhood being cared for by her German governess, by her aunt Francesca and by the nuns at her boarding school, she would come to bitterly resent her mother's neglect; and she would resent it all the more deeply because she had no brothers or sisters to mitigate her isolation.

It's not clear if Luisa actively resisted getting pregnant again. Camillo needed a male heir (later he would fight Italian law for the right to pass his title on to the son of his second marriage) and Luisa, as a very young wife, may not have had the courage or the means to deny him.* She may simply have had problems conceiving or carrying a second child. But whatever the case, Luisa seems to have made no show of maternal sorrow, no pretense of caring about the fate of the Casati bloodline; and in the face of this indifference, the already strained relationship between her and Camillo began to disintegrate.

*   Divorce wasn't legally recognized in Italy until 1974, during which time Camillo's son did not have a fully legitimate status in the eyes of the courts.

Outwardly, the façade of the marriage remained intact. The young couple were seen together at parties and hunts, car races and air displays: he a handsome and apparently decent husband, and she a compliant wife – odd and rather intense, perhaps, but a fine horsewoman and elegantly turned out. In private, however, Camillo had diminishing patience for his wife's peculiarities, and he began to spend long periods away from home, chasing stags and foxes across much of Italy and as far away as England.

For the first time in her life, Luisa was left in charge of her own domestic world; and if she felt abandoned by Camillo, she began to compensate by imposing her visual taste on her surroundings. The Villa Casati, where she was based for half of the year, was a building of impressive scale and history, its parklands modelled on the grounds of Versailles and its rooms heavily decorated with biblical and mythological frescoes. Luisa only dared to make small changes, but she learned how the villa's oppressive atmosphere could be lightened by the hanging of a decorative fabric, the placing of an unusual cushion or an exotic arrangement of flowers. She complemented these flourishes, too, with romantic additions to her own wardrobe: an extravagantly long rope of pearls wound around her neck, a train of old Venetian lace added to a dress, an antique jeweled belt cinched around her waist.

There were, however, few people in Luisa's life to see and admire these innovations and her days were often lonely. Marriage to Camillo had been hard, but it had also prised open the shell of her reclusiveness, making her more restless, not so self-contained. There were times at the Villa Casati where, craving some excitement, she would order the racehorses from the stables to be harnessed to her carriage so that she could be driven around the country lanes at headlong, dangerous speeds. Luisa had discovered boredom, and there were periods in this solitary life when her marriage stretched ahead of her like a long sentence.

The idea of leaving Camillo was not yet imaginable. Divorce was illegal in Italy, and a separated wife could only claim control over her property if she could prove she'd been abandoned by her spouse. Other, bolder women might dare to flout convention, but Luisa was far too inexperienced, far too easily floored by life to have any notion of how to exist on her own. It's possible that she might have lived out the rest

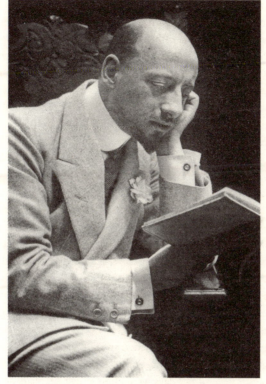

Gabriele D'Annunzio,
Italy's most famous writer and aesthete.

of her life in a state of obscure dependency, the increasingly sad, eccentric wife of the Marchese Casati. However, three years into her marriage, when she was riding to hounds with Camillo, she had her first encounter with the writer Gabriele D'Annunzio – and under the galvanizing force of his personality, the flattering intensity of his interest, she was inspired to rethink her life from a thrillingly new perspective.

Later, D'Annunzio would mistakenly recall that their meeting had taken place in 1906, but if the writer was hazy about dates he had an exact visual recall of how Luisa had impressed him: a 'young slender

Amazon' showing admirable control of her mount as she'd galloped through the 'golden bronze' of the Lombardy heathland.[5] Her skills particularly impressed D'Annunzio because he himself was a newly fanatical convert to hunting, so addicted to the danger of the chase that he would feed his mount with an excess of sugar lumps so that it would become almost impossible to control.

When D'Annunzio spotted Luisa – her face half-glimpsed through the veil of her tall hunting hat, her horse kicking up a fine spray as it forded the river – he made it his immediate business to find out her name. Luisa, however, needed no introduction, for by 1903 D'Annunzio was famous throughout Italy, lionized as a writer and patriot, but also known as a man of wickedly heinous tastes.

He'd gained this reputation back in 1883 with the publication of his *Intermezzo di rime*, a collection of erotic poems that contained images of startling depravity: 'O sinuous moist and burning mouth...Oh great head of hair strewn over my knees during the sweet act...'.[6] When D'Annunzio's debut novel *Pleasure* was published in 1889, its aesthete-hero Spirello acquired a cult-like status, inspiring male readers to ape his mannered speech and dress while female readers dreamed of being seduced, like Spirello's mistresses, among cushions, rose petals and lilies.

Just as D'Annunzio's fiction became the stuff of collective fantasy, so too did the stories that circulated around his life. He was rumoured to drink champagne from human skulls, to practise magical arts, and to believe that great art justified any crime. When he stood for election to the Italian parliament in 1897, it was as a representative for the Party of Beauty, and he actually won his seat. Such was D'Annunzio's genius for self-promotion that when people first met him they were often disappointed. Despite the exquisite vanity of his wardrobe – his emerald rings and tie pins, his dove-grey suits – D'Annunzio lacked the aristocratic *sprezzatura* with which he endowed his heroes. He was short, with narrow shoulders and a pigeon chest; his teeth were yellow, his hairline receding, and his skin had a curious pallor. Yet what D'Annunzio lacked in beauty, he compensated with charm: he had a compelling, hypnotic speaking voice and a gift for insinuating intimacy. As one young girl innocently commented, 'When Signor D'Annunzio speaks it always seems as though he is telling one a secret.'[7]

With women, D'Annunzio used that charm with predatory expertise. Although he was still married to his first wife when Luisa met him in 1903, he'd already seduced more women than he could count – mistresses, prostitutes, anonymous women he picked up in a café or on the street. Promiscuity was a compulsion with him – later it would become a sickness – yet he himself considered it the exercise of a refined connoisseurship. He prided himself on having an eye for subtle variations in female beauty, temperament and style, and when he got himself introduced to the elegant but unfathomable Marchesa Casati he thought she was extraordinarily lovely.

Even though Luisa's angular beauty was not yet in vogue, D'Annunzio had an erotic yen for tall, thin women who, like the heroine of his novel *Il trionfo della morte*, had breasts as 'small and firm as if carved in a delicate alabaster'.[8] He discovered that the Marchesa was very rich, a quality as sexy to him as beauty, and that she was interestingly unhappy. Altogether she seemed to present an intriguing challenge, and in the months following their first encounter D'Annunzio made a point of seeking her out whenever their paths re-crossed, at the theatre, the races, a dinner or a ball.

Luisa herself was guilelessly delighted with her new acquaintance. He coaxed her out of her natural reserve, talking wonderfully about the things that most interested her: art, literature, travel, the world of the occult, even the world of fashion. Unusually among the men she knew, D'Annunzio had an educated and impassioned eye for clothes. The colour, cut and fabric of an outfit, the sheen of a jewel, the drape of a skirt were to him a form of art and a celebration of the senses. In his novels he paid excessive care to the wardrobes of his characters; in real life he paid no less careful attention to the clothes of his mistresses. He particularly admired the rare and sumptuous designs created by Fortuny in Venice – their fabrics 'tinged with strange dreams'[9] – and once he knew Luisa well enough to advise her on such matters, she would fill her own wardrobes with Fortuny cloaks and gowns.

As yet D'Annunzio gave no suggestion that he wanted anything more from Luisa than friendship. He sensed that it would take a long and patient courtship to unlock her guard, and he may have been reluctant to risk the complications of an angry, powerful husband. While his letters to Luisa were full of absurd, courtly tributes – 'Your hair looked so beautifully *Leonardesque* today that I did not dare approach you' – he always remained deferential to her status as a wife and mother, sending 'kind regards' to Camillo and his compliments to Cristina: 'I saw your adorable daughter riding a grey pony this morning. She greeted me so elegantly.'[10]

Later, D'Annunzio would claim that his slow seduction had been deliberately planned: 'my schemes to get close to her were carefully laid'; and that he had deliberately chosen to savour the pleasures of deferred desire, gaining an intense private satisfaction from having Luisa stand near to him at a party and luxuriating in the sensations of frustrated arousal: 'she had on a gray dress, gray of black pearl…I was troubled down to the root of my being.'*[11]

But it was also very easy for D'Annunzio to be patient, since he was fully occupied elsewhere, extricating himself from a long affair with the actress Eleonora Duse and embarking on a new and addictively stormy relationship with the lovely, rich and conveniently widowed Marchesa Alessandra di Rudini.

This affair was much reported on by the press. According to the diarist and amateur historian Tina Whitaker, D'Annunzio and Rudini had made themselves the most scandalous couple in Italy, creating a very public spectacle with their rows and reconciliations and with the speed with which they were running through the Marchesa's inheritance, spending on 'horses dogs carpets and extravagances beyond imagination'. Two or three years earlier, Luisa would have had neither the courage nor the worldliness to associate herself with such people. Yet now that she had met D'Annunzio and learned to identify the depth of her own disenchantment with Camillo, she was inspired to greater boldness, and in March 1905 Tina Whitaker observed to her diary that when D'Annunzio escorted Rudini to the theatre, the Marchesa Casati was seen with them too.

As Luisa was drawn into D'Annunzio's world, it was an education for her to observe the high, flamboyant carelessness with which Alessandra Rudini had shed her widow's weeds. It may have inspired

*   D'Annunzio adored grey, and many of his heroines were dressed in very precise shades of it – pigeon, feather, pewter or ash.

her to imagine that one day she might lead a more recklessly independent life of her own. However, Tina Whitaker would be very premature when, nine months later, she confided to her diary that, 'now people are saying the Marchesa Casati is the lover of D'Annunzio'. Luisa had become sufficiently close to the writer to attract gossip, and close enough, perhaps, for Camillo to raise objections. But all she wanted at this point were the pleasures of the mind: she wanted D'Annunzio not as a lover but as a mentor and a Magus.

The conversations they now shared were of passionate importance to Luisa, for subjects that Camillo had dismissed as female trivia were elevated by D'Annunzio into high-flown discourse. He regarded beauty in all its forms as the goal of his existence, and he abided by the creed of the aesthetic life that he'd plundered from the German philosopher Friedrich Nietzsche.

Nietzsche had argued that greatness could only be achieved through the full and unflinching realization of himself or, as he expressed it, through the fashioning of one's life into 'an unequivocal work of art'. It was for him an essentially moral premise. But it had been appropriated by the Aesthetic movement, led by writers like Oscar Wilde and Walter Pater and by artists like Whistler, and D'Annunzio himself had turned it into a catch-all justification for every passion and excess that he cared to indulge. When he declared, as he frequently did, that 'one must make one's own life as one makes a work of art' he was giving himself moral credit for every act of adultery, every extravagant purchase, every self-promoting gesture of his career.[12]

To Luisa, D'Annunzio's world view was a revelation, making sense of her own tentative strivings for poetry and vividness. It became the basis of a new obsession, encouraging her to view her own small experiments with style as the foundation of a serious creative project. Taking Nietzsche's phrase to its literal and logical conclusion, Luisa began to imagine a life in which everything about herself – her clothes, her houses, her surroundings, even her servants – might be as beautifully and marvellously constructed as an actual work of art.

At first she embarked on her project in orthodox ways. Costume balls had recently come into vogue among the Italian nobility, and these were events at which Luisa could safely test her powers of invention.

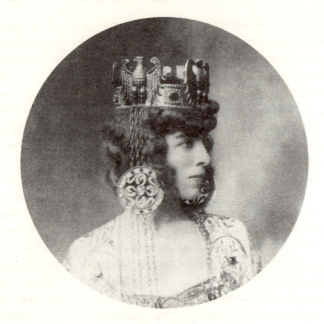

Luisa dressed as the Empress
Theodora in Rome (1905).

In St Moritz in 1904 she was reported to have evinced a 'strange beauty'
in the guise of Madame Pompadour; the following year, in Rome, she
attended a charity ball as the Byzantine Empress Theodora, wearing
a costume based on photographs of Sarah Bernhardt in Sadou's 1884
play, *Theodora*.* Luisa's gown was cut from richly embroidered gold and
silver brocade, and the headdress, which she'd commissioned from the
master jeweler Lalique, was a circlet of linked golden eagles set with
diamonds and hung with loops of pearls.

In this elaborate, costly gear Luisa dominated the room, and also
caught the attention of an American writer, Tryphosa Bates-Batcheller,

---

* D'Annunzio liked to claim Bernhardt as one of his own, calling her 'a divine
D'Annunzian'. Even though she'd rejected his sexual overtures, she accepted the
lead in his 1898 play *La città morta*.

who had devoted her literary career to chronicling the splendours of Italian high society. Bates-Batcheller identified this young Marchesa as a potential star, and from this point she began to attach herself to Luisa and to track her social appearances. Soon the writer was confiding to her readers back home that her friend the Marchesa Casati was regarded as one of the 'best-dressed women' in Europe; and other writers were following her lead.[13] In 1907, when Luisa attended a charity ball adorned with a cascade of peacock feathers, reports of her originality circulated as far as the Scottish press.

By now Luisa's experiments were expanding beyond the ballroom and into daily life. She banned all pastel colours from her wardrobe, dressing only in a monochrome palette of black or white; she also began to play with cosmetics, tinting her hair with henna, drawing dark rings of kohl around her eyes and covering her face with a white powder that, according to D'Annunzio, dusted her skin 'like pollen'.[14] During the first years of the 20th century it was still shocking for women other than actresses to wear make-up, yet Luisa's experiments with her image were so single-minded, so rarefied, that they transcended vulgarity. Creating this new mask for herself, she began to look assertively beautiful.

It was in the first flush of her self-fashioning that Luisa had made her initial discovery of Venice and had begun to envisage the city as a backdrop to her future. Later, when she was asked to describe how she experienced her own beauty, she claimed that as she moved through the world she had the sensation of 'imprinting herself on the very air...leaving behind a succession of impressions that would perpetuate her in the places she had passed through'.[15] In Venice, a city of multiple reflections, of water, marble and glass, Luisa could imagine myriad beautiful ways in which she might imprint and perpetuate her new image.

For the present, though, she was still a married woman, tied to Camillo; and when she returned from Venice, her husband was busy with domestic plans. He had recently been appointed president of the Jockey Club in Rome and, impatient to capitalize on the social advantages of his position, he'd proposed to Luisa that they build themselves a permanent home in the city. It was not yet Venice, but Luisa was glad of the move. Rome was the cultural and political capital of Italy, a far more exciting place than Milan; just as importantly, this new house would not belong to Camillo's family like their other two properties. It would be purchased with Luisa's money and because of that she could claim certain rights – most significantly, the right to dictate all of the decor herself.

The three-storey town house, complete with extensive stabling and garages, was located on the exclusive via Piemonte, and while it may have been Camillo who commissioned the royal architect, the Marchese di Intignano, to design its structure, the rest was to be a blank canvas for Luisa's vision. As with the styling of her wardrobe, she attempted to combine a bold, contemporary palette with elaborate touches of fantasy, and once she'd completed her work No. 51 via Piemonte appeared to its first, curious visitors to be less of a home than a perfect study in artifice.

At the front of the villa, shuttered behind tall gates, was a small garden in which a classically columned fountain was framed by scented shrubs and low-growing trees. Here Luisa may have been drawing on memories of her childhood home, yet the two golden gazelles that stood at the doorway of the house were signs of a far more unusual taste within. Throughout the entire three floors of the interior Luisa had worked with a black and white colour scheme, beginning with a herringbone pattern of black and white marble tiles that covered the oval entrance hall and continuing on through ebony floors, white-painted walls, all-white furnishings and alabaster bas-reliefs.

Luisa was in advance of the times: black and white decor would become fashionable in Europe after the First World War, but in Rome in 1908, drawing rooms were still heavy with colour and opulent drapes. She did, however, dramatize the starkness of her design with rococo splashes of brilliance; a fresco of tropical birds adorned one ceiling; Venetian mirrors were hung on walls to reflect the burnish of gold-plated stair railings; and in one salon Luisa had under-floor lighting installed – an innovation that seems to have been her own idea. When visitors ascended the villa's curving marble staircase, they were serenaded by a choir of clockwork finches singing in gilt cages. Even the pets had a decorative function, the cats an elegant mix of Syrian, Siamese and Persian and the dogs a pair of greyhounds (D'Annunzio's favourite breed): one pure black, the other white.

Luisa had created an interior of such studied perfection that, according to her niece Camilla (Francesca's daughter), visiting 51 via Piemonte was like going to church – one 'was induced to speaking in whispers or walking on tiptoe'.[16] To Luisa's conservative neighbours, however, the house seemed a ludicrous act of pretension. It also became the subject of stiff-lipped gossip as she began to entertain her own guests. Luisa was often by herself in Rome, for Camillo's hunting duties were now consuming most of his time: he'd recently been appointed Rome's Master of the Foxhounds, and had his eye on becoming Master of the Staghounds.[17] But rather than feeling neglected, Luisa was gaining the confidence to profit from her husband's absence. She was beginning to mix with a wider circle, writers, painters and intellectuals whom she'd met through D'Annunzio, and with a house that she considered her own, she was able to entertain her new set without deference to Camillo's interests.

Two of the key men in Luisa's expanding world were the artist Alberto Martini and Filippo Tommaso Marinetti, the lawyer turned cultural terrorist who, as leader of the newly formed Futurist movement, had declared his mission to destroy the past and embrace the new age of the machine. Luisa might very easily have been frightened by Marinetti, whose iconoclastic assaults on all that he considered sentimental, decadent or old had so far included an excoriating attack on D'Annunzio and the shocking idea that Venice must be made modern. As Marinetti would claim in his 1910 provocation 'Contro Venezia passatista', it was time to 'murder the moonlight' and 'rip' the veil off the city's romanticism; the canals should all be filled in, and electric street lights installed throughout.[18]

Yet if Luisa was confused by the aggression of Marinetti's ideas, she was stimulated by their energy, and by the realization that he was drawing her into a milieu that operated by liberatingly different rules. Her new acquaintances in Rome didn't expect her to act the conventional hostess: they were happy to enjoy her food and wine, and to admire her extraordinary appearance, but they were not bothered if she preferred to remain on the edge of a conversation, if she spoke clumsily or misinterpreted the social signals in the room. Among these people, eccentricities were not liabilities but proof of an interesting temperament – and in

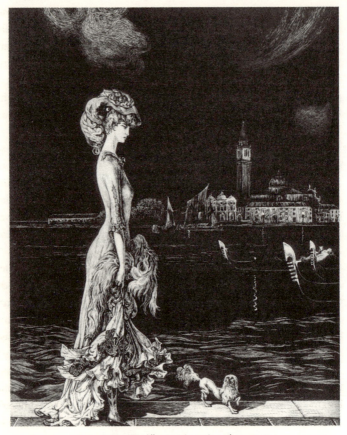

Luisa in Venice: Alberto Martini's early portrait,
one of the first in her personal gallery.

fact Luisa was beginning to learn how to re-present her own awkwardness as a form of social mystique. A few years later, the writer Harold
Acton was at a party with her and noted that throughout an entire evening she had remained almost mute, but for a few gnomic observations.
To Acton, this silence gave Luisa the fascinating aura of a sibyl; it was,
he wrote, 'inconceivable' to imagine 'ordinary sentiments [coming]
from the lips of so chimerical a creature'.[19]

Luisa's confidence didn't just flourish in Rome. Even when she was in residence at Villa Casati, she began to assert herself more forcefully. Tryphosa Bates-Batcheller was invited to a soirée Luisa had hosted, apparently during Camillo's absence, and noted that her taste was everywhere evident both in the decoration of the rooms and in her choice of guests – among them the worldly Princess Helene Soldatenkov, who knew everyone in Europe and was rumoured to have Sapphic tastes in her lovers.

Tryphosa also noted that the princess had brought her daughter to the Villa Casati as a playmate for Cristina. This was, however, one of the very rare instances when Cristina's presence was mentioned in dispatches from Cinisello Balsamo or Rome. Family had no role to play in Luisa's growing dedication to the aesthetic life; and when she began to commission a gallery of portraits to document that life, Cristina appeared in none of them.

Luisa's idea of creating a permanent record of herself and her increasingly varied guises may have been inspired by the Comtesse de Castiglione, a mistress of Napoleon III who was known as the most elaborately dressed woman of mid-19th-century Paris. La Castiglione, bent on posthumous fame as well as on immediate celebrity, had posed for over five hundred photographic portraits during the course of her career, for which she'd dressed in hundreds of different costumes, from Medea to Anne Boleyn. Towards the end of her life these photographs became the Countess's only consolation when, lonely and embittered, she had all her mirrors shrouded in black so that she would not have to contemplate the ruin of her beauty. But if there was a moral to the story of her narcissism, Luisa chose not to see it. She saw only the grandeur of La Castiglione's ambition, and it became her private mission not only to emulate the Countess's gallery but to surpass it.

One of the first portraits Luisa commissioned was by Alberto Martini. It was an unremarkable pen-and-ink drawing in which she was posed against a nocturnal Venetian skyline, with just a suggestion of daring in her coquettishly lifted skirt. But a portrait painted by Giuseppe Vitelleschi a year or two later drew Luisa to the attention of a wider audience – and to the Parisian aesthete Robert de Montesquiou, who claimed that Vitelleschi had found a fascinating subject in Luisa, seeing in the 'devouring restless and unsettling' expression of her eyes a resemblance to D'Annunzio's more daring fictional heroines.[20]

To be complimented in such terms, and by a man who was as eminent as Montesquiou, was a new affirmation for Luisa, and she began tentatively to expand her artistic and social horizons. She'd started to travel more widely to Paris and London as well as Venice, and was becoming conscious of the limits of her life in Rome. Compared to other centres of Europe, much of the city was still culturally isolated, still dominated by the traditions of the church and the nobility. To the young Englishman Gerald Tyrwhitt, who came to Rome in 1910 as honorary attaché to the British embassy, it felt like a city that was still waiting to be 'hustled' into the 20th century.[21]

Luisa not only wanted to see more of Europe, she wanted to be more widely seen, and it became imperative to her that she should become known in Paris. She believed that she needed to make an extended stay in the city in order to immerse herself more deeply in its fashion and philosophy, and to test herself against its demanding arbiters of taste. But she quailed at the idea of being alone without close friends to receive her, or without any justifying purpose; until, in the summer of 1908, she found her excuse.

She was making her now annual pilgrimage to Venice, and D'Annunzio, who was also there for the season, had invited her to join him for breakfast at the Danieli Hotel to meet the distinguished portraitist Giovanni Boldini. Boldini was a painter for whom Luisa already aspired to pose. He was famously discriminating in his choice of subjects – Verdi, Bernhardt and James Whistler had all sat for him – and she knew that to be painted by him would confer her with a reflected celebrity. Boldini's studio was also in Paris, and Luisa was aware that if she could snare the painter's interest it would give her a very plausible motive for staying there.

She dressed very precisely for the meeting, assessing the impression that her black dress and long pearl necklace would make against the gilded pillars, stained-glass windows and great hanging chandeliers of the Danieli's magnificent interior. But as she approached the table where the two men were sitting, her necklace broke and dozens of pearls bounced violently and noisily across the polished marble floor.

Luisa was mortified. Several men leaped from their seats to help as she sank to the floor to scrabble for the scattered pearls. Yet this social disaster proved to be the clinching introduction to Boldini. The stout little painter gallantly joined in the retrieval of Luisa's pearls and, as he later wrote, 'it was under one table that I found myself face to face with her' and saw close up the startling impact of her 'immense eyes'.[22] Captivated by the idea of painting those eyes, he insisted on making some preliminary sketches in Venice, and arranged for Luisa to come to Paris in the autumn to pose for a full-length portrait.

Despite his enthusiasm, Boldini would still charge Luisa a fee of 20,000 francs; yet the money meant nothing to her, for she'd always left it to an accountant in Milan to manage what she assumed were her unlimited finances. Luisa never looked at price tags, never considered the value of what she was getting beyond its beauty, its power or its charm. Money was simply the element in which she moved. And it was with the same financial insouciance that she prepared for her long stay in Paris, booking herself a suite at the city's most luxurious hotel.

When the Ritz opened in 1898 it had become immediately conspicuous for many things – for its smart combination of antique furnishings and modern plumbing, its worldly clientele and its policy of encouraging single female guests. The hotel's dining room was softly illuminated, its waiters carefully trained, so that a woman taking a meal by herself would be made to feel at ease. Discretion was guaranteed for those who wanted to come and go from the hotel with anonymity; yet for those who wanted visibility, the Ritz was also the place to be seen. Rich Americans and French intellectuals, celebrities of the stage and silent screen could all be seen in its public spaces. Proust regularly dined there, and among its permanent residents was Liane de Pougy, the beautiful dancer and *grande horizontale* who kept a permanent suite at the hotel for the pursuit of her many love affairs.

All this was a reassuring ambience for Luisa as she settled into Paris and made preparations for her portrait. The right costume was essential, and having dismissed the older fashion houses of Doucet and Worth, she went instead to the atelier of Paul Poiret, a couturier who was marketing his designs directly to her own generation. When he had established his business in 1903, Poiret had announced himself as an emancipator of women's bodies, signalling an end to the whalebone corsets and voluminous petticoats of the past. With his high-waisted, subtly draped gowns he was re-drawing the image of female beauty, replacing hourglass curves with a longer, leaner, more contemporary silhouette.

It was Poiret who would be partially responsible for transforming Luisa's recalcitrant physique into a template of fashionable style, and the black satin gown she commissioned from him made striking virtues of both her slenderness and her height. It was cut very close to the body until it flared out into a froth of skirt, and its lines were made even more dramatic by the large black feathered hat balanced with a precarious jauntiness on Luisa's head and the black greyhound (transported specially from Rome) that frisked at her feet.

Once the dress had been fitted and sewn, Luisa began the long process of posing for Boldini at his studio, Villetta Rossa. Despite his daunting reputation, the sixty-six-year-old artist was easy company: short, plump and precise, with a thick grey moustache and tiny pince-nez, he painted with a gregarious bustle, darting back and forth between Luisa and the easel, crooning arias from his favourite operas.

She relaxed in his company, and over time Boldini developed a protective affection towards her. What Boldini didn't yet realize, however, was the weight of expectation Luisa had invested in this portrait, believing as she did that once unveiled it would become her calling card to Parisian society.

The role that Luisa imagined for herself in Paris was vague in its outlines. She couldn't aspire to become a rival to the city's leading *salonnières* – the Princesse de Polignac, who entertained musicians, composers and intellectuals at her mansion on Avenue Henri-Martin, or Natalie Barney, whose more bohemian salon drew a mixture of Left Bank radicals and romantic lesbians. Running a successful salon required the ability to manipulate and manage other people, to orchestrate their conversation, to navigate the intricate cross-currents of Parisian society. These talents were far beyond Luisa's scope.

What she hoped to find was an audience, one she could trust to appreciate her new public persona with the discrimination and admiration she craved. Between her sessions with Boldini, she made a start on building a small circle of acquaintants. She held a luncheon party

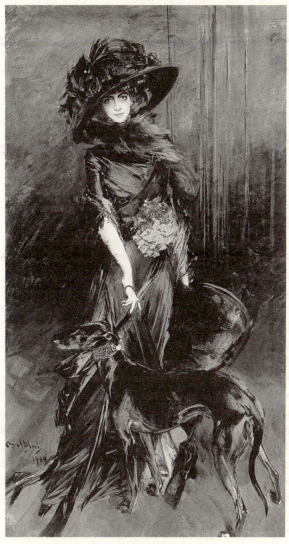

Giovanni Boldini's portrait of Luisa
with her pet greyhound (1908).

at the fashionable Laure Restaurant, and having invited the celebrated actress Cécile Sorel to be her guest of honour she was able to secure the attendance of several others; the actress Ève Lavallière, and the Baroness Ernesta Stern, a woman of cosmopolitan tastes and independence who would become something of a role model to Luisa. Dividing her time between Paris and Venice, the baroness had created the kind of life to which Luisa aspired; answerable to nobody, and dedicating herself to the study of art, literature and the occult as well as to the enjoyment of her young Italian lovers.

Given how few female friendships Luisa had formed in her life, these women were an education and a support. But her most important Parisian connection was Robert de Montesquiou, the slim and dandified aesthete upon whose character Proust would draw when writing the erudite and sexually deviant Baron de Charlus in his novel *A la récherche du temps perdu*. Montesquiou dabbled in poetry and watercolours, but his true medium was society. He was invited everywhere, and his verdict on a party or a dinner could make or break a reputation. He kept a catalogue of every notable woman in Paris, assessing her social and financial worth, and Luisa, unsurprisingly, struck him as a most interesting specimen when D'Annunzio introduced them. Later he would christen her Casaque (a nickname deriving from *kaazk*, the Turkish word for adventurer) and would dedicate three satirical but admiring sonnets to her.

So absorbed was Luisa in developing her Parisian life that even when the portrait was completed she hated to leave; and, breaking her promise that she would return to Camillo and Cristina by Christmas, she remained until after the New Year. It's not clear why she did not subsequently return in April when her picture, *La jeune femme au lévrier*, was unveiled at the Paris Salon. She had no reason to be nervous of Boldini's work, since the portrait was ravishing, its impressionistic brushstrokes giving a dancing animation to Luisa's black-gowned figure and concentrating the impact of her dark, pooling eyes.

Perhaps Camillo tried to forbid Luisa's return, or perhaps she shrank from the exposure of the painting's unveiling: instead she had to read about it in the French papers and magazines that she had sent to her in Rome. The first reports were gratifying. Luisa could hardly have hoped for greater validation than the review in *Le Figaro*, which acclaimed Boldini's portrait as 'the most beautiful piece of pure painting in the whole Salon'; and dwelt admiringly on Luisa's 'beautiful black eyes'; the intensity of her '"witch's sabbat" mien' and her 'long question mark of a body'.

Luisa's satisfaction was further bolstered by the glossy reproduction of her portrait that appeared in *Femina* (a magazine that prefigured *Vogue* in its intelligent coverage of fashion and the arts) and by the short poetic tribute published by Montesquiou, banal in itself but for Luisa pleasingly insistent on the 'grace' and 'mystery' of her painted form. Yet this proved to be the extent of her press coverage, and Luisa's disappointment was made all the more acute by the fact that *L'Illustration*, the magazine she'd revered since childhood, had paid her no attention, despite giving a lavish spread to one other Boldini portrait in the exhibition.

The subjects of that portrait were the recently married couple Philip Lydig and Rita de Acosta. The latter – ambitious, beautiful and American – had used a $2m divorce settlement from her first husband to orchestrate a public image that easily rivalled Luisa's own. She'd amassed a wardrobe that was said to contain seventeen antique lace petticoats simply for wear in the bedroom; she had a circle of friends that included Rodin, Duse, Bernhardt and Tolstoy; and, most mortifyingly for Luisa, the painter John Singer Sargent had commented admiringly of Rita that she did not need to be an artist, because 'she herself is art'.

To be overshadowed by such a woman at her first showing in Paris was a violent upset for Luisa, and she did not handle it well. She'd devoted such care to this moment, invested such hope in it, and her frustration expressed itself in an irrational storm of rage. Such storms are symptomatic of Asperger's, and it is possible that Luisa was simply unable to restrain herself. Certainly Boldini was shocked by the stream of venomous letters she wrote to him in Paris, accusing him of deliberately sabotaging the success of her portrait.

But Boldini did not hold a grudge, and while he huffily rejected Luisa's accusations, he had recognized her vulnerability as well as her continuing potential as a client, and eventually the two became close friends. Yet this setback did make Luisa hesitate in her plans to create a more permanent base for herself in Paris. She'd seen and heard enough of the city to understand how absolute were its criteria of failure and success, how competitive its social stage. As one of its leading players, the artist and writer Jean Cocteau, would claim, 'In Paris everybody wants to be an actor; nobody is content to be a spectator.'[23] And it was while Luisa was questioning whether or not she wanted to spend more time in Paris that she re-focused her attention onto Venice.

During her annual visits to the city she'd tended to stay in a suite at the Danieli Hotel; but, influenced perhaps by Ernesta Stern, she began to think of acquiring her own Venetian home. With a palazzo on the Grand Canal she could entertain on a far more magnificently public scale than in Cinisello Balsamo or in Rome, and Venice would also provide a more beautiful backdrop to the parties she was starting to host. It wouldn't be an easy proposition to find such a property; entire palazzos rarely came vacant on the canal because the old families remained tenaciously possessive of their ancestral homes, even when financial circumstances forced them to rent out floors of their palaces as tourist accommodation. Yet sometime in late 1909, Luisa had word from Ernesta Stern that a very intriguing property had become available to rent.

The very name and history of the Palazzo Venier dei Leoni resonated with Luisa, for Sebastiano Venier had always been esteemed by D'Annunzio as one of the heroes of Venetian history; indeed, D'Annunzio's third son had been christened Veniero in the admiral's honour. Yet there were practical and personal advantages to the palace, too. It was far more compact than most of its neighbours – suitable for a dwelling that Luisa planned to use only for the summer – and while it would need some basic work before she could move in, that too suited her well. As dirty and forsaken as the Palazzo Venier might appear, it was a building Luisa could mould to her own demandingly aesthetic image.

CHAPTER 2

'There was a narrow canal which led to the house between the
gardens and trees, where one could see classical statues, golden
and indirectly lit. There were ruined marble railings covered
with carved flowers and fruit. The house itself could hardly be
seen through its covering of climbing vines. Within was the great
salon; walls, carpets, furniture, decorations, doors, all in gold,
a gold of lost brilliance – a pale aged colour.'[1]

This was the fantasy that would imprint itself on the memories of guests
who visited the Venier palazzo in the years just before the First World
War – among them a young Mexican artist, Roberto Montenegro, who
would become something of a pet of Luisa's. But during the first year
and a half of her tenancy, she effected only basic repairs on the property. Perhaps she was waiting for permission from the palazzo's owner,
Isabelle de la Baume-Pluvinel, or perhaps Camillo was attempting to
block the extravagance – and it was not until early 1912 that a crew of
builders and craftsmen moved onsite to begin an extensive project of
refurbishment.

Disappointingly for all those neighbours who'd been hoping to see
the palace restored to some semblance of its intended magnificence,
almost all of the work that Luisa commissioned was on the interior,
away from public view. She had fallen in love with a semi-ruin, and she
wanted to maintain its illusion of gothic romance. Even though the building was made safe (and one later report suggests that a temporary shell
or 'pavilion' was built within its most dilapidated section), the layers of
grime and ivy remained on the external walls, and sections of collapsed
roof were left exposed. It was only inside, where few of the locals were
invited, that the splendour of Luisa's money became apparent and the
palazzo came into its own as the residence of a rich Marchesa.

There is no surviving ground plan of the building and most of what we know of its internal decoration comes from the descriptions of visitors like Roberto Montenegro. According to him, the palazzo's passageways had been lined with new white marble and irradiated by Murano glass chandeliers. Gold lace curtains hung from the windows, snaring the sunlight from the canal: a gold verdigris staircase connected the ground floor to the basement, and the main salon was painted in matching gold. As a final touch, the black and white marble floor from Luisa's Roman villa was reproduced in the entrance hall.

Outside in the grounds, Luisa preserved an illusion of wildness by retaining some of the dense tangle of trees and vines. But she also filled the garden with strange and lovely artefacts: classical statues painted in gold, fragments of old marble carvings, mechanical songbirds in gilt cages. There were live creatures, too, as the feral cats and pigeons which had once regarded the garden as their rightful terrain found themselves ousted by a startling colony of newcomers. Not only did Luisa import her greyhounds and cats to the palazzo, but she added monkeys, parrots and eventually snakes. She had white peacocks trained to perch

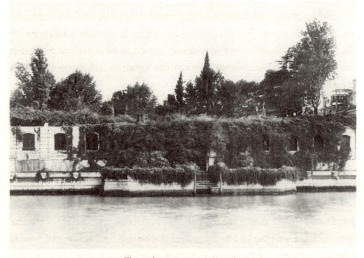

The palazzo as romantic ruin,
its walls overgrown with ivy.

decoratively on her windowsills, and she kept a flock of tame albino blackbirds that were dyed in different colours to match the theme of whatever party she was hosting.

These dyed birds of Luisa's were much copied and admired, although she had possibly got the idea from D'Annunzio. His father Francesco Paulo (a bullish landowner in the Abruzzi region) had shared his son's instinct for the self-promoting gesture and had kept a flock of white doves at his house that, on special occasions, were plunged into vats of pink, green, purple and orange dye, before being released in a spectacular rainbow flight around his inner courtyard. What had been a novelty in the Abruzzi, though, was simply a detail in Luisa's menagerie. Like the 18th- and 19th-century aristocrats who'd shown off their rarefied taste with collections of wild animals, or like Byron, whose own Venetian bestiary had included a fox, an ape and a crow, Luisa aspired to the extraordinary. And the most prized of all the creatures at her palazzo was an elegant spotted cheetah.

There were some locals in the Dorsoduro neighbourhood who speculated that the cheetah was Luisa's way of paying tribute to the lion that, according to legend, had been kept in the grounds of the Palazzo Venier while it was being built. It was true that Luisa liked to emphasize the leonine associations of her new home. She had her summer stationery engraved with the Lion of St Marco (the heraldic template for the eight stone lions on her waterfront terrace), and she liked to shorten the name of the building to Palazzo dei Leoni, which to her ear was infinitely more poetic.

But the acquisition of her cheetah had little to do with the history of the palazzo, and everything to do with the finessing of her image. Even though the animal was carefully controlled when it was out in public, drugged with mild opiates and kept on a very short leash by its handler Garbi (the first and most long-serving of Luisa's black staff), it was a wild creature nonetheless. Prowling in Luisa's garden, padding behind her as she walked through the city, lying by her feet in her gondola as she floated down the canals, it conveyed a frisson of menace. Like the famous Russian dancer Ida Rubinstein, whose delicately boned beauty was dramatically offset by the pet black panther that loped by her side, Luisa intended her cheetah to give her an aura of dangerous exoticism.

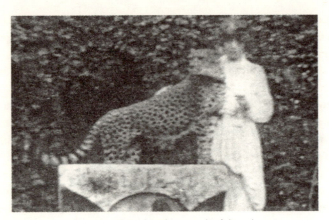

Luisa with her cheetah in the grounds of the palazzo.

It was in 1911 or 1912 that Luisa acquired the animal (some reports suggested there might at one point have been a pair), and she was rarely to be seen in Venice without it. Together they caused a reliable stir: crowds parted nervously when they appeared in the street, and onlookers would line the bridges to applaud when she took the cheetah out on the canals. According to the photographer Baron Adolph de Meyer, one of the great sights of pre-war Venice was the 'Marchesa Casati, at sunset, reclining in her gondola, wrapped in tiger skins and fondling her favourite leopard'.[2] Luisa might have minded the Baron mistaking the species of her pet, but she relished his admiration, for it assured her that she had left behind the life to which she'd been so awkwardly and unhappily ill suited. She could never again be confined to the roles of wife and mother – she was a modern decadent whom D'Annunzio could salute as his equal, a 'divine spirit, edged with wildness'.[3]

* * * * *

The compact geography of Venice made it very easy for Luisa to draw a crowd when she appeared in public with her cheetah. The city, as Henry James observed, was like an 'immense collective apartment' – its cafés, squares, churches, even its bridges all places where people naturally gathered to gossip and observe. And there was no better moment for

Luisa to emerge in public than the hour of the evening *passagietto* in San Marco. One of the first times that she appeared among them, an eyewitness recalled that the summer tourists drinking outside Florian's, the street vendors, the local women in their shawls and clogs, had all been stunned to silence. She was dressed with unseasonal opulence in a red and gold Fortuny cloak, a black fur cap and ropes of gold necklaces; she was accompanied by the tall and turbaned Garbi, who held the cheetah's leash in one hand and in the other the peacock parasol that shaded his mistress from the last of the sun.*

But while Luisa had no difficulty in attracting the attention of strangers in Venice, her challenge was to create a more intimate and discriminating audience. D'Annunzio had already introduced her to some of his extensive contacts in the city, including Fortuny, whom Luisa was tentatively coming to regard as a friend. Yet the writer himself was no longer a dependable support during Luisa's first Venetian summers, because by 1910 he'd got himself so deeply into debt that he'd been forced to flee his Italian creditors and exile himself in France. Alone in her palazzo, and inexperienced, Luisa had to fend for herself in the building of her own wider circle.

There was little point in her seeking introductions to the city's remaining cluster of aristocrats, whose attitudes were no less parochial and conservative than those of her neighbours in Rome. Clinging to the remnants of their former eminence, most of them regarded the bizarrely garbed, attention-seeking and apparently husbandless Marchesa Casati as a most undesirable addition. They would not invite her to their homes, nor would they want to visit hers; and Luisa would have to find her new admirers and friends among more kindred spirits – among the romantics, artists and bohemians who were visitors to the city, and among the seasonal residents like herself.

* * * * *

* The city was apparently very susceptible to the spectacle of a beautiful woman: Annina Morosini, who ruled Venetian society in the years just before Luisa's arrival, was said to have drawn such dangerously large crowds when she went out in public that the authorities begged her to keep her face veiled.

There were now around three and a half million visitors coming to Venice each year, and they made a profound impact on the moral and social fabric of the city. Many came from more liberal societies than Italy (Edith Wharton described the typical summer crowd as thoroughly 'intermarried, inter-loved and inter-divorced') and many came in search of pleasures that the city was famously willing to tolerate. There was gambling at the Casino, there were rumours of discreet orgies in one or two of the Lido hotels; and young Venetian boys were famously compliant, with the self-styled Baron Corvo, an English writer called Frederick Wolfe, routinely pimping out pretty gondoliers to his friends. So dependent was the Venetian economy on its tourists that the city was obliged to be far laxer in its codes than other parts of Italy. In 1914, the Pope would issue an edict that prohibited the tango and other foreign dance imports in Rome; in Venice, however, the jaunty sounds of rag-time and jazz had become commonplace.

But there was a longer history to the city's unusual spirit of tolerance. During the golden age of the Republic, the city's financial and political power had been built on a willingness to embrace foreigners and foreign ideas. Venice had been Europe's main trading portal to the east, and its paintings and buildings, its imports of silks, spices and pigments had reflected an open exchange of cultures. The wonders of the Constantinople court, with its bejeweled opulence, its 'unknown beasts as big as lions' and its 'black eunuch boys', had inspired the 15th-century merchant Giovanni Dario to have his own Venetian home, Ca' Dario, decorated like a small oriental palace.

From the early 18th century, when the financial might of the Republic was in decline, the city's economy relied more and more on servicing the appetites of its foreign visitors. Venice had always been famous for its prostitutes – 'the best sex shambles in Italy' according to one early-17th-century connoisseur – and in accordance with the city's historic spirit of pragmatism, they'd been allowed to ply their trade very freely. It was considered that the sight of these women, their breasts exposed in low-cut dresses as they picked their way through the muddy streets or as they sat on balconies drying their hair, would serve as a check to any transgressively homosexual instincts among the city's youth. Despite the disapproval of patrician senators who mourned the city's degeneration into a marketplace of 'excessive luxuries [and] vain shows',[4] Venice by the mid-18th century had become a magnet for adulterers, debauchees and pleasure-seekers of all kinds. Around 40,000 visitors came each year just for the winter carnival season; others were drawn to the gaming clubs, the theatres, the fairs, feast days and regattas that made the city into a kind of open playground for the rest of the year.

Yet if there had always been a strong financial motive for Venice's tolerance of outsiders, there was also a more disinterested vein of enlightenment running through the city's culture. Even though the 20th-century rump of the city's nobility had grown defensively insular, their ancestors had shown an early regard for the principles of free thought. Literary and musical salons had been a marked feature of the city's intellectual life, and even when the Senate and Church had attempted one of their periodic clampdowns on subversive ideas, the Republic had been a more liberal place than much of Europe.

It had also been unusual in the freedom it granted to certain female communities, and while Luisa may not have appreciated the fact, when she embarked on her new life at the palazzo she was following a long line of Venetian women who'd aspired to lives as unorthodox as hers. Some of these, like the celebrated poet and courtesan Veronica Franco, were also women whose stories were woven deep into the Venier past.

Franco, who was born in 1546, had been the beloved mistress of Marco Venier – a poet himself, and also second cousin to the admiral Sebastiano. She was a member of the privileged community of *cortigiania onesta*, honoured courtesans who operated in Venice somewhat like the *geishas* of Japan.* At a time when only 12 per cent of the city's female population were literate, these women were educated in music, languages and classical poetry and were prized by their clients as much for their conversation as for their erotic skills. Veronica, however, was more gifted than most; in 1566, when her name first appeared in the

---

* Like many *cortigiana onesta*, Veronica came from a family of *cittadini originari* – a social group midway between peasant and nobility which enjoyed certain hereditary rights, including (for the men) the right to work in the lower ranks of city bureaucracy.

city's register of leading courtesans, her listed assets included her rare talent for poetic composition.

Veronica became renowned for the wittily erotic poetry with which she seduced her favoured clients (among them Henry III of France and Poland). Deftly composed in *terza rima*, their teasing sensual imagery was reputed to be as arousing as any foreplay. But her literary ambitions extended far beyond professional titillation; during her lifetime she published several collections of her own poems and letters in which she wrote about politics, philosophy and the details of her daily life, and in which she experimented with a bold variety of literary forms.

She was exceptional too in using her writing to present an entirely female, even feminist perspective. While Veronica had voluntarily embraced her own profession, preferring it to an early, unhappy marriage, she knew that many women – wives as well as prostitutes – were in situations far more brutalizing than her own. In one defiant polemic Veronica called on all of her sex to unite against their long history of subjugation: 'When we too are armed and trained, we can convince men that we have hands, feet, and a heart like [theirs]....Women have not yet realized this, for if they should decide to do so, they would be able to fight...until death.'

Veronica's intelligence gave steel to her writing and personality to her beauty. In one surviving portrait, attributed to Tintoretto, there was no mistaking the nature of her profession: the nipple of her left breast was fully exposed, an artful blush coloured her plump cheeks and lips. Yet it was Veronica's dark eyes that dominated the portrait, the directness of her gaze, the emphatic curve of her brows. She looked like a woman of exceptional character, and early in her career she was recognized as such by Domenico Venier, an elder statesman of the city who presided over its most influential salon.

Domenico was one of the more enlightened members of the Venier dynasty, and he not only welcomed Veronica into his palazzo on Santa Maria Formosa, but appointed himself her literary mentor. It was probably through his salon that Domenico's nephew Marco first met Veronica; and from the evidence of their letters and poems, their union became a long and passionate one. 'When you lie stretched out upon the pillows,' wrote Marco, 'how sweet to fall upon you and that way strip you of any retreat or defense'. At least one of Veronica's six children was fathered by him, and it was said he wanted to marry her. But although a courtesan was effectively allowed much more freedom in Venice than a patrician wife, she could never transcend the stigma of her profession and her class. Veronica might enjoy the protection of Domenico, but other Veniers condemned her association with Marco; his cousin Maffio was particularly hostile, circulating a trio of viciously obscene poems designed to demolish her reputation.

Veronica parried Maffio's assault with poems of her own, but the attack made her vulnerable, especially now that she was approaching middle age. In 1575–6 a catastrophic plague epidemic swept through the city, killing around a quarter of the population. Veronica had sufficient money and sense to escape to the mainland, but when she returned home her house had been ransacked and most of her possessions were gone. A second blow fell in 1580, when she was taken before the city's Court of Inquisition, accused by her son's tutor of practising magic. The man was simply exercising a grudge – Veronica had implicated him in the theft of her belongings, and in 16th-century Europe it was not unusual for a disgruntled man to revenge himself on a woman by denouncing her as a witch. Yet even though Veronica successfully argued her own defense, the accusation had tainted her reputation – and she was now, also, dangerously without friends. Marco was no longer her lover, and Domenico was approaching death. At the height of her success, Veronica had written eloquently about the plight of Venice's most needy prostitutes and had petitioned the city to offer them charitable support. But when she died in 1591, she too was close to poverty. Records indicate that during her last years she'd been living in the slum area of the city where Venice corralled its lowliest whores.

Other brilliant women fared better. Elena Cornaro Piscopia was a courtesan's daughter, born exactly one hundred years after Veronica, but had the luck to be adopted by her rich, enlightened biological father.*

---

* In pragmatic Venice, such a move might have been intended as a solution to a childless marriage, or simply as an act of liberal kindness. Elena's father was unusual, though, in paying the large sum of money necessary to have her legitimized and ennobled.

With his blessing she entered a convent as a lay student (a popular refuge for independently minded Venetian women who might have neither the dowry nor the inclination to marry). At twenty-four she was appointed president of the city's Accademia dei Pacifici; and at thirty-four she gained a doctorate in philosophy from the University of Padua and a post as lecturer in mathematics. For the rest of her life, Lady Elena Cornaro Piscopia was celebrated as Venice's prodigy and pride, and around the same period, other women were striving for comparable eminence – among them the composer Barbara Strozzi, and the poet Sara Copia Sullam, who attracted writers, artists and clerics to her salon in the Jewish ghetto. Venice was unusual for the space and acknowledgment it gave to women's talents. They might be barred from office, but a woman like the 18th-century poet, feminist and free thinker Caterina Dolfin could attain a measure of real political influence through the salon she ran. When Caterina was subjected to an investigation by the Inquisition it would be because of the radical books in her library, not because of her sex.

Within the ranks of these distinguished Venetian women, the story of Cecilia Venier Baffo remains one of most surprising and mysterious. Cecilia was the illegitimate daughter of Nicolò Venier, governor of the Venetian-controlled island of Paros, and it had been her misfortune to be summering with him in 1537 when Turkish troops made a raid on the island and seized two thousand of its inhabitants as slaves. Young European girls were considered a prize at the Ottoman court, where, as concubines to the Sultan and his sons, they were much valued for the fairness of their skin and for the unlikelihood of their making political trouble. Aged only twelve, Cecilia was thrust into the alien world of the royal harem: she was rechristened Nurbanu, converted to Islam and handed over to the young Prince Selim II as one of his several 'wives'.

The Venier family never saw Cecilia again, and the details of what happened to her have become blurred by legend and folk tale as well as by the overlapping stories of other women enslaved in the Ottoman harem. According to accounts that filtered back to Venice, however, the terrified child matured into an intelligent, resourceful woman. By the time Selim became Sultan in 1566 Cecilia-Nurbanu had become his favourite concubine, whom he consulted on affairs of state. And when he died in 1574 she not only out-manoeuvred her rivals to ensure that her son, Murad III, succeeded to the throne, but as Sultan Validé (the Queen Mother), she effectively ruled in his place.*

This was a curious period in Ottoman history – sometimes described as the female caliphate – when a succession of older women became the political powers behind the throne. From her own little court within the harem, Cecilia assumed control over the empire's domestic and foreign affairs. According to the Venice historian Alberto Toso Fei, her policies were so advantageous to her native city that the Senate, in gratitude, used to send her regular presents of gold silk cushions and lap dogs. It was also said that her favouritism towards Venice so outraged the Republic's trading rival, Genoa, that its officials sent a professional poisoner to get rid of her.

Venice's reputation for tolerance and for intellectual pragmatism persisted even during the French and Austrian occupations, and by the mid-19th century Venice was drawing women from other cities and other countries. George Sand, notorious as a cross-dresser and advocate of free love, came to the city in the winter of 1834 with her young lover Alfred de Musset. Luisa's landlady, Isabelle de la Baume-Pluvinel, also chose the city when she was looking for a home for herself and her lover Augustine Bulteau – a female novelist who wrote under the male pseudonym Jacques Vontade. The Countess doubtless had to navigate some local *froideur*, but the money she spent on restoring Ca' Dario would surely have helped to ease acceptance for her unusual living arrangements.

And in the wake of Isabelle and Augustine came Luisa. Even though the local aristocracy might condemn the circus she was creating at the palazzo, with her curious animals and her startling appearances, the city authorities were not going to interfere. Luisa was free to concentrate on the performance of her new Venetian life; and she was fortunate that the previous year she had secured the acquaintance of one of Venice's most eminent summer visitors to help promote her visibility.

*   Several other European women during this period were also said to have risen to political power after having been kidnapped by Turks; but the lack of clear historical documentation has resulted in the details of their stories becoming blurred.

Serge Diaghilev was the founder of Les Ballets Russes, a company whose debut season in Paris in 1909 had already been hailed as the cultural phenomenon of the new century: its expressively modern choreography and poetic designs promised a revolution on the ballet stages of Europe. While Luisa may not yet have seen the company perform, she had been told about it by D'Annunzio, an enthusiastically converted balletomane and a reliable barometer of fame. Diaghilev's arrival in Venice that August, along with his star dancer and lover Vaslav Nijinsky and his designer Leon Bakst, also promised to be one of the events of the summer season. Each morning crowds would gather down on the Lido, the narrow island which lay to the south-east of the city, to watch Nijinsky posing in his bathing suit as Bakst painted his portrait on the beach. Luisa knew how important it was to make an approach to these celebrated Russians, and while she was too reticent to introduce herself, she made use of the American dancer Isadora Duncan (whom she knew through D'Annunzio) to issue dinner invitations on her behalf.

It's not certain where the dinner took place – presumably in a suite or a private room of the hotel where Luisa was staying. Nijinsky's wife Romola wrote about it later, but she was reporting only what her husband had remembered (the two did not meet until 1913), and some of her information was evidently false – Luisa certainly did not welcome her ballet guests with a live snake coiled around her shoulders, although that would become one of her later stunts.

However, there was sufficiently convincing detail in Romola's account to extrapolate a suggestive picture of what occurred. Even if Luisa had not worn a snake, she'd dressed herself to striking effect: long ropes of pearls were looped around her neck and wrists, and a pure white gown set off the pooling darkness of her gaze – made even more intense by the drops of belladonna she was using daily to dilate her pupils. We can imagine her, too, from descriptions in D'Annunzio's 1910 novel *Forse che sì forse che no*, whose heroine Isabella Inghirami was given many of Luisa's attributes of beauty and style: her 'long narrow legs outlined against the slim narrow lines of a Fortuny skirt [and her] eyelids darkened and lips steeped [in] vermilion'.

Yet as skilfully as she'd managed the staging of her own appearance, it seems Luisa was less adept at managing her guests. The dinner itself passed off reasonably smoothly; Bakst proved a little bit dull and Nijinsky, for all his arrestingly Slavic beauty, was extremely reserved. But Diaghilev – suave, plump and charismatic – kept the conversation flowing, talking buoyantly of the success of his company and enthusing about Venice, which he had claimed as his favourite city.

After dinner the mood deteriorated. Duncan had naturally included herself in the evening, but had grown bored with the conversation and decided that she would entertain the company by dancing a waltz with Nijinsky. It would be a historic moment, she said, the first time that the world's two 'dance geniuses' had ever performed together. Nijinsky, however, was a reluctant partner. As naturally introvert as Luisa, he loathed being turned into a drawing-room pet. He glowered throughout the waltz and was plainly furious when, afterwards, Duncan flung herself in theatrical exhaustion onto the couch and declared, 'What a shame he wasn't my pupil when he was two, *then* I could have taught him to dance.'*

As a silence descended, the awkwardness of the room was compounded by the screeching exhibitionism of Luisa's pet monkey, capering around its cage. Yet while the evening had ended badly, the simple fact that Luisa had hosted a dinner for Diaghilev and his friends had been its own form of social benediction. The following year, when she acquired the Venier palazzo, she would be able to invite them again, and where they came others in Venice would follow.

One other key outcome of that 1909 dinner was the professional connection Luisa was able to forge with Bakst. Until then she'd been content to use couturiers like Poiret and Fortuny to create her outfits, but she was ambitious now to expand her wardrobe beyond fashion; and Bakst, whose bold and brilliantly vivid reinterpretations of historical dress were so crucial to Diaghilev's success, would seem to be ideal for her purpose.

Over the next decade Bakst would create over forty different costumes for Luisa, dressing her as a *commedia dell'arte* harlequin, as a golden sun goddess, as the Queen of the Night, and as St Sebastian in

*   Nijinsky displayed similar irritation when D'Annunzio once arrogantly asked for a private performance, meeting his request to 'dance something for me' with the truculent reply, 'Why don't you *write* something for me?' (Scot D. Ryersson and Michael Orlando Yaccarino, *Infinite Variety*, p. 39)

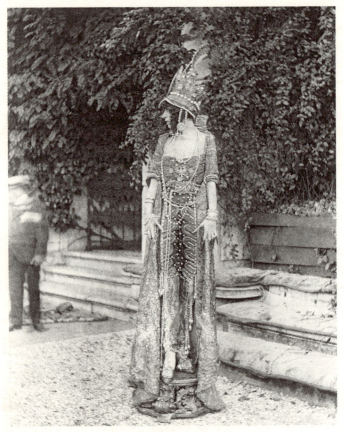

Luisa, dressed by Bakst for her Indo-Persian party
and photographed by Fortuny (1913).

silver armour. Fortuny himself photographed her in the ensemble she
wore for her Indo-Persian party in September 1913: a fantasy of delicate
blue and gold adorned with a pearl-encrusted headdress, long pointed
slippers and gold-painted false nails as lethally sharp as an eagle's tal-
ons. Luisa may have first worn this costume to a ball given by Lady
Cunard in October 1912, but it became one of her favourite Bakst pieces
and remained in her wardrobe for several years.

This was, however, a rare instance of economy, and Bakst's private income was much enhanced by the extravagance of Luisa's commissions. Not only did she pay him to design her own costumes, but also those worn by the waiters, gondoliers and musicians who staffed her huge entertainments. During her first two summers in Venice, before the palazzo had been fully refurbished, Luisa had to limit herself to small dinners and 'water parties' on the Grand Canal – for which she hired a flotilla of gondolas to boat herself and her guests up and down the water. But once the palazzo was ready in 1912, she had the opportunity to let both her imagination and her budget soar.

She had other rivals to emulate: in 1911, Poiret had lavished thousands of francs on an Arabian Nights party inspired by the Diaghilev ballet *Shéhérazade*, and possibly intended to publicize the '*style sultan*' of his own new collection. He'd had the garden of his Parisian home decked out with Turkish carpets and cushions, with fairy lights and red Bengali flares, and had entertained his 300 guests with singers and dancers. The following year the Countess Aynard de Chabrillan had rivalled

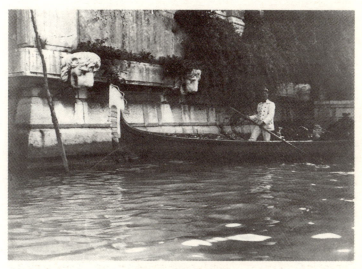

Luisa's gondola awaits her
outside the palazzo (c. 1913).

Poiret with an event so lavish that it was reported in the *New York Times* as exceeding the enchantment of an opium smoker's 'golden dreams'.[6]

But there was a selfless intensity to Luisa's Venetian parties that set them apart from those of her rivals. She didn't just spend staggering sums on feeding and entertaining her guests; she made each event into a special performance whose illusion she dedicated herself to sustaining. At one party she dressed as Sarah Bernhardt and, according to the novelist Michel Georges-Michel (who recycled and embroidered numerous Casati tales), the carefully calibrated climax of the evening was the moment when she suddenly and dramatically staged the actress's death. Without warning, Luisa went rigid and collapsed to the floor, which was the cue for one of her guests – Baron Panatelli – to enter the room dressed as Christ and read out Bernhardt's 'last request' that her body be taken by gondola to the island of Torcello. The evening concluded with Luisa and her guests being floated by candlelit procession across the lagoon.

The power of silent gesture was one that Luisa might have learned from D'Annunzio, whose plays made frequent use of choreography and costume to convey states of rapt emotion.[*] Certainly she was as focused as any stage actress when she performed for her parties, and to her guests the purity of her concentration could be unnerving as well as impressive. The young English socialite Lady Diana Manners was just nineteen when she was first invited to a night at Luisa's palazzo, on 10 September 1913; until then, her experience of parties had been shaped by the dull fruit cups and quadrilles of her debut season in London. But as Diana later wrote in her memoirs, the theatre of Luisa's entertainment had detonated a series of 'glorious shocks' to her imagination. She'd been particularly awed by the silent dignity with which Luisa had handed each guest the welcome gift of a tuberose. It had mortified Diana that while the European arrivals had risen to the moment, murmuring 'Quelle emotion – Madame', as they were given their creamily scented flower, her fellow English guests had only managed a prosaic, 'Doesn't it smell good.'[*7]

---

[*]   One typically detailed stage direction from D'Annunzio's *La città morta* reads: 'The loose hair spreads over the shoulders of the virgin and falls onto the blind woman's dress, flowing like water.'

Five days later, on 15 September, Diana witnessed an even more spectacular variation of Luisa's artistry at a ball themed around the Venice of the 18th-century painter Pietro Longhi. It had started late, at 11 p.m., and when guests arrived at the palazzo garbed as aristocratic carnival revellers and *commedia dell'arte* characters, Luisa greeted them in the white harlequin costume designed for her by Bakst. She was standing on a pedestal with a monkey and a macaw perched on her shoulder, while beside her the ever-patient Garbi (one arm decorated ghoulishly with imitation blood) was keeping tight control of the cheetah. Guests were handed a flower and a Murano glass lantern, and were ushered into the garden where a band played jazz until two in the morning.

It was then that the party moved towards its climax, as a flotilla of gondolas appeared at the waterfront terrace to ferry Luisa and her guests to the Piazza San Marco. Earlier in the day the weather had been stormy, but now that it had cleared there could be no more privileged or entrancing location. Moonlight glimmered palely over the angels and domes of the Basilica, over the lacey stonework of the Doge's palace; flames from a hundred braziers threw the piazza's colonnades into flickering chiaroscuro relief, while beyond, the waters of the lagoon gleamed darkly.

To the accompaniment of a distant melody, played by a small band on an approaching gondola, the guests were directed from the waterfront jetty to a roped-off section of the square. Their path was lit by dozens of candelabra, held up by a hired retinue of staff who, according to some eyewitnesses, were all black, and all identically outfitted in 18th-century uniforms cut from Fortuny's rarest velvet. The guests themselves remained in the masks, wigs and crinolines they had worn all night, but Luisa had changed into a new costume, a hoop-skirted gown of gold satin. She processed into the piazza, heralded by flag-bearers and trumpeters, by falconers with trained birds held ceremonially on their wrists, and she seemed so much an apparition of Longhi's

---

*   A decade later, when Lady Diana embarked on her own slightly rebellious career as a stage artist, she would try to replicate something of Luisa's carefully contrived mystique. Going by her married name, Lady Diana Cooper, she played a starring role in Max Reinhardt's *The Miracle*, touring across America and parts of Europe.

Venice that she drew applause not only from her guests but from the huge crowds who had gathered to watch.[*]

The scale and sumptuousness of this party were rare in Venice now, and rumours of what Luisa had been planning had circulated long before the evening began. Hundreds of local people and tourists had massed around the edges of the piazza; some had taken the trouble to rent rooms that overlooked it, while others had found their way onto nearby rooftops. Luisa herself had been ordered to hire a number of policemen to maintain control (and it was the writer Gabriel-Louis Pringué who reported that these were reinforced by a line of 'gigantic black men dressed...in cloth of scarlet silk...tied to one another by a gold chain'.)[8] But despite these precautions, the onlookers came close to mobbing the party – Diana Manners recalled that some of the guests around her had been violently jostled and subjected to 'shouts and ribald screams', and that the sound of the music could no longer be heard.

It said much about Luisa's reputation in Venice that she had been given permission to stage her party in such a public place, and to risk so public a disturbance. But while the local nobility might spurn her still, Luisa's arrival at the palazzo each summer was keenly anticipated by the city's officials. The money she spent and the employment she provided were significant assets to the Venetian economy – and it was known throughout the city that the Marchesa could be charged criminally high prices for the goods and services she required. Money continued to have no objective meaning for Luisa; she would buy anything on a whim, and refused to consider the possibility that her servants might steal from her or that tradesmen might be charging her double. The wealth that Alberto Amman had so scrupulously accumulated had become for his daughter a fluid, fantastical currency of pleasure – and the city of Venice was profiting handsomely from it.

As well as being an economic asset to her adopted city, Luisa was also a boost to its public image. In 1913 Venice was entering the 20th century, with new hotels being built along the Lido and steam-powered vaporetti zig-zagging along the Grand Canal. Yet it continued to trade

---

[*]   Details of her costume vary between reports, but this description is corroborated by a portrait by Guiglio de Blaas.

on the romance of its past and Luisa, with all her arcane pageantry, was now very much a municipal asset. The golden age of Venetian culture, when the city had been home to writers like Goldini, composers like Vivaldi and libertines like Casanova, had survived only through its architecture, through the paintings that were hung in its galleries and churches and through the cheap carnival masks that were sold to its tourists. For most of the city's visitors, the romance of Venice started to tarnish as soon as they saw the actual squalor in which many of its citizens were housed, the genteel poverty in which its aristocrats eked out their lives. But Luisa, with her parties and parades, was restoring, albeit temporarily, some shimmer of the city's past.

She was, in short, becoming a tourist attraction. Gondoliers who'd formerly ignored the Palazzo Venier when ferrying sightseers down the Grand Canal now entertained their clients with stories of the expensive high jinks that took place behind its ivy-covered façade. A sighting of Luisa in her own gondola, gliding in state among her tiger skins and her pets, was a prized event; even more so, an invitation to one of her parties.*

Stories of La Casati also spread far beyond the city. Details of her San Marco party appeared in the world's press, from Chicago's *Inter-Ocean* to the *Madrid Herald*; accounts of her exploits featured in social columns and in the memoirs of travellers. Writers laboured to catch the essence of her style – 'sheer Tintoretto' according to one, 'exotic as an Aubrey Beardsley' according to another – and her influence began to spread into the wider culture. Couturiers incorporated aspects of her costumes into their own designs, and over time novelists began to raid her life for inspiration (among them Carl Van Vechten in *Peter Whiffle: His Life and Works* and Michel Georges-Michel in *Dans le fête de Venise*).

Some of those who came to see what the fuss was about were disappointed. Mercedes de Acosta, the writer and younger sister of Rita

---

*   According to Luisa's biographers Scot D. Ryersson and Michael Orlando Yaccarino, these parties were also encouraged because they provided cover for sensitive political meetings, allowing foreign diplomats and government officials to make contact as they mingled unnoticed among Luisa's guests. (Ryersson and Yaccarino, *Infinite Variety*, p. 45)

de Acosta, would invite herself to the Palazzo dei Leoni shortly after the war. Luisa greeted her guest in style, wearing a white robe, with a white flower held in one hand and her cheetah padding beside her. But to de Acosta, the effect was just 'bad theatre'. Others opted to supplement reality with their own fabrications. Wild stories accumulated about Luisa's Venetian antics: about the nocturnal walks she took through San Marco, stark naked except for a fur cloak draped from her shoulders; about the gruesome toll her exacting aesthetic was taking on her servants, several of whom had died, it was said, after having their bodies decorated with toxic gold paint. Her sexuality too was the subject of lurid invention. Luisa was rumoured to keep a handsome but mute Tunisian lord as her pleasure slave; she was said to possess such insatiable desires that some of her lovers died from exhaustion in her arms; and afterwards, it was claimed, she commissioned wax dummies in which to entomb their cremated remains.

This last piece of nonsense might well have been put into circulation by Luisa herself, given its suspicious similarity to the legend of Cristina Trivulzio. She was trying very hard to promote her image as a modern maenad, a woman of perverse and fearless tastes, and such rumours were a useful diversion from the truth, which was that Luisa's experience of sex was actually very limited. Even though she'd become progressively estranged from Camillo and in early 1914 would gain a formal separation from him, she seems to have hesitated to take sexual advantage of her single life. The physical and emotional demands of an affair were possibly still too much of a threat to her fragile independence; and in the end it would be D'Annunzio who, after years of careful patience, would finally break through her reserve. When he did, he would boast that the side of Luisa he had successfully coaxed into passion was one that no other man had seen.

CHAPTER 3

'I am in a gondola. I am crossing the canal. I am approaching
the palace. A fine rain falls in the shimmering violet moonlight.
The green door of the low tide. The splashing of the water
against the stairs...I can see gold lace gleaming in the windows.'
(Gabriele D'Annunzio, '*La figure de cire*')

In an undated and unfinished short story, '*La figure de cire*', D'Annunzio
would transpose his love affair with Luisa to the setting of Venice, and
to the Palazzo Venier dei Leoni. In a heady synaesthesia of detail he
would describe the churning anticipation with which he journeyed to the
palace, the violence of his desire as he knelt to embrace Luisa, and
the intensity of her response: 'She is hot, almost burning. All for you.'[1]
In reality, though, the two were rarely in the city as lovers. Until 1915,
D'Annunzio was still in exile, hiding from his Italian creditors; and if
he did dare to cross into Venice for Luisa's sake, it was only once and
for a very brief occasion.

Otherwise, it was in Paris where their relationship evolved from platonic fascination into a sexual affair. The shift began in May 1911, when
Luisa went to meet D'Annunzio for the premiere of his new play *St
Sebastian* at the Théâtre du Châtelet. It was an elaborately poetic vehicle
that he'd written as a homage for Ida Rubinstein, and with spectacular
designs by Bakst, a new score by Debussy and a cast of two hundred,
D'Annunzio was investing high artistic and financial hopes in its success.

Rubinstein herself had been compellingly beautiful on stage: 'a
stained-glass window come to life', according to the youthfully entranced
Jean Cocteau; a 'sibylline presence' according to her infatuated author.
But Rubinstein's untrained voice was too weak to bear the burden of
D'Annunzio's grandiloquent text and Proust's damning verdict on the
production that it was 'boring' and 'crushed by style' was widely shared

by the public. D'Annunzio flung himself into despair when his play was closed after just twelve performances, and it was Luisa who stayed loyally close by him, listening to his perorations of complaint, consoling him with expensive treats and attending him with a patience that she'd rarely, if ever, been able to summon for her husband or daughter.[2]

From this point on, their relationship acquired a newly exclusive charge, and by the following year D'Annunzio was writing to Luisa as his *cara amica*, his 'dearest friend'. Relations between them remained technically chaste; Luisa was still unwilling to threaten the façade of her marriage. Yet D'Annunzio's account of a meeting that occurred in the summer of 1912 suggests the sexual tension had become deliciously palpable: '[Luisa] was supposed to leave for St Moritz [and] I was having breakfast alone with her. I think I already loved her. Without doubt I wanted her as always. I had brought her a long brush, for her bath. It was a way to touch her from afar, with magic fingers. The husband walked in. The brush, wrapped in paper, was on the mantelpiece. He took it in his hands. I don't know what sort of redness stung my face.'[3]

The following July in Paris, D'Annunzio judged that his moment had come. And as Luisa finally succumbed to his long campaign of seduction, he celebrated by conferring on her the intimately erotic nickname Coré. He'd long made a habit of assigning his favourite mistresses the names of classical goddesses – the athletic Marchesa Rudini had been Nike, for instance – and the name Coré was taken from Kore, the Greek goddess of the underworld.[*]

Luisa, having taken this momentous step in her relationship with D'Annunzio – now her Gabriele – was delighted by the new identity he'd conjured up. Although she had proposed the more mellifluous French spelling of Coré, she believed that the name now affirmed her as the dark goddess of D'Annunzio's imagination. Indeed, as Gabriele's mistress she aspired to become his privileged muse. She imagined the

---

[*]   The name was also a reference to the Korai, a type of classical Greek statue characterized by its androgynous form and enigmatic smile. Leon Bakst was also fascinated by the Korai, which he considered emblematic of the 'emancipated hermaphrodite' woman of the future. (Gioia Mori, 'Luisa Casati: A Living Work of Art', from Fortuny Museum Catalogue, p. 7)

two of them rising to heights of creative fantasy and poetry together; and it was for her a precious compliment when, early in their affair, he told her that she had become a permanent presence in his mind and senses, shaping the way he experienced the world: 'I create [you] continually inside me, like yesterday at dusk beneath the trees, along the water which was...more heavenly than the sky.'[4]

D'Annunzio's own expectations of the affair were not, however, so rarefied. He'd been lusting after Luisa's body for years, and had imagined that once he overcame her reticence she would yield as gratefully to his expertise as Eleonora Duse – who'd confessed that his lovemaking had turned her into an 'addict' – or Alessandra di Rudini, who'd declared that until she met him she'd only 'loved like a virgin, cold to the desires of men'.[5]

It was to D'Annunzio's credit as a lover that he did take pride in bringing his women to orgasm, however callously he might treat them in other ways. He was greedily curious about their bodies – the folds of their vaginas, the hair of their armpits, the hidden softness of their feet. At a time when the language of sex was largely closeted, he used it to seductively blatant effect, writing in loving detail to one woman about the velvety heat of her labia, begging another to 'kiss my eyes, slowly caress my lashes with your soft moist tongue'.[6] He took equal care with the staging of his seductions, ensuring that the air was aphrodisiac with lilies and incense and that every surface was a sensual crush of rose petals, cushions and fur. He liked his mistresses to wear high-heeled shoes when they made love – it suited his fetish for tall women, especially during oral sex – while he himself favoured loose silk pyjamas and a liberal application of cologne (a bespoke blend called Aqua Nuntia, which he had specially bottled in vessels of fine Murano glass).

D'Annunzio had every reason to assume that this sexual theatre would appeal to Luisa, who was always most comfortable when her life was structured around ritual and stagecraft. Yet during the intense three-week period in Paris when they came to know each other as lovers, she proved disappointingly erratic in her response. The occasions when he most successfully overcame her physical inhibitions were in fact those when their lovemaking acquired an edge of violence, and despite his sexual experience, D'Annunzio was almost as alarmed as he

was stimulated by this discovery. 'I swear to you that I have no awareness of what happened', he wrote to Luisa on 9 July 1913, 'I only know
that I had the taste of blood in my mouth and that I ached with yearning the whole night long.'[7] In his diary he made cryptic notes of what
had occurred when an intimate dinner in the garden of a restaurant in
St-Germain-en-Laye had turned savagely heated: 'the stinging kiss on
the neck, the mad return to the hotel, the red mark which she displays'.[8]
During that night of raw passion he encountered a new, abandoned
Luisa, calling out in 'the unexpected confession of [her] pleasure'.

In memory of that night he began to call her his 'Divine Marquise',
a reference to the deviant writings of the Marquis de Sade.[9] But while
D'Annunzio had found a way to unlock Luisa's shy, untutored sexuality, it still frightened her to lose control. She fought shy of his ardour,
and from the volatile tone of his frequent letters to her, it is clear that
their relationship was fraught with arguments and cross purposes from
the start. If Gabriele tried to force a moment of passion against her
will, Luisa became vehemently angry, the shock and offence in her
dark eyes matched by the force of her cries: 'NO I don't want it. Don't
touch me.' She was almost as antagonistic when he pressured her into
emotional intimacy. D'Annunzio had assumed that they would now be
seeing each other nearly every day in Paris and that Luisa, like most
of his mistresses, would delight in exchanging confidences and sentimental expressions of love; yet to his wounded surprise, she kept him
at a distance, refusing to commit to any plans beyond the moment and
disdaining any form of conventional romance.

D'Annunzio had reason to believe that Luisa loved him in her
own way. She had not only trusted her sexuality to him, but given him
glimpses of an innocent, childlike aspect to her personality, 'a fresh...
smiling [Luisa]...a sweet creature hidden in the dark'. He adored the
sound of her laughter, 'one of the beauties of this earth'.[10] Yet still she
remained wary of letting him get close: her habits of shyness, self-
preservation, vanity, control and ego were too strongly ingrained to yield
to his demand for intimacy, and she could not bear the idea of the 'great
mystery' of their love being tainted by mundane familiarity. 'If you would
be near to me, leave me,' she urged, and she begged him to respect her
emotional privacy so that Coré's 'opaque exterior' might remain intact.[11]

Luisa was dictating the terms of the relationship in a way that D'Annunzio had never expected, and she was doing so in language that he himself had taught her. He promised to try and subdue the 'profound trembling' of his heart.[12] Yet he remained frustrated and jealous. He tormented himself with images of what Luisa might be doing when she was apart from him, envisaging her 'in the arms of some professional dancer or...at a table with some witty important man'. He was unable to prevent himself from begging for affection, and after one particularly harsh quarrel, when Luisa withdrew into an 'atrocious silence', he cravenly sent letter after letter begging for 'just one word'.[13]

It was also bewildering to D'Annunzio that Luisa appeared so indifferent to the other women in his life. When they had begun their affair in early July he was still deeply involved with his current mistress, Nathalie de Goloubeff, a classically beautiful Russian with a lovely singing voice whom he had no expectation of relinquishing, despite the 'trembling' emotion he avowed for Coré. But Luisa didn't seem to care. She made no claim on Gabriele's fidelity; apparently she felt no jealousy, and so perversely detached was she as a mistress that at the end of their first turbulent, exploratory three weeks together she floored him completely by announcing that it was necessary for her to leave Paris and move on to Venice, where she wanted to prepare for the summer season.

Luisa was actually hoping that she might persuade D'Annunzio to follow her. It had been his inspiration that had first sent her to Venice, and she longed for him to admire the transformations she'd made to her palazzo, the splendour of her menagerie and the scale of her parties (this was to be the summer of the Persian and the Pietro Longhi balls). She probably wanted to show him off as her lover, too, for having so carefully cast herself as a sexual transgressive in Venice it would be gratifying to have D'Annunzio there with her, in person.

But he himself had good reasons for refusing. Engrossed by Luisa these last three weeks, he'd neglected the writing of his new play, and he feared that Venice would be too full of distractions for him to concentrate on his work. Even more problematic was the possibility that in crossing back over the Italian border he might be apprehended by creditors still hounding him for money. Although he tried to explain the danger of exposing himself to 'pestering onlookers in Venice',[14] Luisa was unable to understand why he would allow himself to be subject to such prosaic constraints. Rapidly the issue of Venice became a flashpoint: D'Annunzio was pained by Luisa's refusal to forgo the season for his sake, and she was equally pained by his failure to grasp that for her, the summer parties were no less serious a vocation than his writing. When she declared her firm intention to leave at the beginning of August, they quarrelled with a ferocity that D'Annunzio feared was terminal. Afterwards he scribbled a miserable note: 'I telephoned several times yesterday, hoping to slice through this stubborn and undeserved silence. Are you leaving this evening? Are you leaving without seeing me again? What will I do?'[15]

Luisa had indeed left, and hoping to conciliate her, he sent a vague promise of following her soon afterwards. On 4 August she telegrammed back with credulous delight: 'What a joy. You can come to Venice. I would be very glad.'[16] Yet the days went by and D'Annunzio, having ordered his bags to be packed for the journey, simply ordered for them to be unpacked again. He genuinely believed it would be too dangerous to act on his word and in the end, wearied by his vacillating emotions, he went instead to his summer refuge in Arcachon in south-west France. Luisa, in her palazzo, grew impatient and lonely. She sent a pleading telegram complaining that she was 'so sad' without her Gabriele, and that she longed for him to be beside her so that together they could 'watch the lagoon through the golden windows'.[17]

He responded with letters of solicitously detailed ardour, assuring her that he remained in thrall to her beauty, that the image of her body was always with him, as was that of her 'imperious, childlike' face. Yet now that he had gained some distance, D'Annunzio began to punish and to play with Luisa. Barbs of accusation spiked his love: he claimed that he would willingly have come to Venice if only she had allowed him more intimate access in Paris. 'Presence for you ruins everything, destroys everything. So many times I have felt, beside you, that presence inevitably diminishes or falsifies me.' More viciously, he accused her of being incapable of true feeling: 'If only Coré loved me. If only she truly had a "delicate trace" upon her heart, a crack!' With practised cruelty he informed her that she had only herself to blame for the fact he was now consoling himself with other women, that he was compelled 'once more into intolerable earthly promiscuity'.[18]

Luisa was not equipped to parry this level of emotional manipulation, nor did she trust her own writing skills. Although she liked to devote elaborate care to the appearance of her correspondence, using gold or coloured inks on highly embellished black notepaper, she had little confidence in her powers of written expression. Where possible, she restricted her letters to matters of fact. Her communications to Gabriele during that summer were almost all by telegram, and many of them were limited to a single line, a single observation that was almost poetic in its literalness. One day she telegrammed to say 'I have a fierce turtle dove'; another, to observe that there had been a 'Pure turquoise sky'. But as D'Annunzio's correspondence grew more bullying, she was goaded into more artless and fulsome declarations of emotion: 'Coré is crying. You should never torment Coré. Words are useless. Come if you love her.'[19]

It was a cruelly unequal correspondence. D'Annunzio would follow up a letter of vicious accusation with one of studiedly patient tenderness, claiming that all he wanted from her was an assurance of her continuing love. When she received one such reprieve, her gratitude was naked, almost self-abasing: '*Grazie, grazie, grazie, amico caro, Obbediro*', she replied ('thank you, my love, I will obey').[20] Yet days later some fresh bitterness of spirit moved D'Annunzio to write a torrent of accusations in which he railed against her 'hard and frozen' attitude. The letter was harsh enough for him to send a second, begging Luisa to ignore the first, but his warning came too late.[21] Her response, even though couched in protectively opaque language, was desolate: 'Coré is dead because she has dared to approach the gods. Her heart is asleep for ever. We weep....Souls are impenetrable to other souls and we suffer.'[22]

This poignantly over-elaborate confession was a very rare acknowledgment of the alienation and loneliness that Luisa experienced, even within the edifice of her fantasy life. It was an admission that she felt, very deeply, the gulf between her own fugitive sense of self and the ordinary world of emotional and social intercourse. Yet confidences did not come easily to her and by 5 September, when she telegrammed D'Annunzio again, Luisa had reverted to her usual concerns and her usual tone of impractical command. She promised him that if he could finally come to her in Venice, 'on the evening of the full moon', he would find her waiting for him, dressed in her Persian costume.

There is no evidence that D'Annunzio obeyed Luisa's summons at this late stage, but clearly he immersed himself in the fantasy of having done so. For it was the image of Luisa in her 'wide silvered trousers', her 'corsages of pearls', 'splendid helmet [and] white feather plume' that inspired the short story '*La figure de cire*', which he would later write and dedicate to her.

The bulk of the story would be written in 1922, but its prose was charged with the savage emotional ambivalence that had marked the lovers' first summer together. On the surface, it was a flamboyant trib-ute to her beauty and to her pursuit of the aesthetic life; but in the dark, dreamlike plotting of '*La figure de cire*' lay all the violence of D'Annunzio's thwarted ego. There was a chilling, detached cruelty in the way his narrator made love to the fictional Coré: he described her vagina as 'that other sombre mouth'), he triumphed in her orgasm as a moment of death: 'My heart stops. I have nailed her in the silver coffin. The world vanishes.' But there was even more explicit violence in the way D'Annunzio elaborated the conventional metaphor of *le petit mort* into a full-blown fantasy of murder.[23]

The murder in the story pivoted around the wax figure of the title, which was itself inspired by a collection of wax figures that Luisa had begun to assemble around 1912–13. These were mildly macabre repli-cas of herself, which she liked to dress in garments and jewels identical to her own. One was life-sized, with emerald glass eyes and a coppery wig (during its construction Luisa had telegrammed to D'Annunzio, 'The glass worker has given me two great green beautiful eyes like the stars – do you want them?').[24] When Adolph de Meyer and his wife dined at the palazzo one night Luisa was already seated at the table with the replica by her side; and in the dim candlelight, under the force of their hostess's wilful strangeness, it was momentarily impossible for them to distinguish between the two figures.

Another of the wax pieces in her collection was an exquisite figurine that she had commissioned from the young Russian artist Catherine Barjansky; and for a while it became her favourite companion, taken to

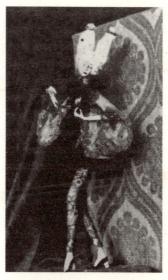

Luisa's wax doll and miniature avatar,
created by Catherine Barjansky.

dress fittings at Poiret's atelier or placed on the seat beside her when
she was driving her Rolls-Royce.*[25]

Figures cast in wax were fashionable during the pre-war years, and
these replica Luisas became key props in the theatre she was constructing around herself. For D'Annunzio, however, they became emblematic
of Luisa's baffling and frustrating behaviour as a mistress, her refusal to
yield him her body, her insistence on hiding behind the remote, unsul-
lied image of Coré. In 'La figure de cire' all of D'Annunzio's frustration
was channelled into the symbol of the wax dummy; and at the story's

* One other artist who worked in the medium was Lotte Pritzel, from whom
Luisa commissioned an 18-inch piece in which she was posed half naked, holding
a crystal ball. Also in Luisa's collection was a life-sized dummy of Mary Vetsera,
allegedly cast just after the impressionable young baroness had been shot by her
lover. The dummy, with a bloody wound clotted on its temple, was taken out of its
cupboard at judicious moments to alarm unwary guests.

surreal point of climax he had his narrator descend into such a perverse delirium of love and hatred that he throttles the flesh and blood Coré, so that the replica can permanently take her place: 'I am not afraid – when I strangle Coré, the Wax is always there....The Wax is alive as if the last breath of the strangled woman passed into the frightening copy.'[26]

D'Annunzio's message to Luisa was brutal: if she demanded to be loved as a work of art, then she could not be loved as a woman. Yet if the story had been written to vent his bitterness, it had also reflected his admiration and his need for Luisa – and this was ultimately all that mattered to her. When he wrote to her about the story in 1922 he gave her eloquent credit for the role that she had played as his muse; he'd been 'transfigured' by the pain he'd suffered in loving her, and as a result had been able to write with a new and 'marvellous boldness of introspection', with 'thoughts more real and potent than my very arteries'. Thanks to Luisa's inspiration, he believed he had written a story of rare 'darkness and brilliance' – and when he finally allowed her to see it, she viewed its murderous subtext simply as a tribute to their special understanding.*

* * * * *

Just as D'Annunzio regarded 'La figure de cire' as his homage to Luisa, he also cherished the small wax doll carved in her likeness that she'd almost certainly given him as a gift. He claimed that it was imbued with her magic and often, in his letters, it became a metaphor for their relationship. When he wanted to admonish Luisa for being too elusive, he would write that her avatar had melted, 'no trace left, not even her eyes'; when she was sweetly attentive to him he promised to treasure it forever.* Their bond of love, sex and mutual support would always be shifting its ground, as over the next two years they moved in and out of each other's lives, sometimes meeting with pleasure and sometimes

---

* The story would not be published until 1935, as part of the autobiographical miscellany 100 Pages of the Secret Life of Gabriele D'Annunzio.

* D'Annunzio also had a wax collection of his own, and just after the war, when he himself was living in Venice, he had a life-sized dummy made of himself which he placed in the canalside window of his rented house in order be on constant view to his public. (Lucy Hughes-Hallett, The Pike, p. 10)

clashing violently. But they had each recognized something irreplaceable in the other: D'Annunzio was uniquely, admiringly complicit in Luisa's mission to turn herself into art; she in turn provided him with a bounty of literary inspiration and imagery. And as early as October 1913, when Luisa returned to Paris, they were clearly attempting to find new terms by which their relationship could continue.

D'Annunzio expressed open delight in their reunion. 'I have seen so much of you...in this feverish solitude, that it seems almost unbelievable to see you again in reality'. A few days later he wrote: 'How you delighted me yesterday Coré. Like never before.'[27] But they were settling as much for companionship as passion; during Luisa's stay in Paris she was discussing with D'Annunzio the advantages of putting her greyhounds into the same kennels that he used while she went with him to consult a famous 'sibyl'. She was also turning to him for help with a legal 'difficulty' – almost certainly connected with her separation from Camillo. And even though Gabriele's love letters would occasionally revert to their former self-dramatizing demands, he seemed willing to accept that this new relationship had been scaled down to something 'perfect and pleasant'.[28]

Key to D'Annunzio's new mood of resignation was his understanding that Luisa's provoking detachment was intrinsic to her mystique, that he could not have one without the other. When he boasted to Robert de Montesquiou about their relationship, he would claim that Luisa was unique among his mistresses: 'she possessed the gift of an omnipotent knowledge of the masculine heart: she knew how to be or to appear, incredible. She was in fact the only woman who ever astonished me.'[29] To his friend and biographer André Germain, he paid tribute to her independence: she was, he claimed, the only woman he'd ever known who was able to commit herself fully to the 'inimitable life', and the only one capable of loving him without 'a trace of bitterness'.

Yet while D'Annunzio could admire Coré's vocation for beauty, could even flatter himself that he had been a formative influence, he remained fundamentally stumped by the mystery of who she really was. Early in their affair he'd written, both as a compliment and a complaint, 'There is in Coré a puzzle that cannot be solved except at a distance' – and for as long as he knew Luisa, he could never satisfactorily put the pieces of her personality together: the childlike innocent, the grandstanding egotist, the artistic soul.[30]

The puzzle fascinated those who knew her far less well. The English diarist Harold Acton met Luisa just after the war and claimed to be hypnotized by her 'chimerical beauty' and 'crystal-gazing eyes'. Yet as he watched her in company, he found it impossible to work out whether she was an extraordinary rarity or a brilliant fraud. 'What was the real essence of this creature? Was she aware of her continuous metamorphosis, or was she impenetrable to herself, excluded from her own mystery? In her expressions how much was artifice, how much was spontaneity?'[31] So many of Luisa's gestures seemed choreographed, so many of her lines seemed rehearsed. On one occasion, when a guest complained about the feral smell emanating from her pet monkey, Luisa's response was to toss a lilac blossom into its cage and, as she watched the animal tear the flower into a hundred fragments, to rhapsodize, 'Don't you think that is beautiful? Isn't it like something in a Chinese painting?' When Luisa observed a rival socialite, the Princess Mananà Pignatelli, arriving at a ball in a costume more gothically black than her own, she declared dramatically: 'I am desolate. Dancing in this room I have just met a woman who is much more dead than me.' On such occasions it was impossible to be sure whether Luisa was being serious, whether she was satirizing herself, or just straining very hard for effect.

The young Russian artist Catherine Barjansky, who came to know Luisa quite well during the creation of her wax figurines, was inclined to take a critical view. From her account of their early meetings, it is clear that Luisa had grown considerably in social competence; very little of the tongue-tied, awkward young wife remained evident in the worldly performer Barjansky encountered. 'She had great charm, much imagination and regarded the world in an amusing and original manner. It was never dull where she was.'

Yet the more Barjansky saw of Luisa, the less convinced she was by the Marchesa's performance: she noted the tight wires of tension in her mannerisms, the restless way her 'fingers played nervously with the long hair of a jet-black Russian borzoi, lying at her feet'; the continuous cigarettes she smoked through her long, diamond-studded holder.[32] She noted too that while Luisa liked to gossip, to be told what was 'unusual and interesting' about the people she met, the relationships she formed were peculiarly limited and rarely deepened into friendship. Harshly, Barjansky formed the judgment that Luisa's commitment to the aesthetic life, so captivating to men like D'Annunzio, Montesquiou or Acton, was simply an expression of the same innate superficiality. 'She had an artistic temperament, but being unable to express herself in any branch of life, she made an art of herself. Because she possessed no inner life nor any power of concentration, she sought wild ideas in her external life.'[33]

It was difficult, of course, for Barjansky to guess that the studiedly glamorous Marchesa might possess a struggling interior life. Luisa was so ill-equipped at articulating her feelings that even D'Annunzio, who'd known her so long, found it hard to read her emotions. But by 1913 she was also becoming so used to living up to her public mask that, with new acquaintances like Barjansky, she was far more inclined to show off the 'wild ideas' and the surface glitter than to attempt the far more difficult feat of opening herself up to social intimacies.

As Harold Acton would ponder, though, it was difficult to distinguish the performative from the involuntary in Luisa's behaviour. She was becoming known for the throwing of extravagant tantrums in public places, her temper exploding if one of her carefully contrived arrangements came under threat. When a hotel once failed to prepare a suite of rooms exactly as she'd ordered, she hurled her jewelry out of the window. When guests failed to participate in her parties as required, she never hesitated to evict them. On one occasion, while wintering in St Moritz, Luisa believed she had an arrangement to go on a carriage ride with Prince Adalbert of Prussia (the third and most handsome son of Kaiser Wilhelm II). She dressed magnificently for him in diamonds and furs, and when she saw him driving off with another woman, she was so unable to contain her fury that she ordered her own driver to overtake the couple and force them off the road. 'The young man is very handsome, but he has no taste!' she was heard screeching. 'He will end up as a travelling salesman.'[34]

What seems to have been absurdly, stagily bad manners on Luisa's part may, however, have been symptomatic of her atypical wiring. Electric panic storms are typical of those with Asperger's, who describe feelings of invading chaos when the structure of their world is undermined. Even if Luisa had only a mild version of the disorder, her response to a frustration or an obstacle was sometimes so extreme that she appeared to be a helpless victim of her emotions, so lacking in control that she was momentarily crazed.

But Luisa had also been given unusual licence to act out these melo-dramatic outbursts, for those who witnessed them tended to applaud and enjoy them as part of the Casati legend. Luisa was rich, she was remarkable, she was entertaining, and there were few who were inclined to criticize her rudeness to her face. It's possible to imagine other cir-cumstances in which her behaviour might have been contained – if her mother had still been alive, or if she had been married to a different man. But performing her life on the stages she'd created, Luisa had almost no one to set her any limits. Even if consideration and restraint had come more naturally to her, they were qualities that her audience neither expected nor required.

For Cristina, who was the principal victim of Luisa's grandstanding performances, there was little to applaud. As a teenager she continued to feel excluded from her mother's life, boarded out to a convent school in France and spending most of her holidays with her aunt or in the care of staff. Luisa herself had little idea of how to manage a growing daughter, and the gestures she made towards parenting veered between excessive strictness (she refused to let Cristina wear dresses appropri-ate to her age) and excessive laxity (during one of her daughter's rare visits to Venice, she sent Cristina out alone in the gondola with just the cheetah for alarming company).

Yet in 1914, when Luisa and Camillo's marriage ended in a formal separation, Cristina would elect to remain in her mother's custody. However inadequate Luisa might be as mother, she had a powerful hold over her daughter's imagination, and the brief periods they spent together provided what little colour and excitement Cristina could hope for in her drab, restricted life. She looked forward to these interludes as much as she feared them; and there was always the hope, too, that she might find herself on the receiving end of one of her mother's unpre-dictable flashes of sweetness and warmth.

When it suited her, Luisa could behave with devastating generos-ity. In Venice she became aware that Emilio Basaldella, one of her two gondoliers, was suffering from a broken heart because the parents of his girlfriend Italia had refused permission for them to marry. As soon as Luisa was told of Emilio's situation, she became determined to make his cause her own. With unswerving persistence she sent a barrage of notes to Italia's family, praising Emilio's character and promising her financial support. When Italia and Emilio were finally married in the spring of 1914, they swore never to forget her kindness; and years later, when Luisa died alone in London, Emilio would be among the small group of people who travelled to the funeral to mourn her.

Another grateful beneficiary of Luisa's sympathy was the young Arthur Rubinstein. The pianist had been in Rome in 1912 to promote his career, and his friend Count Alexandre Skrzynski had promised to introduce him to the city's 'most interesting and charming woman', the Marchesa Casati.[35] Rubinstein chose not to inform Skrzynski at that moment that he'd actually met Luisa before, in a bizarre encounter in the library of a Munich hotel. Late one evening he'd gone into the library where she had been resting alone in the semi-darkness. Startled by his entrance, Luisa had sprung up from the couch, and the sight of her huge dark eyes and wild halo of hair had in turn terrified the young man, who'd given an involuntary scream.[36] As he described the incident later, for one hallucinatory second he had thought he'd disturbed a witch, or a demon.

But in Rome, when Rubinstein accepted an invitation for tea at Luisa's villa, he was very differently impressed. Her intelligence and her personality struck him as 'remarkable' and she was overwhelmingly eager to assist him, not only arranging for him to play at a private concert but assembling an exceptionally discerning audience. 'Aside from a scattering of illustrious names, she had gathered the real intellectuals, the real music lovers, the ones who are part of a concert public.'[37] This gesture of support represented a significant new direction in Luisa's aesthetic life, for even though her money and her energies would always centre on her own performances, she was becoming interested in the power that came from being a patron to others. A year or so after she had helped Rubinstein in Rome she gave generous support to Roberto Montenegro, the young Mexican painter whom she'd first met in a gallery on the Venetian island of Murano.

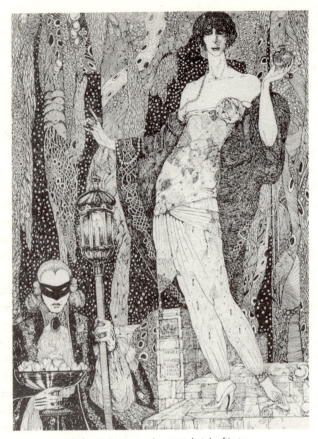

Robert Montenegro's c. 1912 sketch of Luisa,
which she had printed on her Christmas cards that year.

Montenegro recalled that he'd come to the gallery to purchase a distinctively shaped black vase when a tall, thin woman in furs and a veil
had made it clear to him that she was after the same piece. Through
an assistant the woman had communicated her willingness to buy
the artist whatever else he might like in the gallery if only he would
relinquish the vase. Intrigued by her urgency, Montenegro had agreed.
Luisa's gratitude would give a boost to his career. She invited him to

dinner, where she promised to introduce him to the director of Venice's Academy of Fine Arts. She also commissioned him to draw her, dressed in her Persian costume and posed on the steps of her palazzo. And so delighted was she with the result, a highly decorative drawing in the manner of Klimt, that she had it printed on all of her Christmas cards that year, thereby ensuring that his name became known to some of the richest and most well-connected people in Europe.

Montenegro was now one of many artists who were benefiting financially and socially from Luisa's patronage. By 1913 she had begun to expand the scope of her portrait gallery, seeking out painters, photographers and sculptors who would record the progress of her aesthetic life. She was desperate for another Boldini portrait, and was inundating the artist with hopeful photographs of herself costumed in Russian furs, harem pants and veils that might inspire him. But as fond as he had become of Luisa, Boldini was not willing to be her tame artist, and instead she had to turn to the inferior but more willing talent of Alberto Martini.

During the years between 1910 and 1925 Martini became something like a court painter to Luisa, paid an annual retainer by her and always on hand to paint or draw as required. It was, he claimed, a wonderful privilege. The Marchesa was a 'great artist', and he described how she used to arrive at his studio in a state of heightened awareness, studying herself in the mirror with 'a focused even glance' and then deciding how he should portray her: 'Give me a lion's head' she might announce to Martini one day, 'I see myself, I feel as if I am a lion.' Another day it might be a Medusa, or a butterfly, and the artist declared himself fortunate to be so intimate a conduit of Luisa's imagination.'[38]

Yet as willing as Martini was to defer to Luisa's imagination, much of what he committed to canvas or paper was disappointingly bland. He was neither original nor independent enough as an artist to address the more interesting aberrations of her appearance; his tendency was always

* Martini produced over a dozen painted portraits of Luisa, as well as numerous informal sketches. According to him, Luisa signed their contract with immense style, 'shining with byzantine majesty in a costume of gold and pale red [and] twinkling with gems and pearls and shining crosses'. (Scot D. Ryersson and Michael Orlando Yaccarino, *Infinite Variety*, p. 49)

to smooth out the sharp jut of her cheekbones, to disguise her distinctively long upper lip, to veil the penetrating force of her gaze. Even when Luisa herself wanted to appear dangerous – to pose as Cesare Borgia, in a suit of armour and with a boa constrictor coiled at her feet – Martini still contrived to make her look decorative, or merely pretty.

Perhaps Luisa perceived the problem. In 1914, one of Martini's portraits was selected for the Venice Biennale, the international art exposition for which the city had become famous.* But while she triumphed in their joint achievement, when Martini attempted to profit from it further by assembling all his Casati portraits for a public exhibition, Luisa refused permission. In a lofty volte-face from the position she'd taken with Boldini back in 1909, she claimed that to court such publicity would be vulgar. 'What is fortune compared to the dignity of art,' she scolded Martini. 'Nothing.'[39]

Her ideas about portraiture were, in any case, beginning to expand. She had recently posed for a quasi-Fauvist painting by Umberto Brunelleschi in which she wore nothing but a pale-blue wig and blue stockings and was accompanied by several rainbow-coloured animals, including a lavender greyhound. Her gallery of portraits also boasted some witchy pen-and-ink drawings by Hans Henning von Voigt, the self-styled diabolist who called himself Alistair: and, most distinguished of all, a series of expressionistically chiaroscuro photographs taken in 1912 by Baron Adolph de Meyer.

In these photographs, de Meyer had captured a potency in Luisa's presence that had eluded Martini. In one image he shot her face in deep shadow, dramatizing the intensity of her kohl-ringed eyes; in another she was leaning over the back of a chair, a long cheroot between her fingers, her expression fixed in a mordant half-smile. De Meyer had nailed both the force of Luisa's charisma and the force of her will, and D'Annunzio, when he received a copy of the photograph, recognized it

---

*   The Biennale of 1914 was a good one for Luisa. As well as the Martini portrait, a rather etiolated wax sculpture of her by Prince Paolo Troubetzskoy was selected for the main exhibition, while in the unofficial or 'reject' show down at the Lido were two costume portraits by Guiglio de Blaas and a nude by Umberto Brunelleschi. (Fortuny Museum Catalogue, p. 4)

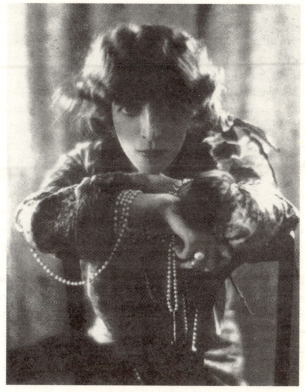

The unsettling force of Luisa's personality
as captured by Adolph de Meyer in 1912.

as the woman who had both tortured and enchanted him. Sententiously he inscribed it with the words 'Flesh is merely spirit betrothed to Death', and for the rest of his life he kept it prominently displayed in his bedroom.

Another significant artist to put himself at Luisa's service was Kees van Dongen. The Dutch painter had begun his career as a rebel Fauvist, but by the time Luisa met him in Paris in 1914 he'd begun to specialize in more commercially erotic nudes. 'I exteriorise my desires by expressing them in pictures,' he asserted. 'I love anything that glitters, precious stones that sparkle, fabrics that shimmer, beautiful women who arouse carnal desire' – and when he was approached, via a third party, with a commission to paint Luisa, he acknowledged that she was exactly 'the type' to arouse those desires. Van Dongen would paint Luisa at least seven times over the next seven years, and with each portrait he would dramatize and exaggerate her in a different way: as a veiled narcissist, leaning towards her reflection in a mirror; as an Amazon astride a rearing horse; as a green mermaid rising from the Venice lagoon. And during that period he embraced her not only as one of his favourite models – 'his naked sorceress' – but also as his mistress.

Luisa had struggled during the early stages of her affair with D'Annunzio, but having dared herself to sexual experiment, she now felt emboldened to widen her experience. Camillo was not even a symbolic obstacle, for he had become alienated by the scandal and discomfort of sharing Luisa's life and had finally agreed that they should part. Divorce was still impossible in Italy; but in early 1914 the two of them met in Budapest and signed papers that not only formalized their separation, but gave Luisa command of most of her inheritance and all of her independence.

Back in Paris, van Dongen proved to be a very accommodating lover. Tall and neatly bearded, with a pale, enigmatic gaze, he was far less interested than D'Annunzio had been in possessing Luisa's soul. He was intrigued by her obsessions and he enjoyed her money, but he was also content for the affair to develop on the terms she set. What Luisa wanted from van Dongen was not so much physical passion as artistic admiration: the climax of her pleasure was the desire and admiration that she could see reflected in his discerning gaze as she undressed for him and posed for him in the bedroom.

D'Annunzio may or may not have been imagining Luisa when he described the sensually choreographed gestures of Isabella, the heroine of his novel *Forse che sì, forse che no*: 'slowly removing her glove, allowing the doeskin to slip over the light down of her arm...taking the pins from her hat by raising her arms in an arc and letting the sleeve slip down to the curly gold of her armpit'. This, however, was the kind of performative sex at which Luisa had learned to excel, and although she was never as promiscuous as she hoped her reputation would suggest, it was with van Dongen that she embarked on an intensive and international period of experimentation, seeking out new lovers as well as new artists across the cities of Europe.

Venice was only her home for the summer season. After late September, peacock-feathered parasols and outdoor parties were rendered impossible by rains and tidal flooding, and also by the ghostly enveloping *caigi*, the city's notorious sea fogs. During the autumn and spring Luisa routinely spent a few weeks in Rome, where, despite the capital's more sedate codes of behaviour, she could still find opportunities to perform. The young diplomat Gerald Tyrwhitt recalled a costume ball at the British embassy in April 1913 where, dressed by Bakst as a sun goddess, Luisa made her entrance escorted by Prince Lichtenstein, two gold-robed 'priests' and the ever-present Garbi – who was keeping control of two greyhounds and a white peacock, decorated for the occasion with a diminutive pearl necklace around its throat.

Between Rome and Venice, Luisa was also making impulsive trips to Poland, Vienna, Munich, the Antibes and the island of Capri. Most winters she went to St Moritz, where she decorated her hotel suites with brocades and tiger skins and dressed herself in a parade of costumes – ermine for sleigh rides, Russian furs and a Cossack hat for skiing. These travels were a logistical nightmare for Luisa's staff, since everywhere she went she took trunks filled with costumes and an expanding panoply of props – pictures, ornaments, mechanical songbirds, books on magic, crystal balls and also her growing menagerie of pets, which now included a boa constrictor called Anaxagoras, travelling with her in a large glass cage.

Luisa was passionately attached to all of her animals, and one reason she preferred to stay at the Ritz in Paris was the saintly tolerance with which the hotel management accommodated her pets. Not only did they provide for the animals' different and often disgusting dietary needs, but when Anaxagoras escaped from his cage and was found coiled up in the bathroom of another guest, the episode was handled with discreet efficiency.

Paris remained Luisa's favourite city after Venice, and she went there regularly, both to see D'Annunzio and to visit the atelier of Paul Poiret, still her preferred couturier. She'd been wearing a pair of the latter's signature *jupe culottes* on the afternoon that she had first met Catherine Barjanksy, and initially the young woman had been shocked by the anomalous glitter of Luisa's appearance. Her long oriental trousers had been fastened around her ankles with diamond bangles, and she was weaing high-heeled gold sandals, an antique lace chemise (through which her small breasts were clearly visible), a powder-blue cape trimmed with chinchilla and a priceless-looking array of pearl jewelry. Yet as Barjansky became used to Luisa, she realized that this kind of artifice looked as natural on her as a tea dress might on another woman. 'The fantastic garb really suited her. She was so different...that ordinary clothes were impossible for her.'[40]

It was hard work, nonetheless, to be Luisa. The drops of belladonna that Luisa used to dilate her pupils were making her eyes extremely sensitive to light, and she would soon need to wear a protective veil or an eyepatch during the day. She was also experimenting with enormously long false eyelashes and sticking strips of gummed black paper around her eyes, adding to the discomfort of the wigs and masks, the heavy props and period costumes she wore at night. Other women in these years before the war were starting to liberate themselves from the heavy, corseted clothes of their mothers' generation; Luisa was wilfully submitting herself to every kind of sartorial discomfort.

But it was worth the pain for the interest she aroused: from Robert de Montesquiou, who painted her picture and squired her around Paris; from Jean Cocteau, who declared to his mother that she was like 'le beau serpent du Paradis terreste'; and from Georges Goursat, the satirical cartoonist known as SEM, whose work was principally published in the magazine *L'Illustration*. Although SEM's cartoon of Luisa was a grotesque exaggeration, portraying her as a beanpole giant dancing with a dwarfish-looking Boldini, she didn't mind – it mattered only to her that the artist had elevated her to his gallery of the rich, the celebrated and the damned.

Even more gratifying, perhaps, was a request that came from Serge Diaghilev in 1914, asking Luisa to perform as a guest with the Ballets Russes. She'd been in Rome when de Montesquiou (who regarded himself as an intimate of Diaghilev's) telegrammed to suggest that 'If Mme Casati would agree to take on immediately the role that was discussed for her' she would have 'the opportunity of a sensational presentation'.[41] That presentation would obviously require minimal dancing, since Luisa had no formal training. Yet she had acquired poise and grace through all of her own public appearances, and in St Moritz during the summer of 1912 she had given two informal dance performances, both inspired by works from the Ballets Russes' repertory, *The Firebird* and *Cléopatre*.* She could certainly have carried off a mime-based role with distinction.

According to the British hostess Mrs Hwfa Williams, who made it her business to know everybody and everything, Diaghilev had wanted to hire Luisa 'for the sake of her marvellous silhouette'. Yet it was more likely that her principal attraction was her notoriety. Diaghilev was under constant pressure to expand his audience across Europe, and a celebrity performer like the Marchesa Casati could be a useful box-office draw. In 1928 he would make a similar offer to Lady Diana Cooper (formerly Lady Diana Manners), who by then had achieved her own fame as an actress and an international socialite. Yet Luisa did not accept Diaghilev's invitation, and it's not clear why. Perhaps she was reluctant to make the commitment, even to so distinguished a company as the Ballets Russes. Or perhaps she simply hesitated too long, and history intervened before she was able to respond.[42]

In early August 1914 Luisa was back in Paris and staying at the Ritz, where the manager, Olivier Dabescat, was proving as accommodating as always – providing live rabbits and fresh meat for her pets, and instructing his staff to work around her very antisocial hours. Luisa was now living a quasi-nocturnal existence and would generally stay in bed until mid-afternoon, ringing for breakfast at a time when the rest of the guests were taking tea.

When she awoke on 3 August, however, she found herself distressingly and inexplicably unattended. No one responded when she rang for her breakfast tray, and when she tried to summon the hotel's magnificently gilded lift to take her down to the dining room, there was no

---

* In the former she wore a Bakst costume similar to that which he'd designed for Fokine's 1910 ballet; in the latter she performed a version of the 'danse persane' arranged for her by a professional ballet master.

attendant to answer her call. Forced to walk downstairs and investigate, Luisa discovered that the management was occupied by far graver concerns: France and Germany had declared war, the rest of Europe looked likely to follow, and already several of the Ritz's staff were being mobilized to join the army.

Luisa was utterly unprepared for this development. Even though political tensions had been mounting across Europe, as a bellicose Germany tested the nerve of the other major powers, few had expected war to break out so soon; and Luisa, living at such a privileged tangent from reality, had ignored all the signs. Her reaction on hearing the news was one of pure selfish terror that the world she'd constructed for herself would be violated and destroyed. So extreme was her panic that Catherine Barjansky, who also happened to be at the Ritz, claimed she'd found the Marchesa convulsed by fits of hysterical screaming. 'Her red hair was wild. In her Bakst-Poiret dress she suddenly looked like an evil and helpless fury, as useless and lost in this new life as the little lady in wax.'[43]

Barjansky's response to Luisa's hysterics was initially contemptuous. All over France, women would be sending lovers, brothers or husbands off to fight at the Front, while it was clear that all Luisa cared about was the disruption to her own concerns. Yet Barjansky could also acknowledge that Luisa's despair was genuine. For the past four years she had dedicated herself to art; she had re-fashioned herself and her surroundings into the *mise en scène* of her imagination. Now, as Barjansky observed, 'War had touched the roots of life. Art was no longer necessary.' And without art, Luisa was terrified that she might herself become nothing.

CHAPTER 4

'The decrepit house of Coré has even more the appearance of an enchanted ruin. The cypresses overlook the great poles from which the carpets of virgin vines hang. From that stairway...on a full-mooned summer's evening that seems so long ago, a masquerade once came out, led by a white Harlequin who carried a blue parrot on her shoulder and one of those little panthers on a leash...'[1]

When Gabriele D'Annunzio came back to Venice in October 1915 he was serving as a commander in the Italian air force, and he found the city much changed by war. He'd rented a modest house, the Casetta Rossa, which lay on the opposite bank of the canal to Luisa's palazzo, and when he looked out of his window he liked to imagine the parties that had so recently been staged there – 'the wigged servants...with their golden lanterns', and Luisa in all her many guises. Now, however, the Venier palazzo was shuttered up; an autumnal mist hovered dankly, and the only signs of life were the seagulls that flew over the palace roof, looking to D'Annunzio like 'large pale supple hands repeatedly rearranging a pearly veil'.[2]

Luisa was sitting out the war in Rome. The last time she'd visited her palazzo had been in June 1914 when, still innocent of the impending international crisis, she'd been making her preparations for the forthcoming season. If war had been the last thing on her mind, it seems to have been of equally little concern to the summer visitors who were already flocking to Venice in record numbers. As the writer and local historian Gino Damerini sardonically reported, 1914 was expected to be an exceptional year for the tourist industry, and the city was bracing itself for a more than usually strident season of 'nudist exhibitionism, hedonist wildness, carnivalesque fancies and pretentious elegance'.[3]

When war was announced, however, the impact on Venice had been immediate. Rumours of closed borders, frozen bank accounts and mobilizing troops had sent the tourists scuttling for home, and Damerini wrote that it was as though '[all] the illuminations, the silk, the jewels, the kaleidoscopic game of devil-may-care sophistication [had] vanished, as though sucked away by a whirlwind.' In May 1915, when Italy finally committed itself to the conflict, Venice was even more starkly transformed. Airbases and military camps were built close by the city, ready to launch attacks on Austrian-controlled territories across the border; blockades were erected across the larger canals, and gun batteries were installed on the Lido. Roof terraces that had once been fragrant with jasmine were armoured with searchlights and sirens. Public monuments disappeared under piles of sandbags, art treasures were put into storage, the angels on the Basilica were covered in sackcloth and most of the hotels were converted into hospitals. At night Venice was almost deserted, as the enforced blackout made the city treacherous to navigate; the tiny alleyways were impenetrably dark, the contours of canals marked only by the faint glimmer of stone that edged the bridges.[4]

Austrian bombing raids began early, and hammered the city so hard that the American resident Ralph Curtis felt 'the whole city shake on its

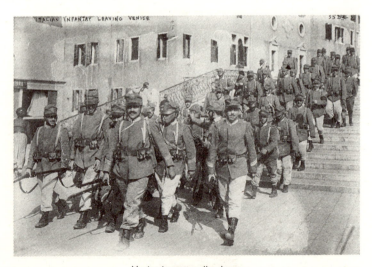

Venice in 1915: a city at war.

piles'. Casualty figures were mercifully low, with only fifty-four deaths and less than a hundred seriously injured. Yet the raids inflicted terrible damage, not only on the city's historic treasures (the beautiful Tiepolo ceiling of the Chiesa degli Scalzi was destroyed during an attack on the nearby train station), but also on its morale. The people of Venice were battered and traumatized, and many of them were hungry. In 1917, when Austrian forces advanced to within thirty miles of San Marco, many fled the city in terror.

Luisa herself would make one or two visits to Venice in order to see D'Annunzio, but she did not open up her palazzo, nor did she remain in the city long enough to witness much of its devastation. During the entire four years of the conflict, in fact, she remained almost as detached from the war as it was possible to be. For many women, these years would be gruelling but transformative. Historic numbers of them would gain their first taste of independent employment: they would volunteer as nurses, drive ambulances and trains, dole out food in factory canteens, take jobs in the police force, engineering and law. Even among Luisa's circle, several women would volunteer for the war effort – Ida Rubinstein serving as a Red Cross nurse (albeit in a uniform designed by Bakst), and Misia Sert, a friend of Diaghilev, driving wounded soldiers to hospitals (albeit in her own smart Mercedes).

Luisa, however, had neither the aptitude nor the interest for war work – she would have been a liability on any hospital ward. Instead, as the war cast its pall over costume balls and ballets, as Poiret closed down his atelier to aid in the production of military uniforms, she drifted around France and Italy in search of company. She went down to Nice to visit Boldini, who'd retreated there from Paris; she was briefly in Venice during early 1915, and then in Sorrento to see her friend, the Princess Soldatenkov. During her travels she sat for several portraits, including a ghoulish drawing by Gustav-Adolf Mossa in which she appeared as a disembodied head, and a more conventional oil by the American society painter Mrs Louise Cotton. If her life was less crowded now, it was not unpleasant – she was a citizen of a neutral country, and she had sufficient money to buy her way around whatever inconveniences and restrictions the war imposed. But when Italy finally entered the war on the side of the Allies in May 1915, Luisa's freedom of movement was curtailed. She returned to her villa in Rome, where, she assumed, she would wait out the rest of the war in an artistically moribund exile.

Entirely unexpectedly, however, the next three years turned out to be one of the most productive, absorbing periods of Luisa's life, bringing her new friends and projects and also rekindling her affair with D'Annunzio. Initially the war had been a divisive issue between them, for as doggedly as Luisa had tried to ignore it, D'Annunzio had embraced it with bellicose fervour. In Paris in August 1914, he exulted at the sight of French soldiers massing in the streets and campaigned feverishly for Italy to join them, regarding war as a crucible in which his nation might regain its former greatness. On 4 May 1915 he finally broke his long exile from Italy and, backed by a battalion of soldiers from the Italian volunteer force, returned home as a demagogue for war.

Along the route to Rome he held mass rallies, making speeches in which he denounced the Italian government and cast himself as the 'demon of tumult' who would cleanse the nation of its pacifist 'turds'.[5] Fanatical and gaudy, his speeches drew crowds of up to forty thousand, and while it was the promise of territorial rewards that officially persuaded Italy to join the fight against Germany and the Austro-Hungarian empire, D'Annunzio would regard it as one of the triumphs of his life that less than three weeks after he'd begun his own campaign, Italy was at war.

Now that her lover was being hailed as the nation's warrior poet, Luisa willingly allied herself to his cause. Typically, and preposterously, her one contribution to Italy's war effort was to meet with him on the Appian Way just outside Rome and conduct a series of magic midnight rituals in aid of victory. By now, her fixation with the supernatural had deepened from a hobby into a faith. She never travelled without her fetish objects and her books of magic, she retained fortune-tellers on her staff for private consultations, and her most prized possession was a crystal ball given to her by D'Annunzio. He, while less credulously committed, was happy to believe in the theatre of the occult; and during that night of 20 June 1915, as the two of them chanted spells, consulted magic books and stuck pins into wax figures, they were Coré and Gabriele to each other once more.

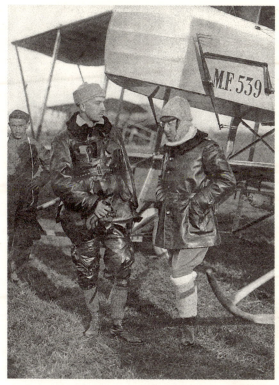

D'Annunzio the warrior poet and aviator, preparing
to fly a mission with his co-pilot Ermanno Beltramo (1915).

For the next three years, Luisa continued to cast herself as
D'Annunzio's wartime helpmeet and muse. Even though the fifty-two-
year-old writer was technically too old for service and had no military
training, he'd been determined to fight for his country, and during the
next three years he managed to advance his career from official speech-
maker to the troops, to a commanding post on the Venetian airbase that
had been built at one end of the Lido.

Flying had long been D'Annunzio's passion. He was among the first
civilians in Italy to pilot one of the new propeller-driven air machines,
and for him the experience of spiralling, godlike, through weather and

cloud formations was the ultimate expression of the Nietzschean ego. Now, as an aviator with the Italian air force, an Icarus of war, he prided himself on his fearlessness. He dressed and groomed meticulously for every mission, and despite being half blinded during one accident in 1916 he returned to his vocation. In May 1917 his courage was acknowledged with the command of his own squadron – which he named La Serenissima, after his beloved city. When he risked almost certain death by flying all the way to Vienna to drop propaganda leaflets over the city, Italy declared him a hero and even the Austrians admired his valour, declaring they had not a single leader to equal his daring.

There were, as always, many eager women to tend and worship D'Annunzio during his wartime career, to admire his medals and his military honours (he was eventually promoted to Lieutenant Colonel). But Luisa reserved a special role for herself. When she was unable to see her Gabriele in the flesh she wrote to him assiduously, promising to keep alight their shared vision of the 'inimitable life'. It had mattered very much to her that when D'Annunzio was convalescing from his injuries in Venice she'd been prevented from joining him, or even writing to him, by an injury of her own. She'd broken her arm in an awkward fall, and as D'Annunzio lay in his darkened bedroom at the Casetta Rossa, hallucinating from the pain of his damaged right eye, Luisa frantically commandeered her friends and acquaintances in Rome to send messages on her behalf.

D'Annunzio was moved by her attentiveness, and fantasized freely about a time when they could be together again. Towards the end of October 1917, when he was travelling to one of the most critical battles of the war close to the border town of Caporetto, he experienced such a powerful urge for Luisa's company that he was tempted to make a detour all the way south to Rome. He had to invoke the name of Eleonora Duse (whom he'd now cast as his guardian saint) in order to control himself, recording simply in his diary 'The temptation to see her [Luisa] at night. Then self denial.'

Evidently they met soon afterwards, since D'Annunzio wrote from a frozen battlefield in December 1917 to thank her for the night they'd spent together. The weather outside was brutal – he'd had to cover his face with petroleum jelly to protect it from the wind – but he assured her that it was the memory of Coré that kept alight his determination to triumph over the enemy ('*ora voglio vivere per vincere*') and he signed his letter with a lover's passion:

> 'I kiss your sublime eyes so tenderly.
> Ten-der-ly'[6]

By April 1918 D'Annunzio was back in Venice, comforting himself with images of Luisa in her palazzo and begging her to write, even to send 'a cabalistic sign' of her love.[7] This combination of wartime ardour and heroics was a mutually flattering extension of the artistic life to which they'd dedicated themselves, but nonetheless it absorbed only fragments of their time. D'Annunzio, as always, was running several concurrent affairs, as well as speechmaking and commanding his squadron; Luisa too was involved with her own lovers, and her own creative activities in Rome.

War had brought a new energy to the Italian capital. Because the battle lines were still distant, the population was able to enjoy a semblance of peacetime existence – there were no blackouts, no threats of enemy fire. And as other great cities were barricaded, rationed or bombed, some of the cultural life of Europe shifted naturally to Rome.

At the centre of the city's artistic life were the Italian Futurists. Several of them, including their leader Marinetti, were serving in the army, and it was impossible for them to sustain the movement at its pre-war pitch (back when the Futurist message 'We want no part of it, the past' had been splashed over giant billboards across Italy, and Marinetti had embarked on the stream of manifestos that would apply his iconoclastic logic to everything from poetry to cooking). But the artists, composers and writers of Futurism remained committed to their cause, and during the summer of 1915 when Luisa was back in Rome with little to occupy her, she found herself being co-opted as their wartime patron.

It may, ironically, have been D'Annunzio who helped to broker this new association. Before the war he had been cast by the Futurists as an enemy, a relict of the decadent past; now, however, he was linked to Marinetti and his followers by their shared enthusiasm for war. It was, they declared, 'the world's only hygiene', and like D'Annunzio, they had made a religion out of the blood, mud and machinery of battle. Luisa, already converted by Gabriele to the philosophy of war (if nothing else) was now very drawn to Marinetti, and in Rome she became his acolyte, his patron and very probably his lover.

Putting herself at the service of the Futurists, Luisa began to host parties for them and to support their wildly various endeavours in painting, music, puppetry and cinema (she may even have been the inspiration for Anton Giulio Bragaglia's film *Thaïs*, since its heroine not only looked very similar to her but was framed on screen by an esoteric assortment of peacock feathers, incense burners and exotic clutter).

Most importantly, Luisa started to collect Futurist art. Until now, her purchases had largely been confined to her own portraits, but in Rome she developed a more disinterested appreciation. She was greatly attracted by the clashing colours, the explosive energies of Futurist artists like Umberto Boccioni, Carlo Carrà, Alexander Archipenko, Giacomo Balla and Luigi Russolo; and as her tastes grew bolder, so did her buying habits. By 1918 the journalist Eugenio Giovannetti (who wrote as Satyricon) would describe Luisa as one of Italy's leading collectors of 20th-century art, and a guardian angel of innovation. 'She is, in the eyes of the public at large, the spirit protector of all the cubists and futurists and avant-gardists of all colours and races.'[8]

All this marked a new shift in Luisa's engagement with visual art – promoting work for its own sake, rather than as a means of enhancing her image. Only a few of the Futurist pieces that she purchased were representations of herself, and they had little in common with the flatteringly decorative or decadent portraits of her pre-war gallery. Balla's three portraits of Luisa, for instance, were radically different in both technique and affect: the pen-and-ink drawing *La marchesa Casati con levriero e pappagallo* was like an abstract diagram of her elusive personality, the solid shapes of her body unravelled into a cobweb of interlacing lines. In *Fluidità di forze rigide della marchesa Casati* she was a force field of geometric shapes; in the wood and cardboard bust he constructed she became a kind of Cubist toy, with black mica eyes that could be made to open and shut by turning a small heart-shaped handle. When the bust was exhibited in public, spectators found it hilarious, but Marinetti admired it greatly and acquired it for his personal collection.

Although there is no hard evidence to substantiate the stories that Luisa and Marinetti were lovers, they were certainly close. The Futurist leader visited 51 via Piemonte regularly when he was on leave, or when he was recovering from battle injuries; and as he recalled in his 1921 memoir *L'alcova d'acciaio*, he always found Luisa a luxurious consolation. War had made no impact on the life of the villa, whose rooms remained fragrant with incense and flowers and whose guests were catered to by a startlingly large staff, including Garbi – now dressed in formal tails, and always on hand with a tray of cocktails.

War had also done nothing to subdue Luisa's appearance. Marinetti recalled that he would arrive at her villa with his mind still churning from the 'onslaught' of the battlefield, but the sight of Luisa would act like an 'onslaught' to his senses, dislodging all thoughts of war. With the 'stormy waves of red hair cascading around [her] face', with her features made strange in the moonlight 'like a bleached tiger' and with the cloud of perfume released by the ring on her little finger which had 'a microscopic incense holder' attached, Luisa represented for Marinetti a perfect Futurist synergy of sensation.

Far from condemning Luisa for maintaining the artifice of her daily life, Marinetti celebrated her as a warrior against mediocrity and convention. When he watched her play with the parrot Abracadabra, he visualized her as a Futurist painting: 'The screams of the parrot tie the colours of his feathers to the red of the Marchesa's hair to the black of her eyes and of her nostrils, to the blood red of her mouth...'. He believed that her obsession with costume made her one of Italy's 'most original national products'; that her 'astounding creation of bizarre oddity and dandyism' had placed her 'sensationally [ahead of] all that Paris can offer'.⁹ He also complimented her for developing a most 'impassioned understanding' of his own Futurist beliefs, and later he would make a point of crediting her role in keeping his movement alive in Rome during the three and a half years of war.

So keen was Marinetti to adopt Luisa as a Futurist that sometime during 1915 he ordered an early 1910 portrait of himself to be re-dedicated to her. The artist, Carlo Carrà, had painted the writer at his desk surrounded by a maelstrom of geometric forms, but in this reworked version a note was added to the desk that read: 'I give my portrait painted by Carra to the great Futurist Marchesa Casati with the languid satisfied eyes of a panther that has just devoured the bars of its cage.'

All this was the public rhetoric of Marinetti's relationship with Luisa, but in his memoir he presented a more intimate picture. He had come to know and love her well enough to observe the nervousness that twitched at the edges of her social manner – 'the circular spiraling arabesques of her mute gaze', the bursts of 'spasmodic laughter...out of keeping with the sense of her words'. He wrote about her with tenderness as well as with an eye for the Futurist flourish; and it is from this memoir, too, that we get an image of Luisa in wartime Rome, animated to a bright, childlike excitement by all the ideas and artistic currents that were stirring around her.

It wasn't only the Futurists who were filling Luisa's life with the rush and clamour of creative interest; Serge Diaghilev, along with several of his close associates, also came to live and work in Rome between the autumn of 1916 and the spring of 1917. The outbreak of war in Europe had come close to destroying Les Ballets Russes, cutting the company off from many of its former theatres and sources of funding, and Diaghilev had retreated to Rome to try and regroup his operations.

As Luisa renewed her acquaintance with the great impresario she was happy to see him approach several of her favoured Futurists as potential designers, among them Fortunato Depero. She had developed particular closeness to Depero, having modelled for him several times and very possibly been his mistress. She may even have been a trigger for the artist's imagination when he was given his first design commission by Diaghilev, for the proposed ballet *Il giardino zoologico* was based on a surreal story about a group of animals who escape from a Paris zoo, and the equally bizarre escapades of Luisa's own pets may well have been in Depero's mind's eye as he worked.*

Also in Rome as members of Diaghilev's inner circle were Jean Cocteau and the young choreographer Léonide Massine, who were collaborating on the ballet that Diaghilev planned to be the most

* Diaghilev had been attracted to Futurism even before the war, making contact with Italian artists and also with their Russian equivalents, Natalia Goncharova and Mikhail Larionov. The Depero ballet, however, would never see the stage.

astonishing production of his career. It was titled *Parade*, and it was to be advertised as the world's first Cubist ballet – not only because of the jumbled, disjointed logic of its storyline (centred on a motley cast of circus performers) but also because it was to be designed by the world's most prominent Cubist artist, Pablo Picasso.

Luisa was thrilled when Picasso himself joined Diaghilev in Rome. The artist had so far eluded her social reach, and determined to make an impression, she held a dinner for him on 2 April. It was so preposterous a contrast to the shell-shocked Paris that Picasso had recently left that he retained a precise visual memory of it for the rest of his life. Forty years later he could still recall the footmen in their 18th-century livery who'd thrown copper filings onto the dining-room fires in order to turn the flames green; the massive boa constrictor that had lounged in golden coils on a polar bear skin rug; the parrot Abracadabra, perched on Garbi's shoulder; and above all, the startling appearance of Luisa herself, dressed in a pearl-embroidered gown with a stiff Elizabethan ruff and a neckline that plunged to her navel.

Luisa may have been hoping that she and her costume would inspire Picasso to a portrait. If so, she was disappointed.* But as a hostess she could claim one compensating success in the impression created by one of her other guests: the Chinese ambassador to Rome. His traditional Mandarin robes and his formal Mandarin manner so fascinated Picasso that he used the ambassador as a model for one of the lead characters in *Parade*, a mysterious and slightly sinister Chinese conjurer.

There was a buzz in Rome now that the Ballets Russes were in town. Diaghilev himself was everywhere, 'eccentrically rouged with an enormous chrysanthemum in his buttonhole', and there was a sense of things being made, of creative alliances being formed.[10] Picasso was very interested in the marionette ballets that were Depero's special invention: productions in which wood and plastic figures were set in choreographed motion against a sequence of bright avant-garde backdrops, and in which Depero made inventive experiments with perspective and scale. Picasso would borrow from Depero when he came to

---

* She did, however, model for Goncharova and Larionov, the two Russian Futurists working with Diaghilev.

create the towering Cubist structures worn by the rival circus managers in *Parade*, and he certainly enlisted Depero's help in constructing them. Meanwhile, another of Luisa's friends, Gerald Tyrwhitt, was helping paint the ballet's sets; he was quietly triumphant over the fact that after he'd taken Picasso to see a 'tiny dirty' music hall near his home, the artist had used the theatre's quaint interior as a visual source for the ballet's drop curtain.

For Luisa, this creative to-ing and fro-ing presented a novel spectacle of collaboration. Her own artistic pursuits – posing for painters and orchestrating parties – were mostly solitary endeavours, and she seems to have begun hankering after a more collective project. Another recent arrival in Rome was Misia Sert, who had long been a friend, adviser and patron of Diaghilev's. He was seeking Misia's guidance now over *Parade* – which she'd warned might be too contentious for a wartime audience – and as Luisa noted the influence Misia wielded, she wondered how she might emulate her. Given the power of her own money, her tastes and her contacts, Luisa considered that she too might merit a place within the impresario's inner circle.

To that end she organized an evening of new ballets to be performed at her home and invited Diaghilev as guest of honour. Two of the works in the programme, *Macchina tipografica* and *Intervenzione meccanica*, had been conceived by Marinetti and their choreography was surely too minimal and too mad for the impresario to take seriously. But they had sets and costumes by Balla, whom Luisa was keen to promote as a stage designer; and she had very real ambitions for the third work of the evening, which was Massine's setting of Satie's *Les Gymnopédies*. The spare, limpid beauty of this piano score was unlike any music Massine had used; and Luisa had high hopes that the ballet – presented, promoted and probably funded by her at via Piemonte – might be taken into the repertoire of the Ballets Russes.

In fact Diaghilev did not act on anything that he saw. None of the works were developed for the stage and Balla did not receive a design commission.* Nor did the impresario request any further input

---

* Although a Massine *Gymnopédies* ballet would eventually be performed by the company, it would be a different and much later work.

from Luisa, for in his mind her value was already well established. The Marchesa was simply one of his key female patrons who brought glamour and publicity to his company. In Rome her most important function would be attending the gala premiere of his other new ballet, *Les Femmes de bonne humeur* (a clever comic pastiche of 18th-century Venice choreographed by Massine), and adding her lustre to other famous guests like Eleonora Duse and the novelist Colette.

Luisa was never to become more than a fabulous but essentially peripheral ornament for Diaghilev. In late April, when the company was finished in Rome, she did not join them as they toured on to Naples and Florence; nor did she attempt to go to Paris for the much-anticipated premiere of *Parade*. Instead she acted on a curious and potentially hazardous impulse, and travelled to Peru.

It's not at all clear why Luisa wanted to go to South America. Perhaps her curiosity was piqued by the fact that the Ballets Russes were planning a tour there later that summer; or perhaps she had a whim to see the great Russian ballerina Anna Pavlova, who was currently performing in the region. The sole report of her visit was an appearance she made at the Teatro Municipal in Lima for Pavlova's final show where, according to one observer, Luisa created almost as much of an impression as the ballerina herself, arriving in her box in a gold-coloured gown matched by a towering black and gold feathered headdress.

If Luisa had simply travelled to see Pavlova dance, it was one of her most capricious decisions. South America had remained neutral during the war, but it was dangerous and difficult to travel there nonetheless. Sea passages from Europe were hard to acquire, now that most available vessels had been commandeered for military and cargo use. Luxuries were scarce, even for first-class passengers, and there was the ever-present threat of German U-boats patrolling the Atlantic. Yet Luisa had a habit of courting risk whenever she was bored or unhappy; and once the Ballets Russes had left Rome, the city must have felt suddenly empty to her. Certainly when she returned from her Peru trip, it was to a far less colourful and purposeful life.

There were creative distractions: one afternoon in July Marinetti dashed off the latest of his manifestos, *Manifesto della danza futuristica*, at Luisa's villa, and in acknowledgment of their recent ballet-inspired endeavours, he dedicated it to her.* During the months that followed she remained busy as the Futurists' 'ambassador', featuring in several of their artworks, including Balla's *Injections of Futurism*. In April 1918 she hosted a party to mark the premiere of Depero's latest marionette show, *I Balli plastici*. From time to time D'Annunzio blazed into town, bringing his unique whiff of sulphur and heroism. Yet morale in Rome was sinking as the Italian army suffered a series of catastrophic defeats. By the time the war was grinding out its final few months, Luisa believed the city had nothing left to offer. She was impatient now to move on to the next phase of her aesthetic life.

* * * * *

Ironically, peacetime seemed at first to diminish rather than expand Luisa's options. She was once again drifting away from D'Annunzio, who, unwilling to relinquish his role of warrior poet, had found a new cause to fight for in the city of Fiume, today known as Rijeka. After the war the Allies had promised to give control of the Dalmatian port to Italy, but they had reneged on the agreement and instead handed it over to the newly created state of Yugoslavia. D'Annunzio became obsessed with the idea of taking back control of Fiume himself, and when he wrote to Luisa from Venice in January 1919 his letter was full of preparations for his war, his personal fitness regime and his plans for mustering his 'troops'.

He suggested that Luisa might join him, reminding her that he missed her and rhapsodizing about the beauty that Venice had acquired during the war: noble, melancholic and free of the 'international hordes'. But Luisa had no interest in Venice – yet. The shell-damaged buildings and exhausted, unhappy population had no appeal for her, and she actively preferred to wait until the international hordes returned.

---

*   This was the least serious of the manifestos, amounting to little more than a rhetorical squib in its demand for a new, industrial style of choreography that would 'pay assiduous court to steering wheels, ordinary wheels and pistons...and make way for the fusion of man with machine'. It would have little impact on the dance world – when Diaghilev became interested in a mechanistic style of choreography in the mid-1920s, he was influenced far more by Russian Constructivism.

Meanwhile she would travel elsewhere, and during the immediate post-war period, one of her regular destinations was London. It was perhaps a surprising choice, given that the city was no less diminished than Venice, its spirit battered by four years of rationing, by German Zeppelin bombs and by the virulent Spanish flu epidemic now sweeping across Western Europe. She may have been drawn there by the Ballet Russes, who'd taken up semi-permanent residence in London since the autumn of 1918, but she may also have been invited by Gerald Tyrwhitt, who, having recently inherited a baronetcy and a modest amount of wealth, had abandoned diplomacy and returned home.

Gerald, now Lord Berners, had been a reliably amusing companion to Luisa in Rome. He was a complicated personality, protecting his chronic shyness and his black depressions behind a veneer of ironic English conservatism; but he was also a man of mercurial talents, a witty, fluent writer, a painter of charming landscapes and a composer of real originality. Like Luisa, he possessed a vein of theatrical eccentricity that he learned to cultivate to great effect. One of his odder habits was putting on a grotesque mask while driving around the country-side, both because he liked to frighten the local children and because he claimed to have become 'very bored' of his own face.

Luisa saw Gerald often in London, where she was introduced to his extensive network of friends, among them the clever Sitwell siblings and the wickedly 'fast' Daisy Fellowes. After Gerald bought a country house in Berkshire for himself and his mother Julia, he also invited her there – although there was some deliberate mischief in his motive. Gerald was not fond of his mother, whom he regarded as a grim embodiment of English complacency and philistinism, and early in 1921 when Luisa appeared at Faringdon with a new admirer (an effetely exquisite youth called Marquis Don Ranieri de Bourbon del Monte) and with her pet boa constrictor Anaxagoras coiled up in his travelling cage, Gerald happily expected Julia to be horrified.

His hopes were further raised when Luisa appeared for supper in tight white satin trousers and wearing two-inch-long false eyelashes – a hothouse vamp amid the faded chintz and fussiness of his mother's furnishings. But far from being fazed by her new guest, Julia was highly entertained. 'I liked her so much better than your other foreign friends,' she told Gerald afterwards, and she particularly enjoyed the novelty of playing host to a snake. Like all boa constrictors, Anaxagoras did not need to be fed every day, but the morning after Luisa's arrival Julia was anxious to know what she could offer it for breakfast. Luisa assured her it had already eaten – mendaciously claiming that she'd given it a live goat – but Julia's sense of duty was not satisfied. 'It does seem so inhospitable,' she fretted, and ordered the stable boy to go and catch it some extra rats.

Julia looked forward to Luisa's subsequent visits to Faringdon (marked by the entries in Gerald's guest book in which she always signed herself as 'Tempteuse de Serpents'). But while Gerald had hoped, and failed, to stir up mischief between his mother and Luisa, it was he who became uneasy during this first visit, when Luisa announced her plan to visit the nearby university city of Oxford. He believed she was quite capable of 'startling the undergraduates' in some unfeasible, indecent costume, or of walking around the streets with 'an accompanying ensemble of flute players'.[11] And although the cold winter weather forced Luisa into a tactfully enveloping fur coat, Gerald had had good reason to be nervous. She'd been to Oxford on several previous occasions, and her appearance at a college luncheon, when she wore Turkish trousers and poured herself a glass of absinthe out of a vessel concealed in her walking stick, had already entered university folklore.

Luisa's earlier visits to Oxford had not simply been prompted by the desire to see its architecture and shock its undergraduates, though. In 1919 her daughter Cristina had finally become too old to be kept in boarding school and Luisa had elected to send her to Oxford to improve her English, installing her in a boarding house with a vigilant chaperone. It pleased Luisa to come and visit Cristina from time to time, especially since her grown-up daughter was starting to resemble her in interesting ways. Cristina had inherited Luisa's narrow build, her large eyes and wiry brown hair, but she was also flatteringly influenced by Luisa's taste and style. In 1922, when she left Oxford and moved to London, the life she made for herself in a rented Bayswater flat would be a poignantly cut-price version of her mother's. She kept a small pet snake in her bedroom, shopped as extravagantly for clothes as her allowance permitted (sometimes pawning her jewels or giving Italian lessons to pay off her debts) and developed a reputation for dancing the tango.

Luisa was intrigued by her daughter's developing tastes, and also by the circle of friends she was forming in London – a group of young aristocrats and smart bohemians that included the painter Christopher Wood, the beautiful, dissolute Naps Alington and the rich and literary Evan Morgan. Now whenever Luisa was in England she made a point of inserting herself into Cristina's social life, accompanying her to parties and dinners and tagging along with her to country house weekends.

For Cristina herself, this sudden gift of her mother's interest was dazzling. Yet it came at a price, for when the two of them were out together Luisa's instinct was, as always, to make herself the spectacle of the room, and she seems to have had no notion of the effect this had on her daughter. Christopher Wood was perceptive enough to observe how anxious and withdrawn Cristina became in the presence of her mother's posing, and he disliked Luisa very much for it. But others, like Evan Morgan and Naps Alington, hung attentively around her at parties, and the more grandly eccentric she appeared, the more they adored her. (It was hilarious to them that when Luisa came to stay at Evan's family estate in Wales, she took a taxi all the way from London and calmly expected the butler at Tredegar to pay her fare).

Overshadowed by her mother, Cristina naturally looked elsewhere for affection, and did so with a needy intensity. She was twenty-one when she met Jack Hastings, and fell precipitously in love with his fresh-faced handsomeness and mildly rebellious temperament. Jack, whose full title was Viscount Francis John Clarence Westen Plantagenet Hastings, was an aspiring painter and a sympathizer with radical causes, and he was hell-bent on avoiding the responsibilities that came with his role as the future Earl of Huntingdon. If he fell in love with Cristina it wasn't just because she was beautiful, foreign and adoring but because, as a Roman Catholic and as the daughter of the Marchesa Casati, she was nothing like the traditional English bride his mother Maud would have chosen.

At first the young lovers were innocently, illicitly happy, meeting for secret trysts at the rackety Cavendish Hotel in London or at the house parties of friends. 'You are the centre of all my emotions,' Cristina wrote to Jack, delirious with the novelty of having someone to reciprocate her affections.[12] Over time, however, the unguarded, almost obsessive force of Cristina's passion made Jack uneasy; if he inadvertently disappointed or slighted her she became disproportionately upset and, in a disturbing iteration of her mother's extreme temperament, would break into tearful, inconsolable rages.

By 1925 Jack had become so alarmed by Cristina's instability that he considered leaving her; but what stalled him, ironically, was his mother's discovery of the affair. Appalled by the possibility that Jack might marry this unsuitable Italian girl, Maud Hastings made arrangements for him to be sent out to work on an Australian sheep farm. Inevitably Jack rebelled, and the day before he was due to sail he married Cristina by special license and took her with him to Australia.

Maud pursued her son by post, railing against his choice of wife: 'She has bad manners & no charm & does not go *down* with people & her appearance is so odd. Must she dye her hair that *dreadful* colour...'.[13] Maud was equally dismayed by the bride's mother, who everyone spoke of as 'an *impossible* person...absolutely *unmoral* & her reputation is in every way of the very *worst*. She always hated her child & only wanted to get her out of the way & that is the reason she was so badly brought up & has learned no manners.'[14]

Maud's rage was stoked by horror at the possibility that she might at some point have to associate with the *impossible* Marchesa; but by this time Luisa's brief flare of interest in her daughter had all but gutted out. She was in Paris when she received the telegram informing her of Cristina's impending marriage, and while she offered no objections, she had no interest in seeing her daughter at this critical moment. Her mind was entirely preoccupied with the planning of a complicated new costume and it would be left to Camillo to try and smooth over their daughter's relationship with her in-laws. Word had reached him that Cristina was behaving badly in Australia (having sensed Jack's cooling affections, she was drinking heavily and flirting with other men), and he wrote to warn her that she would have to moderate herself back in England if she wanted to 'resume the position that is your due'. Camillo's tone was sympathetic and his signature was fond, 'believe me with very great affection, your Papa'; but Cristina considered the letter a betrayal, scribbling angrily in its margin, 'What fools!'[15] As for Luisa, she would rarely concern herself with her daughter again – until her own life was in crisis, and she needed Cristina's help.

* * * * *

Once the wartime restrictions on transport were lifted, Luisa wanted to explore the world more widely, travelling across Europe but also as far as India (where she became so obsessed by the tigers she saw that, on her return to Paris, she ordered her hairdresser Antoine Cierplikowski to dye her hair in stripes of yellow, orange and red). These days she had to carry a passport, as new regulations required; but she typically customized it to suit her taste, altering her date of birth to make herself younger and sticking a reproduction of one of her painted portraits where the photograph should have been.

During a brief interlude in Rome in 1920, she was visited by Catherine Barjansky. To the young Russian artist, Luisa appeared a lost and lonely figure in this post-war world. With her 'enormous agate-black eyes...eating her thin face' she seemed almost marooned in the grandeur of her villa, surrounded by 'charming and utterly useless ornaments' and kept company only by her rank-smelling monkey, 'leaping and screaming' in its gold cage.[16]

Barjansky was right to sense that Luisa's life had lost its creative focus. Futurism was artistically on the wane, and Marinetti's energies were diverted into the emergent fascist movement. D'Annunzio, meanwhile, remained possessed by the fantasy of Fiume. Having entered the city in September 1919 with an army of anarchists, patriots, romantics and mercenaries, he'd managed to retain control ever since in a style so poetic – and so murderous – that Lenin would pronounce him, half-admiringly, to be 'the only true Italian revolutionary'.[17]

But Luisa was not without projects herself. As well as using these years to travel, she was assiduously adding to her collection of portraits, and it was during an exploratory trip to London in late 1918 that she posed for Jacob Epstein, his bronze bust becoming one of the most significant pieces in her gallery. She'd been introduced to the American sculptor at a lunch party given by the English debutante turned artist Clare Sheridan. Sheridan herself was an interesting woman; in 1920 she would make an intrepid voyage to revolutionary Russia to sculpt

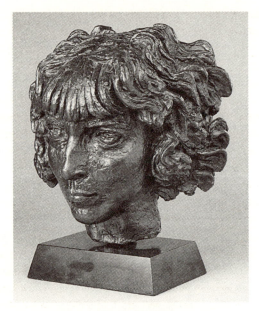

The basilisk stare:
Jacob Epstein's bust of Luisa (1918).

Lenin and Trotsky, and in the same year would make a bust of Luisa herself. But at the time Luisa had taken little notice of her hostess, and instead had spent the entire meal inveigling the notoriously picky Epstein to accept her as a model.

Epstein wrote that Luisa had been so 'very striking looking', so very intent on impressing him with her dedication to art and her wicked tastes, that he'd found her difficult to refuse. She came to his studio the next day, and even though it was snowing hard, she ordered her taxi driver to wait outside in his open cab so that she could stay for as long as the sculptor might need her. Eventually the freezing man had to knock on the door demanding shelter. Epstein was happy to offer a cup of tea and his library fire, but Luisa was deeply irritated by the interruption, shouting out: 'He is a Bolshevik. Ask him to wait a little longer.'

As odd as Epstein considered his model to be, he couldn't help but be impressed by her peculiar commitment. Hours passed in the studio, yet he recalled that the 'tireless Marchesa' sat patiently immobile; and as darkness fell and lighted candles 'formed a circle round [the] weird sitter', Luisa's personality became vividly heightened for him. The bust Epstein produced had emphasized her long nose and long upper lip, and exaggerated the coarse unruliness of her hair; but in the glittering fixity of what he called her 'basilisk stare', it captured the full ferocity of her concentration and expressed, as few portraits ever would, the strange force of her character.[18]

Luisa loved the bust, and she was right to; but just a few months later she found another artist who would succeed in capturing his own personal truth about her. Augustus John was forty-one when Luisa first met him in Paris, at a *thé dansant* (tea dance) held by the impeccably chic Duchesse de Gramont. Ordinarily, the painter liked to consider himself aloof from the social gyrations of the cosmopolitan rich. But he was temporarily in Paris as Britain's official artist to the Peace Conference of Versailles, and in order to keep track of his diplomat and politician subjects he was obliged to attend the numerous parties and dinners that revolved around the conference.

It was while John was helping himself to a quiet glass of port that his eye was caught by 'a lady of unusual distinction'. She was curiously dressed in 'a tall hat of black velvet [and] antique gold', and he watched with interest as she 'moved about the ball-room with supreme ease... looking about her with an expression of slightly malicious amusement'. He asked for an introduction, and if Luisa had at first paid no attention to this tall, slightly dishevelled and bearded stranger, her interest quickened when she discovered that he was the eminent painter Augustus John.[19]

The affair that started between them was unlikely in many ways. Augustus was the son of a suburban Welsh solicitor, born to a world entirely different from Luisa's; as an adult he'd become romantically attached to the idea of a gypsy lifestyle, free from the burden of material possessions. Yet as divergent as some of their tastes and habits might be, the artist developed an unusually intuitive sympathy for Luisa. Like her, he had been abnormally shy as a child, and like her, he had willed his own late transformation into a flamboyant exhibitionist, albeit of a far more vagrantly bohemian kind.

When they first became lovers, Augustus found Luisa intoxicatingly glamorous and foreign – '*Le taxi vous attends. Venez*' he wrote to her impatiently. He also enjoyed the freedom that her money brought to the affair, as they commuted romantically between Paris and London. Once, when they were lunching together in Soho with the novelist Ronald Firbank, Luisa announced that she would like to take all three of them to America that same day, and it was clear to both men that she would have made it happen, had they agreed.

As one fantasist to another, Augustus saluted Luisa's talent for self-invention. He could appreciate the effort she put into her wardrobe; he was amused by her parroting of the latest slang, noting that she'd taken to salting her more poetic D'Annunzian utterances with crude 'borrowings from the colloquial'. He was entertained, if somewhat shocked, by the studied rudeness with which she treated the several young men who now gathered around her – rich, drifting boys who clung to the coattails of her reputation.

In some of the circles where Luisa moved, this rudeness was the norm; malice, disparagement and bitchery were part of the social currency, especially in Paris, where they functioned as a register of wit and power and where Luisa had learned from masters like Robert de Montesquiou. Augustus, however, was perplexed at how blind Luisa could be to the pain she caused. He was riding in a taxi with her and one of her especially worshipful admirers, the young Marquis de Bourbon, when abruptly she announced that the Marquis's face had become intolerable to her. She ordered him to get out, and Augustus felt nothing but pity for the youth as he obeyed her command, weeping tears of humiliation and saying desolately, '*Voilà la femme que j'aime.*'[20]

Augustus's own method of dealing with Luisa's bad behaviour was mockery: when her posturings became too silly and her attitudes too unacceptable, he simply laughed at her. She had little experience of being teased and she reacted badly, calling him a pig and stalking from the room.[21] Yet she always returned. Augustus was good for Luisa, not simply as her lover but as a boisterous, masculine presence in her life, as the brother she'd never had. He made her laugh, he painted 'like a lion' and he made her life fun; it's very possible that in April 1919, when tragedy again struck Luisa's family and her sister Francesca died of the Spanish flu, it was to Augustus's robust embrace that she turned for comfort.[22]

In purely sexual terms, the affair did not last very long. Augustus fancied himself as a man of unfettered impulses; he believed that lovemaking should be spontaneous, and he had limited patience for the artifice and role-play that Luisa required. Yet even when they were no longer lovers, they remained friends, and Augustus would always be generous and kind when she needed him. Like D'Annunzio and Marinetti, he'd been touched by the artless emotional transparency that he'd glimpsed in Luisa and that she seemed only to be able to reveal in the company of her closest lovers and pets. He wrote that when she allowed her calculated exterior to slip she behaved with such a 'perfect naturalness of manner' that she seemed like 'a child of nature', play-acting at life. And it was in that tender, curious, perceptive spirit that Augustus painted two portraits of Luisa during the spring and summer of 1919.

For the first of the two she had posed for him, unusually, without costume or cosmetics, dressed in a simple white jacket and chemise. In contrast to the gaudy, dangerous and erotic Luisas that other artists had portrayed, Augustus had made her look almost ordinary – her uncompromising beauty softened by an almost hesitant expression. Luisa, interestingly, did not like the portrait; it was too unadorned and too conventionally feminine for her taste, and she didn't attempt to conceal her displeasure, quibbling over the fee she had promised Augustus and eventually selling the painting to Naps Alington. But when she sat for him again, a few months later, she was delighted by the result. Augustus had allowed her to dress a little more elaborately, in ruffled evening pyjamas, and had suggested a more challenging assurance in her face and body language. Nevertheless, this portrait was just as personally charged as the first. Luisa's eyes were mischievous, her flesh had a bloom of sensual heat, and as she looked out from the canvas she seemed to be smiling at her lover. There was a sparkle of intimacy in the portrait that drew admiring reviews when it was exhibited in London and was bluntly judged by the writer and adventurer T. E. Lawrence to be 'hot stuff'.

No other artist in Luisa's gallery had captured that liveliness in her, and it would certainly elude the American painter Romaine Brooks, whom Luisa met the following year while summering on the island of Capri.

During the course of her post-war wanderings, Luisa had formed a close attachment to the lush, mountainous island, which lay just off the Italy's south coast. She'd stayed there during the summer of 1919, temporarily abandoning Augustus for a very brief reunion with D'Annunzio – who'd taken time off from his preparations for Fiume and arrived with hundreds of tiny Murano glass flowers that he hung around the grounds of her rented villa. During that holiday Luisa had become interested in the community of artists, bohemians, eccentrics and homosexuals who'd been colonizing Capri since the 19th century, and who she sensed might compensate for the circle she'd lost in Rome. Even though she planned to re-open her Venetian palazzo shortly, she decided to secure herself a second summer home, and the following year, having signed a long-term lease on the same villa, she attempted to take up residence on Capri in commanding style.

The writer Roger Peyrefitte happened to be present on the afternoon that the jerky funicular car connecting the port of Marine Grande to the main square of Anacapri disgorged an extraordinary group of travellers. It was headed by Luisa, who looked to Peyrefitte like some medieval necromancer, although as he wrote later, the afternoon heat had already begun to wreak havoc with her costume. 'The Marchesa...wore an astrologer's hat from which depended long veils enveloping her person. Her face was plastered like a mountebank's...Her make-up, melting in the heat, ran in streams down to her dusty shoes...She carried a crystal ball in her hands to cool them.' Bringing up the rear was one of Luisa's young admirers, Prince Giovanna Battista Sera, and a maid who'd been entrusted with some housewarming gifts sent by D'Annunzio: a number of painted pomegranates and a 'bush made out of wrought iron'. There was also a manservant tasked with attending to the well-being of various pets – including Anaxagoras, some assorted parrots and an owl – and finally a new black attendant, Yarmia, who was clinging to the leashes of the cheetah and two mauve-powdered greyhounds.[23]

Garbi had by now left Luisa's service (his was surely one of the great untold tales), and other witnesses to Luisa's arrival on Capri suggest that Yarmia had not yet grown used to the challenges of the job. Luisa had instructed him to respond to any harassment he might receive – over the colour of his skin or the costumes she required him to wear – with the phrase, 'I am attached to the person of the Marchesa Luisa Casati.' During his first difficult summer on the island, the poor man would have to repeat that line so often he would become nicknamed 'the Marchesa's flea'.

Luisa was renting her holiday home from Axel Munthe, a fashionable psychiatrist and doctor whose life's project had been designing and building the large and graceful Villa San Michele. Ill health and diminishing funds had forced him, reluctantly, to rent out his villa for periods of time, and when Luisa had first proposed herself as a permanent tenant Munthe had been delighted; the Marchesa was rich enough for him to charge a premium rent, and she was unlikely to be in residence for more than a few weeks each year. But shortly before her arrival, Munthe began to hear disturbing rumours – about Luisa's badly behaved pets, her parties and her high-handed ideas of decor – and he was so alarmed at the damage she might inflict on his property that he wrote to cancel their agreement.

Luisa, typically, refused to acknowledge this obstacle to her plans. When she arrived on Capri she argued her way into the villa and, once there, refused to budge, countering all of Munthe's legal threats with bland offers to pay him more rent. It was to be a horrible summer for Munthe, watching from his own more modest quarters nearby as Luisa took over his precious home. He'd designed the Villa San Michele so that the beauty of its island setting would be visible throughout; it was to be 'open to the sun, to the wind and the voice of the seas...[and to] light, light everywhere'. Luisa, however, seemed intent on blocking nature out. She was dressing herself entirely in black this summer, even dying her hair, and she imposed the same colour scheme on the villa, ordering black drapes to be hung over the windows and black carpets to be laid on the floors. She had fans installed in the loggia to create an artificial breeze, and lights hung in the grounds to mimick the effect of moonlight. Under her tenure, even the weather at the Villa San Michele became an elaborate fake.

Munthe despaired over these violations, but others came to be entertained. The writer Compton Mackenzie, invited for tea, was riotously amused to find his hostess stretched out naked on a black bearskin rug; Count Sforza, the Italian foreign minister, came to dinner and was treated to the sight of Yarmia stripped to the waist, with his torso covered in gold paint. Old friends visited, like the Princess Soldatenkov (her once-discreet Sapphism now flagrantly manifested in her tailored white suits, and in the all-female staff who serviced her enormous villa on mainland Sorrento). But Luisa made new friends too, and among them was her neighbour, Baron Jacques d'Adelswärd-Fersen, a self-styled diabolist who invited to her to smoke opium with him in the red 'Chinese Room' he'd installed in his villa.

Opium would prove to be a dangerous temptation for Luisa: it transported her into a world of cloudy delirium, away from the banalities and struggles of real life, but it also impaired her already erratic judgment. The following year, when she was paying more frequent visits to Fersen's Chinese Room, her behaviour became markedly odd. According to the writer Rebecca West, Luisa began circulating lurid stories about her promiscuity, claiming she was in the grip of an 'erotomania' and that she'd been impregnated by a cardinal. Luisa had long been in the habit of vamping up her image, but she miscalculated badly with this sensationalist nonsense; some people concluded she was insane, while West, a feminist of the twenties generation, simply thought she was pitiable.

But during Luisa's first summer on Capri she was only under the intermittent influence of Fersen, and was far more concerned with attracting the attention of Romaine Brooks. The painter was a regular visitor to the island, one of its small colony of lesbian and bisexual artists. Luisa had been encouraged to seek her out by D'Annunzio, who believed she would find her a sympathetic friend: 'Like you she has always wanted to compose her life, handling her senses like her paintbrushes.'*

What Luisa initially wanted from Romaine, however, was not friendship but a portrait. She had admired the severely romantic canvas Brooks had painted of D'Annunzio before the war (when the two had had an intense but short-lived affair), and one of the first social engagements

---

* Compton Mackenzie's 1928 novel *Extraordinary Women* was a comedy based on Capri's lesbian community; its heroine Olimpia Leigh was partially modelled on Brooks.

she engineered on Capri was to invite Romaine to dinner in order to propose herself as model. Romaine, however, was reluctant to accept a commission. She'd been looking forward to a summer of creative 'idleness' during which she would be able to think deeply about her work; and in any case, she found Luisa an unappealing subject. As she reported to her lover Natalie Barney, who'd remained in Paris, 'She is a bit too sloe-button-eyed for my taste and the white of the eye is red.'[24]

Like Munthe, however, Romaine drastically underestimated Luisa's ability to get her own way. All the excuses Romaine proffered (that she had no suitable canvases, that she couldn't contemplate leaving the sanctity of her own villa) were swept aside by Luisa, who insisted that Romaine could paint her wherever and however she chose. By 4 August Romaine was writing resignedly to Natalie that she'd begun work on 'an immense life size nude', and that three times a week Luisa was now making the steep, dusty journey to her home, the Villa Cercola. Gradually, though, Romaine's premonitions of fatigue and frustration were dispelled. Once Luisa stood naked in the studio she could fully appreciate the lines of her 'straight beautiful body' and the purity of her white skin ('chestnut-coloured' sun-tans were already, to the disgust of Romaine's fastidious eye, becoming the fashion on Capri).[25] She could also appreciate the zeal of Luisa's commitment. After one brief hiatus when Luisa disappeared for several days 'on business' and left the anxious Romaine with a 'two-metre-high canvas filling up my atelier', she'd thrown herself into the project with a captivating enthusiasm. 'She is mad for the picture, which has taken over her imagination,' Romaine wrote to Natalie. 'I have never had such an intelligent model.' She went so far as to hope that the collaboration might yield one of the best paintings of her career.[26]

Luisa herself was convinced Romaine was creating a 'work of genius', and her delight in the portrait was heightened by her growing attachment to the artist. She enjoyed their conversations in Romaine's studio, for just as D'Annunzio had predicted, the two women had much in common. Yet Luisa was also fascinated by Romaine's simple, almost solitary, style of living. Her new friend seemed to resist publicity as profoundly as she herself craved it, and the austere, grey palette of her paintings, the plain, practical clothes she wore and the unadorned beauty of her sweet, serious face were the antithesis of Luisa's own created world. It was for good reason that the lover's nickname D'Annunzio had chosen for Romaine in 1910 had been 'Cinerina' – the pale or ashy one.

Luisa had never known anyone like Romaine, and as the weeks passed the curiosity she felt for her new friend deepened. While nothing physical occurred between the two women that summer, and while Luisa had almost certainly never experienced a lesbian relationship before, she became more and more lover-like in her demands, insisting that Romaine accompany her on daily outings around Capri and asking for ever more of her time and attention.

Romaine was flattered by the urgency of Luisa's friendship, but she was also overwhelmed, and by mid-September she was complaining to Natalie that it was making her ill. 'I need my rest,' she wailed; and by the time the portrait was completed, it had become as much a representation of her ambivalence towards Luisa as of Luisa herself. She had painted Luisa's naked figure against a remote, rocky landscape, and in some respects she had made her look disturbingly helpless, her breast and belly as flat and vulnerable as a child's. Yet Romaine had painted violence into Luisa's figure too: the dark shadows around her eyes, the clawing tension of her curled fingers and the wing-like furl of her cloak suggested the image of a predatory Fury, half woman and half bird of prey.

Montesquiou once wrote of Romaine that when she painted portraits she became a 'thief of souls', and when Natalie Barney was shown this painting she judged it to be eerily true to its subject.[27] Natalie would observe Luisa closely over the next eighteen months, and all that she saw of her disjointed emotions, her fixations with the artistic life and with Romaine, convinced her that she was both a victim of her own nature and a menace to others. It was during the summer of 1921, when the three women were together on Capri, that Natalie wrote the poem 'Isola de Capri', in which she described Luisa as a woman 'ever trying by strange disguisements to escape from the inner strangeness'.

For Luisa, the completion of the painting had been a triumph – Romaine had liked it so much that she'd kept it herself, rather than letting Luisa buy it. But their intimate summer was over, and it was when Luisa returned to Rome that Catherine Barjansky visited her at via Piemonte and sensed her isolation. Luisa could turn to other lovers, other friends for distraction, but it was Romaine she wanted. When she went to Paris in December, she invited Romaine and Natalie to dine with her at the Ritz on Christmas Eve, and it was then that she managed to persuade Romaine to come alone with her to London for the New Year.

Once she had Romaine to herself Luisa was determined to prove herself as a lover. Yet it seemed she had learned nothing from her summer on Capri, for she failed to see that the luxury suite she'd secured for them at Claridge's and the gifts with which she began bombarding Romaine were entirely the wrong strategy. Romaine was appalled by Luisa's consumerism, reporting back to Natalie that Luisa was in the grip of a 'real madness' and was 'buying buying buying everything she sees', from a carload of coloured balloons to a pair of 'large hoot owls'. She was angered by Luisa's unwillingness to let her meet up with any of her own friends; and she was horrified by Luisa's clumsy attempt to initiate a physical relationship.

Luisa had wanted to make love to Romaine, but because she had so little confidence in her own sexuality, she seems to have attempted some crude, forceful manoeuvres, her version of male seduction. Romaine was repelled, writing to Natalie that it had been the very opposite of what 'love between women should be'; and that Luisa had frightened her with 'her desire to bring the coarser elements of male love into what...should have been delicate and beautiful'. The charmed tryst Luisa had imagined had ended in ugliness, as Romaine reported: 'We separated somewhat bruised on both sides.'[28]

Yet the affair was not over. Luisa was tenacious, and Romaine was still half in thrall to the intensity of her ardour and the puzzle of her damaged personality. Later, she would acknowledge that the relationship had been one of the key experiences of her life: '[Luisa had] a great admiration for me...and she was beautiful. She was...worth the pain.' And the two lingered on together, through more meetings in Paris and through a second summer on Capri, when Luisa seems to have fled their worsening clashes of temperament by taking refuge in Fersen's opium den.

By the end of that year they had virtually stopped seeing each other. Luisa's portrait had initially been hung on the wall of Natalie's bedroom, in the house on rue Jacob where she hosted her Friday afternoon salons, and Luisa was proud to know that some of the poets, painters and composers who frequented Natalie's salon were taken specially to the room to view it. But eventually the portrait was taken down, removed from its frame and rolled up for storage; and after Romaine had died in 1970 it would be found under her bed, one of the very few pieces she'd kept back after donating the bulk of her work to the Smithsonian Museum in Washington. Romaine never accounted for her motive in setting aside Luisa's portrait: she once evasively described the work as an 'aberration' in her career, but did not specify what that meant. As for Luisa, she seems to have made no attempt to buy the painting back. It had pained and confounded her to be disappointed in her love for Romaine, but once the relationship was over, she was able to forget and move on.

According to Catherine Barjansky, Luisa's opportunistic attitude to her lovers and friends was one of the most unfathomable and least likeable traits of her character. While she could fix on new people with an almost vampiric enthusiasm, 'occupy[ing] herself entirely with them, until she had drawn from them all that was unusual and interesting', she was equally capable of 'dropping' them completely when her curiosity was exhausted. Luisa seemed, to the highly critical Barjansky, to lack any normal instinct of regret for her past relationships: 'she would dismiss them with a shrug. Their day was over.'[29] If Luisa experienced her own emotional world as darker and more complicated than this, she almost never confessed to it.

CHAPTER 5

While Luisa's attention had been scattered between London, Paris and Capri, she hadn't forgotten Venice, and early in the summer of 1921 she was again in residence at the palazzo. Her guest for the season was Kees van Dongen, who was temporarily in flight from Paris and from the controversy surrounding a portrait he'd painted of the literary statesman Anatole France. In gratitude for Luisa's hospitality and in homage to their Venetian surroundings, he was working on his seventh portrait of her, this one representing her as a Fauvist siren, her green-tinted skin electric against a salmon-pink wash of lagoon and sky.

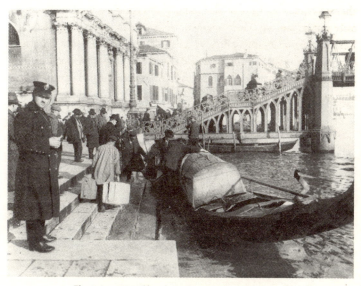

The 'international hordes' return to post-war Venice:
outside the city's train station (1921).

Venice itself was finally back in business. Three summers after the war, the art treasures had all been replaced, the damaged buildings were under repair and the hotels were once again filling with tourists. Luisa's old crowd was returning to the city, among them Lady Cunard and Diana Manners (now Diana Cooper); there were also more recently acquired friends like Ezra Pound, the bearded, combative American poet who had turned out to be a surprisingly gallant conversationalist when Luisa had met him at Natalie's salon in Paris. Pound would later pay passing tribute to Luisa's Venice in his epic poem *The Cantos*, invoking the magic of 'the peacocks in Koré's house'.

There was a new generation of tourists discovering the city, too – many of them young Americans who'd fallen out of love with the brash industrial pace of life at home and were travelling to Europe to spend their dollars on the romance of Old World culture. They would have been a credulous audience for Luisa, had she decided to relaunch the circus of her Venetian life. Yet while she would remain profoundly attached both to the city and to her palazzo, she had, in a way, concluded her moment there. By the autumn of 1921 she was contemplating a permanent move to Paris, confident now that it was the city most deserving of her presence.

During her recent visits to the French capital Luisa had witnessed the dynamic ferment of its post-war culture, the fizz of Dadaism and early surrealist poetry, of black jazz and abstract art, of the fashions of Coco Chanel and the experimental music of Les Six. Luisa was not an intellectual but her instincts were keen, and she was aware that if she wished to sustain her reputation as a living work of art she would need to become a more visible and permanent part of Parisian modernism.

She began to search for a suitable property in the city, and early in 1922 she made her choice: a large Italianate villa just outside the centre, in the exclusive suburb of Le Vésinet. It was called Le Palais Rose after its sweeping pink marble façade (a homage to the Grand Trianon pavilion at Versailles) and Luisa must have known it by reputation at least, since it had belonged to her friend and mentor Robert de Montesquiou. The waspish aesthete had recently died, his kidneys failing after a lifetime of vitriol and excess, and a more sentimental friend than Luisa might have been tempted to preserve the belle-époque artifice of the villa's decor, the painstaking symphony of colour, texture and fabric, Lalique glass and flowers that Montesquiou had orchestrated there.

But Luisa had her own style to assert, and as soon as she took possession of the villa she had its interior repainted in her signature scheme of black, white and gold. Interior walls were knocked through to create an impression of vast, undomesticated space; broken columns and chunks of statuary were displayed in some of the rooms while others were left minimally bare. In the bathroom there was nothing but a giant alabaster tub, supported on the backs of four heraldic lions.

Space also had to be found for Luisa's live menagerie, which now included a tame cobra called Agamemnon who lived in apparent amity with Anaxagoras in a glass case in the entrance hall. The cheetah, now grown stiff and mangy, also made the move to Le Vésinet, but it died shortly afterwards and was replaced by a stuffed, startlingly lifelike black panther. Luisa had commissioned this new toy to be fitted with a clockwork mechanism that caused its eyes to light up, its head and tail to swivel in a menacing fashion and its mouth to emit a low growl, intended, she said, 'to surprise my guests and disconcert burglars'.[1]

While Luisa's builders worked on the transformation of her new home she was often in Paris, monitoring progress from her temporary quarters at the Hotel du Rhin. It was here that she modelled for a series of photographs which would effectively define her image for this next phase of her career. She'd heard about a young American artist and photographer called Man Ray whose work was said to be interesting, and that spring she paid him a call, asking him to take some portrait shots of her.

Man Ray wrote later that he'd known almost nothing about the 'tall imposing woman' who'd appeared at his hotel door, strangely dressed and wearing 'a high headdress in black lace'. Afterwards, discovering that the 'Marquise' was 'well known among aristocratic circles', he assumed that Luisa would require little more than a routine society portrait. He was wrong. When he arrived at her suite she was wearing a silk dressing gown, her eyes were heavily ringed with black and she had formed very forceful ideas about how she wanted to pose, surrounded by what she called her 'curiosities' – the cherished and much-travelled

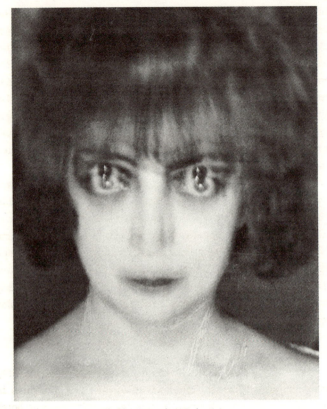

The 'Surrealist Medusa':
Luisa photographed by Man Ray (1922).

crystal ball, and a collection of ornamental flowers made of jade and precious stones.[2]

Man Ray tried to persuade Luisa to stand in one simple position, but she ignored his direction and moved around restlessly, trying out different variations. It was, he complained, 'as if I were doing a movie of her', and he was further frustrated by the fact that he could not use artificial lighting for the session because his equipment had almost immediately fused the hotel's wiring. Afterwards, when he studied the 'blurry and worthless' negatives, Man Ray thought he had wasted his time; but when he printed up the photographs he was able to transform them into something eerie, otherworldly. As Luisa posed in front of her hotel balcony or stared at the camera lens through a glass vitrine, she seemed in these images barely human – wild-haired, transparent and elusive. Most extraordinary was the close-up of her face in which Man Ray had experimented with a double exposure technique that had sent an electric shock of strangeness through her features. As he cheerfully reported, the 'Marquise...now had three pairs of eyes [and] might have passed for a Surrealist version of the Medusa'.[3]

Luisa herself was entranced, declaring that Man Ray had 'portrayed her soul'. She ordered dozens of prints to be sent out to her friends, rivals and lovers – and on D'Annunzio's copy she inscribed the title of their Venetian story, '*La figure de cire*', along with their names, Coré and Ariel (the latter a recent nickname coined by her). As the photograph circulated around Paris it did wonders for Man Ray's reputation: 'sitters began coming in – people from more exclusive circles, all expecting miracles from me'.[4] This quasi-accidental image of Luisa as a 'Surrealist Medusa' became the calling card for both sitter and artist.

* * * * *

When Luisa prepared herself to take on post-war Paris, she was infinitely better armed than she had been as an uncertain newcomer in 1909. She had a list of influential friends and contacts – Cécile Sorel, the Aga Khan, the Duke of Westminster, Baron Maurice de Rothschild – and every evening she could surround herself with people whose language she spoke and whose values, knowingly stylish and fashionably decadent, she shared. But the Paris with which she was familiar was the Paris of the Right Bank, the Paris of princesses, aesthetes and dandies that Proust was immortalizing in his novel *A la récherche du temps perdu*. And there was another Paris that Luisa had yet to broach; the Paris of the younger, more bracing Left Bank generation who were far more likely to be found drinking rough red wine in a workman's bar than sipping cocktails at the Ritz; far more likely to be jazzing to black American musicians in a tiny *boîte*, or arguing Dadaism and communism, than attending the Paris Opera.

Luisa had glimpsed something of this generation while visiting Natalie Barney's salon the previous year, but she couldn't readily understand how to adapt herself to its world. She was too shy and too grand to spend her evenings in the smoky demotic buzz of the Dôme or the Café de Flore; she could not imagine herself in the streamlined fashions, the shingled hair of the Parisian *garçonne*. Yet if this new generation were to take her image seriously as art, she would have to find a style with which to impress them, and over the next decade, as she experimented with different genres and periods of costume, she was frequently oppressed by the difficulties of the challenge. Her instincts were becoming less sure, and there were even moments when her uncertainty about the way she looked amounted to an existential crisis of confidence.

When Luisa had made her first major public appearance in postwar Paris she'd been able to reprise the opulence and fantasy of her pre-war style. The occasion was a Bal Vénitien held at the Opera House in 1922, and Bakst had created an ensemble of transparent, diamond-spangled harem trousers, with a spreading fantail of gold and silver feathers attached to her back from which twinkled hundreds of delicately wrought moons and stars. The costume took the workers at the Worth atelier three months to sew and cost 20,000 francs, and when Luisa made her entrance the press reported that 'the marquise Casati had made the Venetian night her slave'.[5]

It was a gratifying triumph, but Luisa had to be more daringly creative when, shortly afterwards, she was placed on the guest list of Paris's most exactingly exhibitionist event – the annual costume ball hosted by Count Étienne de Beaumont. Beaumont was an aesthete of immense wealth and ambition who cultivated both the Left Bank painters and the Right Bank princesses. Invitations to his balls were determined by strict, if arcane, criteria (Coco Chanel was excluded because she was deemed neither artist nor aristocrat, but merely 'trade'), and the dress code was clear: guests were simply required to look as original and outrageous as possible.

Luisa should have been in her element, and her first appearance at Beaumont's mansion on rue Duroc created a memorable stir: she was dressed as Eve, and while she wore only the simplest of robes, she had one of her pet snakes coiled magnificently around her shoulders and

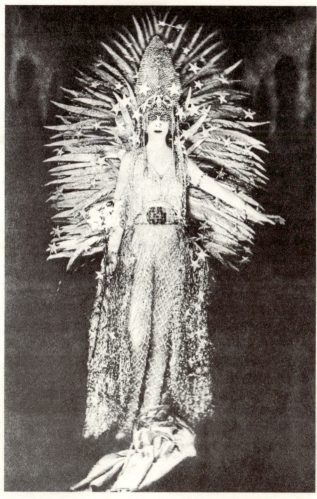

'The marquise Casati makes the Venetian night her slave':
Luisa, dressed by Bakst (1922).

neck. The snake spread a pleasing ripple of panic through the ballroom, but it also set a very high standard for Luisa, and she may well have been feeling the pressure when, for subsequent Beaumont balls, she tried to expand into more unfamiliar tropes of imagery and style.

With at least two of her costumes, Luisa attempted to show off her credentials as a Futurist by incorporating modern technology into her dress. The St Sebastian costume she wore in 1923 was a suit of silver armour pierced by hundreds of slender arrows, each one tipped with a tiny electric bulb; the Cubist 'dress' she wore the following year in homage to Picasso was constructed entirely of wires and lights. On both occasions, however, Luisa's imagination was thwarted by basic physics. During the final fitting for the St Sebastian costume, the wires connecting the light bulbs short-circuited and gave her an electric shock so violent that, according to one onlooker, she was 'sent...into a backward somersault' and was too traumatized to attend the ball. The next year, attempting to make her entrance in the Picasso dress, Luisa discovered that the doorway to Beaumont's ballroom was too narrow, and as she tried to squeeze herself through, the delicate silver wiring of the dress was crushed. According to the artist Christian Bérard, who witnessed the scene, she collapsed like a 'smashed zeppelin' in a humiliating tangle of twisted wire and sputtering lights.*6

After that, Luisa no longer trusted to technology in the creation of her effects, but she was still committed to her experiments in style. She attended a performance of the Ballets Russes in a gown of egret plumes that moulted as she moved, leaving her half naked by the end of the night. For an evening at the opera she wore a headdress of white peacock feathers and had one of her arms, so she said, daubed with the blood of a recently slaughtered chicken. It was probably red paint, but Luisa liked to claim that the sight of it had caused several women in the theatre to turn faint. She was seen dining with Baron Maurice de Rothschild with a pair of gilded rams' horns attached to her temples; she went to costume parties as Medusa in a headdress of writhing snakes,

---

*   When Cecil Beaton reported the story in his anthology *The Glass of Fashion*, the detail that was apparently most mortifying to Luisa was his statement that she'd been consoled with cups of tea – a beverage she loftily disdained.

or as Lady Macbeth with a bloodied wax hand attached to her throat. For the Beaumont ball of 1925 she planned to attend as an ambassador from Mars, and she wrote to D'Annunzio for advice. 'Please send a telegram soon describing the nature of Martians to me. You must know!' This was the event for which Luisa missed her daughter's wedding, and for which, in a grandly idiosyncratic interpretation of alien life, she hired herself a retinue of futuristically attired dwarves.[7]

Throughout the rest of the decade, her search for new imagery would continue. Sometimes she looked marvellous, dressed as a figure from one of Salvador Dalí's dream paintings; but sometimes the effort she made was too obvious – the night she dined at a restaurant wearing the baggy trousers and military boots of a North African Zouave soldier, Luisa was far too ostentatious about sharing her seat with a handsome black youth and feeding him titbits from her fork.

But Luisa still radiated an odd, angular glamour, whatever she wore, however she behaved. Now in her forties, she was as thin as she'd ever been, despite one acquaintance testifying to her having the 'most voracious' appetite of any woman he'd known.[8] For breakfast she favoured fried fish taken with a glass of Pernod, for supper blood-rare steaks with red wine. She did not subscribe to the new cult of exercise (although she liked to ski and occasionally to ride) and given the slight exophthalmic stare of her eyes, it's possible that her slenderness was the result of an overactive thyroid. It may specifically have been the result of Graves' disease, since this hyperthyroid disorder is one whose symptomatic range (from sexual and emotional volatility to severe eye irritation) overlaps interestingly with issues in Luisa's behaviour and own health. Modern medical research is now investigating links between hyperthyroidism and Asperger's – and she might have presented a fascinating case.[9]

But if there *were* any medical issues responsible for Luisa's singularity of style, they did not diminish her impact. The German fashion designer Otto Ludwig Haas-Heye encountered her in St Moritz sometime in the mid-1920s and at first sight her bony figure, wrapped in a riding coat and with an enormous bunch of Parma violets pinned to her chest, had been a disappointment. 'Is she ever ugly,' he'd muttered disparagingly. But then he had seen her 'huge raven-black eyes' and his perception had altered: 'At that moment it hit me like lightning. "She is absolutely beautiful."'[10]

Time, however, was moving against Luisa. While the magazine *Le Gaulois* might still describe her as 'one of the most beautiful and intellectual women of the day', women much younger than her were aspiring to a wholly different template. They modelled themselves on flapper actresses like Tallulah Bankhead or on the supple athleticism of dancers like Josephine Baker. These witty, bouncy, emancipated girls of the 1920s, with their bobbed hair, short skirts, lipsticked mouths and carefully honed slang, represented a new democracy of style. Beauty could now be bought with a marcel wave and with the latest shade of lipstick; fashion was becoming a mass-marketed industry, allowing ordinary young women to purchase factory-made copies of couture through mail-order catalogues and department stores. However modern Luisa tried to be, her expensive idiosyncrasies of dress only made her look progressively old-fashioned.

'Eccentricity is...the most unfashionable thing a woman can indulge in nowadays,' mourned Baron de Meyer, and he ranked Luisa as one of the last great eccentrics.[11] De Meyer's nostalgia was shared by the fashion designer Elsa Schiaparelli, who greatly enjoyed Luisa's conspicuous appearance (she herself would aim for touches of Dalí-esque surrealism in her couture) but regarded her as a rare and almost extinct species, harking back to 'a past age of splendour when a few beautiful and wealthy women adopted an almost brutally individualistic way of living and presenting themselves to the public'.[12]

The writer André de Fouquières also observed the conflict at the heart of Luisa's project when he saw her expensively and elaborately costumed for a charity ball in 1924. The event was themed around her old heroine, the Comtesse de Castiglioni, and Luisa had paid a fortune to the young Russian designer Erté (Romain de Tirtoff) to create a copy of one of Castiglioni's crinolined dresses. She'd planned for this event with even greater care than usual, securing several male friends to act as her retinue and hiring a professional choreographer to orchestrate their entrance. She was also wearing several items of jewelry that had once belonged to the Countess. Yet as de Fouquières pointed out, there was hardly anyone at the Paris Opera that night who knew or cared about the provenance of those jewels, and Luisa, despite her painstaking efforts, seemed to have lost faith in her power to perform: 'she appeared either too painted, or not painted enough; arrogant, but...nervous under her helmet of hair...Instead of an evocation [of Castiglioni] she was a spectral apparition.' Stranded between two worlds and two audiences, Luisa didn't know which to please.[13]

*****

While she was casting around for her post-war image, Luisa's difficulties were compounded by her choice of Parisian home. The appearance of the villa was more splendid than any of her houses, and according to Martini, who visited in 1925, Luisa was entirely justified in christening it 'le Palais de rêves'. As Martini approached the villa its windows glowed with a 'mysterious violet-red light', and the entrance hall into which he was admitted looked, to his admiring gaze, like some 'perfumed temple of Persian amber, filled with luminous Egyptian funereal chimeras [and] a frowning assembly of Roman emperors'. Yet as impressive as the house appeared, its location was too isolated to serve Luisa's purposes. In Venice, she'd only had to step into her gondola or process around San Marco in order to put herself in the public gaze. At Le Vésinet she was ten miles from the centre of Paris, secluded behind high walls, and although she'd planned to lure her audience out to the suburbs, the enormous sums she'd spent on the villa had left her, for the first time in her life, in financial difficulty. She would have to wait until 1927 to host the season of parties with which she hoped to welcome the élite of Paris to her 'Palace of Dreams'.[14]

Meantime, she was very far from being a recluse. She drove into the city for theatre trips and parties; she gave intimate lunches for select groups of friends, among them a circle of exiled Russian aristocrats who found an echo of their own lost splendour in Luisa's home. One of her most enthusiastic visitors was Prince Felix Youssoupov, a once-rich playboy who was now reduced to cadging favours from rich friends. When he'd met Luisa back in 1920 he'd been impressed by the fabulous aplomb with which she'd accepted his introduction, extending her hand to him 'in a slow and undulant movement like a royal cobra'. From that point the two had become closely bound by mutual interest, if not always by affection – Luisa's generous hospitality traded for the Prince's limitless fund of Parisian gossip.[15]

Inevitably, though, there were days when Luisa had no social arrangements and when she was left alone with her books of magic, her pets and her private portrait gallery. She'd kept only a fraction of the hundreds of paintings, sculptures and photographs for which she'd posed, but there were still over one hundred and thirty portraits in the rose-coloured garden pavilion where she'd installed her collection. As Luisa wandered among these multiple images of herself, lost in her Palace of Dreams, it was all too easy for her to ignore the difficult realities of the outside world; and it was also all too easy for her to slip into the beguiling embrace of drink and drugs.

Absinthe, the green 'sorcière glauque' of the belle époque, was Luisa's favourite drink, and opium remained her chosen narcotic – deeply pleasurable to her not only for its tranquilizing effect but for the elegance of its paraphernalia, its antique lamps, its ivory or bamboo pipes. But Luisa was not yet an addict (as Jean Cocteau and Étienne Beaumont were becoming), and she was just as likely to seek relief from solitude by taking impulsive drives around Le Vésinet, either chauffeured by Yarmia in the midnight-blue Rolls-Royce or taking the wheel of her recently acquired canary-yellow Hispano-Suiza. She was travelling a great deal, too, shuttling between her three other homes in Rome, Venice and Capri and exploring further afield in Spain, Morocco, Constantinople and the United States.

Luisa had been imagining this last voyage for some time. Americans like Tryphosa Bates-Batcheller had been among her most enthusiastic admirers; she'd been curious to see more of the vast continent from which they came, and to know how the rest of its population would respond to her. When she boarded the SS *Leviathan* in December 1925 she was clearly planning to make the greatest possible impression, for she'd not only had her usual trunks full of costumes and props loaded onto the ship, but also the travelling glass cage that housed her latest snake.

The beloved and much-travelled Anaxagoras was no longer with Luisa, having recently died of pneumonia. She'd sentimentally kept his skin to drape over her gondola as a 'tapestry' of remembrance, but she'd

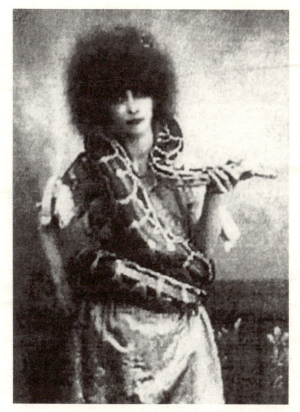

Luisa and snake at the Beaumont ball.

also wasted no time in trying to source a substitute. Snakes were now an essential feature of her image – she 'wore' them as accessories and included them in her portraits – but they had also become her preferred pets. She relished the handling of their dry, muscular, reptilian bodies and admired the beauty of their patterned coils. Perhaps she liked them best for their remoteness, their utter disregard for human affection – for as her acquaintance Mrs Hwfa Williams observed, Luisa seemed to be unafraid of 'the fiercest wild beast' and to have a much more natural affinity with animals than with people.[16]

In her quest for a successor to Anaxagoras, though, Luisa had a run of bad luck. Her first purchase, an Asian python, caught a fatal chill while travelling from London Zoo, and she had to be content with having its body stuffed and put on display at Le Vésinet.* When Mrs Hwfa Williams had visited she'd been urged to admire it, and had assumed from the tender pride in Luisa's voice that the black and yellow reptile lying coiled around a tree trunk was still alive. She'd stared at it apprehensively, waiting for it 'to spring', and when eventually she observed that the snake seemed to be 'very still' Luisa replied without a hint of irony, 'Yes, he is, isn't he? He's been dead quite a long time now.'[17]

She had no more luck with the boa constrictor she'd bought for her American trip. During the voyage the snake managed to escape from its cage, and rumours were soon flying around the ship that a child in third class had been swallowed whole. Presumably some discreet member of the crew was able to find and deal with it, since Luisa was allegedly seen mourning its loss in the Ritz Bar in the *Leviathan*'s first-class lounge. Yet even without her reptilian companion, Luisa was greeted as a figure of rare 'mystery and romance' in America, and her progress around the States was tracked by an enthusiastic press.

'Those who have seen La Casati's portrait would scarcely expect to see her appear that way in the flesh, but it is a fact that she does,' reported the *San Francisco Chronicle*.[18] There she was in Manhattan in a plungingly décolleté dress and matching gold stockings; at the Everglades Club in Palm Beach she held court in a gold helmet plumed with ostrich feathers; and visiting the Grand Canyon, she was photographed in leopardskin trousers, a sombrero and a lace veil. Crowds attending a baseball game in Los Angeles were also treated to the sight of her in a silk nightgown and fur coat, having taken too literally her host's instructions to 'come as you are'.[19]

Luisa was a selective and self-absorbed traveller, concerned principally with the effect she was creating; but she was not incurious.

---

* Luisa had commissioned a leading taxidermist, Marie Phisalix, for the delicate job, and was delighted to find that she considered it so perfect a specimen she had taken it to the Académie des sciences, which published a report in its journal in February 1925.

She was extravagantly delighted by the baseball game and cheered loudly at every home run; she was exhilarated by the scale and majesty of the south-western landscape, and romantically delighted by the remnants of American Indian culture that she saw. She shopped assiduously for Indian souvenirs and crafts, and on her return to Paris commissioned Alberto Martini to paint a commemorative portrait in which she stood posed against the Grand Canyon wearing a feathered Sioux headdress and brandishing a bow and a pistol.

In general, though, Luisa had been ill at ease during her three months in America. She disliked the functional modernity of its cities and the pushiness of its press. To one reporter she declared: 'To be different is to be alone. I do not like what is average. So I am alone.'[20] And while this statement had the ring of a lofty publicity quote, it also had an element of confessional truth. Luisa was lonely. However widely she travelled, however many people she impressed, she encountered few kindred souls who could understand the vocation that lay behind her conspicuous display – few who could see her as an artist rather than a rich and decorative eccentric.

*****

D'Annunzio too was feeling out of step with the times, complaining to Luisa that the modern world was 'drowning in the most unctuous vulgarity' and that he yearned for the 'inimitable life' they'd shared together before and during the war.[21] In their imaginations they remained Coré and Ariel, spiritually twinned, and throughout the 1920s they would try several times to recapture the rarefied essence of their love. Yet in reality they were almost always a disappointment to each other, out of sync; for while Luisa continued to travel and perform, D'Annunzio chose to exile himself almost entirely from public life.

Back in December 1920 his escapade in Fiume had ended in an inglorious rout, and his humiliation had then been compounded by the realization that the emergent fascist rulers of Italy, under Mussolini, had no intention of granting him any power or position. Casting himself as the betrayed hero, he'd exiled himself to Lake Garda, where he began to transform his new home, a modest country villa, into a megalomaniac shrine to his past. All his battle trophies were displayed in the grounds: the bi-plane he'd flown from Venice, the Fiat in which he'd entered Fiume, the hulk of the warship on which he'd delivered his wartime speeches. Inside were shelves and cabinets loaded with his vast collection of photographs, medals and mementoes. One room was dedicated to the satin evening gloves he claimed to have collected from each of his mistresses; others contained his capacious library, his artworks, his array of magic fetishes and his often blasphemously decorated religious statues. D'Annunzio christened his house Il Vittoriale degli italiani ('The Victory Monument of the Italians'), but it was only ever a monument to himself. Even his writing was looking backwards now as he began to assemble the material for his final volume, *Hundreds of pages of the secret book of Gabriele D'Annunzio,* a fervid, heated collage of memory, meditation, superstition and erotic fantasy.

Life was not precisely lonely at Il Vittoriale, where D'Annunzio was served by two devoted mistresses and visited by numerous friends and fans. But it was claustrophobically sealed. The artist Tamara de Lempicka came to stay in 1926 in the hopes of painting his portrait. But she could not tolerate the suffocating atmosphere of his household: the black blinds that shrouded the windows day and night; the religious robes worn by the servants; the clouds of incense that perfumed the air; the random hours at which meals were served; the quantities of cocaine her host consumed.

D'Annunzio had become addicted to the drug while medicating his wartime injuries, but he also used it to fuel his ageing libido. Sex mattered more than ever to him; and in addition to his resident mistresses (Luisa Bacarra, a talented musician, and Amelie Mazoyer, who worked as his housekeeper) he was compulsively slaking his appetite with local prostitutes, bookish female admirers, and pretty young boys procured by Amelie from nearby villages. He was also regularly gripped with nostalgia for the mistresses of his past, and during the first half of the 1920s the expression *rivederLa* ('to see you again') recurred throughout his letters to Luisa like a plaintive refrain.

He missed her acutely at times. 'Why has my imagination been continually preoccupied with Coré these past days?' he wrote in February 1922. 'I do not know where she is. I was even reduced to scanning the society pages, in the hope of finding her name and some clue.

And I do not know whether to say I was happier or yet more unhappy to find nothing.' Luisa was characteristically difficult to pin down. She promised to visit him in March – 'Immense joy. I will come down from the Olympian heights [of St Moritz] to greet you in your ref- uge' – but she was then diverted by the demands of her Paris move, and all that D'Annunzio saw of her that year was his copy of the Man Ray photograph.[22]

For the next eighteen months he pursued Luisa with letters of long- ing and reproach, but the postcards and telegrams she sent in reply were maddening evidence of all that was distracting her: the new friends in England and Paris, the new house at Le Vésinet. It was around this time that Luisa started calling D'Annunzio Ariel, yet for him that nick- name was loaded with unhappy irony: it was she who was traversing the world while he remained in his mausoleum, awaiting her return. While she liked to think of him there, in Lake Garda, she saw no reason to compromise or inconvenience the course of her life; and it wasn't until early December 1923, when a sudden financial crisis brought her to nearby Milan, that Luisa finally wrote with an urgent request to visit. 'Dear Ariel, I want to see you. How can we make it happen? Tell me. I am very sad.'[23]

D'Annunzio reacted to the prospect of their reunion with intense emotion. He wrote to her of the deep psychic bond he believed they still shared, of the 'fear and longing' with which he was anticipating her arrival.[24] When illness delayed her visit by a few days, his anxiety levels soared: he fretted over the disparity in their situations, fearing that Luisa's 'vast and merciless eyes' would be repulsed by his 'disfig- ured [post-war] face' and that she would smile, not quite kindly, at the modesty of his 'old parochial farmhouse'.

Not surprisingly, given D'Annunzio's vaulting fears and expecta- tions, this long-delayed encounter was difficult. Luisa arrived on the evening of 12 December but refused to stay at Il Vittoriale, perhaps because the other Luisa was in residence. The next day she visited, bringing with her an expensive gift – a ring that had once belonged to Byron – but she seemed preoccupied, and after a few hours she disap- peared back to Milan. Hearing nothing further from her, D'Annunzio fired off an aggrieved telegram: 'Byron's ring is painful on my finger.'[25]

But on 24 December, having ensured that they would be alone together at Il Vittoriale, Luisa returned to spend Christmas there. The two dined together at a table set with Venetian crystal and glass and, surrounded by D'Annunzio's magic books, his photographs and mementoes, they were lovers once more.

Luisa was delighted by the reunion, sending D'Annunzio 'infinite thanks'. It would be another six months before he saw her again, during which time she sent eccentric compensatory gifts – a Smith & Wesson pistol, a tortoise from Hamburg Zoo. But when she returned to Il Vittoriale, they spent a night together in the Leda Chamber (the room D'Annunzio reserved for lovemaking) and shared what he, at least, believed to be one of the climactic moments of their affair.

Afterwards he wrote:

The hours which you offered me, in your farewell, are among the most singular, and perhaps the most voluptuously lyrical, of my life. I will never forget them. Among your thousand faces, I have seen one face that nobody else sees and never shall. Of this I am certain.

You go wandering about, while your body leaves me with an enchantment half earthly, half celestial, like some marvellous land both explored and unexplored. And I hear over and over, as if always for the first time, the unexpected confession of your pleasure: 'Molto! Ah, molto, molto!' Do you remember? I cannot rid myself of this cry, trembling in harmony with my musical desires.

Adieu Coré, as per the night of Leda.[26]

Once again, however, D'Annunzio's rapture would be deflated by Luisa's baffling elusiveness. She'd left him at Il Vittoriale with the promise that she would be back within three days, but instead she sent a message saying she'd been unavoidably detained. D'Annunzio raged his protest: 'I was expecting everything from you after that hour...of inimitable life... I consider you as my torture of penance, in the last years of my reckless life. And I love you with relentless agony.'[27] Then as months went by and there was still no sign of Luisa he changed tack, adopting a tone of reproachful renunciation. 'I have managed to transfigure you into pure melancholy, void of a body, void of disillusion.'[28] Yet while D'Annunzio was hurt and was attempting to manipulate and punish Luisa, he did actually know that she had very good reasons for neglecting him. If Luisa remained absent from Il Vittoriale, if she seemed disappointingly less committed to their old 'poetic' connection, it was because she was being confronted by the far harsher facts of real life.

Until now, Luisa had never bothered to question the source of her wealth. She'd left it to her accountant, Lorenzo Saracchi, to manage all her affairs from Milan. But as spectacular as the Amman inheritance had been, it wasn't infinite. The purchase and refurbishment of the Paris villa had made a deep hole in Luisa's capital, and as the Italian lire struggled against high inflation rates and against the strength of the American dollar, the value of her share portfolio had plummeted. Saracchi had regularly warned that her life of travel, parties and property acquisition could not continue, yet by the end of 1923 she'd accumulated so many debts that she was on the brink of bankruptcy. While D'Annunzio, in Il Vittoriale, was complaining of her heartlessness, Luisa had been forced into the painful necessity of selling her shares in the family cotton business, and putting both her Roman town house and her childhood home onto the property market. She was simultaneously having to consult lawyers and travel to Budapest, because she and Camillo were finally getting a divorce. It may have been he who demanded it, in order to avoid being liable for Luisa's debts, and it seems to have caused her surprising, irrational pain, since she refused to have Camillo's name spoken in her presence for a long time afterwards.

But far more difficult for Luisa than either the desertion of her husband or the sale of her family properties was the loss of her Venetian palazzo. Even though she had been spending less time in Venice, Luisa continued to cherish the Palazzo dei Leoni as her special act of creation, the cradle of her artistic life. She might have tried to ignore Saracchi's advice and continued renting it, just as she would obstinately hang on to the tenancy of the Villa San Michele on Capri. Yet back in 1920 the palazzo had been bought by a Venetian financier, Ugo Levi – now, in 1924, he'd found a new buyer for it, the Hungarian industrialist and art collector Baron Marcell Nemes, who wanted to take up residence in the property himself.

Luisa was to be evicted: but almost more distressing to her than the loss of her palazzo was the discovery that the Baron was making extensive plans for its repair and refurbishment. In the planning application Nemes submitted to the Venetian City Council, he asked permission to rescue the roof and walls from their 'serious state of decay'; to re-landscape the garden (now 'feral due to extended neglect') and to modernize the interior. And when Luisa realized how much of her own careful fantasy would be destroyed, she reacted with a howl of anguish. It was pure 'vandalism', she wrote to D'Annunzio – and she commanded him to exert his influence with the city to get the palazzo listed as a national monument, so that the Baron would be prevented from making his horrible alterations.[29]

D'Annunzio had received Luisa's telegram just a few days before she was due to come to him at Il Vittoriale. He'd responded with tactful encouragement, anxious to avoid an argument that might lead to her cancelling the visit. But in truth, he could do nothing to help. He possessed little or no public influence, and with Mussolini's Facist government intent on creating a new efficient and industrial Italy, the Venetians were under pressure to modernize their city. Before the war, Luisa and her romantically ruined palazzo had been an asset to Venice; now, any notion that she had created a legacy there would be dismissed as a sentimental irrelevance.

The two women who came to own the palazzo would have reason to be glad that Luisa had failed to get the building listed; Doris Castlerosse and Peggy Guggenheim would both be free to recreate it for their own very different purposes. But for Luisa in 1924, this defeat marked the effective end of her life in Venice. Having lost her palazzo, she lost heart with the city, and would not return to it for another decade.

It was now, as D'Annunzio had frequent cause to complain, that Luisa became particularly unreachable. He sent out telegrams 'to all the corners of the world' trying to track her movements as she travelled around Europe and America, trying to catch her when she alighted for a few weeks in Paris. By the end of 1926, however, when her finances were on a more even keel, Luisa was settled back in her Palace of Dreams where she was determined to push forward with the next phase of her aesthetic life. The summer of 1927 was to be devoted to a series of entertainments designed to rival the spectacle of her Venice parties, and to show Paris the full extent of her creative powers.

As in Venice, these parties were planned to escalate in extravagance throughout the season. While their number and their dates are difficult to determine, they seem to have begun with a relatively modest event, a '*Bal de noir*', in which Luisa was channelling the current vogue for jazz and black African art by requiring her guests to black up their faces. (Still politically naive, she had no insight into the offence she was causing to the black musicians who played at her party, nor to her long-suffering manservant, Yarmia.) In May she hosted the more ornamental '*Bal de la rose d'or*', where the house and gardens were illuminated by hundreds of pink and yellow lights; where the hired staff were kitted out in gold satin trousers and where each guest was presented with a golden rose, at the centre of which nestled a vial of expensive perfume.

According to a number of flattering press reports, these parties became the talk of Paris: but in reality, Luisa was struggling to replicate the theatre of her Venetian summers. On the night of the Bal de la rose d'or, her carefully choreographed proceedings were disrupted by a sharp shower of rain and by a noisy crowd who'd scaled the garden walls in an attempt to gatecrash the party. She was also battling with her neighbours, who, annoyed by the parties she had already given, were petitioning the local mayor and even the Italian ambassador in Paris to prohibit her from holding any more.

Le Vésinet was a wealthy, insular suburb, and its inhabitants had never taken to Luisa – tutting over her peculiar habits, her dangerous pets, and even her manservant Yarmia (whose muscular physique, packed into a provocatively close-fitting uniform, provoked much prurient gossip about the exact nature of his role in Luisa's household). Now the neighbours became overtly antagonistic. Luisa always started her parties late, around 11 p.m., and despite the high walls encircling her villa the noise, the traffic, the lights and the unruly onlookers prompted outraged local complaint.

Opposition rarely bothered Luisa, though, and she pressed on with plans for her final party of the season. It was to be a costume ball themed around the 18th-century occultist Giuseppe Balsamo, who styled himself le Comte de Cagliostro, and Luisa spent 500,000 gold francs on its staging. The waiters were costumed in white and silver livery; the bartenders were dressed as masked devils in suits of jet-encrusted velvet. In keeping with the period the party was lit by hundreds of Lalique crystal torches and thousands of black candles; ice sculptures and water lilies decorated the garden, and a Savonnerie carpet was laid over the lawns to protect the costumes of the guests. In the centre of it all was to be Luisa herself, dressed as the Count in a gold, silver and diamond-studded trouser suit, and wielding an exquisitely crafted crystal sword.[*]

Afterwards, a photo spread in *Vogue* reported that the Marchesa had conjured the 'dream of an ancient kingdom' that night.[30] Her house had glittered and so had her guests, among them Daisy Fellowes as a glamorous Casanova and the Duchesse de Gramont as an Egyptian serpent, carried on a sarcophagus by four half-naked slaves. Yet many of those present had experienced the party very differently. They'd had a distressing journey, because the signposts that Luisa had been allowed to place along the road from Paris had inadvertently directed them through one of the city's poorest slums. Riding in their Rolls-Royces and Daimlers, in their egregiously embellished outfits, these wealthy partygoers had found themselves the target of abuse, catcalls and volleys of rotten tomatoes.

On their arrival, Luisa had arranged for her guests to form a procession across her garden with two of the guests, the Duchesse de Segonzac and her escort, bringing up the rear in a horse-drawn carriage. However, a storm was brewing, and the procession had only just begun when a crack of thunder caused the horses to bolt. The guests scattered, running for safety, and the Duchess had to be rescued, trembling, from her carriage. For a short while the storm seemed to have blown itself out, but when it broke again in an apocalyptic blast of wind and rain the candles were all extinguished and the band could no longer be heard. As Luisa's sodden guests stumbled off in search of shelter, she was left alone to face the wreckage of her evening.

* * * * *

---

[*] It was rumoured that an unfortunate guest who also arrived in the costume of the Count was shoved by Luisa into a cupboard.

The failure of this party was a tipping point for Luisa; real life had proved embarrassingly resistant to her artistic endeavours, and she had been made an object of ridicule. She doubted herself, she felt exposed and she was made aware that the admiration she was used to eliciting was being replaced by malicious gossip.

Over the next two years lurid stories began to circulate that the Marchesa Casati was cursed. In 1926 the concierge at her villa had been viciously attacked by one of her parrots, and memories of this incident were revived in 1929 when the dead body of her groundsman was discovered in the garden, the mystery of his death made even more gruesome by the fact that his corpse had been half-eaten by her pets.

It was also rumoured that Luisa had caused the death of the distinguished elderly Archbishop Dubois. After the debacle of her party she made a very public show of re-embracing her childhood religion, attending daily Mass and making pious visits to the sick. She was also determined to have the famously strict Archbishop hear her confession, and when he refused to come to her house she lured him there with a message that claimed she was close to death, having suffered serious injuries from a car accident. The Archbishop, unwell himself, struggled out of his bed, and according to various rumours Luisa met him either stark naked or draped in a long penitent's veil. Two days later, when the elderly priest contracted pneumonia and died, all of Paris was gossiping that she had been responsible.

Once, these stories would have heightened Luisa's mystique, adding to the sinister potency of the 'divine Marquise'; but now that she was older and more sidelined from the cultural mainstream they aroused something close to mockery, even disgust.

To Jean Cocteau, who had watched Luisa's decline with a combination of malice and sympathy, she no longer seemed like 'a beautiful serpent', but a performer who'd become pathetically bereft of both her stage and her script:

> *The Marquise Casati...came out of her boudoir as from the dressing room of an actress....It remained to act the play [but] there was none. This was her tragedy and why her house became haunted. The emptiness had to be filled whatever the cost; never for a moment could*

she stop bringing down the curtain and raising it again on some
surprise: a unicorn's horn, costumed monkeys, a mechanical tiger, and
a boa constrictor. The monkeys developed tuberculosis. The unicorn's
horn became coated in dust. The mechanical tiger was eaten by moths,
the boa constrictor died...'

Cocteau saw heroism in Luisa's attempt to keep the performance of her life in motion, claiming that he far preferred the preposterous 'bric-a-brac' of her style to the 'genteel audacity' of modern fashion.[31] There were others, too, who continued to admire. At a costume ball given by Daisy Fellowes, the Duchess of Sermonta could earn a round of applause by dressing up as La Casati in a red wig and pearls. Yet from 1927 onwards Luisa herself received fewer and fewer invitations, and her name appeared less frequently in the press. She was less protected too, as her old circle of familiars and admirers began to diminish: Leon Bakst – her inspired costumier – had died of lung cancer back in 1924, and Isadora Duncan, always a reliable draw at parties if never a reliable friend, had been horribly strangled in 1927 when her chiffon scarf had become trapped in the wheels of her car. Diaghilev, a chronic diabetic, was beginning to fail and would die in 1929; Boldini, nearly deaf and blind, would follow him in 1931.

Luisa could rely on D'Annunzio, at least. Having virtually ignored him for two years, she contacted him again in 1929, offering to visit Il Vittoriale in September. His response was wary: 'if you propose to torment me further it is best you do not come'. Yet he yearned to see her again and, with an unusually blunt arrogance, he wrote to remind her of his claim on her imagination and her heart: 'I own you. One who understands, as I understand you in the sense of your lines and gestures and quintessence, owns.'

D'Annunzio's arrogance was perhaps a compensation for his increasing frailty and his gathering sense of mortality. Earlier that year, the tortoise Luisa had sent him had died (a ridiculously aesthetic death, caused by its having eaten too many tuberoses), and he'd seen the event as frighteningly emblematic of his own decline. Now that Luisa was proposing a return to him he felt it imperative to appear before her as Gabriele, her powerful lover and mentor. To celebrate their reunion, he planned some kind of ritual in which they would take a drug or a potion together, to enhance their spiritual and sexual powers. But he fell ill just before Luisa arrived, and the 'great inebriation' went badly awry. Humiliated and poorly, D'Annunzio had to beg Luisa to leave.

Six months later, though, while he was reworking the still unfinished '*La figure de cire*', he experienced a sudden desire for her return. He wrote to assure her that he was thinking of her constantly; that she was so present in his imagination that during a recent sexual encounter he'd fantasized that it was Luisa in his bed rather than the 'pretty little blonde' he'd procured for the night: 'It was your perfect apparition', he rhapsodized. 'Almost immediately the legs of my nocturnal guest lengthened, the eyes enlarged, the pelvic shadow darkened, the skin matched the purity of the snow.'

Luisa, feeling her own relative age and isolation, might have been pleased by this somewhat addled compliment, but at that moment she was afflicted by too many other urgent concerns to contemplate a return visit to Il Vittoriale. After the first crisis in her financial affairs, Luisa's accountant had begged her to live within her means, yet economy was a concept she was unable to grasp. Between 1924 and 1929 she had managed to squander all the profits she had made on the sale of her assets, lavishing exorbitant sums on her Parisian parties as well as on her continuing addictions to travel and clothes. She still spent on a whim, buying anything that caught her eye, and she was an absurdly easy touch for peddlers and grifters. Augustus John complained that Luisa was 'as credulous as a savage', and at Le Vésinet there was always a knot of gypsies hanging around the driveway, hoping to sell her some new animal or magic charm.[32]

As Luisa frittered away her capital she became reliant on credit; she also began to senselessly trade away her possessions. She settled one minor loan with a priceless ivory statuette, said to have belonged to Pope Alexander I; she paid off taxi drivers and shopkeepers with whatever item of jewelry she happened to be wearing. Because Luisa was titled and had once been so very rich, she was able to survive on longer and longer lines of credit: but when the American stock market crashed in autumn 1929 and the financial aftershocks ricocheted across Europe, it was only a matter of time before her own lifestyle came crashing down. 'Everyone wants money and can think of little else,' Christopher Wood wrote in Paris. *'C'est un belle horreur.'* Among Luisa's circle, the effects were immediate: Princess Violette Murat lost millions, and the Duchesse de Gramont was obliged to seek work as an interior design consultant. Even though Luisa managed to keep up appearances a little longer, by 1930 her debts in France were totalling around 300,000 francs, and those in Italy around twenty billion lire. By today's values, the sums she owed were close to thirty million dollars.[33]

In the end, it was a Parisian coal merchant who had Luisa declared bankrupt. She owed him 29,000 francs, and although she'd tried to pay him in goods (the press reported that she'd offered 'two pictures of the Bouchet school, an onyx statuette set with semi-precious stones, an eagle adorned with diamonds and two pawn tickets'), the indignant man took his claim to the police. With the help of expensive lawyers Luisa was able to avoid jail, and her initial sentence of two years' imprisonment was commuted to a suspended two months. But still she had to face all the penalties of bankruptcy, and was compelled by the court to sell off her remaining assets, abandon the tenancy of her Capri villa and mortgage her Palace of Dreams (it was eventually sold). On 17 December 1932 she sent a wretched telegram to D'Annunzio begging him to salvage a few pieces when the contents of her house went under the auctioneer's hammer: 'I am desperate [at the] offence to Palais Rose. The art objects go on sale on Saturday. Wire me ten thousand lire. Send someone to choose the art you would like. Thank you. With gratitude. Luisa Casati.'

D'Annunzio did not reply. By now he was too ill and too self-absorbed to care about Luisa's latest crisis, and this telegram was almost certainly the last of their correspondence. Although each kept cherished mementoes of the other – the de Meyer photograph, the crystal ball – the bond between them had slipped. Six years later, when D'Annunzio died, Luisa did not attend his funeral, nor was she reported to have shown any regret at his loss. Her own existence, by now, was drastically changed; she and her few surviving pets had left Le Vésinet and begun an uncertainly nomadic life, moving from hotel rooms to rented apartments to the guest rooms of friends. With the assistance of still-loyal admirers like Marinetti and Martini, and with the tiny income she'd salvaged, Luisa was able to maintain some semblance of her artistic life. She tried to impose an ad hoc fantasy onto each of her temporary lodgings – the owner of a Parisian house hastily cancelled her tenancy when it transpired that she wanted to throw out most of the furniture and paint the trees in the garden gold. She was still sought out by the occasional artist – a wooden bust of Luisa and an art deco mask of her face both date from this period. And even with her limited cash, she could still rise to the occasion of a masquerade. In 1935 she made her final entrance to Étienne de Beaumont's ballroom dressed as the Empress Elizabeth of Austria, in a black riding suit trimmed with white ostrich feathers and a tumbling red wig pinned with diamond stars. Man Ray took her photograph, posed against a painting of the Empress's two white stallions, and she looked extraordinary still.

Yet without money, a home or staff, Luisa battled to maintain a day to day appearance of glamour. In December 1936 her wanderings took her back to Venice, where she was the guest of Prince Louis Ferdinand d'Orleans Borbone, and everything about the visit underlined the deterioration of her situation. A decade ago, the prince had been flattered to be among the men who'd squired Luisa in Paris when she made her ballroom appearance as La Castiglioni. Now she was dependent on his charity. Even more poignantly, Emilio and Italia Basaldella – the couple whom Luisa had once employed at her own palazzo – were now the caretakers of the prince's home.[34]

The Basaldellas were shocked by the changes in their former mistress. She'd become even thinner, spending too much of her meagre income on her recently acquired taste for cocaine. Her clothes still aimed for the exotic, but they were mostly remnants of her former wardrobe: 'veils, peacock feathers and...pieces of fur' that seemed to the Basaldellas to be 'kept together by pins'.[35] According to the couple's son, Francesco, who later wrote about Luisa's visit in his book *Giudecca*, her appearance provoked more derision than admiration, and to protect her the Basaldellas took her everywhere by motorboat.

So much had changed in the twelve years since Luisa had left Venice. When she was ferried down the Grand Canal she may simply have averted her gaze from her former palazzo, which had changed hands yet again and was now being refurbished into a smart summer

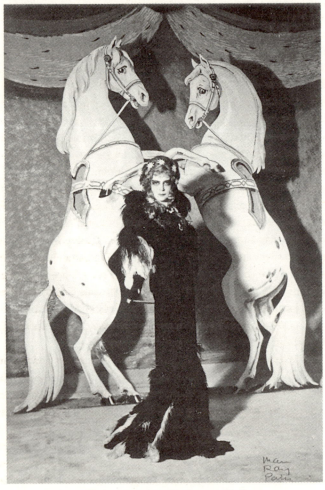

Luisa's final appearance in the Beaumont ballroom,
dressed as the Empress Elizabeth of Austria
and photographed by Man Ray (1935).

residence for the beautiful and reprobate Lady Doris Castlerosse. And if she had any lingering sense of this city as her former home and former domain she was surely disabused when, towards the end of her stay, she had to shift lodgings to a tiny house belonging to Ezra Pound's mistress, Olga Rudge. As Luisa stepped out of her borrowed gondola and began to unload her bags, her candelabra, her dog and her cat, passers-by stopped to jeer, shouting, '*Da dove vien questa vecchia strega?*' ('Where did this old witch come from?').[36]

These days, Luisa was having to move more and more frequently as she began to exhaust the patience of her remaining friends. There was no question of Camillo coming to her aid; in 1926 he'd married again, to an American woman called Anna Ewing Cockrell who'd finally given him the son he wanted.* But Luisa did manage to extract some money from her daughter, with whom she'd resumed sporadic contact. Cristina and Jack had briefly returned to England back in 1927 and the following year had produced a baby girl – named Moorea, after the South Sea island where she'd been conceived. Disappointingly, there are no reports of how Luisa reacted to becoming a grandmother. And she may not even have seen Moorea for several years, since the little girl was mostly left in the care of Maud Hastings while Cristina and Jack travelled on to Mexico and North America, where they became close friends of the artists Diego Rivera and Frida Kahlo, and where Cristina and Frida were briefly lovers.

By the mid-1930s, though, the couple were back in London and close enough for Luisa to make shameless bids for assistance, inviting herself for visits and sending the occasional begging letter to her son-in-law, whom she addressed in polite and careful French. 'Dear Jack I am writing to ask if you could help me at a very difficult time...my situation is very serious and I am turning to you, having always remembered you as most sympathetic and knowing that you understand difficult situations.'[37] Jack was not remotely sympathetic. He found Luisa fascinating

---

* Camillo's son would become even more notorious than Luisa when, in 1970, he shot his wife, her lover and then himself. It was unclear whether the forty-three-year-old Marchese had committed suicide (he was under investigation for tax fraud) or whether the three of them had been involved in some dangerous erotic game.

as a type and in 1934 had painted her portrait, posed in black and with D'Annunzio's crystal ball clasped in her hand. But he considered her monstrous as a mother-in-law, and aside from sending limited gifts of money, he made it clear that he had no intention of supporting her.

Four years later, Jack had even less reason to concern himself with Luisa, as his and Cristina's troubled marriage was headed for divorce. Yet while Luisa could not hope for a home with her family, she was nonetheless drawn to the idea of moving to London, which she associated with two of her closest and kindest friends, Lord Berners and Augustus John. Augustus tried to warn her off the idea, telling her that the atmosphere in England was grim and that people were talking of little but the impending war with Germany; but Luisa was not to be deflected. Sometime in late 1938 or early 1939, she made the decision to abandon the cities of her greatest triumphs – Paris, Venice and Rome – and to settle herself, her Pekingese dog Spider, and her last remaining cat in a tiny flat in central London. To a friend who encountered her there, she announced that she had 'retired from society' and was now prepared to devote herself entirely to the life of the spirit. As she calmly assured him, the Bible was now to become her sole source of consolation and knowledge: 'if studied to the fullest...there is not a more interesting novel in the whole world'.[38]

DORIS CASTLEROSSE

THE SALONNIÈRE

CHAPTER 6

In the summer of 1938 a photograph of Doris, Lady Castlerosse, appeared in the local Venetian press. She was standing on the waterfront terrace of the Palazzo Venier dei Leoni, and she looked like a woman coolly in possession of the moment – dressed in a crisply patterned summer frock, her blonde hair immaculate in the late afternoon sun. Awaiting her on the canal was a private motorboat in which two men were poised to escort her, perhaps to early cocktails at Florian's or down to the Lido to catch the last of the day's heat. In that one photograph was an image of all that Venice could offer a modern woman – the pleasures of the 20th century, pleasingly ghosted but not inconvenienced by the city's romantic past.

It was just twenty-five years since Luisa Casati had posed for the camera at the Palazzo Venier – fondling her cheetah, and costumed as an Indo-Persian princess – yet already she was becoming a distant memory. Back in 1913 there were aspects of Venice that had barely entered the 20th century; only a few areas of the city were wired for electricity, only a few of the palazzos had modern plumbing, and most of the population still earned their living in the old ways, as fishermen, sailors, reed-cutters and lace-makers. Back then, with no cinema in the city and still no radio, there had been few public entertainments to rival the spectacles that Luisa and her parties had offered.

Now the Venice in which Doris spent her summers had become both more contemporary and more functional. A decade and a half of fascist rule had imprinted itself on parts of the city as Mussolini had embarked on his mission to update and homogenize the new Italy. Like Napoleon before him, he'd ordered several of Venice's canals to be paved over; and although there was still no way for motor traffic to drive through the centre, the areas around the rail station (with its new and pompously fascist façade) were becoming busy urbanized areas.

The mainland port of Marghera had also been industrialized, with cranes and tall chimneys belching smoke: new and much-needed housing was built to replace the ancient slums, and the old airbase on the Lido from which D'Annunzio had flown his heroic wartime missions was now a commercial airport.

As visitors crowded into Venice by air, rail and sea, modern hotels were erected to service them; vaporetti and motorboats ferried them busily around the canals, and the Lido was fully transformed into a chic seaside resort. Mussolini respected the economics of the tourist industry, however, and the historic heart of the city remained largely unchanged – the palazzos still placidly regarding their reflections in the brackish water, the gondoliers singing their old songs, the swifts darting around listing chimney pots. But this was not the Venice that Luisa had known, and at the Palazzo Venier all obvious traces of her occupation had been erased. The golden curtains at which D'Annunzio

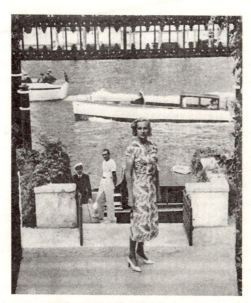

Doris Castlerosse takes possession
of the Venier palazzo in the summer of 1938.

had gazed so mournfully during the war had long been discarded; the symphony of gold in the main salon had been painted over. There were no peacocks in the garden now, and no gilded statues.

The building's basic structure had not, however, suffered the violation Luisa had feared back in 1924, when Marcell Nemes had purchased the palazzo and terminated her tenancy. Despite his plans to rebuild the walls and roof and remodel the interior, Nemes had run out of money before beginning any major construction work. As rich as he was, he was something of a gambler, reckless in his purchases of art and property, often selling at a loss. If it was a lack of solid capital that forced him to delay the palazzo's refurbishment, the banking crises at the end of the decade apparently forced him to sell. It was a provisional sale, with a clause written into the contract that allowed him to purchase back the property with an added 7 per cent interest inside a year. But Nemes never had the chance to profit from that contract because just one month after signing it he was dead, and the palazzo remained in the hands of its new purchaser, Louis Giraud.

Giraud, who was director of French property company the Société Immobilière-Molière Kleber, may have had plans to capitalize on his investment, but when Doris first acquired the palazzo in the autumn of 1936, little had changed. It was still described on the property deeds as 'a garden with the fundamentals of a palace'; ivy still clung to the outside walls, and the interior was still a jerry-built structure suitable only for summer occupancy. While Doris was already picturing the transformations she would make – the new modern bathrooms, the voguish interior design – it was still possible for her to imagine something of what the palazzo had been like during the years when Luisa was so fabulously in residence.

* * * * *

Doris had probably not met Luisa herself, but she knew many people who had. She was a particularly close friend of Lord Berners, Luisa's loyal admirer, and through Gerald had heard many stories of the Marchesa's life. On Doris's own visits to Faringdon House she had seen the grandiose scrawl with which Luisa had signed herself as 'la tempteuse des serpents' in Gerald's visitor's book, and she had also admired the flock of coloured doves he'd begun to keep in tribute to Luisa's flock of dyed albino blackbirds. Once a month Gerald had his own doves dipped into basins of magenta, blue or copper-green dye so that when visitors arrived by car the sound of the motor would send them 'tumbling about like a cloud of confetti in the sky'.[1] It was a gesture of extravagant beauty, Gerald's tribute to an age of spectacular monsters and spectacular excess. Doris planned to create a much more chic, contemporary version of Luisa's world, but as she made her first curious inspection of the Palazzo Venier, and as she surveyed the dense overgrown tangle of its grounds, she may have fancied that she saw a flutter of white feathers in the dark foliage, some descendant of Luisa's legendary flock.

The life of a Venetian grande dame was not one to which Jessie Doris Delevingne had obviously been born. The middle-class comforts of her South London childhood had fallen far short of the magnificent villas, titled circles and theatre of privilege in which Luisa had been raised. But Doris had been a precocious child, sharp-witted and sharp-featured, and she'd been quick to register the narrowness of her family's suburban life. She had also been born with a restless shimmer of entitlement in her genes, passed on to her by her father, Edward Delevingne, who was himself descended from a minor branch of French aristocracy.

Edward had grown up in Paris, but when he was eighteen he and his stepmother Ellen had followed other members of the family to England. To all outward appearances the tall, lean, handsome young man was careful to acclimatize to his new home. In 1899 he'd met and married Jessie Marion Homan, whose character was as sensibly and straightforwardly English as her name, and shortly after Jessie gave birth to Doris, on 25 September 1900, the couple moved from their rented home in Streatham to Coopers Cope House, a roomy Georgian dwelling in the green and affluent suburb of Beckenham, where the two would raise Doris and her three much younger brothers.

Edward was a good father, filling the house with books and music, encouraging family games of tennis in the pretty, rambling garden, but he was not a particularly reliable one, for the demands of his business – importing silk and lace from France – required frequent trips to Paris and to his factory in Lille. Doris adored her father, whom she closely resembled, but she did not have a close or easy relationship with her mother Jessie, whom she learned very early to see as prosaic and dull. Edward's long French absences meant that mother and daughter were too often alone in each other's company; and the three boys, Dudley, John and Peter (born respectively in 1906, 1912 and 1918), were too young to provide Doris with any real form of sibling camaraderie.

Later, Doris would describe her early life as unhappy; and as she grew from a bored, critical child into a rebellious teenager, she became so antagonistic to her mother and so resistant to discipline that in 1914 she was sent away to boarding school. The school was near Windsor, fifty miles from home, and it's possible that the decision to send her away was also prompted by the outbreak of war. Edward and Jessie had additional worries to concern them now: the impact of war on Edward's business, the fear that London and its outskirts might become dangerous, and it may have been simpler for the entire Delevingne household to have the troublesome Doris dealt with elsewhere.

School did at least bring Doris the company of girls her own age, but those four years of war must have been dreary as fuel and food became rationed and as the long evenings were spent knitting for victory. She was protected from danger – Zeppelin raids were a terrifying excitement that happened elsewhere – but her day-to-day life would have been infected by the slow, grinding pessimism that settled over Britain when the casualty lists began to lengthen and hopes of an early victory receded. When Doris was sixteen, however, the war delivered her an unexpected romantic bonus in the form of Captain Gordon Halsey, a young and good-looking army officer. Gordon's father lived in Maidenhead, close to the school, so he and Doris probably met while he was home on leave. There are no accounts of how, or how often, they contrived to see each other, but according to the author Desmond Young, a close friend of Gordon's, Doris fell giddily in love. Gordon's glossy handsomeness and neat military moustache were to her the template of wartime glamour. Almost as alluring were his parents, smart, rich people who divided their time between London society and the French Riviera.

In thrall to her sophisticated new love, Doris grew more rebellious and more precocious; she took up smoking, played truant from school, and by the time the war had ended she was impatient to begin a new life. She'd set her sights on London, where Gordon talked of opening a

nightclub as soon as he'd been demobbed. Even while she was still living at home Doris began taking day trips to the West End, exploring the
streets and shops that she longed to make her own. She stayed out late,
and refused to account for her whereabouts; however forcefully Edward
and Jessie attempted to restrain her with rules and curfews, she was
fearlessly set on independence.

Doris was nineteen when she left home to live in London, and
it's likely she was expecting Gordon to marry her once she was there.
Reading between the lines of Desmond Young's memoir, it's clear
that the two of them had become lovers and that Doris was still sufficiently inexperienced to believe that her 'Gordie' would take care of her.
Yet he apparently had plans that did not include a young wife. In 1920
he headed south to the Côte d'Azur, and Doris was left alone in London
to fend for herself. She received only a limited allowance from her family, insufficient to pay her bills, and now that she had no prospective
husband to support her she was faced with two stark options: suffer the
humiliation of a return to Beckenham, or find herself a job.

Doris's nerve may have momentarily failed her, for while she was
clever, well-read and quick, she had few skills to offer the post-war job
market. She could not type; she had neither the qualifications nor the
desire to teach. But she did have one exceptional asset in her looks.
A photograph taken around this time reveals how much of her father's
golden elegance she'd inherited. With her hair cut short, her bare shoulders set off by a beaded party dress, Doris posed for the camera with
the instincts of a professional mannequin. And when her search for
employment took her to a Mayfair fashion house that was seeking a
young woman to sell discounted end-of-season stock, those instincts
served her very well.

In 1919 the European economies were still battling with post-war
inflation and debts; the couture and beauty industries, however, were
starting to thrive, as a new generation sought to distance and distract
itself from the recent past. That summer, the literary socialite Nancy
Cunard had been in mourning for the lover and friends she'd lost at
the Front; she'd been emotionally fragile, 'exhausted and trembling at
heart'. Yet even in her grief she'd looked for consolation in the new season's fashions, admitting to her diary, 'My god what a help and moral

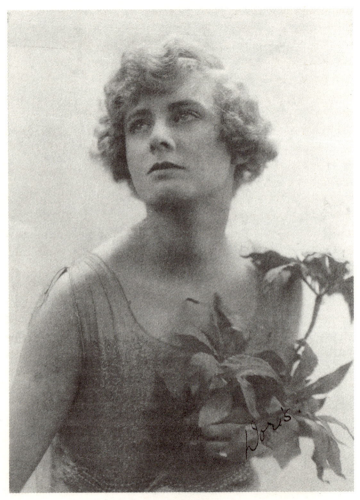

An early studio portrait of Doris, very young
but posing with the instincts of a mannequin.

support clothes are.' Nancy was fortunate in having a sufficiently large allowance to pay for her wardrobe, yet there were thousands of her fashion-conscious contemporaries in less privileged circumstances, and it was these young working women, these secretaries, teachers, actors, dancers and singers, who would form Doris's new clientele.[2]

Doris did well in her job. With her long, pretty legs she was a natural model for the rising hemlines and streamlined silhouettes of the new decade's styles, and although she wasn't exactly beautiful she had a quick, chiselled energy that made her seem so. She'd learned the art of using powder and rouge to enhance her bright, light blue eyes and neatly shaped mouth. And if her customers liked the way she looked, and were inclined to copy her, they also came to the shop because Doris's off-colour jokes, veneer of sophistication and easy manner made it fun to buy clothes from her.

Life in a boarding school dormitory had taught Doris the art of making friends. Later, when she had worked her way up to the higher rungs of London society, she would be criticized as sharp-tongued and arrogant, overly rapacious in her pursuit of wealthy lovers and a title. She would be considered amoral – a Becky Sharp of the times. Yet even Doris's most hostile critics rarely faulted her loyalty to her female friends. She liked the company of women, she made it a point of principle not to betray a confidence or spread malicious gossip, and she was instinctively generous. At the height of her reputation, a profile written in the *London Evening News* made much of Lady Castlerosse's willingness to 'give away or lend things to people in the most impulsive and genuine manner', and the gift she possessed of 'telling delightfully funny stories against herself'.[3]

When Doris had first moved to London she'd surrounded herself with the company of other young working women. They tended to move around the city as a pack: sharing dresses and short-term accommodation, swapping information about parties that could be gatecrashed and men who were generous with money. Their favoured haunts were West End nightclubs, London's newly democratic spaces where women like themselves might easily end up dancing with the sons of aristocrats or industrial magnates. Doris, however, was already aspiring to more than an evening in the company of a well-heeled admirer: she wanted to marry into luxury, to live that life for herself, and when she was about twenty she made her first, crucial advance up the social ladder by becoming a close friend of Gertrude Lawrence.

Gertie ('G' to her friends and fans) was only two years older than Doris and also from a South London suburb, but she was already en route to becoming one of the most popular actors in Britain. She'd left behind her grim childhood years in pantomime and her bleak early marriage, and was now playing opposite Jack Buchanan in the popular West End revue *A to Z*. Soon she would become the star of Noël Coward's debut musical, *London Calling*. Doris was proud of her new friendship, and very pleased to show it off to her family when Gertie accompanied her on her occasional visits back to Beckenham and played tennis in the garden of Coopers Cope House. But Gertie's great gift to Doris was introducing her to a more glamorous London: she made room for Doris in her circle of theatrical friends, promised her access to rich and titled men and even invited her to share her lodgings in a central Mayfair flat.

Gertie had recently fallen in love with a rich cavalry officer called Philip Astley, who had connections to the young Prince of Wales, and had installed her in rooms on Park Lane. She was, however, reluctant to live alone; her difficult childhood and her early professional uncertainties had marked her with a tendency to anxiety and depression. She was also gloomy about her future prospects with Astley, who, while infatuated with Gertie, had made it clear that she was 'too Clapham to marry'. Gertie needed a companion, and Doris, with her wicked tongue and pragmatic optimism, could be counted on to keep her cheerful.

For Doris, the move to Park Lane gave her the crucial Mayfair address from which she planned to pursue her own life's goal – which, as she'd bluntly confessed to Gertie, was to 'marry a lord'. She was far from naive about the obstacles she faced. Even though the Delevingne family were comfortably off, Doris had no real wealth to offer as a dowry, and her connection to obscure French nobility pulled little rank. Within this most competitive of marriage markets, her only capital was her beauty, and her wits; and Doris was clear-eyed in her understanding that if she wanted money and a title, she would have to use sex as a means of trading upwards.

The first stage in her career was to emancipate herself from the fashion house and transform herself into a woman of leisure, and Doris was in her very early twenties when she began to make the transition from shop girl up to professional mistress. It was not a simple ascent – in 1923, when Gordon Halsey returned to London to open his nightclub, the Grafton Galleries, Doris may have worked for him, dancing and flirting with his clients while perfecting the art of separating rich men from their cash. But morals were easy in the circles in which she moved. Doris didn't associate with the kind of bluestocking feminist who might judge her for using her body rather than her brains to support herself; and most of her friends were impressed by the reputation she rapidly acquired of being unusually skilled at her work. 'There's no such thing as an impotent man,' Doris liked to boast, 'only an incompetent woman' – and according to one (unnamed) male acquaintance, she was soon living extremely well off her talent. 'She really was very beautiful...It was obvious and inevitable that she attracted practically every man in town. They used to bombard her with presents. I remember once hearing her describe herself as "Miss Goldsmith's and Silversmith's".'[4] Desmond Young, too, claimed that Doris became so adept at parting men from their money that 'the sons of two prominent jewellers' had to be sent abroad after they'd ransacked the family business for her sake.[5]

Doris would never have considered herself a prostitute, a woman for hire, yet she was defiantly candid about her way of life. She had a touch of larceny in her veins, a high careless style, and she cultivated these qualities as a knowing element of her charm. She liked to flaunt the one obvious flaw in her beauty, the gap between her front teeth, because she believed it made her look 'lucky and sexy – and how'.[6] And according to more caustic wits, when she changed the spelling of her surname to Delavigne it was not because it was more 'modern looking' as she claimed, but because it saved precious seconds when signing cheques. While Luisa Casati had struggled as a young woman through shyness and social illiteracy, Doris prided herself on being at ease in any room. She could be poised, educated and articulate in the drawing rooms of Belgravia, but she was equally at home in racier surroundings, acquiring a raucous vocabulary of swear words that, as she knew full well, made a pungent contrast to her expensively groomed beauty.

Doris's nerve gave charisma to her looks. Yet there were some who thought she'd miscalculated in believing the fearlessness that made her so attractive as a mistress would also make her desirable as a wife. One of her early London haunts was the Cavendish Hotel, where Cristina Casati and Jack Hastings had gone for their first passionate trysts. Its proprietor, the seasoned and cynical Rosa Lewis, took an interest in Doris. But while she was impressed by her rapid progress through the bedrooms of London, Rosa was doubtful of its outcome. 'Young Doris may go far on those legs of hers,' she used to predict, 'but mark my words, she doesn't know how to make a man comfortable.'[7]

Marriage had to be Doris's ultimate goal, however much fun she was having, for she knew that even in the self-consciously emancipated 1920s there remained a cruelly fine line between women who were admired for being fashionably fast and those who were judged as unacceptably loose. A woman like the Honourable Daisy Fellowes could permit herself a reputation for promiscuity because she operated within the security of her inheritance and her married title. Luisa too had been able to dedicate herself to a life of apparent depravity because she was safe within the fortress of her wealth. Doris still had to climb her way to such privileges – and she knew that if she lost her footing on the way, if she became embroiled in a society scandal, if she became pregnant or was known to have had an illegal abortion, her position could become suddenly precarious.

Doris had schooled herself to appear cool, bold and witty, but admirers were sometimes alerted to the possibility that a different, more secretive and troubled young woman lay behind the façade: as one man recalled, 'she had the kind of face you have to study because below the surface there was a most puzzling and enigmatic character.'[8] She had a temper, too, that typically flared if ever she was treated with incompetence or rudeness. When a waiter, maître d'hôtel or shopkeeper appeared to be slighting Doris she reacted with disproportionate anger, as though some deep nerve of insecurity had been touched.

In 1923 Doris's careful calculations appeared to come to fruition when she met the American polo player Stephen 'Laddie' Sanford. Laddie wasn't a lord, but he did fulfil every other criteria Doris had set herself: he was athletically good-looking, with a big, broad chest and broad American features, and he had a large allowance from his family's business which he seemed more than willing to spend on her. As he rented a West End flat for Doris, squired her around London and treated her to expensive gifts, she began to believe he was the realization of her dream. Dropping her guard, she fell in love; and although Laddie was frequently absent, occupied with his busy round of social and sporting fixtures, she convinced herself that he was only waiting an appropriate length of time before proposing marriage.

But months went by, and Laddie showed no signs of committing himself to anything more than an affair. Doris grew anxious and impatient. She'd been unusually guileless in her adoration – everyone in London knew how much she'd hoped to marry Laddie, and it came as a shattering blow to her pride as well as to her heart when he suddenly transferred his affections to Edwina Mountbatten, the fast flapper wife of Dickie Mountbatten. Doris could not laugh off so public a betrayal, and with no close friend to console her (Gertie was currently on stage in America) she turned for support to her brother Dudley. He had recently given up his job with their father's business in France and she now invited him to come and live with her in London.

Despite the six years that separated them, Doris had developed a close affection for Dudley, who not only bore a striking physical resemblance to her but shared her charm and social ambition. According to the writer Beverley Nichols, who became a mutual friend, Doris and the nineteen-year-old Dudley made a compelling double act when they started to go around town together: 'two brilliantly beautiful young people...simply stunning'.[9] In a photograph of the two siblings taken at a race meeting, they could be taken for twins – both lean and rangy, with a slightly predatory edge to their golden good looks.

Dudley would be an additional expense for Doris while he looked for some kind of employment (he had various ideas, ranging from acting to stockbroking), and late in 1925, in search of some long-term financial security, she embarked on one of the most cynical of her affairs. The Canadian merchant banker Sir Edward MacKay Edgar was nearly fifty – an old man compared to Laddie – and there was little about him that appealed to Doris beyond his money. Despite his title he was something of a social outcast in London: his risky financial ventures and his North American Indian ancestry meant that certain drawing rooms remained closed to him. But Edgar, who preferred to be known simply as Mike, was infatuated with Doris, and prepared to spend far more lavishly on her than any other man she'd known. During the eighteen months or so in which she was his mistress Doris acquired a little house in Mayfair, a second-hand Rolls-Royce, a lady's maid called Swayne and a chauffeur.

Although Doris hadn't yet recovered from the heartbreak of Laddie, she was determined to capitalize on her new situation. She'd always been careless with money, walking a tightrope of debts and loans; but now she became wantonly extravagant, as if spending her way towards a version of aristocratic entitlement. When she was invited to a country house party one weekend she discovered that there were plans to visit a neighbour's new swimming pool and, having no bathing costume with her, she coolly sent her chauffer all the way back to London to fetch a selection of six. A recently acquired friend, the dress designer Victor Stiebel, recalled that Doris once returned from a trip to Italy having purchased 250 identical pairs of shoes. She told Stiebel that they had been such a perfect style and fit, it would have been 'too idiotic' not to provision herself with a future supply.

With Mike's money Doris also acquired an extensive collection of earrings, brooches and necklaces. Jewelry was her serious passion: when making a promise she would make her own ritual sign of the cross – touching her forehead, breast and earlobes while reciting the mantra 'tiara, brooch, clip, clip'. With Mike's money, too, she was flamboyantly generous: one freezing winter night she gave a lift home to a young man who'd come out to dinner without a coat. He was the son of the Duke of Bedford, but he had to subsist on a paltry allowance, so Doris scribbled the address of a shop on her calling card and told him to buy himself a proper overcoat on her account.[10]

According to Randolph Churchill, one of her later lovers, Doris 'had a sort of Robin Hood mentality'. She might soak her rich protectors for money, but she was also capable of spending a small fortune on treating 'a whole gang of young officers' to a night on the town.[11] This reckless spending made her loveable, but it was also a manifestation of the gambler's streak, the helpless inclination towards risk and excitement that frequently undermined her strategies for social advancement. By the late 1920s she'd attained a superficial eminence in London. She had a large and well-connected circle of friends, among whom were Diana Cooper and her politician husband Duff, the American actress Tallulah Bankhead, the fashionable novelist Michael Arlen and the even more fashionable playwright Noël Coward. She entertained lavishly from her little house on Deanery Street, and when Mike faded into the background – his money lost on one of his more dubious financial ventures – other lovers were there to take his place.

Yet there were days when Doris could not disguise the strain of maintaining her life as a professional mistress. When gossip columnists wrote about her – as they now frequently did – the more observant commented that her polished beauty was shadowed by a 'wistfully cynical smile'. She was approaching thirty – a dangerous age, she believed – and she was not only unmarried still, but her reputation was acquiring a slightly unsavoury taint. Some of the younger men and women she invited to her parties were forbidden from attending by parents who feared that Doris would corrupt their morals. And while she shrugged off the insult and pretended to enjoy her notoriety, she knew very well that she was sometimes a hair's breadth from scandal.

In August 1927, Doris's life was disrupted by a sudden hitch of tragedy. Her fifteen-year-old brother John had been the boffin of the family, quietly dedicated to the setting up of scientific experiments in the stables next to the house. One day, however, he'd been careless and had begun working on some electric wiring while standing in a puddle of water. The resulting shock had killed him.

The horror of John's death distressed Doris. Although she hadn't been close to her middle brother, she couldn't help but be affected by her parents' grief (her father's death, three years later, may have been hastened by the tragedy) – and she was superstitiously frightened for herself. The precariousness of John's short life was a reminder that her own time as a society beauty was limited; and when an unsuitable but rambunctiously adoring new lover appeared in her life shortly afterwards, Doris was too vulnerable and too thin-skinned to resist.

Valentine Castlerosse had briefly crossed paths with Doris the previous year, when they'd been dining in the same London nightclub.

been lamenting his losses at the races that day and his compan-
an older woman friend, had attempted to distract him by pointing
he beautiful woman who had just entered the room. 'Look at that
an,' the friend had said admiringly. 'Apart from anything it must
n to afford a dress like that.'[12] Valentine, perking up, had made his
over to introduce himself, and had been very disappointed to learn
Doris was planning to leave London for New York that same week.

Jaunts to America were now a regular feature of Doris's life, as they
were for many of her friends. The new luxury liners had facilitated a
transatlantic party circuit in which first-class passengers were transported across the ocean in a ten-day cocoon of swimming pools, deck
games, cocktails and dancing. The previous year, when Luisa Casati
had made her own first voyage to America, she'd been able to console
herself for the loss of her snake with several friends encountered on
board ship, including the painter Guiglio de Blaas and the Princess
de Polignac. Doris herself was visiting America so frequently that she

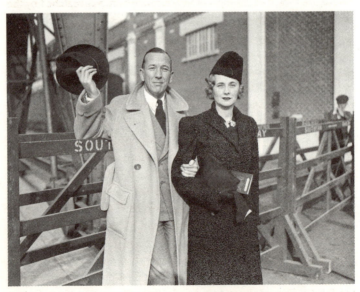

Doris and Noël Coward – their friendship
continued through to the 1930s.

had social circles established in both Hollywood and New York (where Dudley had also temporarily moved). By the autumn of 1927, however, she was back in London; and Valentine, having immediately sought to renew her acquaintance, had fallen so much in love that he was making persistent, persuasive attempts to marry her.

As a potential husband, Viscount Castlerosse fulfilled a number of Doris's criteria. Socially, he ranked as highly as any of her suitors: his family owned a large estate in Ireland, he counted royalty among his friends and he was destined to become the 6th Earl of Kenmare. Valentine was a man who seemed to know everyone, who'd heard all the latest gossip and considered himself an authority on worldly matters. He was also an engaging hedonist and while his appetites would eventually make him dangerously obese, when Doris first met him he carried himself with the attractive swagger of his Guards Officer training. His fat, florid face and rather prim little mouth still gained some distinction from his military moustache; his bulk was still contained by the dandified style of his wardrobe. Unusually for a man, Valentine enjoyed clothes, and his big, clubbable personality was matched by the exuberance of his spotted ties, claret-red waistcoat, striped trousers and salmon-pink tweeds.

Yet as much as Doris enjoyed Valentine's company, she was sharply aware of the reasons why marriage to him might be disastrous. He was constitutionally feckless, addicted to women, horses, cards and luxuries, and his allowance from his family was never enough to fund his appetites – his early attempts to make a profession out of stockbroking had foundered on sheer laziness and ineptitude. By the time he reached his mid-thirties Valentine had become the despair of his family, lurching between unsuitable affairs and running up enormous debts. And it was only in 1926, when his friend, the newspaper magnate Max Beaverbrook, invited him to write a personal column for the *Sunday Express*, that he discovered his saving talent.

The popular press was booming in post-war Britain as editors discovered the selling power of full-page photo spreads, celebrity gossip, lifestyle columns and features on beauty and fashion. Newspapers like the *Sunday Express* aimed to entertain the entire nation, from factory workers to aristocrats; and while Valentine's new column, 'Londoner's

Log', was essentially a diary of his own very privileged life and concerns, he had the gift of appealing to every class.

He treated his readers to confidential aperçus about his gambling ('if I were you I would not be with Gregory Morton of 58 Pall Mall for he does not pay'), and he wrote colourful accounts of the parties he'd attended and the characters he'd encountered. Observing an 'enormously rich Irish peer' dining at his club one day, Valentine was delighted to pass on the fact that the man had only eaten one of his lamb cutlets 'and, wrapping the other one up, [had] put it in his pocket'.[13] He was also an inveterate self-dramatizer, and the image he presented of a rogue bachelor yearning secretly for the love of a 'good-natured jolly woman' was enormously seductive to his female readership. Valentine became a kind of celebrity through his Londoner's Log, and out of the thousands of letters he received each week, most were from women wanting to offer advice about his love life. Some even made hopeful romantic overtures of their own.

By late 1927, however, Valentine had no interest in anyone but Doris. He'd become besotted by her beauty, her sexual ingenuity and her intelligence – she was one of the few women he knew whose quick mind and encyclopaedic knowledge of London society could keep pace with his own. After they became lovers he dogged her round London and, jealous of any other man who paid her attention, he got himself deeper into debt by giving her presents of jewelry, pictures and furs. To the friends who warned Valentine that he was making a fool of himself, he admitted, 'I can't help it. I am not just in love, I am obsessed.'[14]

Doris, however, was proceeding more cautiously. She was amused by Valentine, stimulated by his gusting energies, his entertaining sociability and his public celebrity. But she was also irritated by his possessiveness, and disconcerted by the depth of his need for her. It was clear that beneath his worldly assumption of flippancy he was a complicated and possibly dangerous man, and that he might need a far steadier woman to manage him. When he began talking of marriage, Doris felt obliged to warn him that she didn't know if she could be a suitable wife.

On the other hand, it was clear to her that marriage to Valentine would never be dull; and, as she pointed out to a friend one evening,

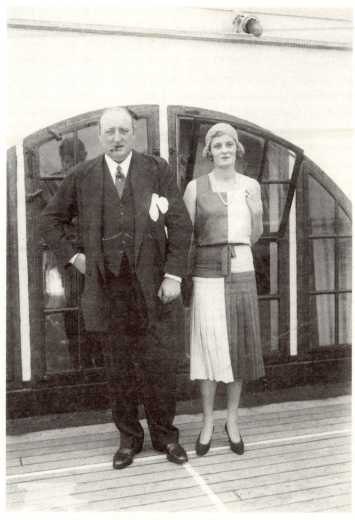

Doris and Valentine Castlerosse:
'It is better to have a few months of happiness
than forty years of boredom.'

his virtues weighed more in the balance of her affections than his vices. Valentine might 'guzzle a lot' and he might be a 'braggart', but beneath the swagger Doris believed that she saw 'a little boy with a warm heart' who'd suffered from an 'unhappy childhood'. She enjoyed his 'great big rascally attitude to life'; she felt she was the last person to 'complain about excess', and she concluded that a man so 'wonderfully suscepti-ble to flattery' might also prove pleasingly easy to control.[15]

Interestingly, Valentine would hold his own debate about love and marriage in one of his columns. A few months after meeting Doris, he devoted an entire Londoner's Log to a conversation between himself and a fictional woman named Margaret. Margaret was clearly Doris, in so far as she was described by Valentine as 'beautiful, experienced, richly successful, extravagant in her clothes but I fancy not over lavish in her morals'. And it was into Margaret's mouth that Valentine put the words he was longing to hear from Doris: in response to the question of what she would do if she fell in love with 'a waster', Margaret declared that, 'providing I was sufficiently in love with him I should marry him... it is better to have a few months' happiness with a waster than forty years of misery and boredom.'[16]

Even so, Doris and Valentine might never have reached the point of marriage had they not encountered so much resistance. Several of Doris's friends tried to warn her away from Valentine; Beverley Nichols had taken a particular dislike to him, considering him 'gross and lech-erous and fundamentally dishonest'.[17] On Valentine's side there was an even more concerted campaign of opposition, led by his mother Lady Kenmare, who was convinced that Doris was a vulgar gold-digger intent on ruining both the family fortune and family name. His uncle, Lord Revelstoke, took the same view, threatening to disin-herit Valentine if 'this notorious woman' looked like getting her hands on the estate.

As the family worked out how to prevent the marriage, they also secured a powerful ally in Valentine's friend and employer, Max Beaverbrook. In principle, Beaverbrook did not disapprove of Doris; he enjoyed the company of women who were free-living, clever and fast. But he'd formed a very close and possessive bond with Valentine, helping him to pay off his debts over the years and encouraging him to develop a modicum of self-discipline. Valentine had loved him for it: 'Max has become my never-ending lord of appeal,' he wrote gratefully. 'He is always there and always indulgent when I have made a fool of myself.'[18] In his gratitude, he had submitted to playing the role of Max's court jester – as mutual friends recalled, Valentine's jokes and Valentine's buffoonery could reliably send the newspaper tycoon 'rocking back in his chair and weeping with laughter'.

But when Valentine had fallen in love with Doris he had become suddenly less malleable, and Max shared Lady Kenmare's fear that Doris was a pernicious influence. Max was used to getting his own way: his talents for manipulating people and markets had won him controlling shares in three of Britain's leading newspapers (the *Evening Standard* and the *Daily* and *Sunday Express*). When he decided it was his duty to separate Valentine from Doris, he assumed it would be an easy task. In late December 1927 he persuaded Valentine to join him and a group of friends in Cannes, confident that by the time they returned to London he would have talked Valentine out of his misguided infatuation.

Yet Max had underestimated his friend's tenacity, and overestimated his own powers of vigilance. It was only after he came to settle the hotel bill in Cannes that he discovered Valentine had been ordering a bottle of champagne every day, to be delivered to the room of an unknown guest. On interrogating Valentine, Max discovered that the unknown guest was Doris and that the two lovers had secretly been spending the afternoons together in bed. In the end Max had only encouraged Valentine, who, irked by his friend's interference and pleased by his own cleverness in outwitting him, became even more intent on marriage. Doris was argumentative, disloyally flirtatious and dishearteningly quick to point out his faults. During the next five months they would have rows so violent they would come close to leaving each other. But they were also complicit together against a disapproving world, and on the morning of 16 May 1928 the two of them met at the Hammersmith Register Office, where, in the briefest of ceremonies, they were married.

* * * * *

It probably didn't matter very much to Doris that the marriage she'd been working towards for nearly a decade had been celebrated with so compromised and clandestine an event. She was perhaps too cynical now to hanker after bridesmaids and flowers, church music and gifts, and was simply ready to get on with her new life as Viscountess Castlerosse. But she had wilfully underestimated how unsuited she and Valentine were as a couple, and how difficult it would be for them to live together once they moved into their married home in Balfour Place.

At first their problems had been camouflaged by the brouhaha that erupted when the rest of the world discovered they were married. Valentine had been so terrified of what people would say that he'd begged a mutual friend, Lady Bridget Paget, to inform Max, and then left it to Max to break the news to his mother. Lady Kenmare's reaction had been as violent as he feared – she'd remained obdurately opposed to Doris and was adamant now that she would not acknowledge her as a daughter-in-law, declaring to Max, 'I will never meet the woman he has married. And she will never enter my house while I am there.'[*19]

But Max's response was no less harsh, and for several weeks he froze Valentine out of his life, issuing no invitations to his home, Cherkley Court, and making no response to Valentine's penitent telephone calls. This ostracism was miserable for Valentine, but Doris understood that the punishment was directed at her. Max wanted her to know that she wasn't to be allowed even the brief illusion of acceptance; and even when he'd relented sufficiently to admit Valentine back into the Beaverbrook court, he would not make a welcome there for Doris, nor would he give up on his mission to break up the marriage.

Doris refused to be cowed. She suggested tactical ways for Valentine to make peace with Max and Lady Kenmare, and she took courage from other, far more exciting well-wishers. When she and Valentine were dining at the Embassy Club one night, it was balm to Doris's spirit that

---

* Lady Kenmare had clung briefly to the hope that since Valentine was a practising Roman Catholic and Doris nominally so, a civil wedding might not count. Even after she was disabused of that belief she bickered with Valentine over the wording of the marriage announcement, insisting that he could not use the word 'solemnized' to describe a ceremony that had been so irresponsibly entered into.

the Prince of Wales sent over an admiring scribbled note to Valentine saying simply, 'Congratulations, my Lord!'[20]

That balm was temporary, though. There had been an under-standing between Doris and Valentine that theirs would be a modern marriage. Each of them had led such self-centred lives that they couldn't be expected to settle into conventional domesticity. They would tolerate each other's flirtations and accommodate each other's diaries: Valentine would gather material for his column from race-meetings, golfing trips and dinners at his club, while Doris would continue going around town with her own circle of friends. But this model, admirable in theory, did not take into account the scale of their respective egos, nor the competi-tive nature of their tempers, and when the first small disputes began to arise in the marriage they escalated with shocking and violent rapidity.

A first, the most divisive issue was money. Both Valentine and Doris had come to the marriage with debts, and his £3,000 salary from Beaverbrook, his allowance and his occasional winnings from the races did not come close to covering their expenses. Writing to Dudley about his newly married state, Valentine complained, only half jokingly, that it was ruinously expensive: 'Doris thinks she pays her own way, has become miserly, yet I can tell you that her casual expenses cost me £100 a week.'*[21]

Doris was certainly profligate. She'd become addicted to lovely things, and she liked to take her pleasures on the spur of the moment. It was normal for her to sweep up a group of friends for a last-minute champagne supper; to go for a weekend shopping trip in Paris; to zig-zag from lunch at Quaglino's to a dress fitting in Mayfair and then on to cocktails at the Café Royal. She expected to dine in the Ritz and to go dancing at the Gargoyle – currently London's smartest club, where actors and aristocrats jazzed amid art deco surroundings. Yet Valentine was no better. Friends reported that money simply 'burned a hole in his

---

*   Dudley had become unofficially engaged to an American heiress, the Countess Felicia Gizycki, though he would not marry her until 1934, by which point the relationship was all but over. They would be married for only six weeks before Felicia sent for her mother's lawyer to begin divorce proceedings, although they would remain good friends.

pocket…and *incited* him' to spend. It was like a sickness; and in 1929, when his debts had risen to over £20,000, Doris had to sell her own sole asset, her little house in Deanery Street, to help him avoid bankruptcy.*

As Doris and Valentine berated each other for their inability to budget, their arguments spiralled into more painfully contentious areas. When Valentine complained too tediously about her extravagance, Doris was inclined to arch her eyebrow and inform him that she'd be happy to take care of the bills herself, which as Valentine knew full well meant she was accepting money from other men. Monogamy had never been one of Doris's marriage vows; few of the married couples that she knew considered it necessary, and she'd been clear to Valentine that she herself had no intention of remaining faithful. Even if she hadn't been looking for financial subsidy from other men, she still craved their sexual admiration. Doris was used to being courted and adored, and now, if ever she doubted herself, if ever she wilted under the hostility of Valentine's family and friends, a sexual intrigue or an affair was her instinctive recourse.

'I went into this marriage with my eyes open,' Valentine wrote several years later. 'Doris was always honest and no matter what happened between us, I knew she was fond of me.'[22] By then he could speak of her infidelities quite rationally, but at the time, he hated her for them, especially because she made no attempt at concealment. 'She is quite blatant,' he complained to a friend, 'and she will soon have all London laughing at me behind my back.'[23] Doris, however, regarded her candour as a badge of honour: she detested sexual hypocrisy, and when Max tried to reprimand her she was flippantly unrepentant, shrugging her slender shoulders and smiling, 'Don't you know an Englishwoman's bed is her castle.'

Valentine himself was no model of fidelity, but his interest in other women was increasingly motivated by revenge. Jealousy had made him vicious, and when he realized that Doris remained unmoved by his peccadilloes, he looked for other weapons. He complained that she was growing ugly, dredged up malicious stories about her past and put into circulation the rumour that she was much older than she pretended

---

* Max also helped to pay some of the debt, as did Valentine's family.

to be. Millicent Hearst, a former mistress of Valentine's, was sympathetic towards Doris, judging that she was essentially a 'nervous flighty' woman who had married the wrong man. When she found Doris in tears one evening after Valentine had been particularly obnoxious, she counselled her to rise above the insults: 'you know what will happen if you have a row...all Valentine's friends will be pleased as Punch.'[24] But Doris was incapable of silence, and her tongue grew sharper and more cruel. When she mendaciously informed Valentine that Max had described him as 'a nuisance and a bore' he lumbered around for days in a furious sulk, and one malicious wit compared the quarrelling Castlerosses to an elephant and a vitriolic shrew.[25]

Some of the conflict might have been deflected or at least postponed if they had started a family. Valentine knew he was expected to produce a son at some point, and Doris was not indifferent to children – later she would become very attached to her infant nephew and niece. But she may have balked at having her life disrupted and her beauty invaded so soon, and in any case the opportunities for producing a Castlerosse heir were dimishing rapidly. After just a few months of marriage, their arguments had become so vicious that they both left home, Valentine going to stay at his club, the International Sportsman, and Doris returning to Deanery Street (which at that point she still owned). It was a long period of separation and by 1929, as their debts got worse and their quarrels became more entrenched, Doris began to toy with the idea of divorce. Knowing there would be a battle, knowing she would need powerful allies, she began to make overtures to Max Beaverbrook. He, ever the opportunist, saw the uses of a grateful Doris, and they came to a rather grubby agreement whereby she supplied him with gossip about her friends in return for a small fee. Later she would admit that sometime during that year they were also, briefly, lovers.[26]

Valentine, meanwhile, felt himself the victim; he grew listless and depressed and, as he was eating even more than usual, his body swelled to an alarming bulk. He professed to loathe his wife, but he suffered even more when the two of them were apart. Max took him away for a recuperative yachting trip, but at their first port of call Valentine was already trying to telephone Doris, and when she failed to answer he was so frustrated that he tore the phone away from its socket.

In the summer of 1929 Max was reporting to Diana Cooper that the Castlerosse marriage had degenerated into 'civil war...the worst I've ever known'; with a distinct tinge of satisfaction, he concluded that it was 'a cesspool...beyond my power to get to the bottom of [it]'.[27] Doris and Valentine attempted a period of reconciliation, moving into a new flat together, but it was a failed experiment. In 1930, when Noël Coward premiered his play *Private Lives*, few doubted that the toxic sparring between its lead couple was inspired by the Castlerosses or that the role of the jagged, sophisticated Amanda (ironically played by Gertie Lawrence) had been very specifically modelled on Doris.*

While Coward's warring couple only assaulted each other verbally on stage, the battles between Doris and Valentine were physically ugly too. Max was drawn in to arbitrate one day and, shaken by the bruises Doris displayed, he was forced for once to defend her. Valentine tried to justify his violence, protesting that Doris had bitten his leg so hard he'd had to 'hammer' her to make her stop, but Max flinched from the idea of any man hitting his wife. If Valentine could not 'live amicably with Doris', he pronounced, 'he should let her go'.[28] Valentine could do neither, however, and, trapped between love and hatred, his behaviour grew more extreme. One night, having learned that Doris had arranged to receive a man at home, he armed himself with a blackthorn stick and waited outside in the street. When the lover arrived, Valentine leaped out of the shadows and began beating him around the head so violently that Doris had to run screaming for help.

Valentine's unidentified victim was probably Alfred Beit, a sweet-natured man who was heir to a South African mining fortune and who was rumoured to be paying Doris a handsome allowance for the privilege of being her lover. But Valentine would have been equally ready to attack Randolph Churchill, the twenty-one-year-old son of Winston Churchill, now also said to be having an affair with Doris. Although she herself denied it, flippantly claiming that Randolph smelled 'too

*   Lady Kenmare was rumoured to have protested to Coward that no couple could possibly quarrel like that in real life, to which he wickedly responded, 'You obviously don't know the Castlerosses.' There may have been no truth to the story, but all of London relished the joke and wanted it to be true.

much of castor oil' (a reference either to his extreme youth or to the brand of pomade he used on his hair), there were witnesses who convinced Valentine otherwise, and for a while London society was greatly amused by the two men as they fought over Doris like rutting stags. When Valentine used one of his Logs to satirize a group of young men who traded openly on the reputations of their fathers ('pigeons aping the habits and fine feathers of peacocks'), Randolph was obviously his principal target. Randolph, in return, published a venomous riposte in the *Daily Express*, dismissing Valentine as a 'corpulent clown' and a 'gossip writer whose greatest tragedy was that he was supposed to be a wit [but had] a wife so much more amusing than himself'. One night, when the two men encountered each other at the Kit Kat Club, violence threatened as Valentine tried to hit Randolph and was infuriated by the latter's contemptuous response: 'Don't do that – I'm not your wife.'[29]

By October 1932 it was Valentine who wanted a divorce, although even now, so close to the brink, he remained addicted to the cycle of rows and reconciliations that bound him to Doris. Having hired a

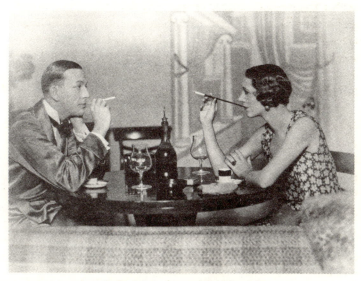

Gertrude Lawrence and Noël Coward
in *Private Lives* (September 1930).

detective to follow her to Paris and secure evidence of her adultery, he had to admit that the man whom the detective observed accompanying his wife into the Ritz was none other than himself. 'I was continually at war with myself,' Valentine conceded. 'I hated Doris lividly, and I loved her too.'[30] By March the following year he had agreed to drop the divorce suit and replace it with an official deed of separation: as Doris would later joke sardonically, 'We were married for ten years. We lived together for one.'[31] But even after they were separated, Valentine could not let her go. That summer, when Doris was holidaying on the French Riviera, he contrived to join her there; when she telegrammed a few weeks later to inform him that she was in Biarritz, he set off in pursuit. Having found her in the Casino with a stranger's arm around her shoulders, he became so upset that he threw his drink in the man's face. Doris would mock him gently – 'If you are going to act like this towards all the men I know, darling, you had better prepare to make duelling your career' – but Valentine was powerless to restrain himself.[32]

'I loved Doris with a folly and futility that passed belief,' he admitted later; and when he couldn't keep track of her in person he followed her through the press, cutting out photographs and gossip items, which he pasted into a scrapbook.[33] It wasn't until 1938 that he was finally able to nerve himself to file for divorce, and still he couldn't feel himself entirely free. When he fell ill with a severe infection, he insisted to his friends that if it proved fatal, he wanted it to be known that the 'green streptococcus' had been the cause of his death: 'I don't want Doris going about boasting that she broke my heart.'[34]

Doris too had ended up clinging to the marriage, for she had loved Valentine in her own ironic fashion, and she was very reluctant to give up the status she'd acquired as his wife. Becoming a viscountess had been a triumph for her, and she'd taken an almost childlike pleasure in having the customary coronet stamped onto her writing paper and onto all her trunks and valises. If Valentine divorced her she could remain Lady Castlerosse, but it would only be a courtesy title, which Valentine could contest were he to feel so vengefully inclined. The divorce itself worried her too. While broken marriages were no longer a cause for social ostracism, they still carried a stigma, especially for women – and Doris, formerly so heedless of gossip, was now reluctant to attract

more notoriety. When Sir John Lavery painted her in 1933 (an untypi-
cally staid portrait for which she posed in an 18th-century riding habit)
she became anxious that if Valentine successfully pursued his divorce
suit, the picture would not be allowed to hang in the Royal Academy as
Lavery had promised.

To all outward appearances, however, Doris rode out the unravelling of her marriage with her usual flair. An admiring paragraph that
appeared in the *Daily Express* in July 1932 described her as a woman of
exceptional self-possession: 'Lady Castlerosse has simplicity, a rare quality in a Society woman...She is well turned out without exaggeration.
She has no habits...she does not twist the ring around her finger. She
does not smoke cigarettes.'[35] Yet the anonymous writer also indicated
that there were cracks of unease in Doris's image. She was inclined to
make ironic gestures of regret about the direction her life had taken,
remarking that she wished she'd been better educated and could dedicate herself to more serious pursuits. She had acquired a defensive
habit of making 'absurd mis-statements', as though to mock her own
inadequacies. And if the writer of the article noted some subtle form of
disappointment in Doris, there were only a few close friends who knew
how deeply that disappointment cut. One of them, Phyllis Boyd (who'd
successfully married her own title, to become Viscountess de Janzé)
recalled a gossipy lunch at Quaglino's restaurant during which Doris
had suddenly bowed her head and said in a savage tone: 'You may think
it fun to make love, but if you had to make love to dirty old men as I do,
you would think again.'[36]

In the rare moments when she allowed herself to reflect on the
gambles she'd taken, Doris was aware that her winnings had fallen
far short of her ambitions. After just four years of marriage, she was
separated from her husband and was subjected to harassing threats
of divorce. She could still surround herself with admirers, some of
them wealthy; but none of them were poised to take Valentine's place
as a husband or long-term protector. Doris was back on the market
again – and now that she was approaching her mid-thirties, it felt like
a treacherous place to be.

CHAPTER 7

'Where is Venetia, who loved to chat so?
Could she still be drinking in her stinking pink palazzo?'

In 1948, when Cole Porter wrote the lyrics to 'Where Is the Life I Led?', the couplet in which he recalled the hedonism of 1930s Venice was said to have been a salute to Doris, one of the great survivors of the age, and one of the more surprising women to take up residence on the Grand Canal.¹ Porter himself had enjoyed a long association with Venice: at various points during the 1920s he'd rented both the Palazzo Barbaroni and Ca' Rezzonica as his summer homes, famously hosting parties at which dozens of handsome young gondoliers did service as waiters and barmen, and tightrope walkers crossed over the Canal in a blaze of light.²

As one of Venice's most extravagant summer sybarites, Porter had also taken over an enormous float that was moored permanently in the shallow waters of the Lido. He'd hired an American jazz band to play on l'Arca di Noe, or 'Noah's Ark' as it was called by the locals, and arranged for lines of flappers to Charleston on the beach while the stout American hostess Elsa Maxwell sang 'I'm a Little Old Lido Lady' dressed in a short skirt and blonde wig. Within this new jazz-age Venice, Nancy Cunard had become a celebrity too: with her cropped hair and stridently modern wardrobe, she attracted almost as much attention from painters and photographers as Luisa Casati had done a decade earlier. Nancy was also seen around town with a black escort, although it was a mark of the changing times that Henry Crowder, a jazz pianist, had not been Nancy's servant but her lover.

Serge Diaghilev, who was still a regular visitor to the city, found much to disapprove of in such antics, and complained bitterly about the corrupting influence of the 'negros and nightclubs'. Despite his professional interest in the avant-garde, Diaghilev's love for Venice had always been deeply conservative; for him the city's beauty lay in its timeless-ness, and he required everything to remain *com'era e dov'era* – 'exactly how and where it was'.

But for Doris, who first got to know Venice well in the August of 1932, the 'negros and nightclubs' were as key to the charm of the place as its ancient stones. She'd come to the city alone, needing to escape the wearisome battleground of her marriage to Valentine and knowing that Venice was filling up with amusing but sympathetic friends. Diana and Duff Cooper were there, also the playboy politician Chips Channon, Noël Coward, Tom Mitford and his coolly beautiful sister Diana (who was soon to become scandalous by running away with the proto-fascist MP Oswald Mosley). Randolph Churchill was among their party too, and according to the local press was enjoying himself uproariously, his loud and inebriated voice heard 'booming down the canals'.[3]

It was a good summer for the privileged English to be in Venice. The European banking crisis was easing, and Britain seemed to be emerging with the value of its currency intact. Randolph and the rest

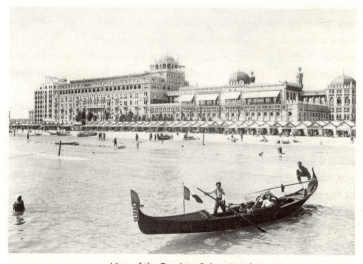

View of the Excelsior Palace Hotel
and the Lido beach, a haunt for competitive sun-worshippers.

of Doris's circle had reason to celebrate, and Diana Cooper would recall the season as the 'wildest' she had ever known. If Diana had looked more closely at the city, however, she would have observed that it was no longer the uninhibited playground that had first captivated her, before the war. Ten years of fascist rule had made their impact, not only in the modernization of certain areas but – far more sinisterly – in the way the city was now policed.

Political repression under Mussolini was less brutally felt in Venice than in other parts of Italy; the Venetians, on the whole, were talented at compromise and accommodation. But still the city was subjected to strict fascist policies. The carnival season had been curtailed, the more illicit sexual trading was driven underground, and Venice's famous tolerance for outsiders was curbed. These days, tourists who were overtly camp in their demeanour had to take care when walking alone in the city at night, for fear of an arrest or a beating. A black musician might be allowed to play in a jazz band, but he would be watched with suspicion.

Nevertheless, it was easy for seasonal visitors like Doris to pretend that Venice remained dedicated to their amusement – especially down at the Lido beach. This had been a relatively popular destination even for 19th-century tourists, ideal for bracing morning swims and with a small development of luxury hotels that were famous for their tolerance of gambling and off-colour parties. But these same tourists had tended to shun the Lido during the summer's height, preferring to retreat into the shaded colonnades of San Marco, the cool interiors of churches and galleries. In 1923, however, Coco Chanel created a vogue for sun-tans, beachwear became fashionable, and from that point the Lido became one of Venice's most bustling 20th-century attractions.

The young photographer Cecil Beaton was one of its early enthusiasts. In 1926, when he first ventured to the Lido, he had been appalled by its drab appearance – 'horrid, bare and ugly like Ramsgate'.[4] Yet he'd rapidly appreciated that the point of this narrow strip of beach was not its views, picturesque or otherwise, but the bronzed, athletic bodies that were stretched out on the sand – and the daringly cut swimming trunks sported by some of the men. '[S]mall little trousers, the smaller the better', Beaton confided excitedly to his diary, and vowed to 'buy a pair immediately'.[5]

By 1932 every inch of the Lido had been dedicated to the swimmers and the sun-worshippers: a double row of jauntily striped canvas cabanas now ran along the length of the sea front, fronted by ranks of deckchairs and loungers. The geography of the beach had also become a clear register of wealth and class, with the most privileged visitors occupying a private stretch of sand in front of the Excelsior Hotel while ordinary locals and day-trippers were relegated to the public areas at the far end.

Doris had naturally positioned herself by the Excelsior during her own summer in Venice, and as she settled on her lounger, her long racehorse legs on display, she was fully alert to the social currents around her. It was here, on lazy afternoons, that crucial gossip was exchanged, games of backgammon (a new craze) were played, and arrangements were planned for the evening. Doris's diary was taken up with the usual Venetian entertainments: cocktails at the recently opened Harry's Bar, dinner at the Danieli hotel. But she was also included in some of the grander private parties: a sumptuous dinner at the Palazzo Brandolini, hosted by the American hostess Laura Corrigan; a candlelit soirée given by Mona Harrison Williams at Ca' Vendramin; a party held in honour of Diana Cooper's fortieth birthday.

That party was memorable not only for the beauty of its setting on the island of Murano, but for the quantities of alcohol that were consumed and the drunkenly bad behaviour of some of the guests. Randolph Churchill wrestled with Richard Sykes for the attention of rich tobacco heiress Doris Duke, while Cecil Beaton and the stage designer Oliver Messel fought 'like bears' over Peter Watson, a man they both adored.

Doris was flirting too. She toyed with Tom Mitford, with whom she'd had an affair when he was just twenty-one, just as she did with Randolph. Yet while she'd been happy to use Randolph in her skirmishes with Valentine, Doris did not take him seriously. She called him Fuzzy Wuzzy, a nickname more patronizing than romantic, and she was inclined to be irritated rather than amused by the boorishness of his behaviour. The Churchill in whom she would take a deeper, more calculated interest was in fact Winston, Randolph's father.

Meanwhile, she was seeking out the company of a man who was more physically attractive to her, more charming and amusing, than

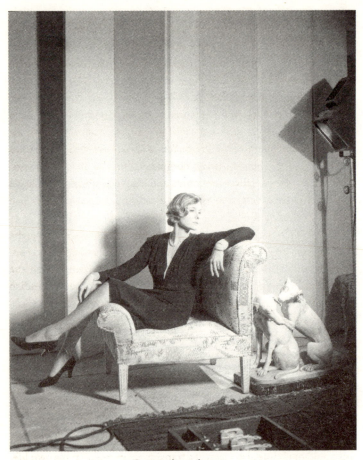

Doris in the early 1930s,
photographed by Cecil Beaton.

either of the Churchills. Cecil Beaton had long been known to Doris
through his photography: his portraits of socialites and film stars were
everywhere in the pages of glossy magazines, and his style was unmistakable. He lit his subjects with artful magic and posed them with
theatrical flair – dressing them in period costumes, surrounding them
with drapes, flowers or balloons, framing them with light-reflecting

cellophane. One of his signature techniques was printing multiple reflections of a single image, an idea he may well have derived from Man Ray's image of Luisa since Cecil had been introduced to the Marchesa through their mutual friend Lord Berners and was also an admirer of Man Ray's work.

Before this summer Doris had only a superficial social acquaintance with Cecil himself. He was just three years her junior, but he'd been at the centre of a very different social generation – his most intimate friends were members of the Bright Young Things, frivolous butterflies of the late 1920s. Their world was dominated by elaborate costume parties, childish games of treasure hunts and charades, and playful sexual inversion: if Cecil wore rouge and mascara, his women friends had their hair cut boyishly short.

The world in which Doris moved was largely more conventional; the men with whom she had affairs were often older, or had powerful connections to the political and financial establishment. Even though she might encounter Cecil and his friends at the Gargoyle or the Cavendish Hotel, her own regular haunts were the more expensive Embassy Club, the Dorchester or the Savoy. These Bright Young Things might be amusing, but to Doris, who'd worked so hard to attain her own social status, they seemed like privileged children. The formal portrait Cecil shot of her some time in the early 1930s was, in its own way, a salute to her more grown-up world. Doris looked beautifully assured in the shot; her face glowingly lit in three-quarter profile, her legs elegantly draped across the arm of her chair. There was none of the fantasy and camp with which Cecil had staged the portraits of his younger friends. But this photograph was also taken at a transitional moment in his own life, when he was attempting to distance himself from the excesses of the Bright Young Things. Conscious of the need to expand and advance his career, Cecil had begun to dress more conservatively and to leave off the paint. In 1928, when he'd begun seeking work in New York, he'd also found it expedient to assume a more masculine demeanour; according to his friend, the artist Rex Whistler, he'd returned to London looking 'very hard and manly and with a much deeper voice'.[6]

Most radically, though, Cecil had begun a determined attempt to re-orient himself sexually. From an early age he had known that his deepest desires were for men. 'My attitude to women is this', he'd confessed to his diary: 'I adore to dance with them and take them to theatres and private views and talk about dresses and plays...but I'm really much more fond of men. I've never been in love with women and I don't think I ever shall.' Now he was trying to convince himself that he could learn. To be queer in England was still to be a criminal, and Cecil found it repugnant to think of himself as part of a shadowy, branded minority. '[F]airies, collectively...frighten and nauseate me,' he admitted to his friend Charles James, and as his professional ambitions rose, he vowed to try and put his 'terrible terrible homosexualist' phase behind him and become a lover of women.[7]

During his New York trip Cecil had become romantically involved with Adele Astaire, the sister and dancing partner of Fred, and while his friends quipped that the affair had been 'as great a surprise to him as to everyone else' Cecil had been encouraged that his conversion to 'manliness' was underway.[8] Doris certainly wanted to be convinced by it, for in Venice in 1932 she not only sought out Cecil's company but began to fall in love with him.

It was, for her, a simple pleasure to look at Cecil: his smooth limbs, wide-set violet eyes and gracefully expressive hands were a beguiling contrast to Valentine's aggressive bulk. But she could also talk to Cecil with a far greater ease; he shared her interests in books, plays and fashion, and he was one of those rare Englishmen who was happy to share confidences about himself. In Venice, Doris discovered how much she and Cecil had in common – how he, like her, had believed himself to be a changeling child, born to conventional parents (who'd wanted him to take a job in the City or join the family timber business) but always dreaming of a different life.

One crucial truth, however, Cecil did not confide to Doris. His travelling companion in Venice was Peter Watson (the man over whom he had fought at Diana Cooper's party); and despite his best attempts to overcome his 'homosexualist' impulses, Cecil was deeply in love. The masculine beauty of Peter's languid, heavy face and the hard cleverness of his mind both intimidated and enthralled Cecil, and so too did the cruel indifference of Peter's heart. Peter had always been clear that he could never love anyone who was in love with him, and for the past two years he'd kept Cecil on a leash of agonized desire, permitting him to sleep in the same bed, yet never allowing him a lover's rights.

Not only did Doris fail to grasp the nature of the two men's relationship, but she was ignorant of the fact that it was Peter who finally goaded Cecil into becoming her lover. Exasperated by the relentlessness of Cecil's devotion, Peter had ordered him to go off and have sex with someone else – and that autumn, when they were back in England and when Doris finally seduced Cecil into her bed, she had no idea that he was essentially using her to wean himself off his other hopeless love.

To the rest of the world, the Doris–Cecil relationship had a delicious comic value. It was assumed that she'd taken him on as an amusing challenge, and mutual friends took a shameless interest in the details of the seduction. It was said that on their first night together Doris had filled the bedroom with tuberoses, trusting that Cecil would find their scent so creamily and carnally intoxicating, he 'wouldn't have to do a thing'.[9] It was said that she'd instructed him to 'think of his sister's wedding' if he worried about climaxing too soon, and that Cecil had proved a willing and grateful pupil. When the two of them were together at Faringdon House one weekend, fellow guests were said to have tiptoed to the landing outside Doris's bedroom in order to eavesdrop on Cecil's orgasmically joyful cry, 'Oh goody, goody, goody!'[10]

In truth, however, Doris was far less in control of the affair than people realized. Shortly after her return to England, Valentine had made his first attempt to file for divorce, and Doris had turned to Cecil for support. His almost feminine talent for sympathy, his playfulness, beauty and youth were as consoling to her as his admiring responses in bed, and for the first time, perhaps, since her affair with Laddie Sanford, Doris allowed herself to become vulnerable to a man.

When Cecil realized the depth of her feelings for him, he was appalled. He'd grown genuinely fond of 'Doritzens', as he called her, and felt guilty about misleading her. Equally, though, he couldn't help resenting the dilemma in which she'd placed him. He confessed to his diary: 'Peter loves people that are not in love with him and I in my turn am now worshipped and adored by Doritzens, for whom I hold no emotion whatsoever....It seems so terrible that I go to bed with Doritzens out of desperation when it could be so celestial with a bedfellow I love and it is doubly hard that though Peter does not love me he is incensed by my relations with Doritzens, whom he loathes, and becomes bitter so that he doesn't want to see me.'[11]

Cecil admitted none of this to Doris. But when the two of them were spending a weekend together at Madresfield Court, the Worcestershire home of the Lygon sisters, she came across Cecil's diary among his belongings and – dangerously – read its contents. She was frightened by its revelations, yet she had become too dependent on Cecil and too attached to leave him. He in turn was too self-absorbed, too confused to put an end to the affair, and both tacitly agreed to carry on as if Peter did not exist. Doris hid her unhappiness behind a façade of knowing worldliness: she joked in public about her weakness for 'homosexuality', and when Valentine, seeing them together in a restaurant, commented loudly, 'I never knew Doris was a lesbian,' she responded with a nonchalant pout.[12]

The affair was serious enough, and public enough, for Valentine to try and subpoena Cecil when he first considered divorcing Doris for adultery. It continued on through weekends at Ashcombe, the hauntingly lovely Wiltshire house Cecil had begun renting in 1930; through trips to Paris and parties in London, including a circus-themed ball for which Doris dressed as an equestrienne and Cecil, costumed as a cowboy, chased her around with a whip. It was possible for the two of them to ignore the fundamental dishonesty of their situation because they were never together for long. Cecil was working in New York for much of the winter of 1932–3, and Doris remained unflaggingly social – attending the usual round of parties and dinners, travelling abroad, surrounding herself protectively with other men.

In May 1933, they were in Paris for a weekend tryst at the Crillon Hotel. Doris had wanted some time alone with Cecil before he embarked on a sightseeing tour of Europe paid for by an American admirer, and she arrived with her usual excess of luggage, determined to make herself beautiful. After a gossipy lunch with friends (the interior designer Lady Mendl and the fashion editor Johnnie McMullin) they spent an intimate evening together, watching a cabaret of black Harlem dancers and a Hungarian gypsy band. Afterwards they retired for what Cecil admitted to his diary was a night of 'very enjoyable' sex.

Yet even during that short and apparently intimate weekend, Cecil kept himself at an emotional remove. While Doris had been touring the Parisian shoe shops, he'd claimed to be visiting an art gallery when in fact he was seeing Daisy Fellowes – a woman he knew Doris disliked, but whom he found entertaining and useful (she was at that moment the Paris editor of *Harper's Bazaar*). Even when in bed with Doris, Cecil was guiltily aware of performing a role: 'Situation the same', he wrote in his diary, 'No truth is ever sought...I am so capable of tying the string a bit tighter and it flatters me a lot. It is an exciting game and I am always fond of anyone that is fond of me.'[13] He recognized that the pleasure he experienced with Doris was essentially the servicing of his own sexual ego: he felt himself become 'a peacock' when he was with her; 'so self assured and even beautiful'.[14]

Cecil had learned to hide these treacherous confessions more care-fully after Doris had discovered his diary, but she could sense from his manner that his heart was closing against her. When she wrote to him during his European travels she permitted herself a pinch of reproach: 'Enjoy yourself darling, and do come back the same sweet Cecil you were before you went to New York.'[15] Later that summer, when the two of them were down on the French Riviera staying with one of Doris's friends, Cecil was unable to sustain the fiction of his sweetness for very long. Shortly after their arrival a letter arrived from Peter Watson, announcing that he was alone in Salzburg and feeling depressed, and Cecil did not hesitate to rush to his side.

Doris was still unable to let go of Cecil, but as the affair dragged on through more intermittent and mostly unsatisfactory meetings she was always the supplicant, and by the spring of 1935, when they were again weekending in Paris, it was clear that the relationship had exhausted itself. As Cecil had networked his way around the city, flirting efficiently with men and women alike, and courting the attention of Jean Cocteau, the depth of his indifference was impossible to ignore. In the end it hadn't been his love for Peter that doomed the affair, but the waning of his sexual fantasy. While Cecil had still been able to see Doris as a worldly enchantress, as the siren of London society, he'd been able to summon up desire for her. But after two and a half years she had become too familiar, too ordinary. It would reveal much about Cecil that the woman with whom he was able to fall most deeply in love was the elusive, unattainable Greta Garbo.

Cecil retained no sentimental attachment to his affair with Doris. When he met her on a crossing to New York in September 1937 he considered that she had noticeably aged, looking 'quiet and alone and sad, under an unlucky star'.[16] But she remained privately and loyally devoted. Noël Coward once said of Doris, 'Her wit when she's in a good mood can be devastating, but she doesn't give a damn about people's feelings.' Cecil proved otherwise: Doris never tried to berate or belittle him after they had parted, and she held no grudge. On the contrary, as their mutual friend Rudolf Kommer observed, she used to speak of Cecil 'with a startlingly deep affection', and she always kept track of his career.[17] When they'd met en route to New York Cecil had been planning an exhibition of his paintings and photographs in the city, for which he had high hopes. Doris not only attended the exhibition's private view but quietly bought up nine of the works on show, signing a cheque for $760 – nearly half his total sales.

* * * * *

Doris had lost Cecil as a lover, but she remained attached to some of his friends, and she became especially close to Gerald, Lord Berners, and his quasi-lover and companion Robert Heber-Percy. Gerald in his fifties had become a plumper, more eccentric but more confidently brilliant version of the diffident aesthete Luisa Casati had met in Rome. He'd achieved distinction as a composer, and after the death of his mother in 1931 he had turned Faringdon House into a court for his own friends and a showcase for his whimsies. He'd filled the house with a mix of fine antiques and inventive kitsch, and in homage to Luisa he'd not only taken to dying his resident flock of doves, but also to winding (fake) pearl chokers around the necks of his favourite dogs.*

Just as he had once been an avid admirer of Luisa's theatrics, Gerald greatly enjoyed the frank bravado of Doris's love life. He was more or

---

*   Although Berners had known about Luisa's albino blackbirds in Venice, he told Heber-Percy that he'd got the idea from a book about ancient China. (Sofka Zinovieff, *The Mad Boy, Lord Berners, My Grandmother and Me*).

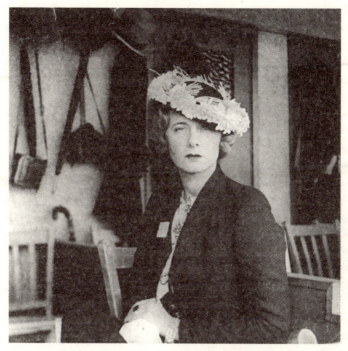

Doris: 'She had the kind of face you had to study
because below the surface there was a most
puzzling and enigmatic character.'

less celibate himself, and the stories of her battles with Valentine, the roll-call of her flirtations and scandals were as marvellous to him as fairy tales. According to Robert Heber-Percy, Gerald always relished the moment when Doris would 'curl up on a Faringdon sofa' and announce that she was ready to 'dish the dirt'. Perched on his piano stool, he would listen with almost childlike raptness to her accounts of her escapades, occasionally accompanying her with a few chords on the piano or interrupting with some 'Puckish suggestion' of how she might resolve her latest crisis.[18]

But Gerald's interest in Doris went deeper than voyeurism. He admired her courage and her lack of inhibition, and he was genuinely concerned for her well-being. When her debts became too pressing he offered to help her out with a loan – although she, touched by his kindness, had to confess, 'Dear Gerald, anything you could do wouldn't last me two days.'[19] She became a pet of Gerald's, a favoured *enfant terrible*, and he even watched with amused benevolence when her sexual gamesmanship extended to his own beloved companion Robert.

Robert Heber-Percy was a very attractive man, tautly muscled with sharp cheekbones and a full, sensuous mouth – and after long nights of drinking at Faringdon, he and Doris sometimes ended up in each other's beds. But what they found most appealing about one another was their shared appetite for risk. In his youth Robert had earned the nickname 'Mad Boy' for the violence of his temper, the extremes of his drinking and the brutishness of his practical jokes. Now Doris liked to test the limits of his wildness against her own. On one occasion, when she invited him to Paris for his birthday, she hired a prostitute who was a specialist in sado-masochistic sex to come to their room. The woman had brought a whip with her, and Doris crowed over the fact that Robert had only been able to bring himself to administer a couple of tentative taps before begging her to put an end to the session, protesting feebly, 'Any more of that and I'll be sick.'[20]

It was not Doris's finest moment. But she was deliberately living up to the role in which Robert and Gerald had cast her – a woman who spurned the conventions of the sexual mainstream, a woman they accepted as an honorary queer. In 1935, when Gerald came to write his camp and gossipy *roman à clef*, *The Girls of Radcliff Hall*, it was significant that only one of its characters would be inspired by a woman, and that woman would be Doris.

The novel (written for private publication only) was a gleefully hybrid spoof on the lesbian novels of Radclyffe Hall and the schoolgirl stories of Angela Brazil. It was loaded with indiscretion, its entire gallery of female pupils and teachers modelled transparently on Gerald's own circle of friends. He himself was the headmistress, Miss Carfax; Robert was the 'very popular' Millie Roberts; Cecil Beaton was Cecily Seymour, 'one of the most charming and talented girls in the school'; and Peter Watson was the 'capricious' Lizzie Johnson. There was only one male character, the school's dancing master Mr Vivian Dorrisk, and Gerald left his readers in no doubt that this was Doris: an elusive, graceful person who, although 'no novice in the art of love', was the victim of a 'decided penchant' for Cecily.

Throughout the vicissitudes of Doris's affair with Cecil, she had regarded Gerald and Robert as among her closest friends. There was a photograph taken of her out walking with them at Faringdon, and it shows her smiling brilliantly at the camera, unusually and unguardedly happy. Yet the two men could not be entirely relied upon, and far less their circle of friends. Among the writers, musicians, aesthetes and work-shy aristocrats who gathered at Faringdon, gossip – especially sexual gossip – was rife. To the novelist Evelyn Waugh, Gerald's set appeared at first sight to be 'so agreeable, so loyal, so charming', but he came to judge that most of them were emotionally feckless, 'aboriginally corrupt'.[21]

When Doris was absent from Faringdon, she was often the subject of crudely misogynist talk – Robert liked to boast about his first-hand knowledge of what he called her 'Cleopatra Grip', a knack Doris had for contracting her vaginal muscles during intercourse which, he claimed, could make a man 'sign away a kingdom'.[22] It was that same skill with which Wallis Simpson was said to have entrapped the Prince of Wales – and as with Simpson, the admiration it elicited among male circles was edged, very often, with a fascinated disgust. Gerald too was capable of using his intimate knowledge of Doris against her, embellishing and re-telling the stories she'd confided to him. In 1942 he would write a play, *The Furies*, in which the character of the 'socially unacceptable wife', a hard-drinking, ruthless tart with a heart of gold, was very obviously and unflatteringly modelled on Doris.[23]

The 'unacceptable wife' in Gerald's play was treated with snobbish hostility by two of the more socially elevated female characters, and here too he was writing from life. In July 1933, he and Doris were staying at Ashcombe when someone, probably Cecil, took a photograph of them together in the garden. Doris was sitting on a rug with her legs curled

*   The Faringdon circle also included Oliver Messel, Rex Whistler, the beautifully aesthetic Stephen Tennant, the composer Constant Lambert and the Mitford siblings.

up beside her and Gerald was painting her portrait, his balding head protected by a straw hat. It should have been a happy scene, but in the background were two older women who seemed to be standing in judgment. One was Lady Ottoline Morrell (a friend of Gerald's, who a long time ago had been in love with Augustus John). The other was Edith Olivier, a local writer, who was particularly possessive of Cecil and particularly disapproving of Doris.

When the two women had accepted an invitation to lunch at Ashcombe they'd expected to find Cecil alone with Gerald, and they were indignant to discover that Doris was present too. This open evidence of Cecil's misguided 'liaison' had most offended Edith, and afterwards she complained to her diary: 'It makes me feel I can never go there again... There is nothing there [in Doris] but a common little *demi-mondaine* and why should one put oneself out for her....As Ottoline says, a woman like Mrs Keppel was on the grand scale – a "king's mistress" – but this is nothing but a woman with physical attraction which she exploits in a mercenary way. It made me feel very depressed and quite unable to enjoy Cecil's society.'[24]

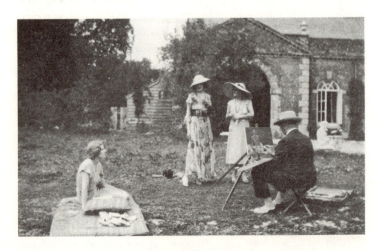

Doris being painted by Lord Berners at Ashcombe:
Ottoline Morrell and Edith Olivier pass judgment in the background.

Edith, many years older than Cecil, had always worried over his poor choice of lovers, yet she had singled out Doris for special disapproval. She herself was a proud bluestocking and a force in country politics, and while she adored the romantic frivolity of the Faringdon set, she considered that a 'professional mistress' like Doris was a betrayal of her sex. She could not see Doris's sexual career as anything more than a tawdry business venture, lacking any redeeming element of rebellion or romance. And it was even more offensive to Edith because Doris, now in her mid-thirties, a separated woman with a husband pressing for divorce, lacked the allure and excuse of youth. In the eyes of society a promiscuous woman of a certain age was beginning to verge on vulgarity, and while Doris herself remained confident of her powers of attraction she was aware of a chilling in certain drawing rooms, a retraction of the welcome to which she'd become accustomed. And it was some time between 1934 and 1935, when Doris was resigning herself to Cecil's indifference and to the impossibility of salvaging her marriage, that she found sympathy from a man who was to become the most touchingly chivalrous but also the most potentially scandalous of all her lovers.

Dating the exact course of Doris's relationship with Winston Churchill is problematic since there were so many reasons why, as a married man and a prominent politician, he needed it to remain secret. The two of them had probably been introduced in the late 1920s – Churchill knew Valentine, and was a close if sometimes combative friend of Max Beaverbrook. In 1929 they had all stayed at Max's villa and Churchill, a keen amateur painter, had been sufficiently struck by Doris to ask her to model for a portrait sometime the following year.

The portrait itself holds only ambivalent clues about Churchill's feelings for Doris – it's an odd likeness in which her sharp-boned face appears both vulnerable and sly. But it seems to have formed a bond between them, which deepened during the summer of 1933 when they were guests of Maxine Elliott, a former actress and possible mistress of King Edward vii who now amused herself by entertaining the powerful and beautiful people of Europe at her gleaming, modernist villa in the South of France.

Doris had arrived first at the Villa d'Horizon, and with her fashionably cut white swimsuit in her luggage, she had been anticipating a

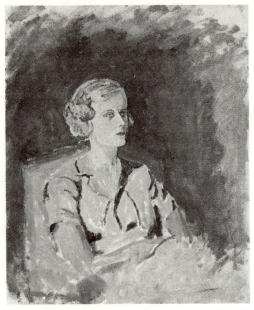

Winston Churchill's
first portrait of Doris (c. 1930).

month of unclouded idleness and good company. But the holiday did
not progress as she hoped. This was the summer in which she'd been
hoping to tend her relationship with Cecil back to its early sweetness,
and when he disappeared off to be with Peter Watson in Salzburg.
Attempting to conceal the humiliation of Cecil's abrupt departure,
Doris then had to contend with the appearance of Valentine, who was
playing the outraged husband, but still lonely and pining for her affection. She behaved well with him in front of the other guests, who by
now included Winston Churchill, his wife Clementine and their daughter Sarah; but the discomfort Doris felt in her husband's presence is
evident from a photograph taken of them beside Maxine's swimming
pool. Valentine, as fat and shiny as a seal in his black bathing suit, has
his arm draped possessively around Doris while she, pale and slender,
seems to shrink from his embrace. How much Churchill intuited of
Doris's unhappiness is impossible to know, but he did ask her to pose

for another portrait, and according to Valentine's biographer George Malcolm Thomson, it was during this summer that 'a romantic friendship... [o]r intellectual affinity' sparked between them.[25]

Churchill was twenty years Doris's senior: he was as closely wedded to his career in politics as he was to his wife, and his gargantuan work ethic had prevented him from forming a more than scant acquaintance with most of her social set. Yet the two of them did have qualities in common. Churchill was in his own way a gambler; throughout his career he had ducked and dived between parties and policies to advance his political agenda (he'd twice crossed the floor of the House of Commons, first deserting the Tory party for the Liberals, then returning to the Tories). He was also something of a social maverick – impatient with the ponderousness of his colleagues, he sought out the wit and wickedness of people like Coco Chanel, Noël Coward and Ivor Novello. In fact, he was rumoured to have enjoyed, long ago, an experimental one-night stand with Novello – his curiosity driven, according to Somerset Maugham, by the desire to know 'what it would be like with a man'.*

Churchill's taste in friends made his political associates wary, but it was even more mistrusted by his wife. When Max Beaverbrook and his mistress Jean Norton were invited to a lunch party at their house, Clemmie (who was absent) wrote to warn Winston that there should be absolutely no kind of 'low conversation' at the table and that the relationship between Max and Jean should not be made publicly 'apparent'.[26] Down on the Riviera, Winston was more than eager to enjoy Doris's easy, worldly company, to hear gossip about their mutual acquaintances. But he was also very protective of her. At one point his son Randolph also appeared at Maxine's villa and, having blundered into the room where his father was painting Doris, he swore loudly in surprise. Winston rebuked him sharply, 'Wash out your mouth, my boy, after using such words in a lady's hearing.' The irony wasn't lost on Randolph, who knew exactly how salty Doris's own language could be, but Winston himself remained doggedly gallant and romantic in his perception of his new lady friend.

---

* According to the same rumour, Novello had composed the song 'I've Caught My Lilacs in the Spring Again' in tribute to their coupling.

Over the following years they continued to meet quite regularly, and to the outside world their friendship seemed an innocent if unlikely one. Winston offered Doris advice when she was having legal difficulties with Valentine; he took her side if he heard malicious comments made at her expense. In return, she charmed and entertained him, and posed for two more portraits. Officially, all seemed above board: in London in 1934, when Doris wrote to invite Winston to supper, she emphasized that she 'very much' hoped Mrs Churchill would be able to come too. When Winston stayed again at the Villa d'Horizon, the letter he wrote home to Clementine did not conceal the fact Doris was one of the other guests.

And yet there is strong evidence that the friendship evolved from a flirtation of sympathies into a love affair. For two more summers Winston contrived to be alone at Maxine's villa at the same time as Doris, and the one surviving photograph taken of them there suggests that, at the Villa d'Horizon at least, their intimacy had become an accepted fact. It is a snapshot of a large luncheon party, typical of Maxine's generous scale of hospitality. Doris and Winston can be seen at their own separate table, seated at a slight distance from the other guests. From the way they are leaning towards each other, mutually engrossed, it is clear they were engaged in their own very private conversation.

Rumours of their relationship did eventually surface elsewhere. There was talk of them spending an unusual amount of time in each other's company in London; of an occasion when they'd been sighted entering the Ritz in Paris. In September 1936, when Winston's daughter Sarah eloped with the Austrian comedian Vic Oliver (divorced and twice her age), Doris was perhaps suspiciously eager in her offer to help: 'I can handle Sarah better than Randolph,' she wrote, 'and give him [Oliver] hell.'[27] When Winston's youngest daughter, Mary, cut Dudley at a party one night, some shrewd observers wondered if the insult might not have been intended for Doris, since Mary and Dudley had been romantically close. The gossip got sufficiently out of hand for a story to circulate that Winston, no less incredulous in his delight at Doris's lovemaking than Cecil, had exclaimed adoringly, 'Doris, you could make a corpse come.'

Further rumours were fuelled by suggestions that Winston's devoted union with Clementine was temporarily in trouble. By mutual agreement, husband and wife had fallen into the habit of spending periods of time apart, allowing themselves a break from the frantically politicized pace of their marriage. During the winter of 1934–5, however, Clementine was away for five months on a cruise of the South Sea islands, and during that time she became very attached to a handsome art dealer called Terence Philip. Later she acknowledged that the initiative for their romantic friendship had come from her, that Philip did not care for her in that way (indeed, he was probably gay). But the fact that she'd briefly imagined herself to be in love – and with a man so utterly different from her husband – suggests that both of the Churchills were looking for sympathy outside their marriage.

A few close friends did know about Doris and Winston's relationship, but no word of it reached the press, nor did it become widely discussed. Doris was fully conscious of Winston's power to help and advise her, and once or twice she would overreach herself. In 1937, when Valentine tried to get her barred from the Royal Enclosure at Ascot, she wrote to Winston to ask him to intervene. But generally she remained circumspect, and the only two people to whom she fully

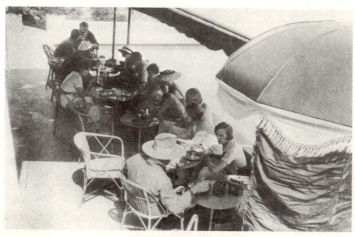

Doris with Winston Churchill.
Both were regular guests of Maxine Elliott
during the mid-1930s.

trusted details of the relationship were her brother Dudley and the woman he would shortly marry, the very beautiful and well-connected Hon. Angela Greenwood.

For a short period the young couple were in fact witnesses to the affair. Early in 1937 Doris had been given the gift of a Mayfair house by a new lover, Arthur Bendir (part-owner of Ladbrokes), and she invited Dudley and Angela to come and live with her there. Although they were tucked away on the top floor of No. 43 Berkeley Square, it was always obvious to them when Winston was expected because Doris would give her staff the evening off – and it was also quite clear what occurred during his visits, since afterwards Doris described them in frank detail.[28]

Many years later Angela would relate some of that detail to her children, recalling that Doris, while proud of her intimacy with the great statesman and genuinely fond of him, had also been quite candid about his lack of finesse as a lover. But at the time Doris swore Angela and Dudley to secrecy, knowing that if the affair became public the scandal could do irreparable damage to Winston's career. Churchill was currently engaged on a long and difficult campaign to reposition himself at the heart of government, having been sidelined for several years by his stubbornly independent stance on a number of key issues – among them, home rule for India. But it wasn't just personal ambition that was driving him; it was his conviction that Britain was sleepwalking into a second war with Germany, a war that it was his duty to try and prevent. He'd watched, appalled, as Britain's coalition government had nodded along to Hitler's successive grabs for power, apparently ignoring all evidence of his ambition to regain the territories Germany had lost in 1918. The people of Britain might not want another conflict; the government might not want to commit to an unpopular policy of rearmament; yet Churchill believed the only chance of curbing Hitler's aggression was to meet it with a credible threat. To argue so drastic a case, however, he had to appear morally unassailable, and if the papers were to get hold of the story of his adulterous affair, it could undermine his reputation. By the summer of 1937 it became obvious that he and Doris could not safely continue as lovers; and in July she was writing carefully to reassure him: 'I am not at all dangerous any more.'[29]

It's unlikely that Doris felt much of a pang, for all the qualities that had drawn her to Winston as a lover – his gallantry, his rambunctious capacity for pleasure, his immense fund of practical sympathy – were those she could hope to enjoy as his friend. (When writing to assure him of her discretion, she'd also taken the opportunity to ask his advice about her impending divorce, complaining that Valentine wanted to cite her as the guilty party even though she knew he had committed at least 'three indiscretions' himself.) The affair with Winston had also occupied only a tiny fraction of her life: she'd continued to see other lovers, as always, and had been travelling widely. According to a 1936 report in *Freepost America*, 'Lady Castlerosse' had become almost as well known in America and 'around the spas of Europe' as she was in London. She was often in Hollywood, where she counted film-star royalty like Charlie Chaplin, Mary Pickford and Douglas Fairbanks among her friends and where she claimed to have been offered one or two minor roles herself, including a cameo part in *Gone with the Wind*.* The offer had come, she said, from the director George Cukor; but although she boasted about it, and apparently fantasized about the possibility of a film career (she had taken a couple of screen tests in the early 1930s), she did not seriously pursue the idea. A photograph taken that year suggests that while Doris claimed she had been too busy to accept the role, she might actually have been wary of exhibiting herself on screen. At thirty-six, she was no longer young by Hollywood standards, and as lovely as she might be in the flesh, there were already dark shadows beneath her eyes and a papery fragility to her skin that the camera would cruelly expose.

Doris was still chasing the good life, but she was far more conscious, now, of its cost. Plagued by mounting debts and worried about the future, she would occasionally try for a rapprochement with Valentine. In 1935 Doris left her rented flat in Ebury Mews and moved into

---

* *Gone with the Wind* would not be filmed until 1939, but it was already being touted as the most important movie of the era. Both Cukor and his producer David Selznick got into the habit of handing out indiscriminate promises of roles: Selznick also offered one to Angela, Dudley's wife. She, while flattered, was pregnant at the time and unable to accept.

Claridge's hotel, where Valentine also happened to be staying. From time to time she would telephone him, knowing he would be unable to resist if she asked him to take her out for dinner. Yet these meetings invariably turned stormy as the two of them raked over each other's marital misdemeanours; and in 1936, as Doris had been scanning her social world for new and potentially generous lovers, she made a leap into what was, for her, an interestingly experimental relationship.

Margot Liddon Flick Hoffman was an American heiress, born in 1905 to the coal-mining Flick family (her mother had initially been married to the oldest son, Reuben, but had moved on, or been passed, to the younger brother Jay when Reuben died). Margot's childhood had been a conventionally privileged one, divided between rural Massachusetts and central Manhattan, yet as an adult she'd exhibited little enthusiasm for the life of a wealthy socialite. Broad-shouldered and tall, her clothes tailored and her dark hair kept efficiently short, Margot had no patience with boys, parties or shopping trips. She owned and ran a dog kennel, she piloted her own airplane and she was the sole female player on the Pittsfield polo team.

One or two gossip columnists insinuated that there was a Sapphic subtext to Margot's sportiness, yet throughout her twenties she managed to keep her romantic affairs private. In 1935, however, she picked a fight with the Flick family butler, William Graham, after he'd barged into her bedroom before she was properly dressed and, she claimed, exhibited offensive signs of inebriation. She had Graham dismissed from his job, but the butler refused to go quietly – not only suing the family for defamation of character, but justifying his demand for $100,000 damages on the grounds that Margot had no moral right to complain of his behaviour. On more than one occasion, he claimed, he'd caught her in compromising situations, citing the evening he'd found her kissing a married woman in front of the drawing-room fire.

The case was taken to court. But while the butler lost and the family managed to keep press coverage to a minimum, Margot's brush with notoriety had been sufficiently alarming for her to seek the protecting cover of marriage. Her new husband was the novelist Richard Sanford Hoffman, and the marriage was clearly one of convenience, for not only had it been orchestrated with unceremonious haste (the press reported that 'Miss Flick will dispense with [wedding] attendants'), but when Margot and Richard were travelling on an extended honeymoon in Europe and the Far East, they were accompanied for much of the time by Doris.[30]

The two women had probably met in London in 1935, but it was when they re-encountered one another in China that Margot fell in love. Doris had been holidaying with friends on a luxury cruise (Jean Cocteau was among their fellow passengers) and according to the American press, she and Margot rapidly developed a 'fast friendship' and continued travelling together. Afterwards Doris returned to America with Margot, staying in her Fifth Avenue apartment and at her family estate in Lenox. It was discreetly reported by local journalists that Margot's marriage to Richard had been quietly dissolved in Reno, with both parties agreeing that the union was a 'mistake'.[31] Among Doris's own friends, however, the nature of the women's friendship was far more bluntly discussed: according to Loelia, Duchess of Westminster, 'you only had to look at her to know what was going on. Doris got more out of [Margot] than from any of her rich men, every jewel the size of a cherry.'

There's no reason to suppose that Doris's feelings for Margot were purely opportunistic. She was open in her sexuality, willing to explore, and she seems to have had genuine reason to care for Margot, who, according to Angela Delevingne, was 'very likeable, and much nicer to Doris than Valentine'. On the other hand, Margot had come into her life at exactly the point when Doris most needed her unconditional money and support – when she'd overdrawn her own social and financial credit in London, and when the idea of reinventing her life had never seemed more desirable.[32]

A decade earlier, the novelist Michael Arlen had prophesied that if ever Doris acquired a sufficiently rich husband she might transform herself into one of the leading hostesses of her generation. She possessed all the necessary style, wit and acumen that would qualify her to inherit the mantle of a *salonnière* like Lady Cunard, Nancy Cunard's mother, who for decades had gathered the great and the good, the rich and bohemian for high-level gossip at her Mayfair house. Doris already possessed the necessary contacts: during the early 1930s she'd hosted dinners for Douglas Fairbanks and for Emerald Cunard herself, as well as for members of the bohemian aristocracy like Naps Alington and Evan Morgan (now Viscount Tredegar). But her marriage to Valentine had become too rancorous and debt-ridden, and her own reputation too dubious, for her to consolidate her position. It was only now, with Margot's backing, that she believed she might finally be able to reinvent herself from professional mistress to social doyenne. Although she wasn't confident that London was ready to embrace her in this new role, she believed she could successfully embark on her new career from a base in a foreign city.

Back in Venice, in 1932, she'd been conscious that the effective queen of the summer season had been the homely, middle-aged American Laura Corrigan. Laura's story had interesting resonance for Doris, for she'd been born without title or wealth (when she'd first met her husband she'd been working as a waitress); and once she'd been propelled by James Corrigan's money into the upper echelons of New York and London society, her early years had been a struggle. Laura had been mocked for the awkwardness of her Wisconsin manners and for the gaucheness of her efforts to impress. Even when she'd finally gained a certain amused acceptance, she'd remained a social novelty, a kind of pet.

But in Venice, where Laura held court over the holiday season, no one was inclined to mock her origins or her style of hospitality. The rich, the smart and the beautiful were more than happy to lodge for free in one of the several palazzos she'd rented, and to enjoy the sumptuous meals she hosted. As Diana Cooper wrote with amazement, Laura was like one of the old Venetian doges: she'd 'married the Adriatic and seemed to be holding most of the palaces in fee'. Four years later, as Doris was considering how to advance her own social career, she seems to have remembered Laura's success and to have set her sights on a Venetian palazzo of her own.[33]

She may have considered it a lucky portent that the Palazzo Venier dei Leoni had come onto the market just as she and Margot began looking for properties. Having heard so many stories about the days of Luisa's residency she could now imagine herself as La Casati's successor. But there were practical considerations, too, that attracted her to the palazzo; for even though it needed extensive building work,

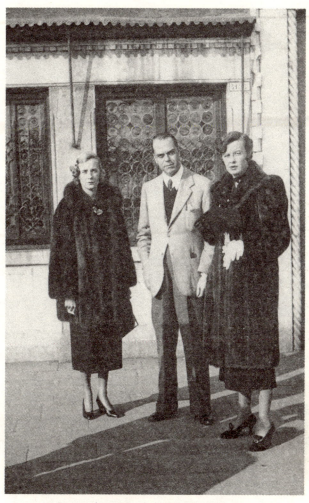

Doris and Margot with their architect Schioppa
outside the Danieli Hotel (c. 1936).

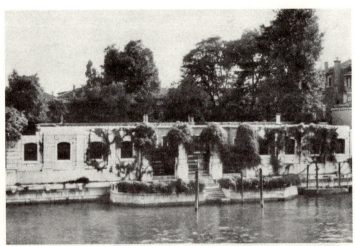

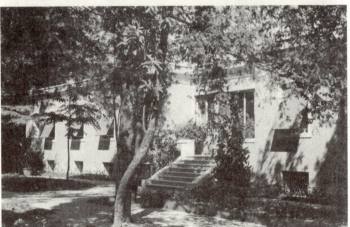

Front and back views of the newly renovated palazzo:
the ivy has been cut back, but not entirely removed (1937–8).

it was far more realistically compact than most other properties on the Grand Canal, and given its unlisted status, there would be no obstacles to prevent her modernizing it as she chose. Doris was very happy to appreciate the historic beauty of Venice, but she didn't actually want to live among ancient tapestries and crumbling marble halls, nor to walk along a long damp corridor in order to get to a bathroom at night.

As soon as the purchase was made, Doris and Margot hired the Venetian architect Schioppa to draw up plans for the palazzo's remodelling, and from late 1936 work progressed at a speed that would have seemed miraculous to the builders who'd laboured on its original construction. The two women visited occasionally to watch (a photograph shows them posed outside the wintry-looking Danieli, dressed in matching furs). And in February 1937 Doris wrote excitedly to Winston Churchill about her new home, sending a photograph and asking anxiously whether a diplomatic stand-off that was currently affecting relations between Italy and Britain might pose any danger to her ownership rights.[34] (Mussolini had just reacted with aggressive pique to the fact that the former emperor of Abyssinia, a country he now ruled, had been invited to the coronation of the new British king, George VI.)

By early 1938, work on the palazzo was complete. On the new ground floor a dining room and kitchen ran along the back of the house; there was a sunny sitting room at the front and six new bedrooms were installed, each with its own marble bathroom and sunken bath. There was central heating throughout, there were new floors of Verona marble terrazzo inlaid with mother-of-pearl, and Doris's designer friend Lady Mendl had been hired to complete the interior, renovating the decorative stucco on the walls with what the English society columnist the Marquess of Donegal judged to be 'superb modern taste'.

Outside, the lime trees and cypresses still fringed the garden (all trees were protected under Venetian law), but the rest of the grounds were laid out with bright new plants and paving stones. Neat green awnings shaded every window, and by the steps of the waterfront terrace a private gondola was moored alongside a motorboat, which had Doris's name painted gaily on its prow. Luisa would have condemned everything that Doris had done, and Cecil Beaton, when he visited, was cruelly dismissive: 'a very expensive house that contains nothing of any value', he wrote priggishly in his diary, judging that Doris's efforts at refurbishment would have been 'as effective if done on the cheap'. But Doris was immune to criticism. She adored her glamorous new home, boasting happily that it was the only palazzo in Venice to have a bathroom for every bedroom; and as soon as she'd taken up residence for her first extended season, she began assembling a list of guests that would grace them all.[35]

Doris had been especially glad to escape to the palazzo, for earlier that summer her divorce from Valentine had been finalized. Although she had also wanted to end the marriage, having become sick of the mud-slinging and the grubby legal machinations, Valentine had declared himself triumphant in getting Doris cast as the guilty party with Robert Heber-Percy cited as correspondent. He had proven himself additionally vindictive by insisting to all of his friends (and Doris's) that he'd been thrilled to be rid of her because she had aged so badly, grown so ugly, that she could now be mistaken for her own mother.

Now she was determined to forget Valentine in a season of parties that would launch her career as a Venetian hostess. Her 'inaugural soirée' that summer was a dinner and drinks reception that was described in gratifying detail by the press, who reported on the number of tables set out on the palazzo's waterfront terrace – 'the biggest in Venice' – and on the eminence of a guest list that included the actor Douglas Fairbanks and his wife; Princess Alexandra of Greece; Noël Coward; and Count Volpi, Mussolini's former finance minister and a prime mover in political and cultural affairs. More guests were brought in for the reception that followed, and Doris's acceptance in the city seemed assured. During the rest of the summer the social columns were full of the bridge parties and dinners Lady Castlerosse was hosting at her new home, which she now, half-mockingly, liked to call by its local name – the *palazzo non finito*. The names and titles of the élite summer crowd were all listed among her guests and Doris was being invited everywhere too, dining with Ivor Novello, Lord and Lady Melchett, José Sert (Misia Sert's former husband) and Lady Juliet Duff.

Occasionally, at the bottom of these social listings, there were references to Dudley and Angela, who had also come to stay at the palazzo. Doris had wanted to make a romantic fuss of their arrival, and late on

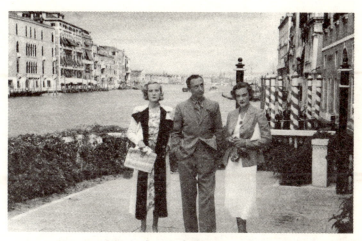

Doris on the waterfront terrace with
an unidentified male acquaintance and Angela,
her sister-in-law and close friend.

their first night she'd come into their bedroom with a small orchestra she'd lured from the party she'd been attending. The young couple were serenaded, in traditional Venetian style, and the sweet silliness of the gesture was typical of the affection that Doris felt for them both. Out of all the photographs that survive of her life in Venice, those in which she appeared alongside Dudley and Angela, arm in arm by the palazzo or lounging on the Lido, are the ones in which she looks happiest.

One name that was absent from the press, however, was Margot's – for even though she'd paid for the palazzo and been consulted in its rebuilding plans, she didn't much care for Venice and was only willing to stay in the city for short periods. She and Doris were still seen together a great deal. Late in 1936 they'd travelled from New York to an all-female house party on a Nevada ranch and Valentine, who'd tracked them down while touring America with Beaverbrook, had been scathing about the Sapphic community he found there: 'a regular mare's nest....Female horses and female humans'.[36] He regarded Doris's latest transgression as an offence against masculine propriety, and it was the following year that he punitively attempted to get her barred from the Royal Enclosure at Ascot. Undeterred, however, Doris and Margot remained publicly on view on both sides of the Atlantic: they were in London in May 1937 to see the new king being crowned; in October they were in Florida, drinking at the El Morocco night club with George Cukor. They spent Christmas at the Royal Hawaiian Hotel in Honolulu, and the following year they were at a house party in Palm Springs, where Doris was painted a second time by Lavery.

Yet Margot did not particularly like cities and crowds; she seems to have required large landscapes and the company of animals to keep her happy. While she was still devoted to Doris – so devoted that she didn't notice Doris's growing impatience with her – Venice in high season was too crowded, too artificial for her to put up with for long. And she didn't, apparently, make an exception for the end-of-season ball that Doris had planned as the climax of this first Venetian summer.

It was a lavish, all-night event, with cocktails on the front terrace and a polished dance floor laid out over the garden at the back. A jazz band played throughout, and fairy lights reflected the night's stars. Cecil came, despite his disapproving eye, and with him the artist Rex Whistler and the writer Raimund von Hofmannsthal. There was an array of European titles, including the young Prince Philip of Greece, and as Doris watched her guests dancing under the night sky; as the music from her band floated across the canal; as the lights of San Marco glimmered in the near distance, she may have believed that she had finally put Valentine and their wretched marriage behind her. She may also have believed that she had guaranteed her place in Venetian society.

But the night of Doris's party was to be memorable for reasons that had little to do with the beauty of its setting or the luxury of its entertainment. Doris couldn't know it yet, but this event was to be one of the last of its kind in Venice before the outbreak of war. Mussolini was drawing closer to Hitler, and already the effects of their alliance were being felt; anti-Semitic laws had been passed in Venice in July, and those Jews who had not had the foresight to leave were suffering segregation and exclusion. Some of the more politically sensitive summer visitors had chosen to stay away entirely – as Margot Asquith had announced grandly in her column for *Vogue*, 'no one likes dictators', and she herself was boycotting the city.

Elsewhere in Europe, tensions had risen after Hitler's annexa-
tion of Austria, and now that he had clear designs of moving into
Czechoslovakia there was jittery talk of another international conflict.
On the night of Doris's ball, while most of the guests were dancing and
drinking in cheerful oblivion, others like Raimund von Hofmannsthal
and his friends were preoccupied by urgent concerns. News had just
reached them that Duff Cooper, as First Lord of the Admiralty, had
ordered the British navy to mobilize in preparation for Hitler's likely
invasion of Czechoslovakia and for its likely political fallout. If war broke
out between Nazi Germany and the rest of Europe, Doris and her guests
might find themselves stranded in Venice, in pro-Nazi territory which
for those of Jewish origin, like Raimund von Hofmannsthal, could
create a suddenly dangerous situation. Even though it was two in the
morning, when Raimund heard the news of Britain's military response
he made the immediate decision to leave Doris's ball. Accompanied
by his lover Liz Paget, Rex Whistler and Rex's girlfriend Caroline,
Raimund embarked on a panicked journey across the border towards
neutral Switzerland, the women still wearing their evening gowns.

Raimund's fears proved premature, as in late September Britain
caved to Hitler's terms and signed the compromised Munich
Agreement. Doris, although primed by Winston to understand the
moral and military arguments for opposing Nazi expansionism, could
not help but be swept up in the general euphoria as war was averted.
When she closed up her palazzo at the end of the season, she had
agreed to lease it out to Douglas Fairbanks for the following spring, but
she had every reason to hope that she'd be returning in the summer,
and for many summers more.

But Doris would never see Venice again. By March the following
year, the British government had reversed its policy of appeasement;
on 3 September, two days after 1.5 million German soldiers marched
across the Polish border, Britain declared war, and by June 1940 Italy
had entered the conflict as a German ally. Venice now lay in enemy
territory. And not only had Doris's palazzo become completely inaccessible to her, her fledgling career as a society hostess had been
summarily terminated.

* * * * *

Doris was in England during that tense summer of 1939, renting a picturesquely rural house called Titlarks Farm in Sunningdale, a village about twenty-five miles outside London. She'd grown sentimental about family now that Dudley and Angela had become parents, with a small daughter called Venetia and a new baby, Edward. Doris doted on them both, especially Edward, and she held an extravagant christening party for her little nephew. Edward Senior was now long dead, but Jessie was still sturdily alive and seemingly happy: in a photograph with Angela and Venetia she displayed a rather girlish elegance, wearing a small black hat at a rakish angle on her head, and shoes tied with ribbons.

During the first few months of the war, as the Germans made no move to attack, Doris moved back to London, where life continued almost as normal. There were precautionary air raids, some of her friends were disappearing into war work and Dudley was commissioned in the army. But still there were parties, dinners, weekends away: over Christmas, Doris went to stay at Madresfield Court, and during January she was preoccupied by Maxine Elliott, old and failing now after a severe stroke.

By the spring of 1940 the 'phony war' was turning serious, and Doris was very tempted to abandon London, and her family, for the safety of neutral America. Her relationship with Margot had soured; perhaps Doris had spent too much of Margot's money, or perhaps she had been too unkindly blatant about the other lovers she'd continued to see. But she now confided to Angela that during her last trip to America she had become involved with a very wealthy man who was heir to the Mellon banking fortune. Later Angela would be hazy about the lover's first name, but it was almost certainly Paul Mellon, and according to Doris he had promised to leave his wife and marry her if she would come and live in the States. He had even got a house prepared in readiness, she said – and by the spring, as Hitler unleashed his first aggressive moves against Northern Europe, it seemed madness not to accept his proposal.

Doris made her plans to leave London, but as she did so she became guiltily concerned about the safety of Angela and Dudley's children. She was terrified of them being exposed to German bombs, and begged Angela to let her take Edward, the baby, away with her to America, promising that Paul would find a suitable nanny to take care of him.

Angela, not surprisingly, refused. She and Dudley had bought a little house in Surrey, a reasonable distance from London were the Germans to attack; if their situation became at all dangerous, she planned to take the children down to her parents' rented house in Cornwall. So in June 1940, Doris was on her own when she travelled to Galway in Ireland to board the SS *Washington*. The American liner was offering one of the last civilian crossings out of Europe, and as Doris set sail with her precious collection of jewelry, her best clothes, and two of the portraits that Churchill had painted of her, she knew it could be many years before she saw Angela, Dudley and the babies again.[37]

The guilt Doris felt at leaving her family – and the lesser guilt at leaving her country – were alleviated by the familiar rush of pleasure she always experienced on arriving in New York. After London, the city was blessedly free of sandbags, blackouts and gas masks. Neon lights blazed, the shop windows were full, and Paul Mellon seems to have been waiting, ready to give Doris an even more charmed life than Margot had offered. What subsequently happened between them, however, remains unclear; for Paul did not marry Doris, nor did he technically leave his wife. Rather, he seems to have undergone some crisis of nerves or conscience. A few months after Doris's arrival in America, he suddenly joined the US army – despite the fact that America was not yet at war, and conscription was not yet an issue.

Whatever Paul's reason for breaking off his relationship with Doris, he had effectively left her stranded. She was now alone in New York, without an income or a home; and while she had various friends in the city, among them Lady Mendl and other Londoners-in-exile, her situation had become very uncertain. Even though she knew she was lucky to be away from Britain, safe from the bombing raids that were now hammering its cities, Doris began desperately to wish herself back home.

Returning to London, however, was a far from simple option. Civilian crossings by air or sea were expensive and scarce. By December 1941, when America entered the war and virtually all transatlantic traffic was commandeered for official use, they became all but impossible. Doris had no idea now how long she would have to remain in New York, nor how she was going to support herself. Her best and sanest option would have been to find herself some paid employment: Doris had a quick brain, charm, and some basic retail experience, and with those assets she could have talked her way into a job of some sort. Had she done so, the story of her life might have been very different. But Doris opted to hope that, as always, a new lover would come to her rescue, and that while she waited for him or for her, she would be able to get by: running up debts in shops, hotels and restaurants, keeping the most bothersome of her creditors at bay by pawning her most valuable jewels.

It was, however, a meagre and a shifting kind of life. Doris had a circle of admiring young men around her who were willing to escort her for an evening, and she was helping with the war effort, attending charity dinners and serving in a milk bar run in aid of British War Relief. But when she wrote to Dudley (who was serving in North Africa with the African Rifles), she made no attempt to conceal her unhappiness. 'I am so homesick and miserable being away from England,' she confessed, and she begged to be distracted with news of Angela and the 'lovely babies'. It was May 1942, and by now she'd had to give up her rented apartment for the 'nasty and cheap' Hotel Domenico on Park Avenue. Her social circle was equally bleak: 'Went out with Lord Carow the other day', she reported to Dudley, 'but no other news.' Although Doris still owned a car – probably a gift from Margot or Paul in better times – stringent petrol rationing meant she could rarely use it to escape the confines of her shrunken life.

She'd been sufficiently desperate to send a telegram to Valentine, asking if he would marry her if she was able to get back to London; but when he replied with a tentative yes, and urged her to come home immediately, she didn't see how she could manage it. As she complained to Dudley, 'it's so easy to write that'. Valentine clearly had no idea of the practical and financial difficulties she was facing, and she confessed she was feeling overwhelmed by them, trapped and scared. Rudolf Kommer, who ran into her later that summer, was shocked by the changes he saw, writing to Cecil Beaton: 'Time and the war have not been kind to her...She looks, I'm sorry to report, devastated, and has become an acid misanthrope. She speaks with impotent bitterness of most people, feels herself persecuted and seems to have nothing to fall back upon.'[38]

Doris's unhappiness had also been evident to Winston Churchill back in January 1942, when he'd sought her out during an official trip to America. Churchill now wielded extraordinary power, combining the roles of Prime Minister and Minister of Defense, and he had come to Washington for a series of crucial negotiations, pressing America for maximum financial and military aid. He was playing now for some of the highest stakes of his career, and he was very concerned that Doris would undermine his position. Gossip had filtered back to him in London that her mental state was volatile and, less accurately, that she'd been making unpatriotic comments about Britain's faltering progress in the war. But of far more immediate concern to him was the possibility that Doris might be trying to make financial capital out of their shared past by selling the story of their affair to an American magazine.

Doris still had in her possession the two portraits Winston had painted, which she could present as illustration, if not proof, of their intimacy. And while there is no hard evidence that she intended to sell their secret, he was sufficiently concerned to make time in his demanding schedule to summon her to Washington for a private dinner. In June, when he returned to America for further negotiations, he again sought her out, and they spoke several times on the telephone. The writer and painter John Goodwin, who used to see Doris when they were visiting mutual friends on Long Island, recalled that there would always be much excitement in the household when a phone call came though for her, in case it was Churchill on the line.

Doris's circle pressed her for any inside information that Churchill might have given her about the war, but their conversations were nearly all about her desperation to get home and his desire to make it happen. Although she'd convinced him that she wasn't going to sell their story and that she certainly wasn't spreading unpatriotic talk, she was no longer being as discreet about their relationship as she'd once promised. He feared she was a liability – and so, possibly, did certain high-ranking Americans. When Doris told Kommer that she felt persecuted in New York, she wasn't only referring to the fact that her friends no longer seemed so willing to help; she genuinely believed she was being spied upon.[39] Certainly Doris knew potentially damaging secrets about Churchill, and she also knew things about Beaverbrook, who was very close to the British wartime government. And although there is no evidence that she was being watched by the FBI, she could still have been considered a person of official interest. According to George Malcolm Thomson, who was Valentine's close friend as well as biographer, it was Harry Hopkins, aide to President Roosevelt, who organized Doris's travel permit and her priority seat back to England on a Pan Am Clipper, even though it was Churchill who put pressure on Hopkins to get it done.

* * * * *

Doris was relieved to be aboard the Clipper as it flew her back towards Southampton in late October 1942, but she had little sense of what she was returning to in London, or of how she would survive. She'd racked up debts of over $10,000, which she had no means of paying, and her only hope was to seduce Valentine back to her side. She didn't yet know that he'd thought better of his willingness to remarry and was actually close to proposing to an old flame of his, Enid, Lady Furness. When he turned up promptly to meet Doris's train at Waterloo Station, looking reassuringly huge in his winter coat, she still trusted that it was a positive sign; and when he escorted her by cab to the Dorchester Hotel and stayed on to have dinner with her, she was confident that she could keep him with her for the rest of the night.

According to many of his friends, and to his own testimony, Valentine had never stopped loving Doris. The film director Carol Reed, with whom he'd been working as an occasional script consultant, recalled him speaking of his ex-wife with nostalgic tenderness: 'Doris always liked yellow,' he'd comment wistfully when passing some daffodils in a florist's window.[40] But while Valentine had ached for the memory of Doris, when he encountered her in the flesh he felt very differently. The worries and disappointments of her American exile had scored lines onto her face, and her once beautifully maintained figure was turning puffy and slack. Valentine was shocked by the change, and although he pitied Doris immensely, the sight of her made him more inclined, not less, to stick with his courtship of Enid.

While he paid for Doris's dinner that night, he did not attempt to go back to her room. Nor was he present when she had her first experience of a London air raid. As the sirens wailed and Doris was hustled with the rest of the guests down to the hotel cellars, she felt more traumatized than she could have anticipated from reading about the Blitz in the American press. She'd chosen to stay at the Dorchester because the hotel's reinforced concrete walls made it one of the most secure buildings for rich and privileged Londoners to sit out the war. Yet down in the cellar, as the more blasé of the guests chatted and passed around hip flasks of brandy, Doris flinched at the boom of the anti-aircraft guns in Hyde Park, the shaking of the ground when a bomb struck nearby. The next morning, her first views of London were almost as terrible. No photograph could have prepared her for the reality of bombed-out buildings, the wreckage of cable, joist and rubble to which solid structures were reduced, the film of dust and ash that caught sickeningly on the breath. The streets were crowded with military personnel and firefighters as well as with civilian workers; yet the absence of private traffic, the patient queues forming outside shops, the tension and pallor on people's faces made the city seem like a ghost town to Doris after New York.

She had not realized, either, how few people she would know in London. Robert was away fighting; Cecil was working as a war artist; and Gerald was hiding away in Faringdon and Oxford, his nerves shattered by the war. Nor had Doris understood how much bitterness she would encounter from those who had remained. After enduring a year and a half of bombs and rationing, Londoners were inclined to brand defectors like her as cowards or worse. Doris, generous as always, had brought back a case full of nylon stockings from New York, knowing that they were a precious luxury in London now. But when she'd attempted to offer a pair to a fellow guest at the Dorchester the woman had angrily refused the gift and had berated Doris harshly for her disloyal flight from England. Shaken by the attack, Doris had retreated to her hotel room – and en route she had encountered another guest, the Duke of Marlborough, who had snubbed her polite greeting with a contemptuous comment about 'people who deserted their country in wartime'.[41]

London operated by a new morality, stoic and patriotic. Even Luisa Casati, tucked away in Knightsbridge, had developed her own version of the Blitz spirit. She was reduced to far worse circumstances than Doris, moving between tiny rented apartments and dependent on the charity of Cristina as well as friends like Gerald, who paid her a small annual stipend. Yet Luisa was far more serene and resilient in adversity than she had been when rich: happy to use shoe polish to darken her eyes; to recycle her last, few moth-nibbled gowns; to conceal the ravages of age behind lace veils; to skimp on meals in order to buy food for her pets, and whisky for herself. The only occasion on which her spirit broke was when the Italian grocer's where she stored her most precious possessions was bombed. The crystal sword she'd worn to her Castiglioni ball back in the Palace of Dreams had been in that shop for safekeeping, and Luisa wept as she searched frantically and futilely though the rubble to find it.

Otherwise Luisa seemed eerily content, reliving her past and enjoying her few remaining friends. When Augustus John painted her in 1942, a thin and witchy figure with a black cat crouched beside her, he gave her a sweetly contented smile. Cecil Beaton, who visited whenever he was on leave, spoke reverentially of Luisa as one 'whose character and pluck could overcome all mediocrity and create nobility out of poverty'.

Doris, though, had apparently forfeited all right to approval or kindness. The woman who'd rejected her gift of stockings had tartly suggested that Doris try and redeem herself by volunteering for war work, but a day or two later her reputation was further imperilled when detectives arrived at the hotel to interview her. Before she'd left New York Doris had pawned some of her last remaining jewelry, leaving instructions for the money be forwarded to her at the Dorchester. When it had failed to arrive she'd telegrammed to enquire about the delay, and something about the phrasing of the telegram had aroused the suspicion of the wartime censors, who had passed the matter on to the police.

Doris wasn't sure what offence she'd committed – it had, in fact, been made illegal to sell diamonds during the war – but she was frightened. She worried that she was still under surveillance; she worried about the expense of a lawyer, if she were to be arrested on some false charge. And when she telephoned a friendly London bookmaker to ask for a loan of £500, she was shocked to learn that such a sum of money was now impossible to obtain. The bookie later recounted that Doris had been sarcastic and panicky on the phone: 'If I can't borrow five hundred pounds from an old friend when I need it,' she'd snapped down the line, 'then it really is time I left this vale of tears.'[42] She'd been home for barely a month, and already her situation felt worse in London than it had been in New York.

Compared to the abject misery so many others were enduring across Europe, Doris's position was far from dire. She might be unable to afford her room at the Dorchester for very much longer, she might find it hard to pay the wages of her maid Edith (who'd looked after her before the war and now rejoined her) – but she still owned her house in Berkeley Square, and she could presumably have found some temporary shelter with Angela in Surrey. Valentine too was not entirely off the scene – she believed he was showing small signs of feeling for her, despite his commitment to Lady Furness – and to maximize her chances with him she had already booked herself into a clinic for a facelift (cosmetic surgery was still an option, even in wartime London).

The younger, jauntier Doris would have calculated her assets and trusted to her luck that either Valentine or somebody else would come to her aid. But in London she was finding it increasingly hard to summon her former insouciance. During her last few months in America she'd struggled with a profound and isolating depression, and now she was also suffering from a bone-deep exhaustion.

Even on nights when there were no air raids, Doris slept very badly. Fears stalked her long into the night, and in order to achieve even one or two hours of sleep she had to medicate herself with barbiturates and alcohol. There was no one to monitor the doses she took or the effect on her health, and one night the quantities Doris ingested were fatal. When she did not respond to Edith's arrival the following morning, the maid assumed she was in a deep sleep and, knowing how fatigued Doris had become, she made no attempt to rouse her. Had she done so, Doris might have been saved; but by the time Edith realized that something was badly wrong, Doris had fallen into a deep coma. She was rushed to St Mary's Hospital in Paddington, and for the next few days she hovered between life and death. Angela came up from Surrey to sit by her, as did Dudley, who was fortuitously on leave. Both of them were traumatized by the sight of Doris's motionless body, made almost unrecognizable by the paraphernalia of tubes and medical equipment surrounding her. They also had to deal with Valentine, who refused to leave the room, tormenting himself over his neglect of Doris, his failure to respond more generously to her hopeful overtures. By 12 December, when she finally slipped away, Valentine not only believed

Doris's death had been suicide but had become convinced that he himself was the cause.

Writing to Max Beaverbrook, he castigated his selfishness. He'd failed to see that 'a crisis had arisen', and had been so determined to guard himself against Doris that he'd been unable to offer the love she so obviously needed. 'I could have lifted Doris up, given her hope, but I did not. I let her die and all because for once I was going to be wise.' It had been his moral duty, Valentine believed, to take Doris back, and he poured out his guilt in florid torrents to Max: 'without a doubt she treated me ill...but that argument to me bears no strength for, if a man is not full and generous in forgiveness, there can be no place among the angels for him.'[43]

At the funeral, Valentine wept fat tears of remorse. However, the coroner's report put a more ambiguous gloss on the death than his own anguished interpretation. In concluding that Doris had died 'from barbiturate acid poisoning...the drug being self-administered in circumstances not fully disclosed by the evidence', the report did support a verdict of suicide, yet it equally allowed for the possibility of an accident.[44] There was no note to confirm that Doris had intended to kill herself, and those who were closest to her, especially Dudley and Angela, remained adamant that she had not. It made no sense to them. Just before her death Doris had been conferring busily with Angela about her planned facelift; about the little nursing home in Surrey into which Angela had booked her to recuperate; about the time she would be able to spend with the two 'lovely babies' while she convalesced. This was not the behaviour of a suicidal woman, they argued. Nor did they accept that suicide was in Doris's nature.

It was Angela and Dudley's belief that Doris had become so fuddled by alcohol, so desperate for sleep that she had simply taken more pills than she intended, and that her death had been a tragic mistake. Later, a rumour would surface that perhaps it had a more sinister aspect – that Doris and her inconvenient past had posed too much of a threat to Churchill's wartime image, and someone had decided she should be removed.* Even at the time, the police had received a letter claiming that Doris had been deliberately poisoned. But the sender was dismissed as a crank and after the war, when Doris's estate was finally settled, the details of her financial situation were sufficiently grim to discredit a conspiracy theory. Not only had she run up enormous debts in America, but she owed money in France, Venice and London, where she also had a large mortgage outstanding on her house in Berkeley Square. She could not have raised money from any of her few remaining assets: the Rolls-Royce, which she'd left for safekeeping with Gerald, had become a white elephant during these petrol-rationed years, and the Venetian palazzo had been completely inaccessible to her, since it was in enemy territory. These facts alone might not have been enough to drive Doris to suicide, but they were sufficient to depress and destabilize her.

Doris had the last copy of her will drawn up in 1941. She clearly felt some sense of outstanding loyalty to Margot, since she left both the London house and the palazzo to her – with the proviso that Margot also paid off any of her outstanding debts. But after the war Margot had no sentimental interest in the properties of her former lover, nor did she have any practical use for them. By now she had lost any taste for the travelling and parties that Doris had so much enjoyed. Dropping her former husband's surname, Margot Flick lived out the rest of her life in relative anonymity.

In her place, it was Dudley who was left to handle the debts and the properties that Doris left behind, and in 1948 he made his way to Venice to inspect the condition of the palazzo. He and Angela had dazzled memories of their summer there, and would have liked to keep it in the family (Doris had willed that any remaining assets from her estate should be kept in trust for her nephew and niece). But during the war years the building had been used as a soldiers' billet by three successive armies: the Italians, the Germans and the Allied forces. Its polished interior had become scuffed and vandalized, its grounds overgrown, and the furniture had all been stolen or burned as firewood. Dudley, recently demobbed, had a growing family to care for (he and Angela would have four children). And with little income left over with which to repair the property or maintain it, he had no choice but to put it up for sale.

---

*   Alistair Forbes suggested this possibility in one of his columns in the *Spectator*; it was echoed by Doris's American friend, John Goodwin.

In 1948, with much of Europe in rubble, economies struggling and the tourist industry in abeyance, few people were in the market for an idiosyncratic luxury like a palazzo on the Grand Canal. But Peggy Guggenheim, the American art collector and heiress, had arrived in Venice two years earlier looking for a new home in which to settle herself and her collection. She'd just turned fifty, and she had a failed marriage and many failed affairs behind her; with a clear sense that she could no longer be happy in the competitive New York art world, she was determined to reset the course of her life. Like Luisa and like Doris, she saw the Palazzo Venier dei Leoni as a place of romantic potential and characteristically she settled the deal immediately: 'I'll have the house,' Peggy said to Dudley – and, with an eye for his still-golden charm, she added, covetously, 'and I'll have you too!'

PEGGY
GUGGENHEIM

THE COLLECTOR

CHAPTER 8

'To live in Venice, or even to visit it, means that you fall in love
with the city itself. There is nothing left over in your heart
for anyone else. After your first visit you are destined to return
at every possible chance or with every possible excuse.'[1]

When Peggy bought the Venier palace in 1948 she was fulfilling a long-
held dream. She'd been to Venice several times previously, and on each
occasion had fallen under the spell of what she called her 'miracle city'.
She was entranced by the quality of 'floatingness' that seemed to per-
vade its every aspect: it was a city 'sprung from the sea', she wrote,
where 'no time exists'.[2] And like so many before her, she'd fantasized
about finding a refuge there, imagining it as a world away from the
conflict and noise of modern life, and from her own private difficulties.

Peggy had been twenty-six, a troubled, self-doubting but determined
young woman, when she'd first lost her heart to Venice. It was the
autumn of 1924 and she'd arrived in the city with her husband Laurence
Vail, hoping to carve out an interlude of tranquil family life from a marriage already grown chaotic and quarrelsome. Laurence knew the city
well, having lived there as a child, but Peggy had only known it as a tourist, and she was determined now to discover her own 'authentic' version
of Venetian life. Rather than renting the floor of a palazzo or a suite at
the Danieli, she took rooms for herself and Laurence, their infant son
Sindbad and their nanny Lilly in an old-fashioned hotel on the shabby
end of the Riva degli Schiavoni. To complete the fantasy of a bohemian
dolce vita, she'd also paid for an artisan studio where Laurence could
work on his current novel.

Peggy described in her memoir, many years later, how she had
come to Venice determined to imprint her senses with 'every painting and stone'. Every day, either alone or with Laurence, she trekked
the city on foot, learning to distinguish each of its six *sestieri*, the small

neighbourhoods that could still be distinguished by their own dialects. She made favourites of the secluded *campi*, where locals still drew their water from a central well. She learned the pleasures of getting herself lost: the unexpected glimpse of a leafy garden or medieval cloister; the dead end of an alleyway that forced her eye upwards to a vista of tall chimney pots or a wooden *altana* flowering with late geraniums. Raised in Manhattan, she was beguiled by architecture that, even in the poorest areas, could spring the surprise of a gothic staircase, a building decorated with ancient carvings of a camel, a turbaned Turk or a Madonna.

Peggy collected impressions of Venice with the same diligence she would later apply to the collecting of art. She became a connoisseur of the city's changing light: the mother-of-pearl softness of dawn, the kingfisher blue of the late afternoon, the crimson theatre of sunset, the silvered sharpness of a full moon. She learned to appreciate the city's distinctive smell, the tangy ozone of sea that overlaid the brackish odours of drain and canal. And as Peggy discovered Venice, she was stirred by the

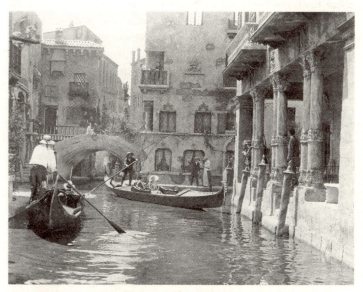

Venice in the 1920s: Peggy collected impressions
of the city with the diligence that she would later apply to collecting art.

idea of owning a small part of it. Although she was not as spectacularly rich as many assumed a Guggenheim heiress must be, she was wealthy enough to buy and maintain a modest canalside property.

Had she come to the city six months earlier, when the Palazzo Venier dei Leoni was on the market, Peggy might have looked it over with an acquisitive eye. She'd heard about Luisa Casati and her Venetian life though the gossip of mutual friends. In Paris, too, their social circles had overlapped a little; Peggy had attended Natalie Barney's salon on a few occasions, she could claim acquaintance with Jean Cocteau, and she'd had her own photograph taken by Man Ray. But by the time she arrived in Venice, Marcell Nemes had already acquired the palazzo; and in any case, the trust that controlled Peggy's inheritance might not have allowed her such an extravagance. All she could do, in 1924, was shop for a few beautiful objects with which she might one day furnish a Venetian home. Aided by an old friend of Laurence's (an art forger called Favai, whose long, elegant face and beard reminded Peggy of an El Greco), she scoured the city for beautiful antiques, acquiring a 13th-century chest carved with religious scenes and a 15th-century oak buffet with shreds of its original upholstery still clinging to its metal decoration. Twenty-five years later, after many moves and many upheavals, these pieces would end up in the dining room of the Venier palace, arranged among Peggy's prized Cubist paintings.

* * * * *

That first stay in Venice had not been a completely straightforward idyll, despite Peggy's rose-tinted expectations. As a native New Yorker, she'd been confused by the slow and, to her, inefficient pace of daily life. She'd disliked having to haggle for goods, the nanny had got pneumonia, and Laurence had grumbled and stalled over his writing. Yet still she yearned to come back some day: 'I have never been in a city that gave me the same sense of freedom,' she wrote. Venice seemed so ancient and unjudging a place to her, so serene in its attitude of *dolce far niente*, that she – no less than Luisa and Doris – imagined it as a city where she could refashion her life as she'd always wanted it to be.[3]

The actual life into which Peggy had been born had left her, she claimed, with 'no pleasant memories of any kind'.[4] She'd been cursed, she believed, with the misfortune of a neurotic, unhappy mother and an absent, philandering father. But she had also grown up within the insular community of the New York Jewish rich, and that world had felt to her both dully claustrophobic and anxiously pressured. Money – the obligation and the status of it – had been a burden that Peggy understood from an early age. Like the rest of her generation of Guggenheims, she'd grown up under the shadow of her grandfather Meyer, a small, square, energetically whiskered man who in 1848 had braved a long and dangerous crossing from Europe to make his fortune in America. Starting out as a peddler, Meyer Guggenheim had founded his first small enterprise on the marketing of a new type of stove polish; but having expanded into the smelting and mining industries, he'd ended up with a business that in 1914 handled roughly 75 per cent of the world's copper, silver and lead output, and earned annual profits of over one million dollars.

It was expected of Meyer's seven surviving sons that they would not only manage the business, but use their father's wealth to advance the family's position in society. As rich as the Guggenheims were, they were Jewish immigrants, and as such they remained excluded from New York's gilded élite. To families like the Vanderbilts, whose Protestant ancestors had arrived in America back in the 17th century, the Guggenheims, like the Loebs, the Liebermans and other wealthy Jewish clans, still carried the taint of the European ghetto. Even though anti-Semitism wasn't legally sanctioned in America, they were effectively excluded from the wealthiest schools, clubs, hotels and drawing rooms.

Peggy's maternal relatives, the Seligmans, were socially a cut above the Guggenheims, having arrived in America slightly earlier and having ploughed the profits of their own businesses (trading in precious metals and manufacturing military uniforms) into the more respectable sphere of banking. Peggy's mother Florette was regarded as lowering herself somewhat when she fell in love with Benjamin in 1894 and married into the 'smelting Guggenheims'. Yet even the Seligmans, with their connections to high finance, remained defined and confined by the stigma of their faith. They remained part of the privileged ghetto which the Jewish rich had been forced to create for themselves: educating their children in the same schools, attending the same temples, socializing among those they arrogantly and defensively referred to as 'our crowd'. When Peggy was old enough to understand the limitations of the community in which she'd been raised, she not only became impatient to escape, but developed a confused and often angry relationship with her own Jewishness.

Marguerite Guggenheim (the diminutive 'Peggy' came later) was born on 26 August 1898, and along with her two sisters, spent much of her early childhood in the grandeur of the Upper East Side. Their family home was an immense limestone mansion on 72nd Street that properly reflected the Guggenheim and Seligman wealth. Its large, high-ceilinged rooms were decorated with a clutter of expensive ornaments and artworks, and it was scrupulously maintained by a large resident staff. Yet to Peggy, the house was always hideous. When she was very small it seemed to her a place of menace, filled with booby traps to spook her childish imagination: the mysterious maze of servants' attics at the top of the house; the stuffed eagle that loomed over the front hall; even the old bearskin rug whose dead, dry muzzle was studded horribly with broken teeth. More terrifying still was the nanny who for years held tyrannical sway over the nursery; an inventively malevolent woman who threatened to cut out Peggy's tongue if ever she complained to her mother about the punishments she suffered.

There were few opportunities to escape from either the house or the nanny because, like all girls of her class, Peggy was educated at home. She had no friends of her own age, certainly none who came to the house – in fact, the only visitors she ever recalled at East 72nd Street were the select crowd of middle-aged matrons who came once a week to take tea with Florette. Despite daily outings to the park and annual family holidays, it was a small, isolated life. And while Peggy worshipped her sister Benita, who was almost three years older, she frankly disliked their younger sister Hazel, resenting her as the petted baby of the family.

It was the tensions between the adults, though, that made life in the Guggenheim mansion so 'excessively unhappy'.[5] Florette was a loving mother, but she was prone to gloominess and to a streak of obsessive-compulsive behaviour that manifested itself in a terror of germs (she insisted on the house being sprayed daily with a disinfectant called

Lysol) and in an agitated tic of repeating certain words three times over. There was a genetic history of instability within the family: Florette's mother and her siblings suffered from varying degrees of hypochondria and delusion, and Peggy herself came close to a nervous collapse at several points during her adult life. But Florette's anxieties were principally caused by her husband Benjamin, who, having turned her head with his smooth-skinned handsomeness and college-educated conversation, had proved to be an incorrigible adulterer.

Benjamin had grown up with different expectations from most of his Guggenheim relatives. In 1901, just six years after marrying Florette, he'd retired from the family business, sacrificing his multi-million-dollar share of its profits. His plan was to live the life of a cultured gentleman, dabbling in his own investments while indulging his taste for art and women. He made little attempt to conceal his infidelities, and Peggy recalled that from a very early age she felt miserably divided between her parents: 'I adored my father because he was fascinating and handsome and because he loved me. But I suffered very much because he made my mother unhappy...I was perpetually being dragged into my parents' troubles and it made me precocious.'[6] She was only seven when, over dinner, she blurted out angrily to her father: 'Papa, you must have a mistress since you stay out so many nights.'[7] Even though she didn't fully understand the concept of a mistress, she knew enough to consider Benjamin both wicked and glamorous for having one, and to pity and resent Florette for being unable to intervene.

The battleground between her parents taught Peggy to believe that love was a contest – something to be competed for, rather than given – and this belief sowed the seeds for what she later described as her mass of 'inferiority complexes'. She was a quick little girl, eager and curious, with fine bones, thick chestnut hair and lively green-blue eyes; yet from an early age she regarded herself as the ugly duckling of the family, eclipsed by Hazel's blonde cuteness and Benita's more classically refined beauty. By the time she was a teenager, her appearance became even more of a disappointment to her as, alone of the three girls, she began to develop the long, bulbous nose of her grandfather Meyer. Peggy considered her Guggenheim nose to be a hideous infirmity; even as an adult, she felt disqualified from the love and admiration that other, more beautiful women enjoyed. Yet no less damaging to her teenage confidence was the sudden and traumatic death of her father.

By the time she was thirteen, Peggy had grown used to Benjamin's frequent absences from home. He'd invested capital in a French steam pump company and used his business as an excuse to spend months away in Paris where, as Peggy now knew, he kept several mistresses. But Benjamin always came home to see his girls, and in the spring of 1912 he was due back to celebrate Hazel's ninth birthday. There was a last-minute hitch when the crossing onto which he'd initially been booked was cancelled; however, he believed his luck had turned when he managed to secure a first-class berth on the RMS *Titanic*, the new steamship that was making its maiden voyage across the Atlantic and was promising its passengers a journey of unparalleled luxury and speed.

Benjamin's body was never recovered after the catastrophic collision that sunk the *Titanic*, and all of its superior ambitions, on the morning of 15 April; and it was four days before Florette and the girls knew for certain that he was dead. One of the ship's surviving stewards eventually came forward to report his last sightings of Benjamin, and to confirm that his final hours had been heroic; still dressed in his evening clothes, he'd refused to take his place in a lifeboat and instead had helped load women and children to safety. He and his secretary Giglio had declared that they 'were prepared to go down like gentlemen', and it was the glamour of Benjamin's heroism that made his death all the more damaging to Peggy. From that point onwards he became a romantic ideal for her – the template of the perfect man – and she would seek to replicate him over and over again in her choice of lovers and husbands. Even in middle age she would write, 'It took me...years to get over the loss of my father....In a sense I really have never recovered as I suppose I have been searching for a father ever since.'[8]

Peggy did not waver in her idealization of Benjamin even once it was discovered that the combination of his poor business sense and extravagant lifestyle had got him deeply into debt. The Guggenheim uncles rallied round, securing what capital he had left, paying off his creditors and pitching in with money of their own. But still Florette and the girls had to relocate to a modestly scaled apartment on the corner of Fifth Avenue and 58th Street and sell off the more valuable family assets, the artworks and the jewels. Over time a succession of legacies, including a chunk of the Seligman fortune, would restore them to some degree of wealth; yet by the standards of the Guggenheims, they'd become the poor relations. Peggy felt the difference acutely: '[F]rom that time on I had a complex about not being a real Guggenheim....[I] suffered great humiliation thinking how inferior I was to the rest of the family.'⁹

Florette was stoically resigned to the drop in her fortunes, but Peggy grew into a rebellious and restless teenager, and when she was fifteen and finally allowed to go to school it felt to her like a deliverance. She'd been deprived so long of the company of her peers that she plunged into the teenage culture around her with avid enthusiasm – mimicking the affected drawl that was fashionable among her classmates, and helping to organize the monthly dance club where, in the summer of 1915, she had her first kiss.

She also enjoyed her studies. Some of the teachers at the Jacoby School for Jewish Girls were clever, progressive women, and one in particular had spotted Peggy's academic potential, drawing up ambitious reading lists of Browning, Shaw, Ibsen, Wilde and Strindberg that gave her a revelatory glimpse of worlds beyond her own. As an adult, Peggy would regret that she'd lacked the willpower and confidence to persuade Florette to allow her to go to college. But she was still determined to learn, and when she graduated from school she continued her education with private tutors, one of whom taught her enough Italian that was she was able to read the works of Gabriele D'Annunzio. The florid complexities of D'Annunzio's prose must have been a challenge to Peggy, but her teenage imagination was gripped nonetheless by his stories of swooning sexual raptures in Venice and Rome. This version of Europe, a place redolent of romance and wickedly colourful possibilities, would stay with her for the rest of her life.

A more immediate influence, though, was the young woman she hired to tutor her in current affairs. Lucille Kohn was a feminist and socialist with a doctorate in classics from Columbia, and Peggy had never before met a woman of such intellectual fire and integrity. She herself had been raised to believe that money came with philanthropic responsibilities; she knew that even as one of the less wealthy Guggenheims, she would be expected to do some good in the world.

But it was Lucille, with her radical passions, who gave Peggy her first inkling that 'doing good' might involve far more liberating excitements than sitting on committees or making charitable donations.

Later, she wrote that Lucille had been the catalyst who'd emancipated her from 'the stifling atmosphere in which I had been raised'. Yet it was a slow process – at eighteen, Peggy's consciousness was still woolly and unformed. Even while she was studying the labour movement and women's suffrage with Lucille, she was also immersed in the frivolities of her coming-out season, in the clothes fittings, tea dances and parties that filled much of her diary during 1916. Although she complained loftily that none of the boys she met was capable of serious conversation, Peggy was still assuming that it was only a matter of time before she settled down and married one of them.

*****

Like many young women of her age and class, Peggy's world shifted with the advent of the Great War. America didn't enter the conflict until April 1917, but once it did, the rhythms and texture of her life were altered. New York was filling up with young uniformed officers, with whom respectable girls like Peggy were encouraged to flirt; and the war also made it respectable for girls like her to find employment. Even though Florette remained anxiously opposed to the idea of any of her daughters working, in 1918 Peggy volunteered to become a clerk at a military supplier's. For a while she thrived on the novelty of having structure and purpose in her life, on the satisfaction of meeting new and different people.

Yet the war was also a profoundly unsettling period for her. Reports of battles and casualty figures revived the trauma of Benjamin's death, and Peggy suffered over the fact that she was helping to outfit young soldiers with the very uniforms in which they might be killed. She agonized over the kisses and the foolish, impulsive proposals of marriage she received from officers whom she knew she might never see again. And as she worked and partied for longer and longer hours, her distress was exacerbated by the deteriorating state of her health. Peggy had never been a robust child, and had suffered a bad bout of whooping cough as a teenager. Now her system began to cave under stress: she

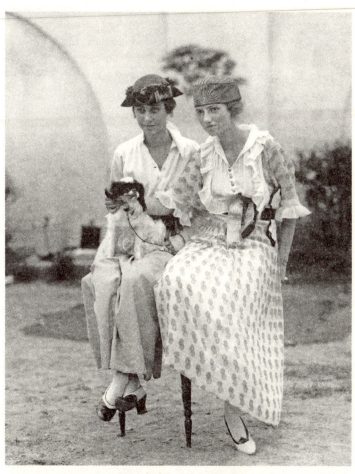

Peggy (right) and her adored
older sister Benita at a dog show (1919).

stopped sleeping and eating properly, and her nerves frayed. Oppressed by the atmosphere of death around her, she developed a tormenting fear of fire – she could not go to bed without making sure there were no unused matches lying around the apartment – and, wracked with a vague philosophical guilt, she began to talk so strangely, so darkly about questions of free will and morality that Florette had to hire a nurse to watch over her.

It was to become a pattern in Peggy's life that her surges of enthusiasm were often deflated by exhaustion, muddle or defeat. After the war, when her health was restored, she enrolled in business classes, determined to equip herself for some kind of serious peacetime employment. Yet stenography, finance and typing proved much harder work than she'd expected, and amid a room full of tougher, less privileged young women she felt herself to be a 'rank outsider' and lost heart.[10] In the early summer of 1919, when she was reunited with a young demobbed aviator with whom she'd flirted during the war, his proposal of marriage came as a relief. It seemed much easier, at that moment, to settle for being a wife than to struggle along the path of Lucille Kohn's feminism. But the couple barely knew each other, and when Peggy visited the aviator's family in Chicago and tactlessly complained of being bored, the engagement was broken off and she was left once more without a plan for her future.

Throughout her teenage years Peggy had liked to think of herself as the 'black sheep' of the Guggenheim family, the rebel and the bluestocking, but her boldness was continually undercut by her doubts and indecision. When she turned twenty-one and came into her inheritance, she could have chosen to do almost anything she liked. With a capital sum of $450,000 (roughly $5 million by today's values) kept in trust for her, and an annual income of $22,500, she might have been a lot less wealthy than some of her Guggenheim cousins, who'd inherited millions; but still, she could set herself up in her own apartment, she could study or see the world. Yet the scale of her options felt too paralyzing, and Peggy could not commit herself to anything. In the end, her first act of adult independence was to spend $1,000 on getting her nose fixed.

She claimed later that it was boredom that drove her to have the operation, although in truth she'd probably been planning it for a while.

Numerous photographs attest to Peggy having matured into a striking young woman – slender and long legged, with hair that curled around a strong, heart-shaped face. Yet she had remained miserably at odds with her appearance, convinced that her coarse Guggenheim nose negated every one of her good features; nor was it just the size and shape she disliked, it was the fact that it made her look, she believed, so obviously Jewish. Peggy had by now tried to distance herself from the family's religion; she rarely went to Temple or observed the holy days. She had also become far more sensitively attuned to the bigotry that her Jewishness attracted. The previous summer, when she'd been on a motoring holiday with her mother and sisters, a hotel in Vermont had made it mortifyingly clear that a party of Jewish women was not welcome. And that moment of humiliation may have been a factor in arming Peggy's resolve to do something about her offending Guggenheim nose as soon as she was in possession of her own money.

Early in 1920 she travelled to a clinic in Cincinnati where a surgeon famous for his skills in reconstructing the war-shattered features of soldiers promised to give her the neat, 'tip-tilted' nose for which she longed. Cosmetic surgery was still in its infancy, though, and halfway through the operation the surgeon had to admit the operation wasn't going as he had hoped. The pain Peggy had already endured was so bad that she could not bear for him to tidy up the work he'd already started. Nor, years later, could she countenance the idea of repeating the operation when surgical techniques had become more advanced.

For the rest of her life, Peggy's Guggenheim nose would remain a focus of her self-doubt; yet as inferior as she felt herself in so many ways, she was also armoured by a thick-skinned sense of entitlement and an obstinate streak of resilience. Ever since childhood, Peggy had learned to compartmentalize her emotions, to repress the hurts and disappointments and allow her curiosity and optimism to propel her forward. As she admitted years later, she was 'moving through life in a kind of dream' at this point, drifting between places, people and projects without any clear idea of what she was doing, instinctively rebounding from each setback. And in the summer of 1920 her life once again seemed flooded with possibility when, almost by chance, she found herself working in a small radical bookstore called the Sunwise Turn.[11]

The store was part-owned by Peggy's cousin Harold Loeb, a writer and publisher who, like his late uncle Benjamin, was something of a rogue Guggenheim.* It was run on a shoestring and, always in need of volunteer staff, Harold had suggested that Peggy might enjoy helping out. At this point she was grateful for any excuse to escape the family home, which had become especially tedious to her now that Benita, her main ally and still 'the love' of her life, had married an airman called Edward Mayer, whom Peggy intensely disliked.

But what Peggy found at the Sunwise Turn was far more than a temporary refuge. The two women who'd founded the store, Mary Mowbray-Clarke and Madge Jenison, had made it one of the cultural hubs of downtown Manhattan, a meeting place for writers and paint-ers, a venue for poetry- and play-readings and exhibitions. When Peggy arrived for her first day of work, innocently wearing her expensive mole-skin coat and string of pearls, it seemed to her that she had stumbled across a new world, one that was governed by the principles of bohemi-anism and art. Although her tasks at the store were menial – sweeping the floors, running errands, doing the filing – she did them willingly. She felt she was serving a higher cause, and never more so than when the poet Margaret Anderson invited her to make a financial donation to *The Little Review*, the small and struggling literary magazine that was contro-versially serializing James Joyce's novel *Ulysses*. Peggy was delighted to volunteer $500 of her own money and also to broker a meeting between Anderson and her rich uncle Jefferson. And as she committed herself to this first independent act of artistic patronage, she began to realize that in using her money to assist the work of writers and painters she might find a way of living among them and sharing in their lives.

Certainly the Sunwise Turn was giving Peggy an entrée to a commu-nity very different from anything she'd previously known. Most of the store's clientele lived around Greenwich Village, and in contrast to the formalities of the Upper East Side, life among the scruffy brownstones, jazz cafés and Italian grocers seemed to Peggy a whirl of impromptu dinners, drinks and parties. Manners and dress codes were vague, and people wore their eccentricities with pride. When she caught her first

---

*   Harold was the son of Benjamin's sister, Rose.

glimpse of Baroness Elsa von Freytag-Loringhoven – a well-known Village character with a sense of theatre as extreme as Luisa's – Peggy's eyes were opened to extraordinary new levels of dissenting behaviour. She could only imagine what Florette would think of this gaunt-looking artists' model who walked the streets wearing false eyelashes made out of porcupine quills, yellow face powder and a breastplate constructed from empty soup cans.

Two of the most important new friends Peggy made through the Sunwise Turn were a young married couple, Leon and Helen Fleischman. Leon was a rakish, handsome publisher, Helen a beautiful rebel, and Peggy developed a crush on them both equally. Hanging around their Village apartment, she became a wide-eyed observer of the emotional and sexual dramas of their very open marriage. She admired the radical literature on their bookshelves and listened to their discussions about art (although when they introduced Peggy to her first abstract painting, a Georgia O'Keeffe, she admitted she had no idea 'which way to look at it').[12] It was through the Fleischmans, too, that Peggy met the man with whom she believed she might build her own version of the creative, emancipated life.

Laurence Vail seemed to Peggy to have crammed a lifetime's exotic experience into his twenty-eight years. He was an aspiring writer and painter (with one published play) and having grown up in both America and Europe, he had acquired what was to her an enchantingly cosmopolitan habit of rolling his Rs and gesticulating flamboyantly with his hands. Laurence was the first man she'd ever met who didn't wear a hat, and who grew his hair long. With his impromptu dandified wardrobe, his brightly coloured jackets, canary-yellow trousers and patterned shirts, he seemed to Peggy a god among dull Manhattan mortals: 'I felt when I walked down the street with him that he might suddenly fly away – he had so little connection with ordinary behavior.'[13] His energy, his confidence and his strangeness hypnotized Peggy – and when Laurence began to talk of going back to live in Paris, she began to wonder if she might go there too.

Already a stream of clever, creative young Americans was leaving home for Europe. Disaffected by the recent war and by the hardening materialism of modern American values, they regarded Europe, and

principally Paris, as a centre of artistic freedom – and, almost as importantly, a place where the cost of living was cheap and where alcohol
(soon to be prohibited by US law) was joyously central to the culture.
Peggy herself had no concrete reason to be in Paris, no friends, work
or project to occupy her there. Yet in her imagination it was Laurence,
and Laurence's Europe, that formed the shape of her future, and her
plans were now focused on how she could join the bohemian exodus
from America.

Ironically, it was Florette who actually orchestrated Peggy's departure. She had grown alarmed by the direction her daughter's life had
taken with the Sunwise Turn (she used to appear at the store almost
every day to check on Peggy, bringing her galoshes if it was raining)
and in order to get her away from this new, disreputable milieu, she
offered to take her on an extended tour of Europe. It was very far from
the romantic exit Peggy had imagined; she would not only be travelling
with her mother but with a middle-aged cousin, Valerie Dreyfus. Yet it
would, nonetheless, alter the course of her life: for when she sailed out
of New York in December 1920, she would not return to live in America
for over twenty years.

* * * * *

Initially the European tour differed very little in pace and style from
the family holidays of Peggy's childhood. Diligently, she tried to extract
some cultural insights from the cities they visited, touring the art galleries of London, Amsterdam and Madrid and tutoring herself on the
wing with Bernard Berenson's classic seven-volume history of art.
But while she was in a 'frenzy to see everything', she later admitted
that she'd been the most superficial of tourists and had 'felt' very little of the culture surrounding her. In the undemanding company of
Florette and Valerie, she'd retreated into a comfortable cocoon, and by
the time the three women reached Paris in the autumn of 1921 Peggy's
high aspirations had become atrophied by luxury. Rather than ventur-
ing into the little art galleries and jazz clubs of Montparnasse, or even
seeking out Shakespeare and Co. (the Left Bank bookshop that was
the Parisian equivalent of Sunwise Turn), she spent most of her time
with a young Russian émigrée called Fira Benenson visiting fashion

houses, experimenting with cosmetics and talking about boys. By the time Laurence and the Fleischmans finally arrived in Paris her veneer of Greenwich Village bohemianism had been all but erased. She was elated to see Laurence, of course, but when he invited her for a walk along the Seine she was aware of the gulf that had opened between them: she'd overdressed anxiously for the occasion in a mink-trimmed suit, and when Laurence suggested a drink in a local bistro, she asked for a Porto Flip – a rich, sugary cocktail that was served only in the lounges of international hotels.

But Peggy was an enthusiast. The fantasy of nonconformity had not lost its hold, and now that Laurence was in Paris she wanted to be initiated into his version of the city. She believed him to be the 'King of Bohemia' and in his company she imagined herself in the heady, smoky crush of a Left Bank café, mixing with the city's most important artists and writers (of whom she naively believed him to be one). It was with Laurence, too, that Peggy hoped to experience an even more crucial initiation: into sex. Ever since her teens she'd been falling in and out of love and the fact that she was still a virgin at twenty-three felt ridiculously burdensome to her. She wanted to understand the physical sensations that the kisses and the petting had promised, and as soon as Laurence made his first exploratory pass, she was ready to seize her moment.

Peggy's eagerness was somewhat disconcerting to Laurence. Possibly he expected some formal show of modesty, but she demurred only in suggesting that they move to the privacy of his hotel room, where they would be safe from Florette – and once there, she proved to have elaborate and demanding expectations of his performance. Recently she'd discovered some photographs of the erotic frescoes at Pompeii, and rather than lying quiescently while Laurence took her virginity, she assumed that he would be initiating her into the positions and manoeuvres she had seen in those images. It was genuine, sensuous curiosity that motivated Peggy's expectations, a curiosity that would remain with her most of her life. But even at this stage she was competitive about sex. One consequence of Benjamin's philanderings had been to instil in her the need to prove herself a more potent woman than her mother; and afterwards, when she was dining with Florette and one of Florette's friends, she spent the evening 'gloating' over her new sexual knowledge and 'wondering what they [the two women] would think of it if they knew'.[14]

Now that she had secured Laurence as her lover, Peggy wanted to spend all her time with him; and having persuaded the still-unknowing Florette to travel on to Rome, she threw herself heart and body into the new affair. Laurence *did* seem to know everybody in Paris: tirelessly sociable, confidently articulate, he inserted himself into the most exciting crowd in every room. Peggy sat with him shyly as he drank and talked with the surrealist poet Louis Aragon, the writer Robert McAlmon, and artists like Man Ray and Marcel Duchamp. She watched with amazement as he, Aragon and Malcolm Cowley launched a violent assault on the proprietor of the Rotonde café because they believed him to be a snitch for the police. At a riotous party held by Laurence in his parents' flat, a notorious lesbian 'got down on her knees' to beg Peggy for sex.

'Strange things were happening everywhere,' she recalled, and she tried to make herself look the part.[15] She took up smoking, sporting a 20-inch cigarette holder; she painted her mouth with a vermilion lipstick decadently named *Eternal Wound*; she shaved off her eyebrows and drew on new ones, finely arched. All the while she believed she was falling deeper in love with Laurence, addicted to the 'fantastic' vitality of his personality and to the glamour of his friends; and Laurence himself was happy to encourage her. Having initially regarded Peggy as no more than an impressionable society girl, he now saw interesting long-term possibilities in her: she was attractive, adoring and unexpectedly adventurous in bed, and she was also, by his standards, very rich.

Laurence was still dependent on the $1,200 annual allowance he received from his parents, his writing as yet yielding niggardly returns; and as early as Christmas 1921, he was wondering if marrying Peggy and her dollars might be a wonderfully effective way of gaining his financial independence.* Late in December he took her up to the top of the Eiffel Tower, fully prepared to propose. But while he liked Peggy,

---

* Living costs in France were roughly half of what they were in America, with a meal for two in Paris costing between two and three francs. The exchange rates were also very favourable, with a dollar buying twenty francs. Expatriates could thus live quite well on less than fifty dollars a month.

he didn't know if he loved her enough to tie himself down to marriage, and when he tried to utter the words, panic so choked his throat that he could barely speak. Another woman might have been warned off by such obvious reluctance, but Peggy had been longing so hard for this moment that she accepted with a radiant 'Yes'. During the weeks that followed, she could see how unhappy Laurence was – 'Every time I saw him look as though he were trying to swallow his Adam's apple, I knew he was regretting his proposal' – but she had got what she wanted, and she would not give him an opportunity to back down.[16]

While Peggy was riding out her fiancé's resistance, she was also having to manage the opposition of family and friends. Laurence's mother, Gertrude Vail, disapproved of the marriage because she disliked the idea of a Jewish daughter-in-law: Florette opposed it on the parallel grounds that Laurence was neither Jewish nor rich. Even Leon and Helen Fleischman argued against it, urging Peggy to see that she and Laurence were too temperamentally unsuited to make a marriage work. Weeks of indecision passed. At one point Peggy came close to losing Laurence when he disappeared off to Rouen to 'think things over' and on his return tried to persuade her to go back to New York, where he said he would join her later if they 'still felt like marrying'. Peggy, however, possessed more than enough conviction for both of them, and in the end her determination prevailed. On 9 March Laurence appeared in her hotel room, 'as pale as a ghost', to announce that he had made up his mind, and the next day, in a short civil ceremony, the two of them were married.

There had been no time for Peggy to buy anything beyond a new hat for her wedding, which took place at the Mairie of the 16th Arrondissement. Nor was there time to arrange for any celebration beyond a small reception at the Plaza Athénée hotel, followed by drinking and dancing at the Boeuf sur le Toit, Paris's most avant-garde night club. In the midst of this impromptu partying it was easy for Peggy to convince herself that she'd had the wedding she always wanted – unburdened by Guggenheim and Seligman relatives, and heralding a new era of freedom. Nor did it occur to her to worry that in her haste to marry Laurence, to secure her 'King of Bohemia', she had not really questioned how deeply she either loved or knew him. Almost inevitably, as the first flush of her triumph receded, Peggy began to feel 'let down'.

The fault lines in the marriage appeared even during their Italian honeymoon. They spent much of it on Capri, and at first Peggy believed that she and Laurence had found paradise. She declared herself 'enchanted' by the island's beauty and by its colony of artists, whose picturesque lives seemed to her as amusing as an 'opéra bouffe'. She heard stories about Luisa Casati, 'who roamed around the island with a leopard'; she met the dissolute Baron Fernsen[17] and was entirely captivated by Laurence, who was charming to the locals, chatting easily in his fluent Italian. He seemed willing to dedicate himself to her intellectual as well as her sexual education, encouraging her to expand her reading with authors like Dostoyevsky and Henry James, and to embrace new ideas. As the weather turned warm the two of them swam in the sea and roamed bare-legged around the island, and in this seeming idyll Peggy's confidence bloomed. Her happiness, however, was rudely invaded when just three weeks after their arrival on Capri they were joined by Laurence's lovely and accomplished younger sister.

Clotilde Vail was the kind of woman who triggered all of Peggy's deepest apprehensions about her own self-worth. She was blonde and beautiful, experienced with men, and she had claims to be an artist, her small but professionally trained singing voice having gained her a minor performing career. Her greatest threat to Peggy, however, was her relationship with Laurence. As siblings the two were unusually close, so possessive of each other, so jealous of each other's lovers that Peggy later concluded it was only the force of social taboo that prevented their relationship from becoming incestuous. Even on Capri, brother and sister became so immediately engrossed in each other that Peggy was made to feel like an interloper in her own marriage. 'It was', she recalled, 'as if I had wandered by mistake into a room that had long since been occupied by another tenant.'[18]

Not only did Laurence openly adore Clotilde, but in her company he became more openly critical of Peggy. He complained about her sheltered upbringing and about the limitations of her intellect. He grew irritated by her mannered style of speech (the drawl Peggy had picked up as a teenager would remain with her for the rest of her life). But above all, he was irked by her Jewishness. The two Vails were not immune to the prevailing anti-Semitism of their class and kind, and even if they were sophisticated enough to eschew blatant bigotry, their prejudices coloured their language, their jokes and above all their sense of superiority. Laurence might be happy to spend the Guggenheim money but, goaded by Clotilde, he saw no ingratitude in mocking the family itself, making unkind jokes at the expense of their faith, their cliquishness and what he regarded dismissively as their old-fashioned *shtetl* ways.

Peggy wept when Laurence mocked, and wept even more when he grew impatient with her tears, scolding her for being 'inferior...an awful baby'.[19] Yet, believing as fervently as she did in his brilliance, it didn't occur to her to question or complain. When Laurence and Clotilde were critical she tried to accept her own inferiority; she tried to laugh at herself when she was the butt of their jokes. So completely did she acquiesce to their bullying that when they were due to leave Capri she meekly accepted their decision to continue travelling around Europe together while she returned to New York to visit her family. It was in the same spirit of self-abasement that a few weeks later, when Peggy discovered that she was pregnant, her main concern was how Laurence would take the news, how Laurence would be affected. She was feeling tired and nauseous when she returned to him in Paris, but she was determined that he would not find her dull or disappointing as a wife. Peggy accepted that Laurence was a man who would 'never miss a chance to give a big party', and she would never, yet, expect him to.

It was in Paris, though, as Peggy schooled herself to live up to Laurence's standards, that she realized there was a darker aspect to his gregariousness. He had a quick temper and there had been isolated arguments during their honeymoon; but only now did she glimpse the violence underlying his anger. Small incidents or irritations could flare into full-blown tantrums, into the smashing of crockery, the breaking of mirrors and physical as well as verbal assault. After several years of marriage Peggy would dimly grasp the sources of Laurence's anger, and realize that his tantrums were fuelled not only by alcohol but frustration too. As he approached thirty Laurence was having to face the fact that his ambitions for himself might far outstrip his actual talents, that he had compromised himself in becoming dependent on a marriage he half-despised. Sometimes he picked an argument with Peggy simply in the hopes of sparking their relationship into more dramatic life, and when she sensed this she learned to fight back. But in the early days Peggy was too much in Laurence's thrall, too masochistically uncertain of herself, to do more than weep passively at his rages.

Her lack of confidence was itself infuriating to Laurence. She had a nervous habit of pursing and licking her lips; an expression of darting fearfulness that flickered through her gaze. These signs of vulnerability were at times so maddening to him that he would take a sadistic, needling pleasure in disparaging her; reminding her that she was a person of no talent or significance, and that it was only because she was rich, and because she was married to him, that she had been accepted by his Parisian friends.

But in between the rows, there were good times in the marriage. As Peggy's pregnancy advanced they moved south to the French Riviera, where she read quantities of books and where Laurence learned to drive; in April 1923 they went to London and rented a large house to await the birth of the baby. A crowd of friends tagged along from Paris, and they were actually in the middle of a large and noisy dinner party when Peggy went into labour on the evening of 14 May. Apparently the party continued while she retired upstairs with the doctor and midwife and spent a night of what she recalled as 'excruciating' pain. The labour ended in a traumatic forceps delivery, and afterwards Peggy was too tired and too groggy with chloroform to hold her infant son. She didn't have sufficient energy, either, to object to the unwieldy combination of names, Michael Cedric Sindbad, that Laurence and their friends had riotously proposed for the baby during the previous evening. Of the three, it was Sindbad that stuck (a name picked out from *The Arabian Nights* and always misspelled with that extra 'd'), although in adult life their son would revert to Michael, the name Peggy had initially preferred herself.

Yet despite the ordeal of the delivery, despite the wobbling misery of her hormones and the terror that she might prove an 'unnatural mother' (breastfeeding was very difficult for her), Peggy adored the new baby, his smallness and his smell. She was overjoyed too that Laurence, having been very resistant to the idea of fatherhood, was now 'crazy' about his son. Paternal pride made him unusually tender to her for a time and even though they had a more hectic summer than Peggy would have chosen, renting a house in Normandy that they shared with a demanding stream of guests (among them Clotilde and her lover Louis Aragon), Peggy at least had the support of her own good friend Peggy David, a young woman whom she'd known in New York and whose intelligent, steady sympathy was Peggy's greatest help and comfort during the first disorienting weeks of motherhood.

By the early autumn Peggy was sufficiently strong to travel, and she, Laurence, Sindbad and their new nanny Lilly headed first to Capri and then, more adventurously, on to Egypt and Israel. As a couple, Peggy and Laurence were at their best when they were travelling: intrepid and curious about the sights they were seeing, but also freed from the social pressures of Paris. They had rows still – one over a prostitute whom Laurence had insisted on visiting, and who Peggy feared might give him 'a disease' – but they shared genuine pleasures too: pride in their willingness to explore beyond the guide books, and in the clever trinkets they found together in the local souks.

They were back in Paris by early winter, where they found an apartment to rent on the Boulevard Saint-Germain, across from the Café de Flore. They filled it with rustic tables and chairs, brightly patterned rugs, pictures and books; and Laurence also began filling it with friends. Peggy was less pleased by the parties that now seemed to occur spontaneously, and nosily, several times a week. Having inherited Florette's horror of polluting germs, she hated it when amorous couples strayed into her and Laurence's bedroom, and afterwards would spray all the surfaces with bleach. Yet by slow degrees, Peggy was finding her own personal niche in Paris. Stimulated and emboldened by the cultural electricity of the city, she made her own way to the salons of Natalie Barney and Gertrude Stein, to performances of Diaghilev's Ballets Russes. Even if Laurence had tried to persuade her that she was a non-entity, she was now able to claim people like Man Ray and the alarmingly original Nancy Cunard as her acquaintances, if not her friends. By 1927, when Peggy held a party of her own to honour Isadora Duncan, she was able to boast a guest list that included Jean Cocteau, Ernest Hemingway, Ezra Pound, André Gide, Marcel Duchamp and Janet Flanner, the *New Yorker*'s witty and influential correspondent in Paris.

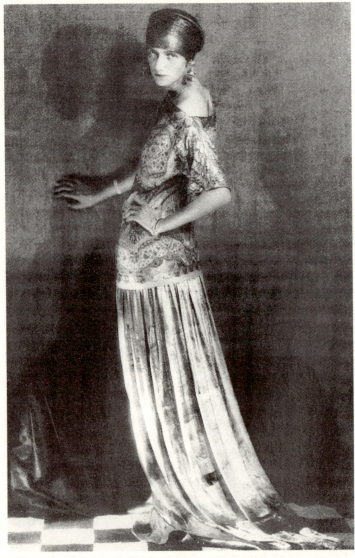

Peggy's favourite photograph of herself,
dressed by Poiret and photographed by Man Ray in Paris (1924).

Some of those who met Peggy in the mid-1920s, like the writer Matthew Josephson, saw her as still very much under Laurence's sway – a 'young matron, somewhat shy in manner and plain in appearance but always beautifully dressed'.[20] Yet a far more confident Peggy appeared in the series of photographs taken of her by Man Ray. She was dressed in an embroidered gold gown by Poiret, a gold turban and dramatic pendant earrings: and while her appearance had none of the singular mystery of Man Ray's portraits of Luisa, she looked glamorously assertive, posed in fashionable flapper stance, her back arched and pelvis jutted forward, her gown draped flatteringly around her body. Even her nose looked elegant, photographed at an angle that gave striking character to her face.

Later that season, Peggy also had her hair bobbed short. Laurence was interestingly furious; as fashionable as he liked his women to look, he considered long hair to be sexier and more 'natural'. She, however, was too relieved to be rid of the weight and bother to worry about her husband's complaints: more importantly, her new style was being applauded by the small group of female friends she'd started to form. Among them was Mary Reynolds, a young American widow and former girlfriend of Laurence's, whose willowy, graceful assurance was matched by a fine intelligence, a rare capacity for sympathy and a strikingly original eye: in Paris she papered the walls of her apartment with maps and created a hanging art installation out of her collection of earrings. Peggy loved Mary, and was greatly impressed by her being the lover of the artist Marcel Duchamp. The latter's reputation as a conjurer of brilliantly improbable ideas, his ability to persuade the world to look at objects like a hatstand or urinal as if they were works of art, had endowed him with a guru-like status among his peers. According to Peggy, all of the men sought Duchamp's approval, while the women all wanted to sleep with him.

Peggy's other closest friend in Paris was the American writer Djuna Barnes. She'd initially had complicated feelings about Djuna, another former mistress of Laurence's who was as intimidatingly attractive as she was talented, a magnificent-looking woman with dark auburn hair, white skin and an elegant nose. She'd felt slightly put-upon when Leon Fleischman had asked her to fund Djuna's passage to Europe, before she had actually met her. Yet over time the two of them developed an intimate if spiky camaraderie: Peggy became more articulate and witty in Djuna's company, talking with her about books they'd read, about mutual friends, about sex and clothes. She admired Djuna greatly for her feminist views as well as for her writing; and in Paris she began supporting her with a monthly stipend which she continued paying for the rest of Djuna's life.

Theirs was a genuine intimacy, but Laurence had been cruelly on the mark when he'd needled Peggy about the role money played in her friendships, for it was an issue that made her feel conflicted and confused. Her first impulse was often to be generous. During the mid-1920s, in addition to paying out Djuna's $40 monthly stipend, she lent 5,000 francs to the photographer Berenice Abbott for the purchase of a professional camera, and she became a patron and business partner to the artist Mina Loy. She was supporting political causes, too: sending money to Lucille Kohn for her various activities, and in 1926 donating a lump sum of $10,000 to the striking miners of England. By the end of the decade, Peggy worked out that she was paying $10,000 a year in regular subsidies to 'artists and old friends'. Yet the closer she was to those she assisted, the more compromised and awkward these arrangements became: some friends, like Djuna, began to chafe under the obligation they felt towards her money, while others tried to press her for more generous handouts.

Peggy was sensitive to the idea that she might be buying her friendships, yet it didn't prevent her from feeling that some of those she helped had shown inadequate gratitude. One of her later beneficiaries, the political activist Emma Goldman, would write that her own relationship with Peggy had 'cracked' over money: 'I have always known that there could be no real lasting friendship between those who have lots and those who must fret for every sou,' Goldman observed. '[Peggy] gives more readily than others of her class [but she] has an awful inferiority complex...She can not imagine one would care for her if she had no money.'[21]

Peggy herself found it impossible to live by a consistent view of her wealth. As a wife and mother she was happy to take on the domestic expenses of houses, food, staff, travel and clothes. As a patron of artists she was open-handed. Yet when she and Laurence went out with friends, it irked her that the bill was almost always passed to her. She disliked the automatic assumption that she would pay, and it bothered her natural instinct for economy. Peggy had seen her father dissipate a large fortune, and knowing that her own wealth was far from limitless, she was always upset by senseless waste. Her caution infuriated Laurence, who considered it narrow and mean. But Peggy could never adopt the grand indifference that Luisa Casati displayed towards finance. She needed to know exactly how her money was being spent, and exactly how much was in her account.

Laurence's distaste for Peggy's budgeting instincts was given spiteful expression in the novel *Murder! Murder!*, which he wrote during the final phase of their marriage. He portrayed Peggy as a woman obsessed by laundry lists and bills, moving her lips in her sleep as she 'dreamed of sums'.[22] It was an ungrateful, vengeful portrait, and it was coloured by all the anti-Semitic disdain he'd felt for her family. Laurence continued to mock Peggy's relatives, openly irritated by Florette when she came over to visit and equally dismissive of Benita, whom he considered 'a prig and a bore'. When Peggy tried to retaliate by pointing out the faults of his own sister, he was so offended by her assumption that Clotilde could be compared to Benita that he smashed every item in Peggy's favourite and very expensive set of tortoiseshell brushes and combs.

By now, Laurence's tantrums had become more frequent and more abusive. Sometimes Peggy suffered no more than bizarre acts of humiliation – once or twice Laurence had angrily grabbed handfuls of jam and rubbed them through her offendingly short hair. But sometimes she felt he wanted to kill her; on one occasion he pushed her under the water while she was taking a bath, on another he slammed her hard against a wall. Afterwards, he was always remorseful; and because he stopped short of inflicting serious injuries, Peggy always forgave him. As adept as she was at blinkering herself to the truth, she preferred to interpret Laurence's violence as proof of his superior, passionate nature, as a necessary characteristic of their bohemian life.

The fighting was always worst when they were in Paris, partly because they drank more heavily when they were in the city and partly because they had so little to occupy them, beyond maintaining the façade of having busy and colourful lives. Like so many of their generation, Peggy and Laurence had come to Paris with the illusion that freedom and happiness were theirs for the taking, simply by being young and in Europe; yet often, they struggled with the essential emptiness of their days, and they took their frustrations out on each other. Life tended to be better, calmer, when they were travelling outside Paris, or playing at house elsewhere. Their Venetian autumn together in 1924 had been an interlude of unusual accord, and while Peggy could not afford to make it permanent then, through the buying of a palazzo, the idea of creating a safer place for their marriage had taken root. The following year, when she was pregnant again and travelling with Laurence through the South of France, she believed she had found them just such a refuge.

It was a seaside house, a former inn that stood just outside the small town of Le Canadel, midway between Toulon and St Tropez. While the building itself was quite primitive, its setting was extravagantly lovely, with a private beach, orange trees and a terrace with wide Mediterranean views. Peggy fell in love with the house, which she named Pramousquier, and she believed that she and Laurence might finally put down roots there, creating a proper home for Sindbad and for their daughter Jezebel Margaret (who was born in August 1925 and whose name, suggested by a writer friend, was rapidly commuted to Pegeen). They took up residence in Pramousquier that autumn, and although Peggy had been fatigued and emotional after Pegeen's birth, she became contentedly absorbed in making the house beautiful and comfortable. It was a talent she was beginning to recognize in herself: even though she wasn't domesticated and barely knew how to cook, she had an eye for property and an instinct for home-making. She and Laurence were in unusual accord as they got the Venetian antiques out of storage, discussed the installation of a new modern kitchen and the building of two garden studios – one for his writing, one as a guest house for friends. She didn't object when Laurence ran up enormous bills – stocking the wine cellar and buying new pictures and rugs – nor did she quibble over the expense of hiring a large staff to service their luxury arcadia: a gardener, a chef, several maids and a new nanny called Doris.

Peggy and Laurence would spend three years in Pramousquier, on and off, and both would regard it as the place where they were happiest.

There were days when the sea was delicious and the sun was hot; when Laurence was writing well; when the children seemed adorable and the friends who came to stay were entertaining and appreciative. Yet as benign an influence as the house exerted, it could not solve the fundamental conflicts in their marriage, which boiled up with renewed ugliness as soon as they were back in Paris. Peggy had by now acquired a taste for alcohol, so it was her drunkenness as well as his that precipitated their rows; and she had also learned to identify and manipulate Laurence's areas of weakness. If he made a slighting comment about her intellect, her family or her looks, she would retaliate with taunting comments about his lack of money and his dependent situation. Alternatively, she would provoke his sexual jealousy. Laurence had always operated by lordly double standards, believing that it was his right to visit brothels or seduce one of the credulous young women who hung around their circle, while retaining a fiercely possessive claim on his wife. During the first years of their marriage Peggy had more or less resigned herself to her husband's behaviour. But as she grew more confident in herself and more consistently angry with him, she began to fight back with infidelities of her own.

During the winter of 1925 she went with Laurence and Clotilde on a skiing holiday in Switzerland but returned to Paris early, pleading the excuse of her weak ankles but also looking forward to 'ten days of freedom' on her own. Celebrating her independence, she hosted a large cocktail party in the studio Laurence used for his writing, and during it she behaved much as her husband liked to do: drinking too much, and making love with one of her guests. She had only ever gone so far as flirting with another man before, but this act of defiant self-gratification was, she claimed, 'exactly what I sought'. She knew the incident would hurt Laurence more than any other weapon she'd used against him, and as soon as he returned to Paris she made sure that he found out about it.

The repercussions were as dramatic as she'd hoped – and feared. Laurence forced his way into the hotel apartment where they were now living, throwing most of Peggy's belongings out of the window and terrifying the children, who had to take shelter with their nanny behind a locked door. During one exhausted lull in his threats and his bellowing Peggy tried to take Laurence for a conciliatory meal, but he turned

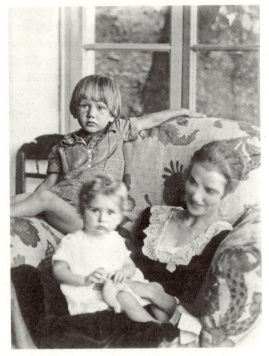

Peggy with Sindbad and baby Pegeen (1926).

his rage onto the other diners, hurling bottles and glasses around the bar. Eventually the police were called, and he was carted off to jail in a wheelbarrow. The following morning, when Peggy collected him, he was still ranting: demanding first that the two of them go straight down to Pramousquier and then, when they were on the train and about to depart, forcing Peggy to get off again and accompany him to a brothel – to spend the night with 'whores' like herself.

In his own egotistical way Laurence was as needy and insecure as Peggy, and to the extent that she was able to sense this she was able to put up with his temper. She continued to tolerate the marriage, too, because she did not know what would happen to the children if they separated, and because she had no idea of how she might live on her

CHAPTER 8   257

own. Yet in the summer of 1927 Laurence behaved so unforgivably badly, according to Peggy, that she developed a splinter of cold, hard hatred for him and began finally to wish that she could leave.

Her sister Benita had suffered a cruel succession of miscarriages during the first decade of her own marriage, but she was now bloomingly pregnant, and Peggy had been anticipating an autumn visit to New York to see her and to rejoice in her new baby. In July, however, a cable arrived at Pramousquier with news that Benita had gone into labour early, and had suffered a fatal haemorrhage from an undiagnosed placenta previa. The shock and the grief were traumatic for Peggy: 'I felt virtually as though I had been cut in two,' she wrote, and for several weeks she was barely able to eat or sleep.²³ At first Laurence was very gentle, yet as Peggy remained locked inside her mourning he grew childishly resentful, complaining that her tears were a boring inconvenience for everyone and an insult to him. Finally, incensed by her refusal to respond to his complaints, he committed what Peggy regarded as the most heinous of his crimes: tearing up all the photographs she'd carefully assembled into a kind of shrine to Benita, some of them precious snapshots from their childhood.

'I never thought about him the same way again,' she wrote. Her own memory of these events was partial, and she later accepted that she'd played her own part in the breakdown of their marriage. Laurence had been an abusive husband – at times criminally so. But she had taken an obtuse pleasure in provoking his demons, and she had lacked the skill and patience to sympathize with the emotions that drove them. Empathy was not a lesson that Peggy had learned from her narcissistic father or her neurotic mother; and as an adult she was too self-involved and insecure to imagine herself readily under the skin of other people's feelings. A new friend of Peggy's, Emily Coleman, would say of her, 'She is as absorbed in herself as any human being I ever saw...She cannot *think* of another person's life.'²⁴

But even Peggy would concede that she had failed Laurence, and that the next woman he married, the writer Kay Boyle, was far more adept at 'managing' both his temper and his unhappiness. Arguably she came to love Laurence most in the years after they'd been divorced, when they were free to appreciate each other's better qualities and to accept one another as friends. But in 1927, Peggy was incapable of such clarity. She was glued to Laurence by habits of drama and dependency that she was unable to unpick, and she might never have found the strength to leave the marriage, had it not been for the bracing arrival of a new friend and ally.

Peggy had been introduced to the feminist and socialist Emma Goldman sometime in the mid-1920s, but it was in the spring of 1928, when Goldman moved to a small villa near St Tropez to write her memoirs, that the two women grew close. It had been Peggy, in fact, who found and paid for the villa. And while Emma, a fifty-nine-year-old veteran in the fight against oppression, might otherwise have dismissed her as a spoiled socialite, she was not only grateful to Peggy but spotted in her a beguiling eagerness for life, a strong if confused impulse for self-fulfilment.

During the early summer they met quite often, and it was now, for the first time, that Peggy was forced to confront the state of her relationship with Laurence. Other friends had witnessed his rages, but they had never tried to interfere; nor had Peggy asked them to. Emma, however, had no such reticence. Appalled by what she saw of Laurence's temper that summer, she asked Peggy how she could possibly 'lead this kind of life'. Peggy admitted reluctantly that 'things were too bad to continue', but she resisted Emma's advice that she must act immediately.[25] She was terrified of losing custody of her children – and, she admitted helplessly, she was just as terrified of facing life without a man. Unlike Emma, who had braved prison, revolution and political exile, and who had lambasted the concept of love as 'a stupid romantic notion, destined to keep [women] forever dependent on the male', Peggy had never attempted to survive alone.[26] After her early experiments with work she'd moved almost seamlessly from being Florette's daughter to being Laurence's wife. And while Emma Goldman's fierce advocacy of freedom made an emotional impact on her, Peggy could not yet act on its message. It was only later that summer, when she found a new lover, that she was able to nerve herself to the point of physically leaving her husband.

CHAPTER 9

'It had never occurred to me before that I could be happy alone.'

In 1936, when Peggy found herself staring at yet another failed relationship, she took herself back to Venice, hoping to find consolation among its familiar beauties. The ten days she spent there, however, proved to be an unexpected revelation of her own, inner resources. 'I walked miles all over the city, at any time of the day or night, and ate anywhere I happened to find myself. I revisited all my favourite churches and museums... I was unhampered by any influence and criticism and could enjoy Venice to my entire delight.'[1] Peggy finally understood what Emma Goldman had been trying to tell her in Pramousquier eight years previously: that she had to learn to be responsible for her own happiness. Back in 1928, however, she'd only been capable of seeing herself in relation to a man.

John Ferrar Holms was an English writer who had been staying in St Tropez that summer with his common-law wife Dorothy, a woman of rather earnest, heavy beauty who was seven years his senior. Peggy had been emotionally susceptible the night she met him; it was the first anniversary of Benita's death, and Laurence had insisted they go out drinking and dancing in St Tropez. The combination of jazz, alcohol and grief had, Peggy believed, induced in her 'a kind of desperation', and she'd not only ended up dancing with John Holms that night, but kissing him in a passionate embrace.

Although the kiss had been a moment of drunken release, John himself had left an impression, and when he and Dorothy came for dinner at Pramousquier a few days later, Peggy contrived to get him alone on the beach. They talked and made love; and the short time they were alone together confirmed Peggy's impression that this Englishman was unusually attractive. He was tall, lean and pale, with soft brown eyes and a dark reddish beard that gave him, she thought, a resemblance to Christ. He also had something of the untethered quality that she'd first admired in Laurence, his limbs so naturally flexible that when he walked or danced he seemed 'barely to be knit together', his movement as fluid as a cat's. Yet it was John's mind that beguiled her most. Like Laurence, he was 'bursting with ideas', but his conversational style was more gracefully impressionistic, woven together with poetic aperçus and arcane references that implied to Peggy a rare depth of knowledge, a touch of genius: 'He talked like Socrates. He held people spellbound for hours, he seemed to have everything at his fingertips...a very old soul that nothing could surprise.'[2]

Peggy was not immediately conscious of being in love, nor of having any desire to separate John from Dorothy. Even though the night on the beach led to other assignations, she told herself that she was only 'borrowing' John for a summer fling. Nevertheless, she was making little effort to hide the affair from Laurence, and as she later recognized, she was wilfully using John as a catalyst to end her marriage. The crisis came when the Holmses were staying in the guest studio at Pramousquier for a few days, and Peggy recklessly seized her moment to go to John after Dorothy left him on his own one evening. She knew full well that Laurence could see her crossing the garden in the moonlight, and that he would be immediately suspicious; and the scene did in fact play out as though scripted, with Laurence bursting in through the studio door and reacting so violently to the sight of Peggy and John in each other's arms that the gardener had to intervene in the ensuing fight.

After this dramatically conclusive scene, there was no question of the marriage surviving. Peggy fled Pramousquier the following morning, leaving Laurence's rage to abate. By the time she returned she was relieved to find him gone back to Paris, but appalled to discover that he had also taken Sindbad; it had been Peggy's great fear that if ever she tried to leave Laurence, he would punish her by claiming possession of the children. While she had the obvious financial advantage in a custody battle, and witnesses to testify to her husband's adultery and abuse, she was afraid that her own infidelities, especially her affair with John, would be more damaging in the eyes of the court and would brand her an unfit mother. Even though she received bracing sisterly support from Emma Goldman and hired a good divorce lawyer to square up to Laurence's demands, the stress and anxiety made Peggy ill.

Early that winter she was also struggling to make sense of a second family tragedy, the deaths of her two small nephews, Hazel's boys, who had somehow fallen from the terrace of a sixteenth-floor apartment in New York. The horror of it was so shocking to Peggy that the fight more or less went out of her. Perhaps she felt contaminated by the tragedy, fearing that she and Hazel were doomed by their upbringing to become bad mothers. Whatever the reasons, she gave in to most of Laurence's demands, offering him not only a $300 monthly allowance as part of divorce settlement, but legal custody of Sindbad. At the time, she rationalized her surrender on the grounds that it would be wrong to separate a son from his father, that Laurence knew better than she how to raise a boy. It did not seem to occur to her then that in splitting up Sindbad and Pegeen, she and Laurence could do lasting harm to both of the children.

The embattled divorce proceedings were not an auspicious start to Peggy's relationship with John; yet she was very good at living with conflicting emotions, and while she ached for Sindbad she was determined to be happy with her new lover. Once John had engineered his own separation from Dorothy, he and Peggy spent much of the next two years on a protracted honeymoon, driving around Europe in their new Citroën with Pegeen, Doris the nanny and the family sheepdog, Lola, all packed together into the back seat. Travel always calmed Peggy, giving her the illusion that she was outrunning her troubles. 'I feel', she wrote to Emma Goldman later, 'as though I am getting away with something really important.' John also appeared to be the easiest of companions, serenely content to enjoy whatever good food and good hotels Peggy put his way; discoursing brilliantly on the places through which they passed.[3]

He was also, for Peggy, a source of sexual joy. Although she and Laurence had been physically passionate, their lovemaking had become inextricably tied to their battles. With John, however, Peggy felt only adored, confident and desirable. A close but not entirely disinterested observer of their affair was Peggy's new friend Emily Coleman, who had been working as Emma Goldman's secretary in St Tropez and had herself developed a romantic crush on John. Emily now attached herself to the couple, visiting them when they were in Paris between travels, sometimes even accompanying them. And as she watched Peggy and John together she reported, not quite kindly, to her diary that Peggy had never looked more physically confident: 'She is shaped perfectly, thinly...she turns her head upon her neck and snaps her hand. Her shoulders are narrow and she walks with assurance which she has not, but so she walks.'

Just as Peggy bloomed under John's sexual admiration, so she delighted in the attention he paid to her mind. Laurence had become too busy, too critical to offer her the mentorship she'd craved. John, however, seemed to delight in making a project of Peggy's education, giving her new books to read, playing her records of baroque and contemporary music, introducing her to new ideas of religion and psychology. 'He was fascinated by the idea of remoulding me,' she recalled with pride: 'he held me in the palm of his hand...he directed my every move, my every thought.'[4]

Emma Goldman had been far less impressed by John, shrewdly perceiving that behind his conversational panache lay a weak, ineffectual man, a would-be writer who lacked the energy and courage to commit his ideas to paper. She considered him an intellectual snob whose 'education' of Peggy was fundamentally a way of diminishing and controlling her. But Peggy herself remained deaf to Emma's misgivings, regarding John as the savant who would lead her on the path to self-enlightenment. She believed that until she'd met him she'd never tried to examine her own emotions or her motives, but had merely acted on 'blind impulses', unconsciously feeling her way towards each new thing in her life. Now that John was directing her to Freud, D. H. Lawrence and E. M. Forster, now that he was talking to her about psychological cause and effect, Peggy was convinced that her mind was being opened up, irradiated. 'To be in his company was equivalent to living in a sort of undreamed of fifth dimension...with him, I began to learn everything I know today.'[5]

Even so, Peggy's self-knowledge remained very partial, and while she was earnestly learning to identify the emotional patterns of her past she was frequently blind to the issues in front of her – especially those affecting her children, who were both naturally distressed by their parents' divorce. It had been six months before Laurence had allowed Peggy to see Sindbad again, and the meeting had been harrowing. They had walked in a park together, and to Peggy it seemed that her six-year-old son was already a stranger, wearing his first pair of long trousers and responding stiffly to her attempts at conversation. The stress of the situation was exacerbated by Laurence, who insisted on hovering a few inches behind in case Peggy should try to steal Sindbad away. Yet when Peggy came to describe this wretched scene in her memoir, it was only her own anguish that she recalled; she made no attempt to imagine the confusion and fear that her little boy must have been feeling.

For the rest of Sindbad and Pegeen's childhoods it would continue like this, as the emotional demands of the parents took centre and front of the family stage. When the terms of the divorce were finally settled, it was agreed that Sindbad would stay with Peggy for sixty days each year and that Pegeen, when she was old enough, would spend part of the summer with Laurence. He was now living with his new lover Kay and her daughter Sharon (always known as Bobby); he would shortly begin to father a second family; and as his and Peggy's situations became more complicated, the custody arrangements became correspondingly

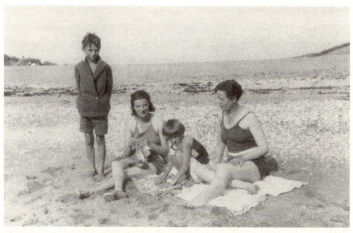

Peggy and the children on the beach
in France, with Djuna Barnes (c. 1930).

chaotic. Dates of visits were swapped around; and as Kay and Laurence settled first in Nice, then in Austria, and as Peggy continued to tour Europe, the children were forced to travel long unfamiliar distances by boat, train or car. None of the adults seemed to consider how unsettling it was for Pegeen and Sindbad to be shuttled around in this manner; how hard it was for them to be divided from each other and from at least one of their parents for much of the year. As they grew older the children were fully conscious of how they'd been used as pawns in the adults' games – not only shunted between their different homes in Europe but drawn into their hostilities, made witness to Laurence's complaints about Peggy's meanness, and to Peggy and Kay's continual bitching about each other's failures as mothers.

Peggy loved her two children, especially when they were small, and early photographs show her smiling and cuddling them with unaffected physical joy. Yet the care she gave them was always filtered through her own needs. Pegeen had become anxious and clingy after the divorce, but most of the time Peggy was too much in love with John and too absorbed in her own self-improvement to give the little girl the attention she needed. Perversely, though, when Pegeen turned to her nurse Doris for love, Peggy reacted with unreasonable petulance, as though she herself had been slighted.

Laurence was no more reliable as a father. When he was sober and happy he could be very affectionate with the children, easy to talk to and fun; but if he was drinking, busy with his writing or wrangling with Peggy, he too became blind to their interests. He failed to recognize how profoundly unsettled Pegeen would be made by the births of her three half-sisters, how afraid she would become of losing her portion of his love. There would be other reasons why Sindbad, as an adult, began to drink too much, why Pegeen hurtled self-destructively towards alcohol, pills and unstable men – yet the children themselves would place most of the blame on their parents.

* * * * *

Once her divorce from Laurence had been finalized in the autumn of 1930, Peggy did attempt to build a calmer and more effective home life. She and John found a house to rent in the south of Paris – a tall, thin, eccentric building surrounded by trees that was conveniently close to the Anglo-French school where Pegeen was now enrolled. Yet once they had stopped travelling, their relationship began to change. John seemed somehow diminished by Paris; he complained that he missed England and that he could not speak French well enough to feel intellectually at home. But he also seemed unable to settle to his own writing. Peggy had furnished a studio for him in the house, but he rarely went near it, preferring to spend his days on the drawing-room sofa reading and listening to records. By the time it was evening he would become charged with an irritable restlessness, insisting that Peggy invite friends over for dinner, or drive him into the city for a meal or an evening of jazz and dancing.

Paris had altered in certain ways from the city Peggy had first discovered with Laurence: many of the expatriate Left Bankers had been forced home by the 1929 crash, and the atmosphere of her old haunts had changed. (Laurence, returning to the city on a rare visit, was dismayed to find the Dome's rackety clientele had been replaced by 'happy German families...and Scandinavian raw fish eaters, who took hours to finish two beers').[6] Nevertheless, Peggy and John still had a wide circle of friends between them in Paris: Harold Loeb, Djuna Barnes, Edwin Muir, Emily Coleman and Helen Fleischman, now married to James Joyce's son, Giorgio – and at the end of a long night, Peggy could still be left to pick up a drinks bill that ran to 1,700 francs.

Peggy enjoyed these evenings in the city – she liked to be gregarious and tipsy in the middle of a crowd – but she was starting to realize that they always ended with John becoming very, very drunk. Ever since she'd known him he had consumed steady quantities of wine and spirits, but he'd always remained lucid and equable. Now he was rarely sober, drinking moderately during the day and much more heavily when they were out with friends. The alcohol was not only making him depressed, but diminishing his interest in sex, and Peggy was frightened and angry to see her mentor so reduced. She couldn't stop herself picking on his failures – as a writer, a lover and a provider – and one of the more shameful moments of her life was when she told John that she'd become pregnant by him but had an abortion, because she did not think him fit to be a father.

John blamed Paris alone for the lowering of his spirits, complaining over and over again that he was 'so bored, so bored'.[7] But when Peggy took him away to Venice, trusting that her miracle city would work its balm, he was moody and unresponsive, claiming that he felt oppressed by so much beauty and history. His reaction disappointed her badly: 'For the first time since I had been with John he let me down.'[8] But still hoping for happiness, she agreed to his suggestion that they spend less time in Paris and move to England for their summers. After much critical dithering from John they settled on the south-west county of Devonshire, where Peggy found a large manor house for them to rent. Although the interior of Hayford Hall was quite hideous – a classically English mix of ancestral grandeur, shabby chintz and spartan plumbing – its location was glorious enough to please even John's demanding eye, set in rambling grounds that extended into the rolling expanse of Dartmoor and away to the sea beyond.

They would spend the summers of 1932 and 1933 at Hayford Hall, and during their first visit Peggy and John were able to regain a semblance of their early contentment. They fell into a companionable routine: walks and games of tennis with the children in the morning; quiet afternoons of reading and writing, followed by long evenings of cocktails, dinner and more drinks. They had several guests to stay, and to Peggy the household assumed a delightfully literary atmosphere. Many of John's friends were writers, and their after-dinner conversations rambled at erudite length into discussions of Aldous Huxley and the modern novel, Elizabethan poetry, religion and ideas. Hayford Hall was good for the children, too. Sindbad was growing into an active, sporty child and while Peggy had begun to find him difficult to manage in Paris, in Devon he had the tennis court, the rudimentary swimming pool and all of Dartmoor to explore. Pegeen, who had by now accepted John as a surrogate father, was also more tractable. In a photograph taken of the four of them in Devon that first summer they look relaxed, outdoorsy, like a conventional English family.

The second summer, though, was far less successful. Emily Coleman, still half in love with John and still half-begrudging of Peggy, was in almost permanent residence at Hayford Hall, and so too was Djuna Barnes. Peggy was happy to see so much of her old friend, and delighted to offer her house room as she worked on her latest novel, *Nightwood* (Djuna would return the favour by dedicating the novel to Peggy and John). She liked Emily, too, even though she was wary of her, and she knew that John's mood would brighten in the presence of these two educated, amusing women. Yet over the summer a malign chemistry developed between the four of them that brought out the worst in all of their characters. Emily, sensing the stresses in Peggy's relationship with John, began to flirt competitively and opportunistically, and even Djuna, who was generally more interested in women, began to make a sardonic play for John. She developed a seductive, sparring intimacy with him and liked to sit herself beside him late into the evening, pitting her intellect against his in literary or philosophical debate.

As John and Djuna argued over the merits of obscure 17th-century poets, Peggy felt herself belittled and exposed. Her discomfort at such moments was evident to William Gerhardie, a novelist friend of John's who came for a short visit to Hayford Hall that summer. He observed Peggy as she sat hesitantly on the fringes of the conversation: 'patiently waiting to go to bed while [John] talks and talks...[She] as always said very little. Her face had a vague look. If she opened her mouth it was to give vent to a general unfocused irony.* Five years earlier, when John had presented himself as the serene, loving pedagogue, he might have drawn Peggy into the conversation, guided her through its difficulties, explained its references. Now he was impatient, and sometimes cruel. If Peggy made a remark that he considered wrong or ill-informed, he didn't move to enlighten her but complained that she was a typically 'pea-brained' American, incapable of rational thought. Peggy, wounded by these shafts of contempt, tried to convince herself that John had never wanted 'an intellectual woman' as his companion, that it was her sexual energy he desired; and defensively she vamped up her role as the raw outsider, disrupting the others' high-flown conversation with sarcastic jokes and deliberately gauche comments. This behaviour, however, only antagonized John further, amused Djuna and gave the watchful, rivalrous Emily cause for delight.

* The description is from Gerhardie's novel *Of Mortal Love*, in which the character Molly is closely modelled on Peggy.

After dinner, when Peggy, John, Djuna and Emily were alone at Hayford Hall, the four of them often played 'Truth', a fashionable parlour game that required its players to comment on each other's talents, personality traits and sex appeal. It was a hazardous pastime, given the tensions between them, and its confessional, confrontational dynamic encouraged them all to behave badly. After one long evening of drinking and truth-telling Peggy lapsed into a doze, and when she awoke she found Djuna locked into an embrace with a visibly aroused John, nuzzling and kissing his neck. She tried to object, but the atmosphere in the room was already sliding into an erotic free-for-all: Djuna retaliated to Peggy's possessiveness by slapping her hard on the buttocks, and then began slapping Emily, who admitted to her diary that she'd been unable to contain her excitement: '[Djuna] hadn't hit me four times before I had an orgasm.'⁹

These febrile evenings blurred the lines between playfulness and treachery. Peggy, already undermined by the waning of John's sexual interest, became paranoid when he stayed up late talking to one or other of the two women. When she accused her lover of being unfaithful he

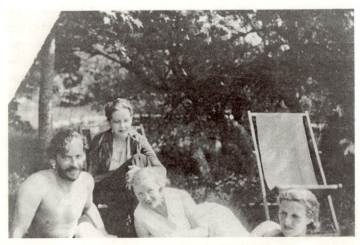

The second summer at 'Hangover Hall':
Peggy with John Holms, Antonia White and Djuna Barnes (1933).

lost his temper and Emily, who took great satisfaction in following their disputes, recorded everything in her diary – from Peggy's screams of fury to John's intemperate response: 'You dirty little bitch, you falsify everything. You lie and lie like a serpent.'[10] The fights and the drinking were off-putting to other guests. Marian Bouché, a close friend of Djuna's who was married to the surrealist Louis Bouché, spent a brief period at what she called 'Hangover Hall', and vowed never to return: 'Too drunken, too hectic. Seems an unhappy household underneath.'[11] Yet still Peggy believed she could fix her relationship with John, if only the conditions were right. Accepting now that he could not tolerate Paris, she agreed that they should move permanently to London; and with the help of a new friend, a big, capable, free-spirited woman called Wyn Henderson, she found 'a very English, 18th-century house' in Woburn Square, where John would be close to all his bookish English friends and where he might finally settle to his own writing.[12]

Having moved John to London, Peggy was also hoping to engineer a more formal relationship between them. Even though she liked to consider herself a bohemian, she'd retained an instinctive attachment to the status and symbolism of marriage. She liked to be properly attached to her man, and she found it tiring to have to deal with other people's responses to her living arrangements – the prurient gossip of neighbours, and Florette's very vocal dismay. John, however, seemed in no hurry to propose. He had agreed to marry Dorothy when they had separated, so that she could continue using his surname,* and he didn't now want the bother of a divorce. But his love for Peggy had become noticeably sketchy and detached, and it seemed to her that the passions she could most reliably arouse in him these days were jealousy and anger. The previous year he'd introduced her to an extremely attractive man called Douglas Garman, a publisher, would-be poet and socialist; and because she was feeling neglected by John, she had impulsively written to his friend to suggest an assignation. Garman, innocently failing to decipher her meaning, had made no move, and afterwards Peggy had all but forgotten the incident. However, late one night in December

---

*   Peggy had smoothed the way to this outcome by offering Dorothy a £360 annual allowance.

1933, when John was being unkind and they were both very drunk, she remembered the bolt of attraction she had felt for Garman, and recklessly informed John how close she'd come to acting on it.

Sexual humiliation was a strategy Peggy had learned in her battles with Laurence, and she had already tried it a few times on John. Early in their relationship they'd fallen into a quarrel – possibly about Laurence, who happened to be dining in the same Parisian brasserie as them – and to punish John, Peggy had gone to sit with her ex-husband and made a play of flirting with him. Her behaviour astonished Emily, who was also present at the scene: '[Peggy] did this to pique him. She is like a child playing with dynamite.'[13] Now, in Woburn Square, the dynamite was very real; for while John's temper was slow, it could be as violent as Laurence's when roused. Peggy later wrote, 'He made me stand for ages naked in front of the open window and threw whisky in my eyes. He said, "I would like to beat your face so that no man will ever look at it again."'[14]

There was for her an ugly kind of triumph in eliciting this proof of jealousy, yet Peggy shrank from the violence of it too, and in the weeks that followed she began to wonder if she and John were done. Sindbad came to Woburn Square for the Christmas holidays, and when it was time for her to take him back to Zürich for the handover to Laurence, Peggy was suddenly wretchedly angry at the situation she was in and irrationally inclined to blame John for having broken up her family. Sindbad had wept miserably at Zürich Station, saying that he hated to leave her and hated to think of her travelling back to London alone. The touching concern of her ten-year-old son moved Peggy to tears and prompted her to re-edit the facts of her former marriage, convincing herself that if John hadn't come between her and Laurence, she wouldn't be suffering now. Standing on the station platform, weeping for herself and for Sindbad, Peggy swore that she hated John, that she wished he was dead. And for years afterwards, that wish would haunt her – because thirty-six hours later it came true.

* * * * *

The previous summer, at Hayford Hall, John had taken a fall while out riding and had injured his wrist. It had not healed properly, and because it continued to give him pain he'd been advised to have surgery to break the wrist and reset it. It was a simple operation, easily done at home, and it had been scheduled to take place at Woburn Square the day after Peggy returned from Zürich. John seemed in perfectly normal health, and although she'd been fleetingly worried by the amount he had drunk the evening before the procedure, she was too embarrassed to voice her concerns to the medical team when they arrived in the morning (they'd already had to cancel their first attempt at the operation when John had contracted flu).

Instead Peggy obediently held John's hand while the anaesthetic was administered, then went downstairs to the drawing room to wait until the operation was over. She'd been assured it would take just five minutes, yet over half an hour passed, during which time one of the two attending doctors slipped downstairs to get a bag from the hall and ominously said not a word. By the time the surgeon and the GP appeared at the drawing-room door, Peggy did not even need to see their professionally grave expressions to know something appalling had happened.

No one would confirm the exact cause of death beyond the fact that John's heart had failed during the operation. He might have suffered an allergic reaction to the anaesthetic, and he should certainly have been questioned more closely about the levels of alcohol in his blood. But the autopsy exonerated the doctors from any dereliction of their duties. Given the state of John's drink-damaged organs, it seemed that even if the operation hadn't killed him, he would have been close to killing himself.

As for Peggy, she recorded with startling, even heroic honesty that her first instinctive reaction to John's death had been relief. 'It was as though I were suddenly released from prison.'[15] But almost immediately her emotions had boomeranged back into grief and dread. She believed that John had died because she'd wished it, and when she looked at her sagging, unhappy face in the mirror she imagined that she could 'see her soul' leaking out of her mouth.[16] She was unable to recall why she'd hated John so much. And just as she had sanctified her father after he was dead, Peggy now whitewashed her memory of John, recasting him as the one great love of her life, the saintly mentor, the brilliant mind without whom her life would have been 'bankrupt'.

Yet Peggy survived; and she did so, yet again, by moving on to a new relationship. When a letter of condolence arrived from Douglas Garman, her grief was so raw that it took her a moment to remember who he was. Then, with a guilty clarity, she recalled how attractive he'd been to her, and how easy it would be to 'use' Douglas now to save herself.[17] Within eight weeks of John's death, she started an affair with him; and while she knew she was acting with shameful haste, the prospect of being on her own was too frightening for her to contemplate. Douglas slotted into her life so easily and naturally. Having grown up with seven sisters, he had an instinctive sympathy, a straightforward liking for women; and although his finances were precarious he seemed to wrap Peggy around with a simple kindness she had never experienced with another man.

Douglas's life at that time was based in Sussex, where he lived with his mother and his eight-year-old daughter from his former marriage. And it was at his suggestion that Peggy found a property nearby, a beautifully weathered house called Yew Tree Cottage, close to the small country town of Petersfield. The move from London allowed her to keep the Douglas affair secret (most of her friends would judge her, Peggy was sure). But it also gave her the chance to settle Pegeen, who had been very upset by John's death and even more upset by Peggy's dismissal of her beloved nanny, after Doris had announced she was engaged. Later, in one of her devastating moments of honesty, Peggy would admit that her real motive for sacking Doris hadn't been the fact that her marriage might be incompatible with her remaining a nanny, but rather the jealousy she continued to feel over Doris's attachment to Pegeen. Doris had often been more of a mother than Peggy had, and as Peggy guiltily acknowledged, in sacking her she'd deprived her nine-year-old daughter of the one stable presence she'd known. At the time, however, she smothered any instinct of regret with the hope that Douglas would become a new father figure to Pegeen and that his daughter Debbie, an affectionate and precociously thoughtful child, would become like a sister to her.

In some respects Peggy's hopes were realized. Douglas and Debbie were soon living full-time at Yew Tree Cottage, and although Peggy grieved for John, and at her darkest moments toyed with the idea of killing herself, this new family unit seemed to function contentedly around her. Douglas was happy and busy, either pottering through repairs to the house or writing in his studio. The two girls went to school together and in 1935 the custody arrangement over Sindbad acquired a merciful simplicity when Laurence enrolled him into the free-thinking boarding school Bedales, which was very close to Yew Tree Cottage.

There were days, more and more of them, when Peggy believed she could be happy again. She took herself on long walks through the surrounding South Downs; she had a heated swimming pool built in the garden – a rich New Yorker's privilege; she worked on her cooking skills, read Proust, and spent a great deal of time writing letters to friends and scribbling down ideas for a novel. To Emily she boasted that her life had become admirably transparent: 'I think [it is] very good for me to be a simple woman and do normal domestic things for a change...I feel I am acquiring poise and better manners and being less vulgar – without trying...'[18]

Without John's intellectual snobbery to diminish her or Laurence's anti-Semitic jokes, Peggy's confidence flourished. She liked herself in the country; she believed she was a much better mother to Pegeen and she even wondered, briefly, about having a baby with Douglas. Yet as so often in Peggy's life, she was building a fantasy. Domesticity was not natural to her, and however easy-going Douglas might be as a lover, he was not a match for Laurence or John. He didn't rouse her to the same physical exhilaration or the same intellectual awe, and the more time she spent with him, the more limited he appeared. Even his socialist principles, which had initially been so admirable to Peggy, became a source of irritation once he'd committed to joining the Communist Party in 1934.

'Douglas now wanted to live his own life under Moscow laws,' Peggy wrote; and more irksomely still, he wanted to convert her too. He denounced Proust as the voice of bourgeois decadence and urged Peggy to study Marx instead; he began to fill the cottage with the gratingly demagogic presence of his fellow comrades, and he tried to veto the visits of Peggy's own more apolitical friends. He even commandeered her new Delage for Party work – blind to the irony that when he was driving to meetings or recruiting new members he was at the wheel of one of the world's most expensive motors. Although Peggy had not abandoned her own socialist sympathies, and in a placatory move had even agreed to join the Party herself, she came to hate the communists and all they stood for. Douglas left her alone for days as he went out to serve the class struggle; and although Peggy had a maid to help with the cleaning and a gardener to tend the extensive grounds, running Yew Tree Cottage was much harder work than she was accustomed to. The house felt chill and damp in winter, while in summertime it was overrun with rats; when the two small girls fell sick with flu and she had to feed and nurse them single-handed, Peggy had rarely felt more put-upon or alone.

But life didn't much improve when Douglas was at home. Peggy had become so bored by his decency that she behaved badly, trying to poke and prod his emotions. Even in his anger, though, he proved a disappointment: Douglas considered it demeaning to abuse a woman, which meant that his best attempt at insulting Peggy was to accuse her of being a Trotskyite. When she once succeeded in goading him to slap her, there was no torrid scene of reconciliation afterwards; Douglas simply wept quiet tears of shame. By the summer of 1936, Yew Tree Cottage had stopped feeling like an idyll to Peggy. Her blood boiled every time she heard Douglas utter the word 'comrade', and she was disgusted by the return of the rats, whose poisoned corpses had to be fished out from under floorboards and from the water tank. Sindbad's arrival, once his school term had ended, made the house even more difficult to manage, and Peggy was euphoric when the time came for her to escort her son to the French Alps, where Laurence and Kay were now living. She eked out the journey for as long as she could, meeting up with Mary Reynolds and travelling with her to Venice; and it was acting on some blind impulse of self-preservation that she remained there on her own for another ten days. Reconnecting with her favourite city, she experienced for the first time in her life the pleasure of being alone.

Appreciating the value of her own company, appreciating the point of self-reliance, was a key moment for Peggy, and she regarded it as a watershed in her life. But afterwards, when she was back in England and trying to terminate her relationship with Douglas, it was not always easy to retain that initial clarity. For her, as for him, it was painful to dismantle the little family they'd created, and they tried to maintain some continuity of care for the girls, arranging for Debbie to come and stay with Peggy and Pegeen every third weekend in the month. But it was also difficult to accept the ending of their own relationship, and for several months after they'd agreed to part, they continued to drift back to each other for consoling sex. By the early summer of 1937, however, Peggy knew she was free – and, as she admitted ironically to herself, that unusual state now left her 'rather at a loss for an occupation'. Having essentially been nothing but a wife for the last decade and a half, she needed a new role. And it was while she was casting round for some job, some project or cause to fill her life that Peggy, almost incidentally, settled on modern art.[19]

CHAPTER 10

Today, the Peggy Guggenheim Collection is acknowledged as one of the treasures of the modern art world. Over 400,000 visitors come each year to the Palazzo Venier dei Leoni, drawn by the intimate collection of Picassos, Kandinskys, Pollocks, Brancusis and Klees that are displayed within its walls. While Venice goes about its noisy commercial business – the vaporetti and motorboats chugging along the canal, the savvy gondoliers singing to their clients, the street hawkers trading their fake designer goods – the atmosphere inside the palazzo is as calm and orderly as a church. Some of the works exhibited here are icons of modern culture, quasi-religious artefacts considered so fine, so rare, that the collection itself is beyond quantifiable price.

Back in 1937, when Peggy first decided to open a gallery, she would have been confounded by this future vision. She claimed to have known nothing, then, about modern painting or sculpture; and when she'd initially begun looking for an occupation, art had not been her immediate choice. Many of the people closest to her were writers – Laurence, John, Douglas, Djuna, Harold Loeb – and literature had long been the social and the romantic element in which she moved. When she talked about possible projects with her New York friend Peggy (now, by an odd twist, married to Hazel's ex-husband, Milton Waldman), some form of literary venture had been the obvious choice. Peggy Waldman had urged her that running a literary agency or a small publishing press would be satisfying – 'better still', she might try writing a novel herself.'

Yet Peggy suspected that she lacked sufficient income for publishing and sufficient talent for a writing career, and instead she began to veer towards the idea of dealing in art. Her father had always bought paintings, and her uncle Solomon was building himself up to become one of New York's leading collectors. Art was in the family blood, and even though Peggy herself had limited capital and as yet no actual works in her possession, she believed she might make her own contribution to the Guggenheim tradition by running a small commercial gallery.

Already she'd had some dilettante-ish experience of that world. Back in the 1920s her friend Mina Loy had developed a side line of pretty and saleable artefacts to fund her more avant-garde projects: lampshades with curious cut-out patterns, paint and paper collages in ingenious junky frames. Peggy was charmed by the objects and, eager to help, she had rented a small shop in Paris in which they could be sold. Mina herself hadn't stuck with the partnership for long, taking offence at Peggy's well-meaning attempts to introduce other, more profitable lines into the shop – novelty items like couture lingerie and painted slippers. But Peggy had sensed an appetite for business in herself: she enjoyed the occupation and the challenge, and she was optimistic now that she could make her gallery a success.

It was a difficult period for her, nonetheless. She was in the final throes of separating from Douglas and she was also coming to terms with the knowledge that her mother was dying. Peggy had heard from New York that Florette had been diagnosed with lung cancer and already undergone several operations, but it was only when her mother came to London in the summer of 1937 that she learned Florette had just six months to live. It was 'a fearful shock': even though Peggy had so often wished herself a million miles away from Florette, and so often despised her way of life, she had depended more than she knew on her mother, not only on her generous gifts of money but her fussing version of love. They did at least have this one last summer together, during which the two women became as close as they'd ever been. Peggy learned to admire her mother's stoicism and accept her idiosyncrasies of character, and she was genuinely bereft when Florette died on her return to New York, her health failing so fast that Peggy was unable to see her again. 'I think my life is over,' she said wretchedly to Emily Coleman; and Emily, in her typically obtuse fashion, replied, 'If you feel that way, perhaps it is.'[2]

Grieving and insecure as she was, Peggy might have put her gallery plans on hold; but she was urged on by her London friend and neighbour, Wyn Henderson. Wyn and her irrepressible pragmatism had been an essential support throughout the break-up with Douglas:

she had refused to indulge Peggy's fears of being alone, and encouraged her to embrace her sexual freedom. Yet she possessed a wealth of practical skills that were to prove more useful still. As a trained secretary and typographer, she had worked for Nancy Cunard when the latter was running a small literary press in France, and now she offered her services to Peggy. It was Wyn who found premises for the new gallery on Cork Street (already the centre of London's emerging modern art scene), and it was Wyn who managed the details of its launch – assembling the guest list, designing the invitations and publicity and overseeing the printing of the first catalogue. It was even Wyn who thought of calling the gallery Guggenheim Jeune – a name that acknowledged Peggy's family background, yet emphasized her own more youthful independence.

Peggy, of course, had to find the works to put inside the gallery, and initially her instincts had been to look backwards to the art of the past. During her years in Left Bank Paris she had drunk, dined and partied with some extraordinary artists, but she hadn't acquired a confident appreciation of their work. When a major exhibition of surrealist art had been held in London in 1936 she hadn't bothered to attend, despite the fact that it had created waves across the city, with even Harrods introducing surrealist themes into its window displays. Now, however, as Peggy made her first tentative sketch of a business plan, she rapidly grasped that classical art was far beyond her financial reach. Even with the additional $450,000 she'd inherited after Florette's death, she would need to adjust her sights downwards to the cheaper, less competitive market of contemporary art.

Her first guide to this market was a skinny experimental painter called Humphrey Jennings, 'a sort of genius who looked like Donald Duck'.[3] He was briefly Peggy's lover too, and although a disappointment to her in bed he was a galvanizing professional inspiration, proposing infectiously 'wild ideas' about the artists she should approach for her gallery and about the ways in which she could exhibit their work. Jennings was also well connected in the London art world and it was through him that Peggy met several of the key figures who would steer her early career: the eminent writer and historian Herbert Read, and the painter and collector Roland Penrose.

Peggy's choice of husbands and lovers might have turned out poorly so far, yet she showed good instincts in the men to whom she turned for expert help. With Jennings' ideas already stirring her imagination, she travelled to Paris to seek further advice from Marcel Duchamp. She knew Duchamp well enough to be able to ask him, very humbly, if he would explain the exact meanings of surrealism and abstraction to her, admitting that she had bluffed her way through art conversations for years without fully understanding how one genre differed from the other. More importantly, she knew that Duchamp would be wise and generous in brokering introductions to his circle of artist friends, and it was through him that she experienced her first epiphany as a lover of modern art. He had arranged for her to visit Jean Arp at his foundry in Malakoff to observe one of his sculptures being cast in bronze. Peggy, who had never witnessed a work being made, was awed by the mystery and charisma of this new-born presence: 'I fell so in love with it that I asked to have it in my hands. The instant I felt it I wanted to own it.' It was the start of an addiction that would define the rest of her life.[4]

Arp agreed to exhibit with Peggy in the spring of 1938, but for her inaugural show she had to aim for an artist like Jean Cocteau, who could guarantee her more publicity and more international éclat. Cocteau, at forty-eight, was now unassailably respected as the Renaissance man of the Parisian avant-garde: he was the witty iconoclast who had helped Serge Diaghilev to 'astonish' his ballet public; he was the writer of adult fairy tales, the artist of elegant, subversive erotica. Peggy appreciated the wisdom of Duchamp's advice, but she was slightly nervous of approaching Cocteau. Even though she had known him quite well in Paris – well enough to invite him to several of her parties and ask him to become unofficial godfather to Pegeen – he had always seemed to inhabit a more rarefied atmosphere than the rest of her circle. In 1937, when she was summoned to his hotel suite in the rue de Cambon, Peggy felt rather as though she'd been granted a royal audience.

During this first visit, Cocteau remained disconcertingly aloof; he'd been smoking opium, and as he lay on his bed his long brittle hands were so quietly folded, his narrow ivory face so composed, that Peggy was unsure if he was even listening to her. But at a second, more animated meeting Cocteau proved enthusiastically receptive to Peggy's proposal, and the works he offered her were ideal: a series of fine pen-and-ink drawings, some archly mannered theatre props, and a huge, political and profane work that was drawn in charcoal and pencil on two sewn-together bed sheets. *La peur donnant des ailes au courage* ('Fear Gives Wings to Courage') was Cocteau's gesture of support to the Republican cause in Spain, depicting a group of semi-naked lovers, bandaged and spattered with blood. It was the detail with which the genitalia and pubic hair had been rendered, and the rumour that it was Cocteau's own blood on one of the figures, that made this drawing the *succès de scandale* of Peggy's launch. Although it was deemed by the British censors to be too shocking for public view and had to be hung discreetly in Peggy's office, it brought a frisson of the illicit to the Guggenheim Jeune, establishing the gallery as a daring outpost of the continental avant-garde.* When Peggy held her launch party on 24 January 1938 (wearing a pair of dangling brass earrings created for her by the sculptor Alexander Calder), she and Wyn were able to drum up a promising crowd. And while some of the London critics hesitated over the merits of individual works in the show, no one quibbled over Cocteau's status as 'the leader and impresario of the moderns', nor over the scale of Peggy's coup in acquiring him for her gallery.[5]

Guggenheim Jeune was launched. Yet among the good wishes and congratulations that Peggy received, the message that pleased her the most was a brief telegram signed enigmatically, 'Oblomov'. It came from the writer Samuel Beckett, whom she'd recently met in Paris at a family dinner given by Helen Fleischman and Giorgio Joyce. Beckett's own literary fame had yet to flourish, but Peggy had sensed reserves of brilliance in this laconic young Irishman, tall and lanky in his ill-fitting suit. She was intrigued by the combination of arrogance and awkwardness in his manner, by the latent authority in his bespectacled, green gaze. After dinner Beckett walked Peggy back to her borrowed flat, and when he suggested that they might 'lie down' together on the sofa, she responded with alacrity. The sex was unexpectedly good; and although

---

* Peggy liked the piece so much she bought it herself, though eventually Pegeen would transform it into another kind of artwork entirely by scrawling telephone numbers on it in lipstick.

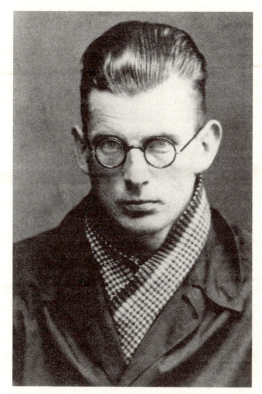

Samuel Beckett: 'Oblomov'.

Beckett's polite words of parting suggested it would not be repeated, when they met in the street a few days later Peggy convinced herself that the two of them were fated to become lovers.

The timing of this new affair could not have been more ironic. Peggy had only just been boasting to Emily that she felt more contented as a single woman than she'd ever been with Laurence, John or Douglas. '[T]o live without love & a man & to be happy is almost too good to be true,' she wrote; and she swore that from now on, sex would only be a 'sideshow'. She would never again allow herself to become emotionally and spiritually dependent on a man: '...everyone needs sex. It keeps one alive & loving & feminine...but now thank god I have my own inner strengths & my inner self to fall back on.'⁶ Yet with Beckett, Peggy's good intentions collapsed. After their accidental meeting they went back to her flat, where they spent most of the next twelve days together; and to her at least, that period felt like an 'ecstasy of physical and intellectual communion'. Several of Beckett's biographers have doubted that he reciprocated Peggy's enthusiasm, arguing that she was too much the rich American socialite to appeal to his fastidious intellect and his careful habits of emotional detachment. But the writer had a taste for rich, unconventional and sexually adventurous women. He'd already had one brief liaison with Nancy Cunard, and for those first twelve days at least he seems to have enjoyed Peggy too, attracted by her strong face and pretty Manhattan legs, by her idiosyncratic sense of humour, by her grand enthusiasms and by her willingness to pay for the quantities of expensive champagne they drank together in bed.

He was also flattered by Peggy's guileless admiration. Intellectual brilliance was as sexy to her as physical beauty, and when Beckett could be bothered to exert himself to lecture her on modern art and literature, Peggy listened with uncritical ardour. With equal spirit she tackled his published works, and even when she lost her way among the more experimental tropes and arcane metaphysics of his writing, she accepted them as proof of his genius. Yet it was Beckett's elusiveness as a lover that bound her most helplessly to him. During the weeks that followed, Peggy returned to Paris as often as she could. Beckett, however, would frequently fail to meet her as agreed, sometimes pleading mysterious business matters and sometimes simply evaporating out of sight. Peggy realized that he was seeing another woman;* yet his absences sprung from a deeper, more obdurate and irrational streak of reserve. If ever Beckett felt she was presuming too much on his affection, he would turn abruptly away from her, insisting the affair was over; if ever he dropped his guard sufficiently to say that he cared for her, he would retract his words soon afterwards, saying that he hadn't meant them, that he'd been drunk.

---

*   The musician Suzanne Déschevaux-Dumesnil, who would eventually become Beckett's wife.

Peggy knew herself well enough to understand the perversity of her attraction to Beckett, whom she'd nicknamed Oblomov after the chronically indecisive hero of Russian fiction. She accepted that his emotional slipperiness was key to his fascination: 'I went home with him [one night] thinking how much less I should really like him if I ever had him. In fact, as he took my arm...I thought "how boring".'[7] Yet even while Peggy understood that Beckett could never be hers, there were nights when the two of them were drunk together on champagne and walking through Paris in the early dawn, when she dreamed that she might have a real future with him as his mistress and muse. Wyn scolded Peggy for her romantic folly and warned that she was making herself as vulnerable to Beckett as she had to John Holms. Yet Peggy believed she had changed: she'd made herself take other lovers, and, more crucially, she was too bound up with the running of Guggenheim Jeune to obsess too hopelessly over her absent Oblomov. Following the Cocteau launch she'd arranged an ambitious schedule of exhibitions: a solo Kandinsky show (the painter's first in London); a group showing of contemporary sculpture, with works by Constantin Brancusi, Jean Arp, Alexander Calder and Henry Moore; also one-man exhibitions for the Dutch painter Geer van Velde (whom Beckett recommended) and the surrealist Yves Tanguy. Peggy was ambitious, too, about the themes and ideas she worked into her programme, and over the next eighteen months she mounted a pioneering exhibition of children's art (featuring works by Pegeen and a very young Lucian Freud) as well as a one-woman show for the portrait photographer Gisèle Freund, making Guggenheim Jeune one of the first galleries to promote photography as art.

If Peggy was too busy to pine for Beckett, she was also armoured by a new public poise. Her gallery was gaining a reputation as one of London's most interesting showcases of modern art, its regular clientele drawn from members of the general public as well as from the world of students, critics and dealers. Peggy felt herself to be successful, useful and admired in ways she'd never experienced, and she recognized the progress she'd made when she had her first professional clash with her uncle Solomon and with the might of his New York collection. During the Kandinsky exhibition she'd offered to sell him a painting that she knew he'd particularly wanted; but the response that

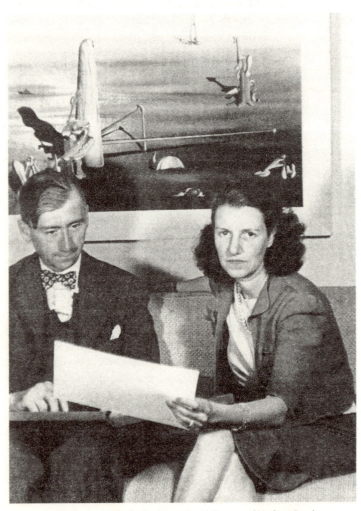

'I blush now to think of our innocence': Peggy and Herbert Read
planning the ambitious launch of their Museum of Modern Art.
Tanguy's *Le soleil dans son écrin* hangs in the background.

came via his mistress and adviser, Baroness Hilla Rebay, could not have been more offensive. Solomon was currently in the process of founding a new public art museum (which he would call the Museum of Non-Objective Painting), and Rebay scoffed at the idea that he and his 'great philanthropic' enterprise could ever stoop to deal with 'some small shop' like Peggy's. She went so far as to denounce Peggy's impudence in attaching the Guggenheim name to her own commercial gallery, and to accuse her of trading in 'mediocrity, if not trash'. Given Peggy's complex about being the poor relation, this letter might once have crushed her. Now, however, she was able to respond with a clear, calm confidence, assuring Solomon and Rebay that despite the modest scale of her gallery she was dealing with some of Europe's finest living artists and was able to offer their work a public space and public prominence in London that they had previously lacked.[8]

* * * * *

Perhaps it was Peggy's first romance with a serious painter that made her feel she truly belonged to the world of art. In July 1938, Yves Tanguy arrived in London to oversee the hanging of his debut exhibition at Guggenheim Jeune. Peggy found his work both transfixing and terrifying; his remote lunar landscapes with their atmosphere of alien menace seemed uncannily evocative of her own dream life, and the two works she bought from him (including *Le soleil dans son ecrin*) formed the core of her early collection. But she was equally captivated by Tanguy himself, a man so eccentrically enthusiastic that the tufts of his fine blond hair seemed to bristle around his head with static electricity. The novelty of falling in love with both a painter and his work was a heady experience, and having seduced Yves in London (while Wyn distracted his wife), Peggy trailed shamelessly after him when he returned to Paris. The affair continued through secret and not-so-secret liaisons on both sides of the Channel, and for a brief period of madness Peggy actually believed that she and Yves might marry.

Yet her experience with Beckett had been salutary, and even though she was infatuated with Yves, even though she was willing to fight for him against his righteously angry wife, Peggy retained a saving commitment to her vow of spiritual independence. She still wanted to prove she was capable of having 'little affairs...without hysterics', and she defended herself against Yves with other lovers (Roland Penrose, and the English painter Julian Trevelyan) and with the absorbing daily business of running her gallery. In many respects, Peggy's life was as steady as it had ever been. In 1937 Kay and Laurence had bought a chalet in Megève, a ski resort in the French Alps; Pegeen and Sindbad were now spending regular holidays there, along with their three half-sisters Apple, Kathe and Clover, and stepsister Bobby. The children's lives were settled, if not happy; Pegeen had started boarding school and finally appeared to be adjusting to its routines, while Sindbad at Bedales had discovered cricket, which was to become his lifelong passion.

So immersed was Peggy in balancing her life, and balancing her books at the gallery, that she was entirely unprepared for the political crisis of August 1938, when Europe drew close to war. For years Churchill and his allies had been warning of Hitler's military ambitions, and Peggy's left-wing friends had been prophesying a fascist Armageddon, yet she herself had been paying little attention. Now when German forces invaded Czechoslovakia and British forces were put on high alert, she was suddenly frantic with dread. 'I have never been more scared in my life,' she wrote later, and in a state of panic she made hurried arrangements for her small but already precious collection of art to be transported down to Yew Tree Cottage and begged Djuna, who was currently living in Ireland, to have the two children come and stay with her.[9]

The threat of war receded after Neville Chamberlain returned from Munich, waving his promise of peace, but Peggy had been shaken by this vision of how rapidly life might change; and it may have been this new sense of precariousness that galvanized her to scheme, professionally, for bigger and bolder things. After barely a year of running the Guggenheim Jeune Peggy was growing impatient with the gallery's limitations: it was operating at a loss despite its critical and public acclaim, and she was inclined to think that if she were going to lose money on art she might as well do so in style. Rather than continuing to struggle in the commercial market, she decided she would emulate her uncle Solomon; she would pin her name and her money to a public collection, and she would found London's first Museum of Modern Art.

There was a self-aggrandizing motive to Peggy's plan; an attempt to prove herself the equal of her Guggenheim relatives, to carve herself a position of power. Yet there was an element of selflessness, too, for Peggy had formed a deep attachment to the London art world and she felt she'd already made a significant contribution through her little gallery. Continuing that work on a much larger scale seemed to her a worthy vocation, and in a mood of exhilarating piety she vowed to dedicate all her available money to planning the new museum and to eradicate all unnecessary luxuries from her life.

Peggy knew that this project was too enormous to manage by herself, and she had her eye on the admirable, scholarly Herbert Read to take on the role of director. It had long been Read's own dream to see a modern art museum in London, an institution that could challenge the prevailing insularity of the British scene, although for him it felt like a greater risk. Working for Peggy would mean resigning his job as editor of the *Burlington Magazine*, and, as he wrote to a friend, he wasn't entirely convinced by her plan: 'The thing bristles with snags.'[10] Even though Peggy had enough capital to pay for the museum's running costs, which she'd estimated at $40,000 per year, she had no money left to purchase works for its collection, which would have to be begged or borrowed by Read and herself. She also had no experience of running an institution, and when Read asked around about Peggy's credentials as a patron and partner he was slightly perturbed by Emma Goldman's enigmatic assessment that she was perhaps '*allzu-menschlich* – all too human'.

But others were more encouraging – the poet T. S. Eliot judged Peggy to be perfectly 'serious'; and once Read allowed himself to yield to the project's temptations the two of them began zealously to plan for a late autumn launch. A few years later, however, Peggy would blush to recall their 'innocence'.[11] She and Read passed happy disputative hours debating the wishlist of works they wanted to show, arguing whether some very early paintings by Cézanne and Matisse could be included (Read loved them; Peggy didn't consider them sufficiently modern). But they had enormous practical problems still facing them in securing additional financing for the museum, and even suitable premises for it. Even more recklessly, neither of them was acknowledging the fact that despite Chamberlain's assurances the previous summer, the menace of war had returned.

It was typical of their mutually complicit optimism that when Kenneth Clark (then director of the National Gallery) came to Read and Peggy with the offer of his huge town house in Portland Place they congratulated themselves on their luck in securing so ideal a location for the museum, rather than worrying about why it had become vacant. Clark, far more attuned to the political tensions in Europe, was sufficiently convinced of the likelihood of war that he'd already moved his wife and children out of London, to the safety of his country estate. Yet even as the summer advanced, as precautionary barrage balloons began to float over Hyde Park and gas masks were distributed, the gravity of the situation remained unreal to Peggy. She was planning to go to New York in the early autumn to discuss the loan of some artworks, but she wanted to spend August in France to see her children in Megève and to scout out possible artists and patrons for the museum.

* * * * *

Peggy felt she was owed a holiday. She'd been working close to the edge of exhaustion as she'd wound down her business affairs at Guggenheim Jeune and begun plotting the new museum; but she'd also recently undergone an abortion, the result of her brief affair with Julian Trevelyan, and while she later claimed to have had no less than seven terminations during her life, this one had left her both physically and emotionally weak. Now, as she packed up her new car (a small, functional Talbot that she'd bought in place of her cherished but now unaffordably expensive Delage), she was determined to make up for wasted time. A new friend, Nelly van Doesburg (widow of the Dutch artist Theo van Doesburg) was to be her companion. Small and chic, a former dancer and self-styled Dadaist, Nelly had a game spirit of enthusiasm. And as Peggy wrote to Emily – a little pointedly – she expected their travels together to be fun: 'She is very gay & alive & her life goes on very full & *active* in every sense of the word.'[12]

After Peggy had picked Nelly up from Paris, the two women motored east to the French Alps, close to where Sindbad and Pegeen were summering. Peggy had never yet risked a visit to Megève, fearing that she would find the children too happily ensconced in their alternate family life, and too fond of Kay – against whom she continued to harbour a bitter rivalry. Yet buoyed up by Nelly's energy, she'd survived the encounter, and her spirits were high when they set off in pursuit of adventures and art.

Their eventual destination was a mountain retreat on the Swiss border, where the artist Gordon Onslow Ford was entertaining Yves Tanguy and a group of fellow surrealists. Peggy was looking forward to seeing her former lover; she had vague hopes of resurrecting their affair, and she had definite plans for showing his work in London. But before going to Ford's retreat her first destination was Grasse, where she had arranged to stay with an American businessman who might be a potential sponsor for the museum. And it was here, in the dry, beautiful southern heat of Provence, that Peggy heard over her host's radio that Hitler had invaded Poland, and that Europe was again at war.

Curiously, Peggy was less terrified now than she had been over the Munich crisis. She and Nelly had been having a distractingly pleasant time, eating and drinking well, meeting new people and visiting Peggy's old Riviera haunts. In the drowse of the late Mediterranean summer it was difficult to believe the world was in danger: the soldiers who'd begun mobilizing in the area looked reassuringly amateurish, and their American host was bullishly insistent that the crisis was just another round of sabre-rattling that the politicians would resolve. Of course, Peggy had alarming issues to confront – what to do about the London museum, where best to send the children should this war prove dangerous. Yet she could not feel the urgency of her situation, and even when she drove back to Paris with Nelly and discovered the city already in a state of panic, she remained calmly optimistic.

Many of her closest friends were already departing for America – Peggy had paid for some of their tickets – and the most sensible plan was for her and the children to go too. When she went to the Gare d'Austerlitz to say her goodbyes to Yves and Djuna, she found the station 'almost in darkness' with 'a terrible tension in the air'; yet she felt like an observer, detached from the agitation around her. 'I did not have the slightest desire to leave and was not in the least afraid.'[15] Her stoicism was partly influenced by Laurence, who'd convinced her that Paris (and certainly Megève) would remain safe for the time being: but her unwillingness to leave was also strengthened by her loyalty to Europe. Peggy no longer regarded herself as an American, and she did not want to have to return to New York. Staying in France also meant she could remain close to the art world she loved: and having agreed with a reluctant Read that they must suspend their plans for London, she was determined now to divert her money and energy into the planning of alternative projects.

Peggy's first, romantic plan was to create a wartime artists' colony in France; a remote chateau in the south where lodging, studio space and sanctuary could be given to a select community of painters and sculptors. Disappointingly, there were few takers for the scheme – as she discovered, artists were generally too egotistical to manage a civil meal together, let alone co-exist as a commune. But if Peggy couldn't rescue artists from the war, she could still rescue art, and late in 1939 she made the decision to remain in Paris for as long as it was safe from German attack and to dedicate herself to the simple but grandstanding mission of buying up 'one picture a day'.

It was, she discovered, exhilaratingly easy. Art prices had begun tumbling around her, and the abstract, surrealist works in which she was most interested were especially cheap. In 1937 Hitler had made it clear that the Reich had no place for 'degenerate' art, and had taken punitive action against all Germans associated with the European avant-garde. Now, as France began to contemplate the awful possibility of an enemy invasion, many of the artists and dealers in Paris felt particularly threatened. During the winter of 1939–40 large numbers of them were leaving the city, selling off whatever works they could not get safely into storage. The market was going into freefall, and for Peggy and her disposable dollars there were astoundingly rich pickings.

Early in 1940 she moved into a borrowed apartment on the Ile Saint-Louis, a charming attic space with views over Notre Dame and a silver-lined bedroom where watery reflections from the river Seine played gracefully over her ceiling. From here Peggy set out every day in pursuit of her mission; trekking around the studios and galleries; approaching all the artists whom she knew, but also taking advice from an American collector, Howard Putzel. Putzel, a 'big fat blond' with a disabling stammer and a near-religious dedication to art, had contacted Peggy during the early days of the Guggenheim Jeune, expressing fulsome admiration for her achievements there. In Paris he was eager to put himself at her disposal; yet much of the time she had no need of his assistance. In fact, she barely had to exert herself: 'Everyone knew that I was in the market for anything I could lay my hands on. They chased after me and came to my house with pictures. They even brought them to me in bed, in the morning before I was up.'[14] Although Peggy didn't quite manage a picture a day during her six months of intensive shopping, she did acquire around 150 works, many of which were treasures. She measured the progress of the war not by the movement of armies or the forging of alliances but by the accumulation of what she was now calling her 'war babies'; pieces by Dalí, Klee, Pacabia, Miró, Tanguy, Kandinsky, Braque, Ernst, Mondrian, Giacometti and Man Ray. On 9 April 1940, when Hitler invaded Norway and shattered the unreal calm of the phony war, the day was made memorable for Peggy both by the beautiful Léger she secured for $1,000 and by her discovery of a large vacant apartment in the Place Vendôme where she might put her rapidly expanding collection on display.

One of the few artists who tried to stand his ground against Peggy's frenzy of consumption was Constantin Brancusi. For a short time in Paris he'd been her lover, and Peggy had been hoping for generous terms when she went to his studio to buy one of the works he'd made in the series *Bird in Space*. The bronze was an exquisite piece, its slender, curving lines miraculously conveying both gravity and flight, and the tiny Romanian sculptor was fully aware of its worth: he demanded $4,000 for it, over $1,000 more than Peggy had budgeted. She raged at his mulishness, insisting that no one in wartime would pay such a sum, but Brancusi refused to budge. It was only by getting him to accept payment in francs – a currency so devalued that Peggy could claw back $1,000 profit on exchange – that she was able to finalize the sale.

Later Peggy gloated over her cleverness, and she truly believed that all her bartering and badgering was justified; allowing her to save the maximum amount of art from German bombs and German vandalism. It is true that without her hard-headed negotiations, masterpieces like *Bird in Space*, Dalí's *The Birth of Liquid Desires* or Léger's *Men in the City*

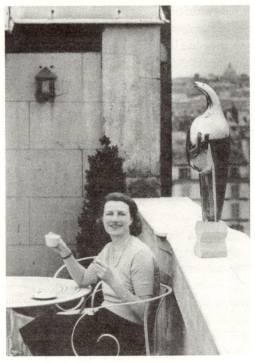

Peggy on the balcony of her Ile Saint-Louis
apartment with one of her wartime spoils,
Brancusi's *Maiastra* (1912).

might conceivably have been lost. Yet in her enthusiasm for the bargain, in her thrill at the chase, Peggy could be bluntly insensitive to the feelings of the artists themselves as they shut up their studios and sold off their work. On the day that she collected *Bird in Space* from Brancusi's studio, the news bulletins were particularly dire: German forces were advancing through Northern France, the outskirts of Paris were being bombed and the French government was contemplating surrender. Brancusi, who was making his final preparations to leave, wept openly as the bronze was packaged up for transport. Yet even though Peggy was touched by his grief, she was unable to understand its depths. Assuming that he was simply mourning the loss of a beloved piece, she failed to grasp that Brancusi might also be mourning the loss of Paris, and of the culture in which he had lived and worked for nearly forty years.

It was a failure in Peggy's character, this lack of emotional perception; but in Paris in 1940, she genuinely failed to accept the gravity of the wider situation. So engrossed had she become in her hunt for art that she had managed to shut out most of the war news, and even when she was forced to confront the possibility of Paris falling to the Germans, her immediate thoughts were not for her own safety, only for her collection. She'd originally assumed that she could hide her war babies away in the cellars of the new apartment she'd found in the Place Vendôme. But as the enemy planes circled closer the cellar had been commandeered for use as an air raid shelter, and Peggy was left to scrabble for other solutions. Léger suggested that the Louvre might take care of her collection, but the museum turned Peggy down on the grounds that it was too modern and 'not worth saving' (a rebuff she would later take pleasure in deriding). In the end she contacted her friend Maria Jolas, who'd run the bilingual school that Pegeen had attended, and who had recently evacuated her staff and pupils to a rural chateau near Vichy. With free space in one of her barns, Maria was willing to give temporary shelter to Peggy's art, as long as she could find some way of transporting it there.

As Peggy tried to secure a lorry, a driver and sufficient fuel for the journey, she received few offers of help from her remaining friends in Paris. The city was filling up with refugees, crowds of the homeless, hungry and wounded who had been fleeing the German advance through Northern Europe and were now in desperate need of help. Mary Reynolds was working tirelessly among them, and she was scathing about Peggy's continuing obsession with her art. It was 'indecent', Mary believed, to be spending money on paintings rather than people at this time, and during one ferocious argument she accused Peggy of being so lost to humanity that she would think nothing of mowing down a refugee or two, as long as the *camion* transporting her collection made it safely out of Paris.[15]

Peggy wept in mortification and later, in her memoir, she acknowledged how 'idiotic' she'd been, how oblivious to the suffering around her. She admitted that she had been blinkered by her art addiction, but she acknowledged too that she'd been blinkered by happiness because, perversely, these last six months in Paris had been one of the most contented periods of her life. She had been very sociable, throwing dinners at the Ile Saint-Louis flat and relishing the gay, careless camaraderie that had grown up among the remaining community of foreigners. She'd also started an affair, with an American called Bill Whidney who used to steal afternoons away from his invalid wife and drink champagne with her. Hypnotized by good sex, drink and the sheer unreality of her situation, it was only when the fall of Paris became shockingly imminent at the beginning of June that Peggy was forced out of her inertia.

Her plan had always been to join Laurence and the children near Megève if Paris was in danger, and she had at least had the foresight to store up sufficient petrol for the 600-kilometre drive. Yet her other preparations had been minimal. She had stupidly allowed her travel permit to expire – a minor infringement of the law that could suddenly turn perilous if she were stopped en route by German soldiers. She had also failed to consider that huge numbers of people (an estimated two million) would be fleeing the city alongside her. By the time Peggy had picked up Nelly, whom she had promised to take along with her, and packed up the Talbot with her two Persian cats and most precious belongings, it was 9 June. Just five days later the Nazis would be jackbooting their triumphal march down the Champs-Elysées, and even now the invasion was so close that all routes out of Paris were jammed. When Peggy manoeuvred her little Talbot onto the road heading south, it was touch and go whether they would even manage to leave the city, the road was so choked with every kind of motor vehicle, with horse-drawn carts, bicycles, even pedestrians pushing wheelbarrows and prams. As the Talbot crawled slowly forward Peggy had to navigate around broken-down cars, dead or exhausted animals; on sections of the route the air was noxious with thick black smoke, evidence of the German machine-gun fire that earlier in the day had been strafing this desperate, slow-moving column of humanity.

But while most were heading south, Peggy and Nelly were travelling east, and eventually they arrived at Megève, exhausted but unhurt. Peggy found a house to rent on the shore of Lake Annecy, which would allow her to keep a tactful distance from Kay and Laurence while still being close to the children; and for a short while she was high on the adrenalin of escape and the relief of being reunited with her family. Yet in Paris she had become used to a life of busy purpose, and exile bored her. She embarked on a couple of half-hearted affairs to fill the time, and took a meddlesome interest in the romances Pegeen and Sindbad were forming with the teenage son and daughter of a neighbouring family. Peggy believed in being open about sex, quizzing the children bluntly about the extent of their experiences and making little effort to conceal her own. Yet while she believed she was liberating Pegeen and Sindbad from the repressions she had suffered as a girl, she was often crassly insensitive to their adolescent sensibilities. When Peggy was finally able to get her collection driven from Vichy down to Grenoble, a manageable 100 kilometres south of Lake Annecy, it was a relief not only to her but to everyone else that she had a serious project on which to focus her frustrated energies.

The Musée de Grenoble had offered Peggy storage space, and in the autumn she moved down to the city, ready to begin the complicated process of cataloguing her art and getting it shipped out to America. The next few months were enjoyably productive as Peggy photographed all of the 150 works in the collection and typed up the details of their titles, artists and provenance. They were made additionally pleasurable by the arrival of René Lefebvre-Foinet, a partner in the shipping business she'd used for Guggenheim Jeune. René provided her with astute advice about the transportation of her artworks – his suggestion that Peggy should crate them up with some 'essential household goods' meant she was able to secure space on one of the vanishingly few cargo crossings to America. But he was also a very attractive man, and in Grenoble, just as in Paris, Peggy was able to blur the pleasures of art and the pleasures of sex into a sweet state of denial. For a few more months she could remain oblivious to the realities of war.

By the end of 1940, however, it was obvious even to Peggy that it was time for her and her family to make their plan of escape. The Germans were threatening to extend their zone of occupation south and east and the Vichy government, which had been set up to govern the rest of country, was clearly no more than a puppet regime. With

Nazi policies coming into force across France, French Jews were now being targeted in non-occupied zones, and even for a Jewish foreigner like Peggy there could be no guarantee of immunity.

The family's best option was to fly back to New York on one of the Pan Am Clippers that still ran civilian passages out of Lisbon, and Laurence and Kay had already begun to investigate the chances of getting tickets. But the logistics of this plan were alarming. They would be a large party: three adults, six children and the teenage daughter of a family friend, Jacqueline Vendatour, whom Peggy had promised to take care of. She herself would be paying for nine of the ten tickets (which were $550 apiece), but while she had the money in her account, it was difficult for her to access because the flow of cash was now being strictly regulated. She would have to make special applications to the Banque de France both to withdraw the money from her account and to get the sum for each ticket registered on their individual passports. Extra cash would also be needed to fund the journey across France, through Spain and into Portugal, and to secure travel permits for both Peggy and Laurence, whose visa had also expired. A year ago these might have been harassing details only, but now that borders and banks were being so strictly policed Peggy was facing a daunting task. It was just now dawning on her, too, that in order to acquire the necessary papers and cash in time, she would have to deal with the gangster-run world of the black market.

This world operated largely out of Marseille, and Peggy had her first glimpse of its frightening lawlessness when she went to the city in the early spring of 1941. Her business there was to set in motion her own travel plans, but she was also acting on a request to help the Emergency Rescue Committee, an American volunteer organization that had been founded early on in the war by classics scholar Varian Fry. It was dedicated to getting endangered artists, intellectuals and Jews out of France before they could be incarcerated by the Vichy government or handed over to the Germans, and it was always urgently in need of funds. Peggy had been specifically asked to assist the escape of two of the Committee's most distinguished clients, the French surrealist poet and activist André Breton and the German surrealist painter Max Ernst. Although she had been slow to react to the plight of refugees while in Paris, now her imagination leaped at the chance of becoming saviour to Breton and Ernst – especially if she could also seize the opportunity to buy some of the latter's work.

Fry and his committee were running daily risks with their operations. All of them were known to the Gestapo, all were under surveillance by the Vichy police, and they were also having to deal with some of Marseille's most hardened criminals as they obtained counterfeit passports, exit visas and black-market currency for their clients. When Peggy first arrived in the city and had to do business with its gangs – both on her own and on the Committee's behalf – it was for her almost the greatest shock of the war: 'Living in Grenoble and thinking only about art I was completely unconscious of the underground and had no idea what all this was about....Later I got used to it, but in the beginning I was terrified.'[16] As she became acclimatized to this world of violent, shadowy transactions, however, Peggy also began to experience a frisson of wartime glamour. Fry's Committee was run from a semi-dilapidated chateau just outside Marseille, and when she visited it was sheltering a number of prominent surrealists. Painting and writing by day, playing games of Truth and Free Association by night, they had brought an atmosphere of festive anarchy to the chateau – André Breton had famously decorated the dinner table one evening with a vase of praying mantises. Visiting the chateau, Peggy felt embraced by a common cause; and although she spoke little about her experiences afterwards, she did some invaluable work in Marseille, donating at least 500,000 francs to the Committee and exposing herself to some degree of jeopardy as she helped with the paperwork for refugee artists.*

It was Max Ernst, though, who dominated Peggy's interest when she returned for a second time to Marseille. She'd met the painter two years earlier and had already half-fallen in love with his fine, fierce handsomeness and with the unsettling mysteries of his art. Since then Ernst had spent two periods in prison (incarcerated first by the French as a

---

* As well as receiving financial support from private individuals like Peggy, Fry had help from an American diplomat who, defying the official US policy of limiting the number of incoming refugees, was issuing as many extra visas as he could get away with. By the time it was forcibly closed down, the ERC had rescued at least 2,000 Jews, communists, artists and other 'undesirables'.

German spy, then briefly by the Germans as a 'degenerate'), and at first Peggy thought his sufferings had left him looking 'much older' than his fifty years, his hair even whiter, his face gaunt. Yet as Max showed her around the impromptu exhibition of paintings he'd mounted at the chateau, the twin aphrodisiacs of art and fame did their work. To Peggy he now 'looked very romantic, wrapped in a black cape', and when he asked if he might see her again she made her own interest very clear, replying bluntly, 'Tomorrow at four in the Café de la Paix and you know why.'[17]

To Max, such directness was sexy and stimulating, especially after the recent and bruising dissolution of his marriage to the artist Leonora Carrington (who had suffered a breakdown while he'd been interned). His admiration burnished Peggy's confidence, and the ten days they spent together in Marseille felt like a delightful interlude to her, one of the most successful of her 'little affairs'. When the time came for her to spend Easter with the children in Megève, it was Max who wept a little as he put her on the train.

Yet Peggy's emotions worked by their own masochistic logic. Before she'd parted from Max he had promised to try and visit her in Megève, and as the days passed without any message her 'complexes' flared. She began to torment herself with the possibility that Max no longer wanted her, that he was even now comparing her unfavourably with his former wife, who was both exotically beautiful and artistically talented. As so often with Peggy, the more insecure she felt about a man, the more she desired him. And when she returned to Marseille with her family two weeks later to make final preparations for their exodus to New York, Peggy was not only determined that Max would be travelling alongside her; she was already working out how to include him permanently in her life.

*****

It would be a long, tense month, however, before she and her party were able to leave. Peggy had to secure the last tranche of money to pay for their tickets, and organize an emergency exit permit for Max. But her anxieties were also focused on Max himself, whom she was now finding difficult to read. As a lover he was stimulating in bed, capable of the occasional gallant flourish; yet his manner towards her remained oddly formal, even remote, and Peggy was nagged by miserable thoughts of Leonora. Marseille was also darkened for her by the presence of Laurence and Kay, who were barely speaking to each other now except when they were fighting. Their marriage had been disintegrating over the last few years as Kay had become worn down by Laurence's drinking and his temper, and irked by what she regarded as his spineless politics – he'd remained infuriatingly impassive to the rise of fascism in Europe. The breaking point had arrived in the person of a left-wing Austrian, exiled by Hitler just before the war, who'd come to Megève to tutor the children. Kay had fallen in love with the Austrian's politics, his suffering and his romantic aristocratic heritage, and was now talking openly of divorce.

Laurence was maddened by Kay's betrayal, and made angrier still once she began angling for her lover to join their escape party. When the four adults met for dinner one night with Marcel Duchamp, Mary Reynolds and René Lefebvre-Foinet, who'd all recently arrived in Marseille, it was destined to turn out badly.

They were eating in a black-market restaurant where a decent meal could still be had at great expense, but no one was in a mood to appreciate the menu. René was smarting from Peggy's defection to Max, while the habitually serene Marcel was quietly enraged by Mary, who had become so committed to helping the Resistance in Paris that she was refusing to go back to America with him. The tension mounted when Kay, angered by Peggy's support for Laurence in the arguments over her lover, vengefully announced that she'd heard the ship transporting Peggy's art collection had been reported missing, sunk somewhere in the middle of the Atlantic. She and Laurence then had a 'terrible row' over Kay's failure to help him pack up the house in Megève, and the night ended in one of the most spectacular, crockery-smashing displays of Laurence's career.

Marcel and René were barely able to restrain Laurence, who seemed bent on killing Kay and destroying the entire restaurant; and while Peggy would later write about the incident with a frivolous bravado, it was a hazardous moment for them all. If the police had been called to investigate the scene, their plans and their identities could have been exposed. Max could have faced re-internment and Peggy too was at special risk, both because of her illegal dealings with the black market and because she was so vulnerable now as a Jew. Threats of imprisonment and deportation had spread to the non-occupied zones, and Peggy had already come close to arrest one morning when a plainclothes detective arrived at the hotel to question her. Suspicions had been aroused by her surname (even though Max had instructed Peggy to insist that 'Guggenheim' was Swiss) and the detective was demanding to search her room for any evidence that might point to her being Jewish. When none could be found he began questioning her over her expired travel permit, on which she'd recklessly forged a new date. Peggy pretended that the forgery was the clumsy penmanship of an incompetent official, but it was only the intervention of a more senior officer, who was more inclined to defer to the rights of a rich American, that saved her from being taken down to the police station for interrogation.

Although Peggy tried to brush off the incident, it was a measure of how risky their situation was growing. When everything was finally in place for them to leave Marseille, they had to travel in small groups to avoid drawing attention to themselves. Max went first, with as many rolled-up paintings as he could carry in his suitcase; Laurence, Kay and the children followed; and Peggy, with Jacqueline Vendatour in her care, was last. Nothing could be counted on, despite the long, careful weeks of preparation. Max was almost turned back at the French border, and even when they were all reunited in Lisbon they faced another ominous setback: their flight to America had been overbooked, and no one could inform them when more seats would be available.

By now everybody was exhausted, jumpy and quarrelsome. Laurence and Kay were fighting their way towards an irreconcilable separation and in turn creating real grief for Pegeen, who had come to love Kay and was afraid of losing her. Jacqueline, meanwhile, had fallen mopily in love with Sindbad, who was himself floundering in teenage guilt over the girlfriend he'd left behind in Lake Annecy. Peggy found her family's emotional dramas exasperating, but Lisbon was made even more wretched for her by the appearance of Leonora Carrington. As soon as Peggy was told of her arrival by Max and saw the stiff, guilty expression on his face, she suspected the worst. Leonora was travelling with a Mexican journalist whom she was planning to marry in order to secure a US visa, but it was clear to Peggy that Max was deeply moved and disturbed by the presence of his ex-wife.

During the seven weeks they spent stranded in Lisbon, Peggy had to listen to Max debate endlessly with himself about whether or not he should try to resurrect his marriage. She had to endure the tormenting proximity of Leonora's beauty, the 'alabaster' skin and 'enormous mad dark eyes' that made Peggy herself feel homely and dull. 'We used to sit for hours in the little English café overlooking the sea wondering if we would ever leave,' she recalled;[18] and at one point she felt so hopeless about Max, so pessimistic about their chances of getting to New York, that she fantasized about leaving her family behind and making her own way alone to London.

By 13 July, when the party was finally able to board their Pan Am Clipper, they were far too miserable to appreciate the luxuries of the flight. The Clipper line had been developed just before the war to provide the most advanced comforts of commercial air travel, and even now passengers were provided with hotel-prepared meals in a dining area, an elegant saloon and individual sleeping berths. To Peggy and the others, however, the two-day flight was yet another ordeal. They were terrified during the take-off, when the boxy sea plane bounced so violently that it became temporarily submerged under waves and spray; they suffered from the plane's turbulence, which made the children sick; and Peggy, who dreaded the boredom and confinement of the flight, tried to get drunk as fast as possible on tumblers of whisky. They would have had far greater cause for worry had they known that on its return journey this same plane would crash, and none of its passengers would survive. Yet even in their enervated state, as the Clipper soared into clear blue sky and as the smoke and rubble of Europe receded, Peggy and her party could recognize that they'd been granted the most privileged of lucky escapes.

CHAPTER 11

As London burned, as German-occupied Paris learned to accommodate, resist or somehow survive, Peggy's other favourite city was enduring a less traumatic war. Both sides in the conflict had agreed that historic Venice was too irreplaceable to be bombed and although some of the outer industrialized areas came under heavy bombardment and blackout had to be enforced, it was one of the few major European cities not to be evacuated or boarded up. Most of its immediate war casualties were the two hundred or so people who had lost their bearings during lampless nights and had fallen into one of the canals. But Venice was changed, and Peggy would have mourned to see how the pageantry had gone from San Marco; how most of the gondolas were put into dry dock; how the city's pigeon and cat population had dwindled as hungry Venetians sought to supplement their rations. From 1943, when the Germans occupied Venice, there were swastikas hanging from public buildings, and fear and acrimony spread through the city as the last of the Jewish community who'd survived Mussolini were rounded up for deportation.

Venice also became a city of soldiers as it was taken over first by the mobilizing Italian army, then by the Germans, and finally by the liberating Allies. The Palazzo Venier was commandeered as a military billet by each, and suffered progressively worse vandalization and neglect. Camp beds filled the rooms where Doris Castlerosse and her guests had recently slept, dirty boots muddied and scraped the marble floors, the stucco grew chipped and filthy, graffiti was scribbled onto the walls, and the planted, paved garden was trampled to mud. Doris knew none of this, sunk as she was in her own wartime troubles; it would be for Peggy to discover when she bought the Palazzo in 1949 and made Venice her home.

Eight years earlier, as she returned to her native New York (and as Doris was making her own desperate efforts to go home to England),

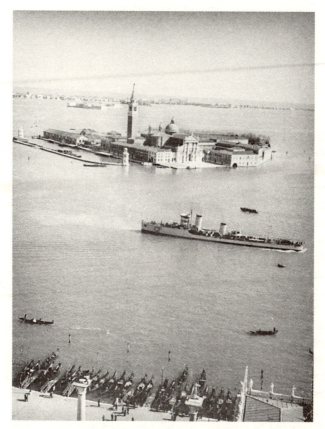

Venice shuts down for war (c. 1940).

Peggy had very different priorities to deal with. The most pressing of these was Max. His fame had preceded him, and a crush of journalists was waiting at the Marine Terminal of LaGuardia airport to photograph the travellers and ask 'a million stupid questions'.[1] Also waiting were the immigration officials – like all arriving refugees, Max had to be taken into custody while his papers were processed. Peggy suffered through an anxious three-day wait while he was removed to Ellis Island to have his right to American entry confirmed. But it was when he was delivered back to her that she had more private cause for worry: for while she had got Max safely to America, she had yet to find out whether he actually wanted to remain with her.

Max had never yet said that he loved her; he did not even use the intimate 'tu' when they spoke together in French; and the stress of the last two months had inevitably taken some of the sexual bloom off their affair. Even now, Leonora was on her way to New York, the Pan Am Clipper having actually flown over the ship on which she was sailing. And Peggy was made painfully conscious of her own uncertain standing with Max when, on his release from Ellis Island, he was whisked off by New York friends and admirers for celebrations at the Belmont Plaza Hotel. So large was the crush of well-wishers around him that he allowed himself to be driven off to the party without Peggy, and as one observer noted, she was left standing alone on the pavement, 'trying to maintain her poise at this insensitive slight with rapid intakes of breath'.[2]

'I always felt that when I would no longer be useful to Max he would have no further use for me,' Peggy acknowledged, and she was determined to prove herself indispensable.[3] Playing to Max's vanity, she bought him a new 'American trousseau' that flattered his spare frame; and she presented him with a diamond and platinum *lorgnon* she'd inherited from her mother, which gave him, she fancied, the look of an English aristocrat. Assiduously she showed him around the art collections of New York, translating for him as they went; and she exercised untypical tact and patience in helping him deal with the awkwardness of his reunion with his twenty-one-year-old son Jimmy, who was now living in New York. Jimmy was the product of his first marriage, and the two hadn't seen each other since Max abandoned his son when he was just two years old. Inevitably their first meetings were stilted: Jimmy wanted to get to know his father, but Max's English was sketchy and Jimmy had little French; so it was Peggy who translated during their first prickly encounters, and Peggy who tried to include Jimmy in their new American life. She liked Jimmy very much – he was far more interested in art than her own son, and far more independent than either Sindbad or Pegeen. He was currently working in the mailroom at the Museum of Modern Art, and when Peggy began to attend to the task of getting her collection through American customs and into storage she hired him as her secretary, paying him almost double what he'd previously earned.

She felt, proudly, that she was becoming 'a sort of stepmother' to Jimmy, and he in turn became fondly protective of her. He was a sensitive man, and claimed that even at their first meeting he'd spotted the flicker of neediness in Peggy's 'anxiety-ridden eyes'; he'd sensed that there 'was something about her that wanted me to reach out to her even before she spoke'.[4] As he observed Peggy's relationship with his father, he became troubled at the sliver of icy detachment in Max's manner, and he grew even more concerned when Leonora arrived in New York. Although Max now assured Peggy that his relationship with Leonora would remain platonic, his behaviour suggested otherwise; he spent hours in his ex-wife's company and relaxed into a warmth and spontaneity with her that he rarely permitted himself with Peggy. When he started painting again in New York, it was Leonora's face and wounded charm that seemed to inspire the dreamlike women in his work, and a cowed, unhappy Peggy had to acknowledge that if Max had a muse, it was still his former wife. (One of the few paintings in which Peggy's own likeness is thought to be discernable is the *The Antipope* (1941); she seems to have been placed at an alienated distance from the other figures, a presence both lonely and furtive).

Peggy's ego was so deflated by Leonora that she was on the verge of relinquishing Max for good when, in late July, an invitation arrived from her sister Hazel proposing a visit to California, where she was now living with her third husband. Leaving Sindbad behind to visit Laurence (who'd temporarily joined an artists' beach community on Rhode Island), Peggy set off with Max, Pegeen and Jimmy; and her optimism soared as they flew west, their plane passing high over a chequerboard of fields and mountain ranges that seemed to her more beautiful 'than any picture abstract and surrealist'. She began to hope that once they landed, the epic south-western landscape would fill Max's imagination, ousting his lingering attachment to Leonora and to his European past.

Peggy had judged well. Having come so recently from the relatively domesticated countryside of southern France, Max was awed by the wind and sun-flayed deserts, the rocky mesas through which they drove in the new grey Buick Peggy had bought for the trip. Like Luisa before him, he was delighted to encounter remnants of North American Indian culture, buying up kachina dolls and totemic art to take back to New York; and seeing her lover so stimulated and engaged, Peggy began to hope that the trip was doing its work.

Jimmy, though, had a less glowing perception. The four travellers were closely confined to each other's company, and it seemed to him that relations between Peggy, Max and Pegeen were becoming a minefield of potential conflict.[5] Pegeen, now a precocious, rebellious sixteen-year-old, was naturally inclined to bicker with her mother, but her attitude to Max was more complex. She resented him in the way that she'd always

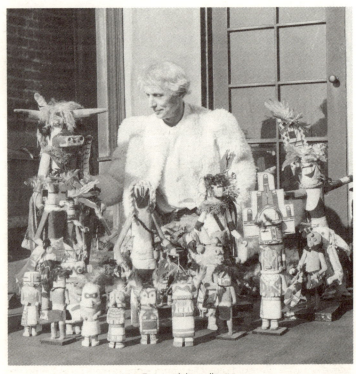

Max Ernst with his collection
of kachina dolls on the terrace of Hale House.

resented any new lover who'd diverted Peggy's attention away from her; but she was also flattered and fascinated by him. Max enjoyed beautiful women, and Pegeen, with her silvery hair and wide green eyes, was maturing fast; she was also developing a small but original talent as a painter, and it pleased Max to position himself as her flirtatious mentor. As the four of them toured the south-west and then took the long road trip back to New York, it was clear to Jimmy that mother and daughter were setting themselves up as rivals for Max's attention.

Yet what Jimmy had seen as a disturbing dynamic between the three of them, 'a staccato of twists, eccentricities and combat',[6] Peggy preferred to interpret as intimacy. Obstinately she chose to see this two-month trip as the foundation of their new family life together, and to believe that Max could be persuaded into marrying her. Even though he'd frequently asserted that marriage was a bourgeois institution to which he never again wanted to be shackled, she believed that he could be made to see the practical necessity of it – the fact that it would free him financially to focus on his painting, and grant him crucial rights of citizenship if America were to enter the war against Germany (in which event he would be reclassified as an enemy alien).

'It is my fate to go through with the impossible,' Peggy later declared. 'Whatever form I find it in, it fascinates me, while I flee from all the easy things in life.' For the next few months she continued to chip away at Max's resistance.[7] By 7 December, when the Japanese bombed Pearl Harbour and America was goaded into declaring war against the Axis powers, he had none left to offer. Three weeks later he allowed himself to be taken down to Virginia, where the marriage laws were lax and where Peggy was able to use her cousin Harold Loeb's address to fake their rights of residence. It was a victory for Peggy, but as jubilant as she tried to feel, none of her family or friends were inclined to embrace her happiness. Pegeen was fiercely critical, condemning her mother for coercing Max into a union he clearly did not want: Jimmy despised his father for having taken cynical advantage of Peggy and her money. To him the marriage was 'horrible' from the outset, and Emily Coleman, now unexpectedly living with a cowboy on a ranch in California, had added her own share of predictive gloom when Peggy visited her during the summer road trip.[8] Emily had assured Peggy that she had no chance of finding happiness with Max because she was simply repeating her old masochistic patterns – attaching herself to a man who did not love her, and triggering all her deepest doubts and insecurities. 'That pained me,' Peggy later acknowledged, 'I had hoped to hide it.'⁹

There were other aspects of her love for Max that didn't bear much scrutiny. She was only half joking when she admitted to Emily that she'd fallen for him because he was so beautiful, so talented and so famous – and it was characteristic of her particular combination of egotism and enthusiasm that in her battle to win the painter, she'd failed to discover much about the man. Beneath Max's cool, proud veneer he was often irresolute and unhappy in America: he felt himself to be an exile in a foreign land, barely fluent in its language, and tied, now, to a wife about whom he felt ambivalent at best. While Peggy blithely claimed that being married to Max had brought her a new 'feeling of safety', she was blind to the fact that for him, the marriage felt more like a prison.

It was a very privileged prison, of course. Peggy had moved them all into a new home, a spacious brownstone on East 51st Street with broad river views, a dramatic, double-height living room and accommodation for both the children (Pegeen was enrolled in the nearby Lenox School for Girls and Sindbad was studying at Columbia). Peggy boasted to Emily that all was 'heavenly' at Hale House and that Max, installed in his own painting studio, was producing marvellous art, but she couldn't yet admit that, just as Emily had foreseen, the marriage was already in trouble. She and Max found potential for argument in nearly every aspect of their life: they quarrelled over trivial issues like who should drive the car, and they quarrelled incessantly over money. Peggy, fearful of being taken for granted as always, had wanted Max to make some symbolic contribution to household expenses and to assume the symbolic role, at least, of husband and provider. He refused, for although he was beginning to earn money from his painting in America, he was anxious to shore up some small portion of financial independence. He was also taking a stand against the allowance that Peggy still paid Laurence – a quirk that offended his old-fashioned notions of propriety, and made him deeply sensitive to the fact that she openly sought the support of her ex-husband during their own marital disputes.

Max's tactic during these quarrels was to retreat behind a wall of silence. He was as 'cold as a snake', Peggy complained, and sometimes he would refuse to communicate for days at a time, the silence at Hale House growing ever more costive with malice. Even when the two were on more cooperative terms Max allowed Peggy only meagre rations of his affection. She never got over the fact that a book he gave her as a present came with no message of love, but only the distantly polite inscription, 'For Peggy Guggenheim from Max Ernst'.[10] It became apparent that Max's way of surviving this marriage was to edit her out of his life as far as was practicable. When journalists came to the house he discouraged them from including Peggy in a photograph or interview. And while he could always find a spare lunchtime for Leonora, a spare evening to spend with the young women who liked to flutter around 'the grand maître' of surrealism, he seemed too busy to spend very much time with his wife.

Peggy, drawing on her half-baked knowledge of Freud, tried to excuse Max's behaviour and explain it away as some form of defense against her intimidating wealth. But that did not stop her resorting to her old punitive tactics; needling him over his dependency on that wealth, and flirting provocatively with other men, among them Marcel Duchamp. It was a fundamentally miserable state of affairs and Peggy, who had already endured one abusive marriage and several dysfunctional affairs, should have known that it could not improve. Yet she continued to cling to Max. And while it was fear that kept her so stubbornly attached – a fear that at forty-one she might never have another chance at love – Peggy was also reluctant to renounce Max, the great artist whom she had so triumphantly netted. It was magical for her to have daily, privileged access to his genius – 'to see his latest paintings on an easel was like being present at their birth'. And she was undeniably just as thrilled by the social status that came from being Max's wife.

Within the Manhattan art world, Peggy and Max were aristocracy. He, by common consent, was considered the greatest of all the émigré painters, yet she was gaining her own reputation as a collector. It was clear, from the limited works she'd been able to put on display at Hale House, that Peggy Guggenheim had accumulated some masterpieces in Europe; and now that she was settled in New York she was continuing to buy at an impressive rate, acquiring several works by Max, along with two Picassos (her most expensive purchases) and significant works by Calder, Moore, Duchamp, the surrealist Roberto Matta and even Leonora Carrington. In January 1942 she began putting together the complete catalogue of her works, commissioning additional scholarly essays from Piet Mondrian, André Breton and Jean Arp; and when it was published, under the title *Art of This Century*, it was greeted as a seminal document of European modernism, greatly enhancing her own standing.*

But Peggy was most enjoyably conscious of her joint power with Max when they held court together at Hale House. In the autumn of 1941 they'd given a 'big and rambling' housewarming party where a drunken fist-fight had exploded between two of the guests (over a clash of surrealist principles) and blood had all but splattered across a nearby Kandinsky. After that instantly notorious event, many more parties had followed; and while Max was inclined to dominate, sitting on the outsized throne he'd placed for himself in the vaulted sitting room, Peggy was also a figure of fascination. She was rich (although not as rich as New York rumour was painting her to be), she owned great art, and, as one contemporary recalled, she had the special bohemian glamour – the 'zing' – of having lived through 1920s Paris. Peggy understood that guests at Hale House didn't require the conventional catering that was still mandatory in most Manhattan drawing rooms, and that most people would consider it modern of her to provide little more than cheap whisky, potato chips and the occasional curry cooked up by Max. She knew that the lure of her parties lay in the mixing of her guests – a famous baseball player or two, the burlesque artist Gypsy Rose Lee and a glitter of European legends like Duchamp and Max. The composer John Cage was twenty-nine when he went to his first party in Hale House, and afterwards he wrote with awe that he believed no other room in Manhattan could boast such variety and brilliance: 'These were people whose names were written in gold in my head.'[11]

---

* Breton's contribution was an encyclopaedic history of surrealism, printed in green ink. It was also his idea to illustrate the biographies with photographs of the artists' eyes.

During these occasions Peggy was at her most charismatic, radiating what Jimmy remembered as 'kinetic flashes of brilliance [and] charm'; she and Max were also at their married best as, playing off the admiration of their friends and associates, they appeared witty and animated together.[12] It was this public life that gave the marriage its illusion of cohesion and enabled it to struggle on through eighteen months of antagonism and arguments. Yet Peggy's own personal lifeline in this unhappy period was the project to which she began devoting herself as soon as she was settled in Hale House: the creation of a new gallery that she intended to be different from anything New York had seen.

She had in her mind the concept of an 'art centre' – a novel kind of space that would combine the functions of both museum and commercial gallery, allowing her to exhibit her own core collection but also present shows of new work. She was committed to avoiding the grim piety of institutions like her uncle Solomon's Museum of Non-Objective Painting, and to channelling something of the transgressive playfulness she'd admired at a surrealist exhibition in Paris in 1938: the artworks there had been displayed by shop mannequins, and the gallery decor had been dominated by a thousand coal sacks, stuffed with old newspapers and suspended from the ceiling.

Towards the end of 1941 Peggy found the premises for her new centre, a double loft over a grocery store at 30 West 57th Street, which was close, but not too close, to the small galleries that were clustered around East 57th Street. Sounding out her friends for a suitable architect, she hired the brilliant and visionary Frederick Kiesler to give shape to her ideas. He was a tiny man 'with a Napoleon complex' whose radical design agenda was often too much for his paying clients; but he perfectly understood Peggy's ambitions to create something beautiful, iconoclastic and rare. Even though she fought over nearly every cent of Kiesler's $7,000 bill, even though she wavered nervously over some of the more extreme elements of his design, when her new gallery was ready to open on 20 October 1942, Peggy acknowledged proudly that he had made it 'special and wonderful'.

The gallery was called Art of This Century, like her catalogue, and Kiesler's genius had been to conceive its layout as four arrestingly different spaces, each one housing a different genre of work. The white-walled

Daylight Gallery, which would host the temporary exhibitions, was the most conventional, but the other three were almost art installations in themselves. The Surrealist Gallery was a dark tunnel of a room with a black ceiling and curving wooden walls, and the works inhabited the space in appropriately subversive ways: some of them were mounted on projecting wooden 'arms' so that they appeared to float towards the viewer, while others were displayed on curved, amorphous furniture designed by Kiesler himself.

In the Abstract Gallery, the walls were created out of curved aquamarine canvas with the paintings suspended airily on strings. In the long, narrow Kinetic Gallery the art was displayed like an entertainment arcade, with seven works by Klee mounted on a large rotating conveyor belt whose speed could be controlled by a lever. The contents of one of Duchamp's portmanteau-style *Boîte-en-valise* pieces were put on view through a peephole in the wall.* Peggy had also agreed that some of the less valuable items in her collection could be placed in racks, so that the public could browse through them at will. According to a captivated John Cage, there was a spirit of jauntiness and generosity about Art of This Century that transformed the concept of what a gallery might be. Between them, Peggy and Kiesler had created 'a kind of fun house...You couldn't just walk through it, you had to become part of it.'[13]

At the party held to celebrate the gallery's launch Peggy strove to emphasize the seriousness of her venture: 'Opening this gallery and its collection during a time when people are fighting for their lives and freedom is a responsibility of which I am fully conscious.' As she reminded the assembled guests and journalists of the circumstances in which she'd accumulated her works, she declared, too, her fundamental belief in the enduring spiritual significance of art. Lucille Kohn would have been proud. Nevertheless, once Peggy had paid her moral dues, she couldn't help but gloat over the buzz of compliments that were now coming her way from the fashionable crowd who had flocked through the gallery's doors. She'd dressed very carefully for her party in

---

* Each *boîte* was a leather case containing reproductions of sixty-nine of Duchamp's works. He produced a few dozen of them over his career, in a project to question the value of the 'original' work of art.

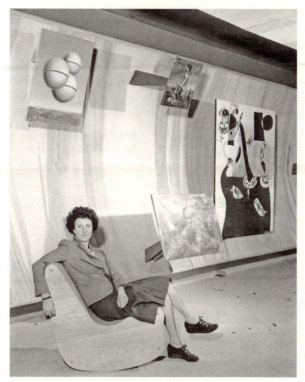

Peggy in the Surrealist Gallery
at the newly opened Art of This Century.

an elegant gown made startling by a radically mismatched pair of ear-rings (a tiny brass mobile made by Calder, and a painted miniature by Tanguy). Framing her was the collection, proudly on display; while by her side, and flamboyantly in his element, was Max, 'a cross between prince regent and the museum's biggest star'.[14]

As for the gallery itself, Manhattan was impressed: the *New York Times* described it as the 'last word' in originality, and the reviewer in the *Sun* was blunt in his admiration: 'Frankly my eyes have never bulged further from their sockets.' The adulatory press coverage and the enthusiasm of the public confirmed that Peggy and her gallery had caught the cultural moment as exactly as Luisa had with her parties in Venice, and that for Peggy herself, Art of This Century was no less of a personal apotheosis.

In subsequent years, critics and biographers would debate exactly how much credit Peggy could claim for her success and how much she owed to the vision of others (all of whom would be, interestingly, men). When talking about her art career she always undersold herself, and was modestly exact in acknowledging those who'd mentored her: Herbert Read, Breton and above all Duchamp, whom she described as 'my great, great teacher'.[15] Yet despite the assistance she'd received, it had been Peggy's own impulse to make her gallery so democratic and entertaining a space. And it had been her continuing willingness to experiment that kept Art of This Century so uniquely abreast of its times. While the Daylight Gallery gave solo shows to many established names, among them De Chirico, Giacometti and Arp, Peggy was always willing to challenge the canon. She programmed a number of group shows that were inventively themed around minor genres such as collages, surrealist objects and papier-mâché art. More pioneeringly, she organized an all-female show in 1943 which included works by Leonora Carrington, Méret Oppenheim and the then little-known Frida Kahlo.[*] It was titled simply 'Exhibition by 31 Women', and even though Peggy disclaimed any sisterly credit for the idea and acknowledged that it had first been mooted by Duchamp, she was active and staunch in her support of women. Up to 40 per cent of the works she exhibited in the Daylight Gallery were by female artists, and in 1945 she organized a second all-women show featuring work by the young Louise Bourgeois. Within a male-dominated art world these gestures had a feminist resonance, and despite Peggy's apolitical demurrals, she gave these women both publicity and a platform.

But for Peggy herself, as for most of the art world, her greatest achievement was not the promotion of women but the nurturing of the New York School – the generation of painters who emerged during the

---

* Georgia O'Keeffe refused to be included; perhaps regarding herself as a more established talent than the others, she said disdainfully that she was not 'a woman painter'. (Mary V. Dearborn, *Mistress of Modernism*, p. 240)

war. Peggy was eager to back young American talent, and even though she'd initially required some advice, her support for several painters would prove career-changing. As Charles Seliger, one of her grateful protégés, testified: 'If you were one of her artists she was really there for you...everyone – artists, critics, art historians, celebrities – came through her gallery.' Robert Motherwell concurred that the privilege of having his own early work displayed in the same building as Ernst, Klee and Picasso had been 'amazing'. According to Joseph Levy, who was running his own small commercial gallery at this time, the New York art scene had been fired into life by Art of This Century: 'When Peggy opened her gallery it was as if she'd lit a match.'[16]

* * * * *

Peggy was loved by her grateful artists, and she was popular with the public. Yet this was a period when the majority of collectors, critics and artists were male, when misogyny was still deeply ingrained in the culture; and there were some in the New York art world who were poised to belittle her, to assume that her role in her gallery could involve little more than the signing of cheques. Perversely, the fact that she tried for a while to charge an entrance fee to the gallery and that she was seen almost every day in her office, keeping vigilant control of her accounts, was taken as evidence that she had no creative vision of her own – that she was a daughter of the Guggenheim tribe, unable to separate money from art.

Perhaps there would have been fewer attempts to diminish Peggy if she had conformed to a more acceptable version of middle-aged femininity – a groomed Manhattan hostess or a bluestocking intellectual. But she was a confusing figure in wartime Manhattan: a rich Jewish princess with a patrician edge, but also a *soi-disant* bohemian with a string of lovers and a rackety past. She was evidently a potent woman and brilliantly connected, yet her authority was often undercut by the nervousness of her manner, her gauche attempts at humour, her flinching gaze. There was something unresolved about Peggy's personality that made different people see very different things in her, and this discordance was reflected in her physical appearance. Several photographs from the period attest to Peggy having retained her early gamine

elegance, her wrists and ankles still gracefully slender despite her thickening waist. But she rarely dressed to flatter herself. Unlike Doris, who
would never look other than polished, Peggy was often too busy to do
more than shrug on an old winter skirt and scuffed ankle boots, a cotton
dress and socks: frequently her only concession to Manhattan sophistication was a smeary dab of lipstick, and the cheap black hair dye with
which she concealed her first signs of grey.

Some men and women found Peggy's style attractively unpretentious,
but others were crudely disparaging. The artist David Hare used to complain that she was 'ugly as sin'; while Jackson Pollock, who would gain
more than anyone from Peggy's patronage, used particularly repellent
language to deny that he'd ever been her lover, claiming that if he had, he
would have needed 'two towels' – one to cover up her face and one to cover
her body. No one doubted Peggy's claims to beauty more than herself,
especially since the effects of her botched nose job were becoming more
pronounced in middle age. And like many women of this period, she
tended to internalize the prevailing misogyny, to make herself complicit
in its attitudes. One night a drunken sex game was proposed at Hale
House, during which all the men present had to compete to restrain their
arousal while the women undressed. Both Peggy and Xenia Cage (the
wife of John Cage) participated, and the game ended with the two women
going off with each other's husbands. Afterwards, however, Xenia wept
privately with mortification, and Peggy too was ashamed.

That game had been a low in Peggy's marriage, but it was symptomatic of how febrile her life with Max had become. She was now
having to deal with a new rival, a young painter called Dorothea Tanning
whom Max, ironically, had met while helping to select artists for Peggy's
'31 Women' show. The two not only became lovers, but were very public
in their infatuation: Dorothea went around in a dress that she'd decorated
with tiny photographs of Max's face, and he invited her to accompany
him to gallery openings and to meetings with his fellow surrealists.

Peggy fought back as best she could, denouncing Dorothea as a pretentious mediocrity and railing at Max's poor judgment. Yet it was clear
to her that Dorothea's youth, beauty and painting talent had stirred
her husband to feelings he'd never shown for her; and by 19 January
1943 (the anniversary of John Holms's death) she was ready to concede

defeat. She announced to Max that she would no longer live with a man so 'incapable of real emotion'[17] and that she wanted him to leave. Max, however, was shaken by this ultimatum – he'd got used to dominating Peggy (and very used to living on her money), and he wasn't ready to have his comfortable life ripped apart. Rather than taking his chance to leave, he begged for a second chance, promising Peggy that the affair was a temporary madness and that he was trying to get Dorothea 'out of his system'.

Rarely had Max made so open or emotional an appeal to Peggy, and she wavered under its force. However, in allowing the marriage to struggle on for another three months, she made a disastrous choice. Max showed no signs of relinquishing Dorothea, and the pain Peggy suffered on his account was exacerbated by anxiety over Sindbad who, having recently received his call-up papers from the American army, might soon be sent off to some distant and dangerous front. When Peggy went to visit her son at his training camp in Atlantic City, he seemed such 'a baby' to her in his military uniform and his brutal GI haircut that the sight of him wrung her heart.[18] And as always when she was distressed, Peggy drove herself towards a nervous collapse. Eating and sleeping very little, she became extremely volatile: at one moment she would sink into blank, suicidal exhaustion, at another she would be seized by a manic restlessness that sent her cruising around New York in search of random sexual distraction. Pegeen watched over her mother in terror, Jimmy suggested psychoanalysis, and Marcel Duchamp, with whom Peggy had finally and ineffectually sought to satisfy her crush ('it was really too late and was almost like incest') tried to talk her back into sense. Like everyone else, he wanted her to end the marriage. But it was typical of Peggy's pattern that it was only when she'd found herself a new lover that she finally had the courage to let Max go.

* * * * *

Peggy had been introduced to Kenneth Macpherson shortly after arriving in New York. A charming, cultured Scot, tall and sandy-haired, Kenneth apparently lived on an allowance paid by his wife, the English writer Bryher (Winifred Ellerman), while freely enjoying what he was pleased to call 'the Athenian community' in New York. He and Peggy had met a few times over dinner or at the opera, and she claimed she had always felt 'a peculiar current' pass between them. Evidently Kenneth felt it too, for in the spring of 1943 he decided to make a project of Peggy, drawn to her by a combination of curiosity, compassion and a very fleeting sexual attraction. His interest, though, was not entirely benign for Peggy, for as damaged as she was by Max and as desperate for kindness as she was, she was all too quick to mistake the affection he offered for love.

As Kenneth took over her life, instructing her to get a good divorce lawyer, persuading her to invest in a smart wardrobe, taking charge of her taste in music and books, Peggy gave herself up willingly to his direction. It seemed to her that Kenneth existed in a beautiful oasis of calm: she would lie in his arms, listening to his favourite gramophone records, and feel herself wrapped in an unfamiliar sensation of 'peace and ecstasy'.[19] If she'd only been content to enjoy the friendship for what it was, she might have allowed herself to be happy. Yet Peggy was hardwired to demand more of the people she loved, and even though Kenneth's sexual interest in her was rapidly exhausted and his intimacy restricted to chaste, almost brotherly embraces, she became obsessed with the idea of them setting up house together.

She believed she could make a fresh start with Kenneth and, as always with Peggy, that meant finding a new place to live. Having told Max to move out and find himself a new studio, she terminated her tenancy of Hale House and located a property that she persuaded Kenneth would suit them very well: an exceptionally spacious duplex on East 61st Street that would allow each of them their own separate floor. They moved in during the autumn, and for a while the arrangement seemed to work: Peggy tried to resign herself to the platonic relationship that Kenneth preferred, and she learned to enjoy the funny, camp and gossipy milieu of his 'Athenian' friends. Writing to Emily, she claimed she had never been happier: 'I love my independent life...my lesbian friend McPherson [sic] and my hard working girl's life.'[20]

But Kenneth was both more cryptic and more self-centred a man than the graceful, charming aesthete to whom Peggy believed she had entrusted herself, and often she found him hurtfully difficult to read. He still liked people to assume she was his mistress: her celebrity reflected well on him and she provided convenient social cover for his homosexuality (which in certain circles in wartime New York was not safe to reveal). When it suited him, he made himself entirely available to Peggy, helping out at the gallery, hosting joint parties at their duplex. Yet there were periods of time when he simply turned his back on her, demanding his privacy and keeping the door to his apartment closed. He resented it when Peggy used their joint kitchen, which was located up on his floor; he resented it when she invited Jean Connolly (a new friend and also Laurence's lover) to come and lodge with her, and he minded still more when they were joined by Pegeen, who'd recently returned from a traumatic series of misadventures in Mexico.

The noise of the women's chatter, the wet nylons left out to dry in the kitchen at night were all felt by Kenneth as infuriating intrusions on his territory. He was tiring of their domestic experiment, and however hard Peggy tried to appease him, the atmosphere in the duplex was becoming impossible. By the time they agreed to dissolve the arrangement the following year, even Peggy was resigned to the inevitable. Yet while she was able to part from Kenneth on unusually rational and amicable terms, the loss of their life together felt like a form of bereavement. She missed Kenneth's gossip, his friends, his physical proximity. And now that she was adrift, without a new love to move on to, Peggy once more began resorting to the sexual comfort of strangers.

It was during this period that malicious talk began to circulate about Peggy's promiscuity. Sex had apparently become as necessary to her as food and drink; and she was frequently driven to pick up men in the street, even to pay for their services. A young artist Jock Stockwell came to her gallery one day to show his portfolio of work, but having been complimented by Peggy on his 'nice tush' he found himself in her private office, where he was both startled and impressed by her 'demanding' stamina.[21] Several of Peggy's relationships were more intimate and more lasting than this, but she was nevertheless behaving in ways that were shocking for a middle-aged woman in 1944 – and she was punished for it. Crudely exaggerated rumours spread through New York about the scope of her 'debauchery'; she was said to have developed a taste for bestiality, and even to have included her daughter in experimental threesomes.

Peggy's sexuality was certainly complicated. As the artist Charles Seliger once commented, 'She really was a much lonelier, sadder person than anyone really realized,' and after the loss of Kenneth and Max she was using these strangers to give herself the illusion of being cherished and desired.[22] Yet it would be wrong to cast her as a victim: Peggy greatly enjoyed sex, the physical pleasure of it and also the sensation of power it brought. Although she was not an active feminist as Emma Goldman or Lucille Kohn were, she did consider it her right as a woman to act on her desires as freely as any man – and not only did she refuse to be cowed by the vicious gossip about her, she claimed to be proud of it, to wear her notoriety as the badge of her sexual independence.

* * * * *

It would also be wrong to paint this period of Peggy's life as bleak and directionless. Art of This Century continued to flourish and although she was employing others to curate individual exhibitions, among them James Johnson Sweeney and Howard Putzel, she remained energetically invested in the gallery's development. She was exploring new areas of interest – in 1944 she flirted with the promotion of experimental music and cinema – but principally she was investigating new artists, and it was after her marriage to Max had dissolved that she began to turn away from the pre-war Europeans and to focus on a younger generation of Americans like Robert Motherwell, Mark Rothko and Jackson Pollock, who would collectively become known as the New York School.

Pollock's potential had been pointed out to Peggy by several advisers, but it had been Piet Mondrian who'd convinced her to take his work seriously. In 1943 she and Mondrian had been assessing submissions for the gallery's annual mixed show and at first Peggy had seen nothing of merit in Pollock's canvas. Composed of sinisterly vestigial human forms, covered in a scribble of mathematical symbols, *Stenographic Figure* looked to her like a messy derivative of Surrealism. She wasn't alone in her doubts; the artist Peter Busa thought that one 'had to work hard to like' Pollock's painting at this time.[23] Yet Mondrian's insistence that the canvas showed signs of a 'most exciting' talent convinced Peggy to sign Pollock to her gallery, and in one of her characteristic bursts of enthusiasm she not only included *Stenographic Figure* in the mixed exhibition but offered the thirty-one-year-old artist his own solo show.

Pollock was a different breed from the sophisticated, cosmopolitan artists Peggy had known in Europe. Raw and taciturn, he was difficult to work with – disorganized, frequently drunk and prone to violent tempers. But Peggy was excited by the idea of stamping her mark on a young career, and was willing to accept Pollock's feral manner as evidence of his genius. With the first show she gave him in November, Peggy nailed her colours defiantly to his talent, stating to the press that she considered him one of 'the strongest, most interesting American painters'.[24] She stuck to that opinion, even though most of New York was not yet ready to agree: the opening of the exhibition was sparsely attended, and only one work was sold. Clement Greenberg, who would become Pollock's most prominent apologist, was still half-hearted in his praise, allowing the painter a certain originality but discerning a too-obvious debt to influences like Picasso and Miró.

Peggy also put hard cash behind her commitment, offering Pollock and his wife Lee Krasner $2,000 to buy a house on Long Island (where she hoped the painter might be persuaded to drink less) and agreeing to pay him a monthly stipend of $150, as a guaranteed advance on any sales. This was not a completely selfless contract – if Pollock's sales were poor, Peggy would take the rest of what he owed her in paintings. Yet it altered his life, allowing him to leave his job as a handyman (ironically at Solomon Guggenheim's museum) and focus exclusively on his art; providing him with a material security that was virtually unknown among his peers. As Charles Seliger recalled, most young artists at that time were 'overjoyed by an occasional $100 sale'.[25]

For Peggy herself, the promotion of Pollock necessitated the making of difficult choices: she had to sell off a number of her favourite artworks in order to release the capital, and she had to scale down her support for other artists. Yet she never regretted it, and would later boast of it as her proudest achievement, knowing that she'd helped to create the conditions for Pollock's talent to take flight; knowing, too, that the very first painting she'd commissioned from him had been a turning point in his work, moving it forward to the huge, visionary abstracts that would become his signature style. That painting, *Mural*, had been commissioned in the summer of 1943, when Peggy was planning her move with Kenneth and was looking for an artwork to place in the entrance hall of their duplex. The scale of what she envisaged was huge – a canvas 20 feet wide and 8 feet high – and it seems to have galvanized Pollock into experimenting with new techniques, laying the canvas out on the floor and using his whole body to power the application of paint so that *Mural* appeared to have exploded into being – a violent stampede of colour, a bacchanal of rhythmic dancing forms.

Peggy adored it. Pollock was to be her own personal 'genius', and over the next two years she doubled his stipend and gave him a second

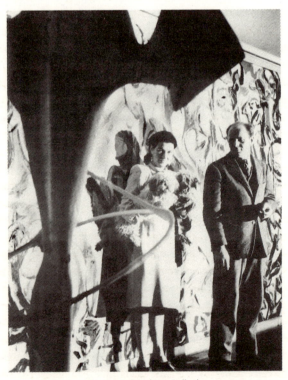

Peggy and Jackson Pollock
in front of *Mural*, the seminal work
he painted for her apartment in 1943.

solo show. Greenberg now added his endorsement, proclaiming Pollock 'the strongest painter of his generation', and as other shows and further critical acclaim followed, more of the works began to sell.[26] Prices remained modest – a few hundred dollars at most – and Peggy gave away several works for which she could not find buyers. It would not be long, however, before she regretted her casual generosity. From 1950 Pollock's career rose on a dizzying trajectory. As New York overtook Paris as the epicentre of the world's art market, and Pollock emerged as its native star, prices for his work rose into the tens of thousands; and when Pollock died, shockingly and prematurely, in a car crash in 1956, he would leave his widow Lee a millionaire.

By then Peggy's formative role in Pollock's career was gaining recognition, as was her wider promotion of the New York School (now more popularly known as abstract expressionism). To Greenberg, she had been as a cornerstone of 'living American art'. Even Lee Krasner – with whom Peggy's relationship had often been embattled – allowed that her influence had been key: 'Nowhere else could one expect such an open-minded reaction [as at Art of This Century]. Peggy was invaluable in founding and creating what she did.'[27] Back in the mid-1940s, however, Peggy had little sense of how far-reaching her gallery might be, and there were periods when she could not see beyond the difficulties of each day. The wartime market was slow, even in Manhattan; it was often heartbreaking work to find buyers for her artists and to juggle the gallery's finances. When an approach was made by the small but reputable Dial Press, inviting her to write her memoirs, Peggy leaped at the flattery and the validation implicit in the proposal.

'I only live and breathe for my book,' she wrote to Emily in October 1944, while to Laurence she confessed, 'Since I started I forget there is a war on.'[28] Peggy had long nursed ambitions to write; over the years she'd scribbled ideas for novels, and kept up a prolific and vivid correspondence with friends. The memoir, which she titled *Out of This Century*, took her just eighteen months to complete, and at its best it was animated by a racy comic directness. The force of Peggy's enthusiasms – her love affairs, her joy in art and travel – jumped off the page with an infectious brightness, and while she wrote incisively about places, she could be wickedly irreverent about people. Gore Vidal, a superb stylist

himself, judged her prose to be 'almost as good as Gertrude Stein....
And a lot funnier.'[29]

But the memoir was a conflicted piece of writing, a very curious portrait of Peggy herself. She displayed flashes of admirable, if masochistic
frankness, acknowledging her ignoble jealousy of Pegeen's nanny, her
tendency to use her money to control family and friends. In the same
spirit of honesty, she was touchingly generous in her appraisals of all
those she considered better, wiser or more talented than herself, giving
ample evidence of what the writer Mary McCarthy would later describe
as her 'huge, gay, forgiving heart'. Yet there were elements in the memoir that were dismaying in their obtuseness and egotism. Peggy made
little attempt to interpret events from any perspective other than her
own; her lovers and friends had no interior lives and, more culpably,
her children were rarely more than footnotes. It was apparently beyond
her abilities as a writer and a mother to accept and describe the damage that had been done to Pegeen and Sindbad during the aftermath of
their parents' divorce. While she could describe in righteously indignant
detail the mistreated, abandoned animals she'd encountered during her
travels in Europe and the Middle East, Peggy lacked the empathy or
understanding to confront the sufferings of her own children.

An even more disconcerting feature of the memoir was the flip-
pant, often clumsily ironic tone Peggy adopted when addressing the
other serious issues of her life: the abuse she'd got from Laurence, the
dangers she'd faced during the war. It was as though she was afraid
of boring her readers, afraid of taking herself more seriously than she
deserved; and it was that same glib instinct for self-deprecation that
seems to have prompted Peggy to make light of her professional achievements in the narrative of her life, and to boast instead about her sexual
career. Lawyers had warned her to conceal the identities of some of her
lovers, but the names she substituted ('Florenz Dale' for Laurence Vail,
'Sherman' for Garman) were all so transparent that when *Out of This
Century* appeared in the bookshops no one talked much about the art,
only about the scandalous checklist of Peggy's affairs.

Some of those implicated in the memoir regarded Peggy's frankness
as a betrayal. Jimmy Ernst was appalled to see his father's inadequacies so baldly recounted in print. Sindbad was angry for Laurence,

whose talents as an artist and a linguist he felt Peggy had trivialized, and whose faults she had magnified. (She had known she was treading recklessly, and when she'd embarked on the memoir she'd warned Laurence, 'I'll write about you and you'll never forgive me.')[30] Others, with no personal connection to the story, simply considered it vulgar: to the art critic Katharine Kuh, Peggy had revealed herself as a woman without 'normal sensitivities', a sad exhibitionist hanging up her dirty sexual linen for all to see. There were double standards at work here, given the acclaim that had greeted the autobiographically erotic novels of Henry Miller, and a few readers did appreciate the courage of Peggy's candour. The *New Yorker* columnist Janet Flanner had only praise for her 'detachment in looking back on life' and her willingness 'to tell the truth' without prudery or evasion.[31] But to Djuna Barnes, who'd tried to edit out the more lurid details of the narrative, Peggy had distorted and debased the true value of her memoir. The times through which she'd lived had been extraordinary – 1920s Paris, 1930s London and 1940s New York – yet too often Peggy gave the impression that she'd spent those years ignoring the cultural ferment around her, and simply notching up lovers on her bedpost.

This, ultimately, was the most damning verdict on the memoir: that in muddying up art and sex, Peggy had undermined her status as a collector and patron. Yet if she was disappointed by her book's reception, she was far from crushed: everyone was talking about it, and as she'd once commented bluntly to Emily, it was far better to be talked about than ignored. In any case, she didn't plan to be in America much longer, for now that the war was over she was impatient to return to Europe, which she regarded as her real home. Despite all that she'd achieved in New York during the last five years, Peggy had never imagined making her stay permanent. She found the city unloveable, lacking in beauty and sophistication; 'the only way to endure [it]', she warned Herbert Read (who was planning a visit), 'is to work hard all day and to drink hard from 6 on.' Others close to her were also leaving: Emily Coleman for London, and Laurence (now married to Jean Connolly) for France. Sindbad was already in Paris, working for the army as a translator; and so too was Pegeen, who had recently married the artist Jean Hélion and, to Peggy's relief, seemed to have found some kind of stability at last.

There had been a very bad period for Pegeen in New York, beginning with the breakdown of Peggy's marriage to Ernst. Terrified by her mother's mental state, conflicted in her loyalty to Max, she had reeled off on her own destructive sexual experiments. During her summer in Mexico she had contracted venereal disease from one lover and formed a hopeless, improbable attachment to another – a young Mexican whose sole employment was diving off high cliffs to amuse the seaside tourists. Pegeen had returned to New York convinced she was 'rotten' and 'moldy'; and Peggy, while distraught with worry over her daughter, was also driven to a deep, irritated resentment, considering that Pegeen had had all the good fortune of being born beautiful, artistically talented and emancipated, yet was unable to appreciate any of her luck.

The two of them had fought constantly during this period – over money, over the living arrangements with Kenneth, and over Pegeen's lingering attachment to her Mexican, which Peggy dismissed contemptuously as 'pathetic'. The paintings Pegeen was producing, emotionally defenseless pictures of flat, winsome, disconnected doll-like figures, had spoken of her pain and bewilderment. However, late in 1943 she had met and fallen in love with Hélion, who, while twenty-one years her senior, was entranced by her pale fragility and apparently delighted to accept the task of caring for her.

With the advent of Hélion, relations between mother and daughter again became affectionate; yet if Pegeen was quickening Peggy's resolve to return to Europe, it wasn't yet clear to her where she would settle. She had already discarded the idea of London because she thought the city would be too depressing in its 'bedraggled' post-war state; and when she made her first exploratory visit to Paris in the summer of 1946, she found it no less sad. The scarcity of good things in the shops and restaurants, the uneasy violence on the streets as collaborators, real or suspected, were held to account, had all but erased the gaiety she remembered. But in Paris she encountered Mary McCarthy, who was planning a tour of Italy with her new husband Bowden Broadwater, and Peggy immediately proposed to accompany them, offering to be their guide when they reached her own special city of Venice.

McCarthy was not particularly happy about the offer. She had not yet learned to love Peggy, and once they began travelling she found

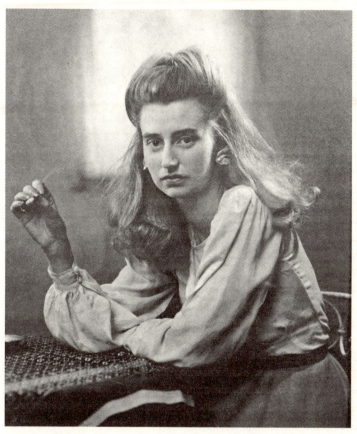

Pegeen as a young woman, beautiful but damaged (c. 1945).

her an annoying companion, boasting about her past adventures in Europe and about her determination to add to them with a new Italian lover. To Mary, Peggy seemed to be more interested in tallying up her experiences than actually living them; she seemed to take 'a quantitive view' of life and seek out 'a *wealth* of sensations'. Later, Mary would channel her irritation into 'The Cicerone', a short story whose heroine, Miss Polly Herkimer Grabbe, was transparently modelled on Peggy. Miss Grabbe was a Jewish-American woman of a certain age who'd become 'hardened and chapped by the winds of rebuff and failure'.[32] Like Peggy, she had learned to conceal the disappointments of her life in a storm of movement and consumption, and like Peggy, she concealed her vulnerabilities behind a forced air of bravado: 'Miss Grabbe', wrote Mary, 'adapted herself spryly to comedy when she perceived that the world was smiling; she was always the second to laugh at a prat-fall of her spirit.'

Peggy, not surprisingly, was hurt by 'The Cicerone', and could not readily forgive it. Yet as harsh as the portrait had been, it did concede the singular virtues of Peggy's character, not least her integrity as a traveller. This was Mary's first trip to Europe but she could see how different Peggy was from most American tourists: a genuine explorer, avid for the tastes, smells, textures and sights of each place that she visited.

Once in Venice, Mary was particularly touched by Peggy's true and knowledgeable love of the city, saluting the emotion, 'as blazing as the native grappa', with which she'd introduced her and Bowden to 'the small hot squares, the working-class restaurants and dirty churches'.[33] She also paid tribute to the absolute certainty with which Peggy had made up her mind, en route to the city, that this was to be her new home. It was twenty-two years since she'd first hazily fantasized about moving to Venice. Now Mary McCarthy observed the unwavering energy with which Peggy began to trawl every estate agent for information, to quiz hoteliers and even strangers in the street, as she embarked on her search for the palazzo that would make the fantasy real.

CHAPTER 12

'I am where I belong, if anyone belongs anywhere these days.'[1]

In the past, Peggy had come to Venice for solace, drawn by the lapping canal waters, the large skies and the serene pace of life that represented for her the city's timeless balm. Yet now that she intended to settle there permanently, she had no intention of becoming an anonymous recluse. Although she was happy to escape the contentious rivalries of Manhattan, she was very far from abandoning her ambitions, and as Jean Hélion astutely predicted, the small, parochial art community in Venice was a world in which she could easily shine. 'Peggy could be a queen in Venice. It suited her and her pictures very well...she could be the first person [there] to show modern art.'[2]

Much had to be organized, though, before the move could be made. Returning to New York in the autumn, Peggy had to finalize her divorce from Max (who'd now moved with Dorothea down to Arizona); she had to wind down the gallery, and ease her way out of her remaining financial commitments. The final exhibition at Art of This Century was held in May 1947, and, in tribute to Peggy's formative years in Europe and as a gesture to Nelly (who'd escaped from France to America in 1942), it was a retrospective show for Nelly's late husband Theo van Doesburg.

If Peggy mourned the dismantling of her extraordinary creation, she did so only briefly. Mary McCarthy observed that she had a talent for always 'looking forward to the next thing', and already she was anticipating a life that would be free from the gallery's financial and administrative burdens. With unsentimental rapidity she sold off whatever she could of the interior fittings and gave away works that she no longer wanted and was unable to sell. With the rest of her collection put into temporary storage, Peggy returned to Venice to celebrate her freedom, staying in a hotel while she resumed her search for a home.

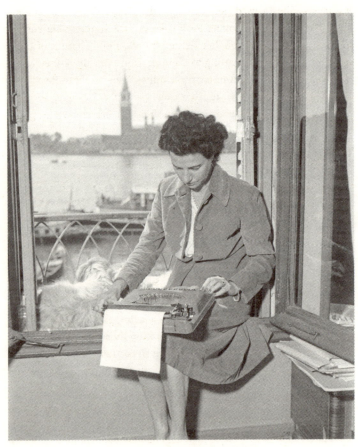

Peggy planning her new Venetian life
from a room at the Danieli Hotel.

In the post-war depression Venetian property was cheap; and Peggy had access to extra capital now, since her New York friend and financial adviser Bernard Reis had been able to break open one of her remaining trusts. She focused her search on the Grand Canal, the location she'd always wanted, looking for a palazzo that would be big enough to house her art collection, her visiting friends and the family of Lhasa Apso terriers she was starting to acquire. 'Don't you think they would be divine trooping about in large quantities?' she wrote to Reis's wife Becky, imagining herself and her dogs parading through the piano nobile of her new home, or cuddling them on her lap as she glided through Venice in a gondola.[3]

Peggy's instinct for grandeur was overtaking her loyalty to bohemia. But her first survey of the market revealed that these larger palazzos were hard to acquire; many had been turned into hotels or government buildings, while others had been subdivided into apartments and often came with immovable tenants. (There was one fifty-room palazzo on which she first set her heart, yet two floors of it were occupied by a tax office that proved impossible to budge.) By the time the first fogs and chills of autumn arrived Peggy was no nearer finding a home, and as Venice emptied of its summer visitors she headed south to winter on Capri. Laurence and Jean were there, and so, coincidentally, was Kenneth Macpherson, staying in the villa belonging to his wife Bryher and paying host to a stream of guests. During those four months there was much drinking and swapping of sexual partners; and when Peggy wrote to Djuna about all the 'mad things' that were going on, and intimated that there were some too sordid to relate, Djuna was concerned that she was falling back into her old destructive ways. But the spring brought Peggy back to Venice, and she was not only ready to resume her search for a home, but soberly and happily concentrated on a new professional project.

That summer Venice was relaunching the International Art Biennale, the global exhibition of painting and sculpture that had long been the centrepiece of the city's cultural life. Founded in 1895, the Biennale had expanded in international scale and ambition over the decades, and the pavilions in the Public Gardens that housed the collections of each participating nation had grown in number and prestige.

During the Mussolini years the Biennale had become distorted into a showcase for fascist values and fascist art, and it had been suspended during the war; but in 1948 its revival was being heralded as a symbolic new start for Italy, and as a resurgence for contemporary art.

This historic Biennale was, however, a difficult event to organize, given the chaos of the war's aftermath. The national pavilions down by the Arsenale required extensive renovations after a decade of neglect; there were problems too with the artworks. Transportation issues delayed America's submission until well after the official opening; Germany was too devastated to participate; and Greece was too busy crushing communist-backed insurgents to concern itself with art. These empty pavilions presented an embarrassing problem for the celebratory launch, but they proved to be a prime opportunity for Peggy. When the Biennale committee were discussing how they could be filled, a local Venetian artist, Giuseppi Santomaso, proposed that the small Greek pavilion could be offered to Signora Guggenheim and her celebrated collection.

Peggy loved to be courted, and she was fully aware of how valuable this invitation could be in introducing her and her artworks to Venice. It also solved two of her most pressing practical problems. She'd left her collection behind in New York because she had nowhere yet to display it, but also because the complications of shipping it to Venice were so expensive, with the Italians' stipulated import tax adding thousands of dollars to her transportation costs. The Biennale, however, was not only offering it a home for six months, but was covering her shipping costs and giving her a temporary pass on the tax.

There were moments when Peggy's gratitude was stretched to breaking point. The city's young and brilliant architect, Carlo Scarpa, had been commissioned to take charge of the Biennale renovations; but he worked with a fastidious attention to detail, and it was only three days before the opening that Peggy was allowed entrance to the Greek pavilion, a faux-Byzantine building of decorative red brickwork and slender pillars that was tucked away at the leafy far end of the Giardini. So frantic were her last-minute preparations as she calculated how best to hang her collection that she had no time to think about her own appearance. On 6 June, as Peggy stood in her pavilion ready to receive

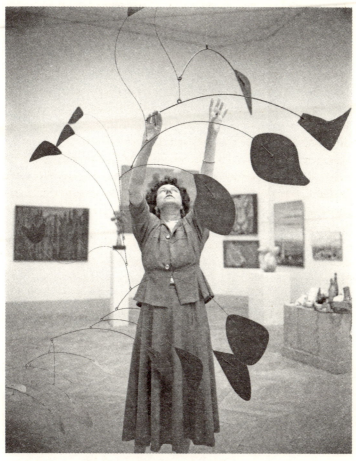

'I felt as though I were a new European country':
Peggy installs a Calder mobile in her pavilion at the 1948 Biennale.

the Italian president and various foreign dignitaries, her stockings and her girdle were borrowed from a friend, and she had to hope that her large Venetian glass earrings would compensate for the fact that she wore no hat.

But Peggy's vanity was all for her art. Seeing her name listed among those of the participating nations gave her a triumphal glow – 'I felt as though I were a new European country' – and it was to her enormous competitive delight that, throughout the summer, her pavilion drew the largest crowds.[4] Italy was hungry for modern art. After the firework show of the Futurists, the nation's culture had been forced back into the sentimental, bombastic and insular aesthetic imposed by the fascists. There had been little contact with the wider European art movements like surrealism, and virtually none with America's post-war scene. Much of Peggy's work was so new, so strange, that to one innocent worker at the Biennale it literally looked like rubbish – a Calder mobile created out of broken glass and china was very nearly lost to the trash cans. To local artists, however, starved of contemporary culture, Peggy's collection was an education and a beacon of future hope. As Venetian painters like Santomaso gathered in her pavilion, they had high expectations that she and her collection would be the start of a post-war renaissance in their city.

Admired, consulted, courted as she was that summer, Peggy felt as much the queen as Hélion had predicted. She'd rented the top-floor apartment of the magnificent old Palazzo Barbaro, within whose library Peggy's favourite author, Henry James, had completed the final pages of his Venetian novel *The Aspern Papers*. Perched above the daily spectacle of the canal, visited by a stream of friends (among them Roland Penrose and his wife Lee Miller, who photographed Peggy for *Vogue*), she was very happy. She went almost every day to her pavilion, where she had become a kind of celebrity and where her dogs grew fat on free ice cream. When she celebrated her fiftieth birthday party in August, she wore a Venetian crinoline dress and her guests drank 'rivers of champagne'.[5]

After the Biennale closed in the autumn, Peggy had to improvise alternative arrangements for her collection. She found temporary lodgings for most of it by loaning works to exhibitions in Florence and Milan. Later in 1950 she was invited to exhibit her precious stock of

Pollocks in the Correr Museum, opposite San Marco. The show was always lit up at night, and Peggy recalled the 'extreme joy' she felt when she sat in the piazza and looked up at her paintings, 'glowing through the wide open windows': proudly, she congratulated herself on the fact that she had installed Pollock in his rightful position as 'one of the greatest painters of our time, who had every right to be exhibited in this wonderful setting.'[6] Yet while the collection was temporarily taken care of, Peggy still needed a home of her own, and it was towards the end of 1948 that Count Zorzi, the press secretary of the Biennale whom Peggy adored for his 'elegant manners and...sense of humour', told her about a 'lovely abode' on the Grand Canal that had just come on the market for around $60,000.*[7]

The Venier palazzo had become so grimed and neglected from its years as an army billet that when Peggy met with Dudley Delevingne to discuss the sale, it was hard to visualize the stories he told her about his recent summer there – the cocktail parties, the jazz bands and film-star guests. But while Peggy was charmed by Doris's handsome brother, and would have happily enjoyed him as an additional perk, she had a very different vision for Doris's palazzo; and as soon as the purchase was complete, in early 1949, she brought in a team of builders to begin renovations.

Her vision for the building was clean, clear and modernist, and above all dominated by the needs of her collection. While she left Doris's decorative mosaic floors intact, she had all of the elaborate stuccowork removed from the walls, leaving them free for the hanging of paintings. She reclaimed a couple of the luxury bathrooms for gallery space, and planned each of the palazzo's main living areas with a specific eye to the works they would house. Her bedroom, painted her favourite turquoise blue, was her most personal space. It was dominated by a silver bedhead that she'd commissioned from Alexander Calder back in New York in the winter of 1945–6; an interlacing of finely hammered metal depicting images of pond life, with exuberantly festive fish and flowers, a dragonfly and ripples of water. The walls were decorated with

* An equivalent by today's values would be approximately $600,000 – far short of the price such a property could now command.

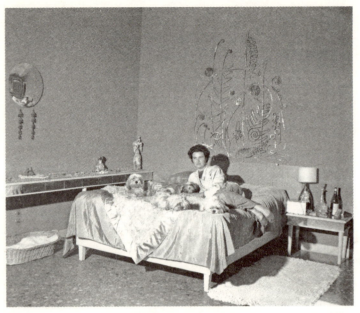

Peggy's bedroom at the palazzo,
with her Calder bedhead.

two paintings of Peggy and Benita when they were children, also her collection of earrings (now numbering over a hundred pairs), which, in imitation of Mary Reynolds, she turned into an art display. Additionally on show were some of her favourite surrealist objects, including several Joseph Cornell boxes and a number of the oddly decorated bottles that Laurence had begun making in New York. Later she would add Francis Bacon's *Study for Chimpanzee*, a work she liked both because it seemed to her the least frightening of his paintings and because, she admitted, its fuchsia background went very well with the room's colour scheme.

The long dining room at the back of the palazzo was hung with a choice selection of Cubist paintings and furnished with the antiques Peggy had bought twenty-five years ago on her first, and spiritually decisive, visit to Venice. She considered that their contrasting patinas and geometries of design, centuries apart, made an 'admirable' complement to each other, and she was right. Peggy had developed an excellent eye, both in the display of her art and the creation of her living spaces. Yet even in the creative euphoria of redesigning her palazzo she kept a careful eye on her budget, tolerating the coat of orange primer on her radiators because it deferred the expense of getting them properly painted. She was a pragmatist, too, and having started to expand her family of Lhasa terriers she opted to make her dark blue living room, in the centre of the palazzo, as modern and functional as possible, installing a pair of plain boxy sofas by Elsie de Wolfe, whose beige leatherette covers could easily be cleaned of dirty paw marks and dog hair.

Peggy was proud her palazzo was becoming so very 'un-Venetian'; and she made a blatant statement of that fact in the Calder mobile that she hung in the entrance hall, in place of the traditional Murano glass chandelier. It pleased her to observe the expressions of distaste and incomprehension on the faces of certain Venetian guests, who considered that Calder's shards of glass and china 'might have come out of a garbage pail'.[8] One of those guests was Princess Pignatelli, who'd once been Luisa's rival in decadent style but had now grown conservatively old; she complained to Peggy that she could have had 'the most beautiful house in Venice', if she would only throw away her 'awful' art. But the 'awful art' made its way into the grounds too: Peggy cleared away enough of the overgrown shrubbery to make space for several of her sculptures. She had an eccentric, Byzantine stone throne installed in the garden from which to sit and view her domain, and in 1961 she would commission the American sculptor Claire Falkenstein to create a gate for the back entrance out of Murano glass and welded iron.

It was on her waterfront terrace, in full public view, that Peggy chose to place her most controversial piece: a bronze statue by Marino Marini called *The Angel of the Citadel*. It was an ecstatic, celebratory piece of a nude man astride a horse, and while the arms, outspread like wings, evoked an angelic kind of joy, the rider's large and lively erection was defiantly pagan. Marini had tactfully made the phallus detachable so that Peggy could unscrew it when 'stuffy' visitors came to her palazzo, or when the nuns came down to the waterfront terrace on holy days to catch the blessing of the Patriarch – the Bishop of Venice – as he sailed past in his motorboat.[9] But despite these precautions, the statue became notorious. Jean Arp had himself photographed 'smoking' its detached phallus as though it were a cigar: the art historian James Lord was snapped astride the horse in a pose which, to his chagrin, made him look as though he were 'fucking' its rider.[10]

*****

At first Peggy's decisions about displaying her art had to be made piece-meal, because until she'd imported it officially and paid her import tax, she was allowed to keep only a limited number of works in the palazzo at any one time. In 1949 she'd been able to borrow her sculptures for a small public showing in the garden, but otherwise the bulk of her col-lection was either lent out to exhibitions or kept in storage at Ca' Pesaro, the city's contemporary art museum. In 1951, however, Peggy managed to bring it all home. It had conveniently travelled out of Italy, touring several museums across Europe, and she had been able to bring it back through a small border post in the Alps where she claimed a few 'ignorant and sleepy douaniers' had been willing to accept her prepos-terously low estimate of its value (a mere $1,000) and charged her a proportionately tiny import tax.[11]

Once she had all the art under her own roof, Peggy was impatient to show it off to the public. Her palazzo wasn't spacious enough to display the entire collection, and some more recent American acquisitions had to be stacked in the basement cellar – where a number of them would suffer the depredations of *aqua alta* flooding and winter damp. The rest was arranged throughout the rooms and corridors, and in the summer of 1951 a notice appeared on the waterfront façade announcing that the Peggy Guggenheim Collection would be open to Venice throughout the summer, on Monday, Wednesday and Friday afternoons.

Compared to the meticulously designed Art of This Century, Peggy's Venetian gallery was a homespun affair. There were no public toilets, which meant that visitors either relieved themselves in the garden or slipped into one of Peggy's own bathrooms; there was no clear bound-ary between private and public space, so that guests who were staying in the palazzo were routinely disturbed by art-loving tourists who strayed into their bedrooms by mistake. While Peggy had had Howard Putzel, Jimmy and others to assist her in New York, most of the daily operations in Venice were performed by her, with her two young maids doing duty as guides (none of the art was labelled, although there was a very basic mimeographed catalogue that visitors could buy). The girls were from the mainland countryside and had no prior knowledge of art, but Peggy took great pride in the fact that she'd drilled them so efficiently, they were very properly shocked by a visiting art professor who mistook a Braque for a Picasso. She also employed the part-time secretarial services of a young restaurateur called Vittorio Corrain, who, with his brother Renato, ran a small trattoria just north of San Marco.

All' Angelo was at that time the closest thing Venice had to an artists' café – the Corrain brothers had a policy of accepting artworks in

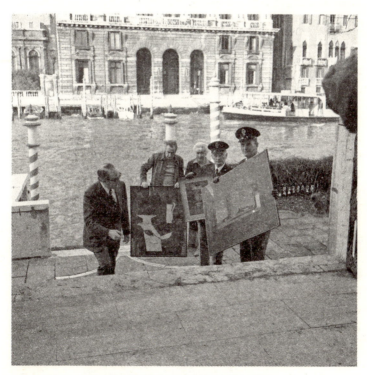

Peggy's collection comes home to the palazzo.

lieu of cash – and it was here that Peggy had been sent in 1946 when she'd first decided to settle in Venice and was searching for evidence of a local art scene. She'd encountered just two modern painters on her first visit to All' Angelo: Giuseppi Santomaso, a genial, tubby surrealist with a passionate knowledge of Venetian history, and the tall, bearded Emilio Vedova. Although she'd had trouble following the men's Venetian dialect, as soon as she'd explained who she was and why she wanted to come to Venice they'd grown very excited and formed immediately high expectations of the impact she and her collection might make on the city. It had been Santomaso, then, who'd recommended to the Biennale committee that Peggy be invited to participate in the celebratory re-opening.

In limited ways, Peggy did succeed in realizing Vedova and Santomaso's hopes for a re-galvanized Venice. During the 1950s, as word spread about her collection, a buzz gathered around the city as artists and art students came from around the world to view it. Art tourists and dealers came too, and it's possible that over the long term Peggy's collection had an influence on the course of the Biennale, as it oriented itself towards the experimental and the new and became, eventually, one of the world's most prestigious showcases for contemporary art. Originally it might have been the foreign merchants and explorers who'd brought an international life and flair to the city; by the end of the 20th century it was the painters, photographers, performance artists and sculptors who energized its culture, and it was the Peggy Guggenheim Collection that had helped to attract them.

Where Peggy failed her Venetian artists, however, was in identifying and supporting local talent. During her early years in the city she was generous in her sponsorship of two Italian artists, Tancredi Parmeggiani and Edmondo Bacci, and she purchased individual pieces from several others. Yet for the most part she saw only mediocrity and provincialism among the region's artists; and, as she later admitted, 'little by little I lost interest' in her vision of discovering an Italian Pollock.[12] Her indifference, however, was also symptomatic of the gradual waning of her interest in post-war art in general, for now that she was based in Venice Peggy had only limited contact with the lively, influential galleries, dealers, critics and artists who'd formerly stimulated her addiction.

She continued to add some significant purchases to the collection: works by Arp and Magritte, De Kooning, her Bacon chimpanzee and some pieces by a young British painter called Alan Davie, whose style reminded her of Pollock. Yet the prices for contemporary art were already rising beyond the reach of her dollars, and Peggy was already beginning to fall out of love with the directions in which painting and sculpture were moving. While she made a modest foray into ethnic art, buying several totemic figures, masks and carvings, she was growing more conservative in every sense of the word, and was increasingly focusing her attention on the works she already had in her possession.

Creating extra gallery space in the palazzo was her prime concern, and one of her early plans was to build a two-storey penthouse on the roof – a feature almost unheard of in historic Venice, but theoretically possible for Peggy, since her palazzo had never been listed. In the end she rejected the idea, disliking the architect's designs and recoiling from the expense – it would have cost her nearly $60,000, close to the price she had paid for the entire property. For a while she temporized, creating extra gallery space out of the basement laundry and moving around the bedrooms of her live-in staff. But as the latter complained about their cramped conditions (and about having to do laundry out on the terrace), the only solution was for Peggy to give up some of her garden and construct an annex in the grounds.

The annex, built in 1958, was a long, low and gracefully arched structure, a modern version of the hay barn or *barchessa* that was traditionally attached to rural farms. It ran at right angles to the palazzo, against the wall of the neighbouring property (a compact 19th-century building, located on the site of the old Venier palazzo, and now occupied by the American consulate);* and it was completed in time for that year's Biennale. When Peggy threw a party to inaugurate her *barchessa* she smugly declared that she'd drawn as distinguished an art crowd as any of the national pavilions. But that party (Peggy called it her personal Biennale) also reflected the way in which her relationship to her art had shifted. Year by year, as she became less of a collector, she was

*   This fact gave Peggy some ironic satisfaction, since it meant she was 'guarded day and night by soldiers'.

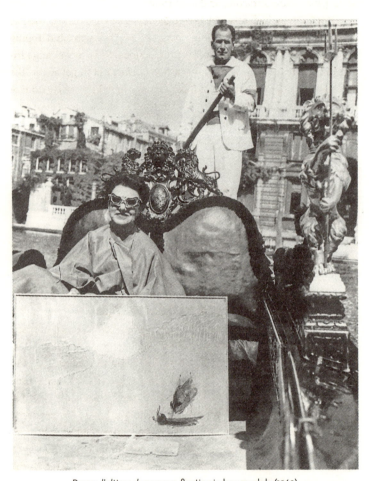

Peggy, *l'ultima dogaressa*, floating in her gondola (1962).

also becoming more of a *grande dame* – and, enthroned in Venice in the midst of her collection, she was starting to relish the fact that she was as much a visitor attraction as the art itself.

When Peggy had first put her collection on display she'd tried to maintain her own privacy, hiding away in her bedroom and roping off areas of the building that were out of bounds. 'It is very strange living in a museum,' she wrote very early on. 'If I want to get across the hall in my dressing gown or a sun bathing costume I find myself out of luck.'[13] But the public wanted Peggy as well as her art, and total strangers routinely appeared at the palazzo outside of opening hours, expecting her to give them a private tour. Some had the decency to claim a distant acquaintance with family or friends, but others simply turned up on spec. Even though Peggy felt bothered, invaded, she could not help but preen a little at the attention she was getting, and by degrees she began to live up to it, making herself a very visible presence in the city.

Like Luisa, she liked to float around Venice every day in her gondola. She had commissioned it for herself in 1956, and at a time when most of the old families had given up their private gondolas and many public ones had fallen into shabby disrepair, Peggy's custom-built craft became the talk of the canals. It was beautifully made – its seats were decoratively carved and its ornate oar rests, or *cavalli*, were cast in the image of the Venier lion rather than the more traditional seahorse.* The two men she hired as her private gondoliers were dressed in turquoise and white to match the striped mooring poles (*palli*) by her waterfront terrace. And if she could not equal the crowd-stopping extravagance of Luisa's appearances – the cheetah, the black manservant, the peacock parasol – she still managed to look extraordinary. Accompanied by one or two of her dogs, Peggy became an unmistakable figure on the water, especially once she took to wearing the outsized sunglasses shaped like jazzy butterfly wings that she'd had designed for her by the painter Edward Melcarth.

So striking and entitled a figure did Peggy cut as she floated along the canals that some of the locals began calling her *l'ultima dogaressa* – the last [female] doge. Centuries earlier, noble families like the Veniers

---

* They were thought by some to be images of her Lhasa Apso dogs.

had made a very public display of their gondolas, decorating every surface with carvings, gilt and paintwork so that the traditional wooden
cabins, or *felze*, looked as ornate as royal carriages. In 1562, when the
Senate passed strict sumptuary laws to purge the city of sinful excess,
all gondolas were stripped of their decorations, painted black and their
ornamentation restricted to a few small details, like the brass *cavalli*
mid-stern. Yet a rich man's gondola could still be singled out from the
general water traffic by the quality of its materials, the livery of its gondoliers and the sumptuous attire of its passengers, glimpsed through
the windows of the *felze*.

In 1956, Peggy's more snobbish and impoverished neighbours were
not amused by the fact that a single American woman could possess a
gondola of her own (in addition to the high-speed motorboat, *Cleopatra*,
that she'd bought three years earlier). Gripping on to the threadbare
remnants of their own ancestral grandeur, these old Venetians resented
the blatancy of Peggy's wealth: the modernization of her palazzo, the
size of her staff (she had a live-in butler and two cooks in addition to her
gondoliers and maids) and above all the effrontery of her hideous art.
Few of them came to see her collection, even fewer invited her into their
homes, and there was certainly an element of anti-Semitism in some of
these rebuffs. Doris, with her very English title and eminent connections, had been far easier to embrace; it was telling that while the city's
leading statesman, Count Volpi, had taken charge of Lady Castlerosse's
welcome, it would take over a decade for the Volpi family to unbend sufficiently towards Peggy to invite her to their annual ball.

Venice was largely a more conservative, less hedonist city than it had
been before the war. Although fascism had been rejected, Mussolini's
puritanical ethos lingered, and there was a particular animus towards the
expatriate homosexual community that had re-grouped in Venice: every
now and again it was ambushed by the city authorities, who brought
trumped-up charges of illegal solicitation against prominent individuals.
Peggy herself was a rogue and possibly undesirable element, and according to Živa Kraus, a young photographer who became a friend in later
years, everybody talked about her, everybody wanted to know what she
was up to next: 'they watched her all the time [– it was] a kind of voyeurism'.[14] Aside from the scandalous positioning of the Marini statue right

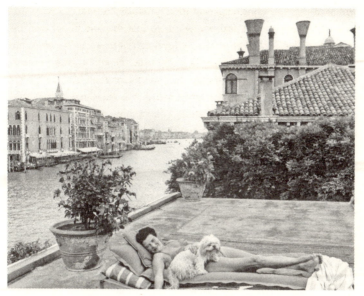

Peggy sunbathing on the palazzo roof.

in front of the palazzo, aside from the daily exhibitionism of her gondola rides, Peggy committed other small but colourful offences against decorum. In hot weather she liked to sunbathe naked on her roof, and even though she couldn't be seen from the street or canal level (and even though this was far more discreet behaviour than Luisa's nocturnal walks around San Marco, when she was rumoured to have been nude under her fur cloak), Peggy was clearly visible from the upper windows of the *prefettura* opposite, where the office workers used to mark the advent of spring by Signora Guggenheim's first appearance on the roof.

Just as Luisa had filled the palazzo with outrageous guests, it was impossible for Venice to ignore the gregarious, noisy, even outlandish people Peggy attracted. In addition to holding small weekly salons, dinners, and occasional large parties, she invited numerous old friends and associates to stay – many of them artists, many of them overtly bohemian by Dorsoduro standards. She always kept a guest book open, to which visitors were encouraged to contribute a poem, a witty epigram, a cartoon or a sketch; and so many guests came to her over the years that she would fill the pages of several. These guests books, in fact, became one of the great autograph collections of the age, including messages from Giacometti, Chagall, Miro, Cocteau and Henry Moore, composers like Stravinsky and Virgil Thomson, and writers like Tennessee Williams and Gore Vidal. Cecil Beaton paid a visit, curious perhaps to see what Peggy had done to the palazzo after Doris's death. The film actor Paul Newman also made an appearance at one of her very last parties, although by then Peggy was in her late seventies and was not entirely sure who he was. There was even an early message from Max, who'd visited Peggy in 1954 while attending the Biennale, and was clearly ready for a truce: 'An old friend is come back forever and ever and ever, darling Peggy,' he wrote – words of affection he'd never granted her while they were married.

Several entries were penned by the American author Truman Capote, who first visited in 1949 and took extended advantage of Peggy's hospitality while working on his memoir *The Muses are Heard*. She always enjoyed Capote. The small, blond, waspish writer was cheap to feed, being very 'careful about his line' and requiring only eggs at lunchtime and a light fish supper at Harry's Bar. He listened appreciatively to her stories, and he entertained her with wonderfully gossipy anecdotes of his own, delivered in his confiding, falsetto squeak of a voice. Capote in turn was quite fond of Peggy, and back in New York would defend her against some of the crueller stories that continued to circulate about her sexual peccadilloes. But he could also be cruel, and as a writer he could never resist the lethal comic thrust: Peggy would have minded very much if she'd known about *Answered Prayers*, the lengthy, Proustian novel Capote began during the mid-1960s in which he represented her as a 'homely' heiress whose habit of 'rattling her false teeth' made it impossible to imagine her ever having an affair with the 'monkish' Samuel Beckett.[*15]

In addition to the friends who came from abroad, Peggy gathered a small circle around her in Venice. She would sometimes complain that

---

*   *Answered Prayers* remained unfinished, and was published posthumously.

the city was too small for her, yet she did find kindred spirits among its expatriate community: Martyn Coleman, a clever, cultivated man who lived opposite her on the Grand Canal; Christina Thoresby, a music writer who played the organ at St George's, the English church on Campo San Vio; and Robert Brady, an American art collector with a rare gift for flattery, who in later years and in other cities would pay court to two other woman whom Peggy had known distantly in Paris, the jazz-age star Josephine Baker and the painter Tamara de Lempicka.

Peggy herself had become more susceptible to flattery in middle age, and when Prince Philip came from England on an official visit to Venice she was pleased and proud to be among those formally presented to him. Nearly two decades earlier, Philip had been guest of honour at the last of Doris's pre-war parties and he reminisced about that night to Peggy, recalling that he'd had a 'great flirt' with one of the guests whom, he joked, had since gone on to become a respectable mother of four. Peggy, eager to respond, quipped 'Ah, she did better than you, then' (the prince having as yet fathered only two children). But as so often when she felt out of her depth, Peggy had miscalculated her tone, and her attempt at humour was left to expire in a royal silence.[16]

* * * * *

Peggy's closest friends in Venice were always foreigners like herself; even though she learned to master the Venetian dialect, with its mellifluous sibilants and slurs, she claimed that she distrusted the 'Italian character' as essentially unreliable and histrionic. But she did nonetheless pride herself on being integrated with the city. When she went for an evening drink at Harry's Bar, she liked to take her two gondoliers for company: when she took her dogs for walks around Dorsoduro she always exchanged pleasantries with local shopkeepers, with the small children who used to splash around the steps of the backwater canals and with the staff who worked in the bars and restaurants that lined the wide expanse of the Zattere.

She was a far more neighbourly figure than either Luisa or Doris had been, and it's significant that the party Peggy said she most enjoyed in Venice was the one she threw for her builders and their families in 1958 to celebrate the completion of her *barchessa*. It had been held in the garden of a local restaurant and amidst the drinking, the conversation and the easy gaiety, Peggy felt she was in her natural element. Someone played the violin for her, someone else composed an impromptu poem, and before she went to bed she wrote in her guest book, 'The nicest night of my life in Venice. 1948–58.'

Peggy was putting down deep roots in the city and she mapped her affection for it with each walk and each gondola ride, becoming as intimately familiar with a particular tumble of bougainvillea around a balcony or particularly limpid reflection of sunlight and stone as she was with her favourite church, the tiny San Giorgio degli Schiavoni with its jewel-bright painted ceiling and radiant Carpaccio paintings. Yet as much as she loved Venice, she was unable to live in the city all year round: the damp chills of winter oppressed her, as did the absence of the summer crowds. It was during these months that she tended to go travelling – often to London to see old friends, and most regularly to Paris to see her family.

During the early 1950s Peggy's relations with the children were still relatively equable. Pegeen had three small sons – Fabrice, David and Nicholas – and although she was drinking too much and had grown disenchanted with her marriage, she was painting productively and well. Peggy took pleasure and pride in her daughter's talent, and during the summers she encouraged her to come to the palazzo on her own to concentrate on her art. She gave over a basement room for Pegeen to use as a studio and from it Pegeen produced numerous Venetian scenes – half-wistful, half-carnivalesque paintings that refracted the city through the pastel colours and childlike forms of her distinctively naif style.

Towards her son, Peggy's feelings had become more detached. Sindbad had ended up marrying his wartime friend Jacqueline Vendatour, and his life with her and their two small sons in Paris seemed reasonably content. He'd now rejected the whimsical embarrassment of his childhood name in favour of his middle name, Michael, and he was running a small literary magazine, *Points*, that he'd launched with Laurence's help. Yet Peggy found it difficult to get the measure of her son, whose greatest love was still, inexplicably, cricket, and who still tended to ally himself with his father rather than with her. Sindbad had always laid most of the blame for his chaotic childhood on Peggy, and although he wanted to love her, he distrusted her. The equivocal nature of his feelings was reflected in a poem he wrote in Peggy's guest book during a visit in June 1955:

Je ne puis écrire plus
Car je dois garder un surplus
pour mon proche retour
A cette ville où on ne trouve pas toujours L'AMOUR[17]

Sindbad had signed the entry with an affectionately filial dedication, 'all my love to Moma'; yet the poem's final line, 'A city where you do not always find LOVE', had read uneasily, as if hinting at Peggy's inadequacies as a mother and at his own underlying sense of betrayal.

Peggy, however, might have read the poem quite differently, for one of the disappointments of her move to Venice had been her failure to find a new husband or companion. She was still as sexually curious as she'd been in her youth and no less eager for affection, but while she'd engineered a few brief liaisons after she'd arrived in the city (one with an admiral), she had never again found the emotional or creative fulfilment of her former relationships. Towards the end of her life she would look back on her first busy years in Venice as essentially lonely ones, and that perception was fuelled by the fact that the one significant affair on which she did embark had ended, abruptly, in tragedy.

Raoul Gregorich was a man utterly unlike the lovers from Peggy's past, a young car mechanic from the industrial suburb of Mestre who was twenty-three years her junior. He had a limited education and an ambiguous past – while he was working with the Italian Resistance during the war, his activities were apparently more criminal than political. But when Peggy first fell in love with Raoul in early 1951, she rejoiced over everything that made him so different. As she boasted to Emily, he was 'completely natural', with a lack of self-consciousness, a simple appetite for pleasure that seemed to her a striking contrast to the competitive intellectual sophistication of her other lovers and friends. He was also 'madly beautiful', dark and muscular with rather flashy, matinee-idol good looks, and in every way a 'real man'. Peggy adored the fact that even though Raoul was years younger than her, he could dominate her physically; that he could put his big arms around her and call her his 'dear child' – *mia cara bambina.*[18]

'I'm terribly in love,' she wrote to her friend Becky Reis in October 1951, 'we get more and more connected even though we don't live together.' Raoul made Peggy feel young and hopeful again, and during the first months of the affair she looked it, too. She dressed well, she drank less and her self-confidence soared on the wings of her lover's finely honed skills of flattery. Raoul was unabashedly eloquent in his compliments, not only praising Peggy's appearance but also the achievement of her art collection, which he assured her would 'go down in history'. He seemed, too, entirely at ease with the difference in their status; casually taking it for granted that Peggy would pick up the bill whenever they went out, assuming that it would give her pleasure to help him when he needed some money to set up his own garage.

Because Raoul accepted Peggy's wealth as part of the natural order, because he appeared neither resentful of it nor threatened by it, Peggy felt emancipated from the niggling paranoia that had damaged so many of her relationships. She didn't even feel her usual disabling jealousy when she discovered that Raoul was having flings with other, younger women, shrugging off his small infidelities as an inevitable consequence of his youth and sexual stamina. She liked it when Venetian society made clear its disapproval of her working-class lover; in September 1951, when the multi-millionaire art collector Charles de Beistegui made a point of excluding Peggy from his annual ball, she flaunted the snub.

But over time, as the sexual intensity began to fade, the stresses and strains in the relationship became more evident. As a couple, their stock of conversation was limited: Peggy had no interest in the life of the Mestre or in the daily running of Raoul's mechanics shop, while he complained that Peggy's friends were snobbish and boring. It also became harder for them to gloss over the disparity in their social and financial positions, and by the summer of 1952 Peggy was reporting to Emily that even though they could be 'very happy' for some of the time, they 'fought like hell' for the rest.[19] The affair staggered on for another two years, with 'various intermissions and lots of rows', but in the summer of 1954 it broke under Raoul's badgering insistence that

Peggy buy him a new and very expensive sports car. Of late he'd been getting progressively more greedy, and Peggy had been growing correspondingly more sensitive to the possibility that he had only ever been interested in her money. But her objection to buying him the car was also motivated by fear. Raoul was a reckless driver, and she had nightmare images of him in his dangerous new toy, careening around the tiny country roads on the mainland. The two of them fought, and when Raoul made it brutally clear that the new car was a condition of his staying with her, that he didn't plan to remain 'a gigolo for nothing', Peggy accused him of blackmail and ended the affair.

But she was acutely miserable. Raoul had given Peggy the gift of his youth – he'd made her feel desirable, energetic, alive – and after a few weeks of lonely regrets, she gave in and purchased the new car. Their reunion, however, was horribly short-lived, because later that autumn Raoul was speeding too fast and too cockily around the mainland in his new car, and when he swerved to avoid a motorcycle he failed to see another oncoming vehicle. The crash was fatal, and as Peggy wrote miserably to Djuna, it had the grim inevitability of a Greek tragedy. She felt responsible for Raoul's accident, and afterwards became overwhelmed by the same superstitious guilt she'd suffered over the death of John Holms. Years later, when she was writing an updated version of her memoir, Peggy would barely mention her young Venetian lover, feeling perhaps that the affair would be of little interest to her readers. At the time, however, she was incapable of such detachment. She felt alone, old, tainted by fate; and after Raoul had been buried on the island cemetery of San Michele, she confided bleakly to Djuna, 'I don't think I'll ever love anyone again; I hope and pray not.'[20]

CHAPTER 13

Two years after Raoul's death, Peggy could write to Djuna about the compensatory happiness she had found in her newly acquired gondola: 'I adore floating...I can't think of anything as nice since I gave up sex, or rather since it gave me up.' But at the time, the city had been spoiled for her by tragedy, and as the winter of 1954 approached she wanted only to get away. She wasn't blind to the melancholy beauty that stole over Venice once the summer crowds had gone: the low, slanting winter sun, the spectral fogs, the gleam of rain-slicked cobbles and the long dark nights during which an ancient silence descended on the city. Yet even in happier years she had found the chill and isolation difficult to endure, and in her grief for Raoul she longed only for sunshine, movement and change.

Late that autumn she headed south, to a tiny, palm-fringed island in Ceylon (now Sri Lanka) that had recently been bought by her friend Paul Bowles and his wife Jane. It lay just a few hundred yards off the mainland, and could only be reached by wading through the warm, shallow coastal waters. To Peggy, it seemed like paradise: 'another dream world, so different from Venice', and as she sunned herself into a pleasurable trance, swimming in the Indian ocean, staring lazily at 'beautiful Singhalese fishermen' on their narrow wooden boats, she allowed herself to drift away from dark memories.[1]

She stayed there for five weeks, after which she continued on to India, joining the photographer Roloff Beny for a sightseeing marathon that took her through twenty-two cities, including the Punjab capital Chandigarh (whose utopian town planning, designed by Le Corbusier, intrigued Peggy with its strict 'socialist' principles). The explorer's spirit that Mary McCarthy had so admired was still strong in her. Just as she'd been happy to tolerate the absence of electricity and plumbing on the Bowles's island for the sake of its remote beauty, so Peggy was an intrepid and very energetic traveller throughout the Indian trip. She even made a special detour to Darjeeling to visit Tenzing Norgay, the Sherpa who had guided Edmund Hillary on his Everest climb, in the hopes of persuading him to part with one of his male Lhasa dogs and so 'put an end to the inbreeding' of her own Venetian 'family'.[2]

Peggy's globetrotting curiosity remained alive throughout the following decade, as she made a habit of escaping the Venetian winters to South America, Japan, Hong Kong, Bangkok and Tripoli. In 1958 she was in Mexico, where she was looked after by a British council official called Maurice Cardiff. The younger man was frequently exasperated by his charge: Peggy's habit of obsessing over some small bit of change from which she believed she'd been cheated; her obstinate refusal to put on sensible shoes when trekking in the jungle; her tactless folly in wearing expensive jewelry while walking through a rural village or city slum were all infuriating to him. But there were better moments when Cardiff also found Peggy entertaining company: sharp, funny and inquisitive, full of questions about how the Mexicans lived, and eloquent in her admiration for the majestic Mayan ruins at Palenque.

In Mexico, as everywhere else she visited, Peggy made it her business to investigate the local art. She thoroughly disliked the polemical frescoes of Diego Rivera, but was glad to deepen her knowledge of his late wife, Frida Kahlo, whose work she herself had exhibited back in New York. Visiting Kahlo's former home (now a museum), Peggy was humbled to see the invalid's chair from which the painter had worked, sensing an 'atmosphere of tragedy' that put her own troubles into perspective. She was unaware, then, of other stories that the house had witnessed back in the years when Kahlo formed a close, sexual friendship with Luisa Casati's daughter. It would have piqued Peggy's curiosity had she known about Cristina, and about the latter's unhappy association with her own palazzo. But while she was in Mexico City Peggy did make one very deliberate attempt to connect with the past, paying a conciliatory visit to her old rival, Leonora Carrington, who was now married to a Hungarian photographer. Because Peggy had recently come to her own pragmatic accommodation with Max, she was in a mood to be generous, happy to admire Leonora's two 'lovely' sons and to appreciate the quality of her painting, which she judged to have 'greatly developed'.[3]

In April 1959 Peggy left Mexico and travelled north to New York; but here there were other grudges, more complicated to resolve. It had been twelve years since she'd left the city, turning her back on the disapproving gossip surrounding her memoir and on the problematic issues of debt and entitlement that had clogged up relations with some of her painters. She had been in no hurry to return, but she was drawn there now by the latest Guggenheim art museum, which was due to open in October and which had been the last project initiated by her uncle Solomon before his death in 1949. Solomon's presidential role in the Guggenheim Foundation had been inherited by his son Harry – Peggy's cousin – while her old friend and adviser, James Johnson Sweeney, had been appointed director of the new museum. Because Peggy had warm feelings towards both men, she came to New York wanting to wish the project well. But the old rivalries and resentments that underlay her relations with the family were not so easily exorcised. That May, when Harry arranged a tour of the new building for her, Peggy found it difficult to be generous in her response.

The Solomon R. Guggenheim Museum had been designed by Frank Lloyd Wright, and there were many who hailed its clean concrete lines and ingeniously structured interior as the late, great achievement of the architect's career. But Peggy was grudgingly critical. From the outside the building looked to her like 'a huge garage' that had been incongruously plonked into the elegant bustle of Fifth Avenue. The inside she liked even less, judging its beige and white colour scheme to be drab, and dismissing as mere gimmickry the long, graceful ramp that spiralled upwards through the gallery's rotunda. Wright had envisaged that space as a vast, luminous seashell, but to Peggy the ramp suggested only coils of an 'evil serpent' and obstinately she claimed that her own modest *barchessa* in Venice was a far more beautiful space.[4] To see the Guggenheim fortune being wasted on such architectural bombast made her glad, she said, to be the poor relation of the family.

Even now, when Peggy was so well established in her own world, it was difficult for her to be confronted by the financial might of her relatives. But it was not only family history that put her on the defensive during this New York visit. When Peggy had left the city in 1947, she had believed that the creation of Art of This Century had been the 'most honourable achievement' of her life – giving a platform to a new generation of American artists, and especially to the genius of Jackson Pollock.[5] Returning now to New York, she found that influential voices like Clement Greenberg were warmly endorsing her achievement; nevertheless, she felt chilled and alienated by the city's art culture, which looked to her now like 'an enormous business venture' with works by Pollock or Rothko routinely bought as investment commodities, as tax write-offs or as cultural trophies for the very rich.

Visiting the shiny, upmarket galleries of Manhattan, Peggy felt bitter nostalgia for the old days of risk and discovery; for the days when dealers and artists were part of the same crowd, driven by the same addiction to art. And it heightened the resentment she'd begun to develop towards her protégé, Pollock, during the final years of his life. Having initially been proud of the media interest surrounding his career, Peggy had grown conscious that the more celebrated Pollock became, the more forgetful he was about crediting her role in his success. Peggy minded the professional slight to her reputation, but she took far more personally the depth of Pollock's ingratitude.

It was still a well-worn pattern with Peggy that her most generous impulses were most frequently ruptured by resentment. Her friendships with Djuna Barnes and Emma Goldman and her relationships with family had been spoiled at various points by Peggy's belief that her generosity was being taken for granted. Pollock's death in 1956 had done nothing to reconcile her to the painter, especially since she'd recently discovered the existence of fifteen early works that had been produced while he was still under contract to her. They should, by rights, have been given to her, and Peggy, suspecting that Pollock had deliberately concealed them, would go on to sue his widow, Lee, for compensation. (The suit proved long and complicated, and in 1961 she eventually had to settle for $122,000, a sum far below their actual worth.)

'I do not like art today,' Peggy wrote fiercely, 'I think it has gone to hell.' It wasn't just the ingratitude of protégés, the cynicism of the market that had disillusioned her; it was the work itself. She disliked the direction that Rothko's painting had taken, and she regarded the emerging generation of Rauschenberg, Oldenburg and Warhol as mere pygmies in relation to giants of modernism like Picasso, Ernst and

Brancusi. It seemed to her that the 20th century had already produced its quota of genius, that its golden age had passed; and when she left New York early in the summer of 1959, she was grateful to return to the enduring consolation of her own collection of masterpieces.

* * * * *

Peggy had now fallen into the habit of referring to the artworks as her children, and as she grew older she frequently found them easier to love than her own son and daughter. Sindbad was becoming even more of a disappointment and an enigma to her. In 1955 his marriage to Jacqueline had ended, and while he was now happily remarried to an English woman named Peggy Yeomans and had fathered two little girls, he seemed to his mother to be drifting through an ineffectual life. His literary magazine had folded and he'd moved on to various jobs in property and insurance that she high-handedly deemed to be 'stupid and sad'. As far as Peggy could see, her son's only abiding passion was for the Paris cricket club of which he'd become president. Friends who were close to Sindbad, and who knew him as Mike, saw a very different man: intelligent, humorous, and one who'd made admirable efforts to achieve some kind of financial independence (a rare phenomenon in the Guggenheim-Vail extended family). Yet Sindbad himself believed that something had gone adrift in him during his childhood as he'd been shuttled between his parents and made a pawn to their quarrelsome caprices. Although he had long come to terms with Laurence (their relationship one of mutual acceptance, fraught by the occasional alcohol-fuelled row), towards Peggy he continued to feel a wary tangle of emotions, a combination of reluctant affection and admiration but also an unbudgeable resentment towards her blind spots as a mother.

When Sindbad had remarried in Paris he'd naturally invited Peggy to attend the wedding; yet she had not only failed to make an appearance, but for several months had shown no interest in meeting his new wife. Sindbad dutifully brought his family to stay at the palazzo during the summer, but it hurt him to see how little interest Peggy could muster in his wife and children, how openly impatient she became by the end of their stay, and how much more affection she seemed to lavish on her terriers. Sindbad's girls took to calling Peggy 'grandmother the dogs'; but she didn't seem to mind. She had blunted her sensitivities towards Sindbad now, and while she loved him because he was her son, as a man he didn't particularly engage her. 'Peggy liked strong people,' according to Jacqueline Vendatour, 'and Sindbad never really had much drive.'[6]

With Pegeen she was far more intensely involved, even through relations between them were often recriminatory and cross. Like Sindbad, Pegeen held historic grievances against her mother, stacking up memories of every crime of selfishness or neglect that she'd committed. Pegeen would not forgive the fact that on the day she'd turned twenty-one Peggy had forgotten it was her birthday, and that she, Pegeen, had felt so betrayed that she'd made an inexpert attempt at suicide, cutting her wrists. Even now that Pegeen was a mature woman, she was jealously alive to every lapse of maternal affection. Like Sindbad, she begrudged the care Peggy devoted to her dogs, and she was even more resentful of the art. One summer when Pegeen was travelling past the palazzo on a vaporetto she startled her companion, a Venetian artist called Manina, by hissing vindictively: 'If that collection goes up in flames you'll know who did it.'[7]

Yet as distant, as thoughtless as Peggy might seem, she was, in her own stubborn and partial way, deeply invested in Pegeen's life. She wanted her daughter to excel in ways that she never had, and she had worked hard to promote her art, displaying several of Pegeen's sad, wonky paintings alongside her own collection in the palazzo and brokering introductions to gallery owners and dealers elsewhere. Peggy was equally eager to save her daughter from the mistakes that she herself had made, and it was around the time that the marriage to Hélion began to fall apart that she made determined (if sometimes crudely misplaced) efforts to try and mend Pegeen's life.

To Djuna Barnes, Pegeen had always looked a soul adrift. With her 'downthrust chin...floating golden hair...her...stubborn and lost wandering walk', she seemed to Djuna to have misplaced her sense of purpose, her belief in happiness.[8] Certainly she had brought her childhood insecurities to her adult life, and while she had initially loved Hélion and doted on her three baby sons, she had been unable to settle. She had embarked on a series of badly judged affairs, the most destructive of

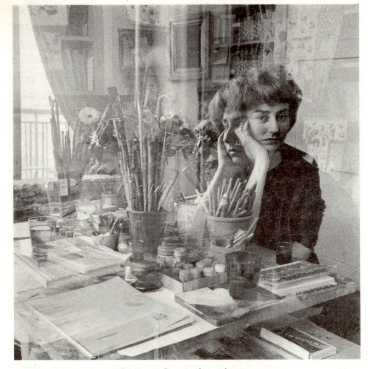

Pegeen in Paris in the mid-1950s,
when her marriage to Hélion was unravelling.

which was with Tancredi Parmeggiani, the Italian artist who Peggy had identified as a potential protégé in 1952.

Back then Peggy had offered the painter a monthly stipend and use of a basement studio in the palazzo, where Tancredi, who insisted on being referred to by his first name only, had produced some rather mediocre work and a lot of mess. Peggy's two maids hated him because he always refused to take off his paint-splattered shoes when leaving the studio; but when Pegeen met him the following summer she fell entirely under his spell, mistaking his histrionic egotism for character and talent.

In fact Tancredi was manipulative and volatile, and he proved very dangerous for Pegeen as he drew her into the melodramas of his paranoid, emotional world. Their stormy relationship continued on and off for two years, after which Tancredi disappeared off to Rome to get married.* Pegeen's own marriage, however, was beyond saving, and although she and Hélion would not divorce until 1958, she stumbled through their final years together in a state of unhappiness and guilt, self-medicating her misery with alcohol, Valium and sleeping pills. Peggy was so worried by Pegeen's decline that she paid for her to go into analysis; yet, as so often, she had her own fixed and subjective views about what was good for her family. Rather than addressing the root causes of Pegeen's problems, she believed that the answer lay in finding her daughter a new husband who might succeed where Hélion had failed. It was the emotional logic she'd so often applied to her own life, and with such unhappy consequences; but this evidently did not occur to Peggy, and in 1957 she took Pegeen on an extended trip to London, hoping to snare her a steady, refined Englishman of the kind she had always rather fancied for herself – and imagined John Holms to be. Almost inevitably, the man with whom Pegeen did fall in love turned out to be the very opposite of what Peggy intended.

* * * * *

At one time in her life, Peggy might have fallen for a man like Ralph Rumney too. He was a young artist, just twenty-three years old, with a sullen kind of beauty and a reputation as a political hell-raiser. His affiliations were both to the Communist Party and to the Situationists (an extreme group of artists who condemned 'the commodification of experience' under modern capitalism and believed that authentic sensation could only be restored through art). There were aspects of Ralph's belligerent self-belief that might have reminded Peggy of the glory days of surrealism – the fights, the protests, the drunken arguments over theory. But as a lover for her daughter, she considered him a disaster. It wasn't only that he was unstable and poor, but she'd convinced herself that his interest in Pegeen was purely mercenary. It seemed evident

---

*   Tancredi, in a last gaudy statement, drowned himself in the Tiber in 1964; but Hélion took a second chance at married happiness with Sindbad's ex-wife, Jacqueline.

to her that Ralph was after a share of the Guggenheim money, and she refused to budge from that view even after he moved to Paris to live with Pegeen. She ignored the care with which he monitored Pegeen's fragile, fluctuating moods; she saw no virtue in his willingness to marry her when she became pregnant with their son Sandro; she was blind to his accommodating generosity in having Pegeen's third son, Nicholas, come and live with them. Most perversely, however, she was disposed to hate Ralph because of the hold he had over Pegeen's heart.

So many contradictions affected Peggy's relationship with her daughter. Ever since Pegeen had been a baby, she had irritated Peggy with her clinging dependency; yet when she had transferred her affections to someone else, to her nurse Doris, to Max or to Kay, Peggy had become jealous. Now that she had no man in her life, no lover of her own, Peggy was even more inclined to be possessive. Convinced of Ralph's base intentions, annoyed at being ousted from her place in Pegeen's life, she made blundering attempts to divide the lovers, offering Ralph $50,000 if he would walk away from her daughter – then, when he angrily rejected the bribe, threatening to stop Pegeen's $150 monthly allowance.

It was difficult and lonely for Peggy to be so alienated from her daughter, and there were few people in Venice with whom she felt able to discuss her family problems. Emily Coleman came to visit from time to time, as did Hazel, although Peggy's hostility towards her sister had revived once the latter began to claim a close friendship with Kay (whom Peggy still regarded as a stealer of husbands and children). Laurence she rarely saw – the death of his wife Jean in 1952 had dashed his last hopes of finding married happiness, and had exacerbated both his drinking and his poor health (he'd suffered from stomach ulcers for years). Nor did Peggy see Djuna Barnes, for while the two women maintained their confiding, scolding, affectionately barbed relationship by post, Djuna was feeling her age, and the combined afflictions of asthma and arthritis made her unwilling to face the long journey from America. These days, Peggy was increasingly reliant on her local circle in Venice, and increasingly ready to welcome the company of passing visitors who came to the palazzo in ever larger numbers, but were sometimes complete strangers to her.

Some of those strangers lingered, however, to become friends. In 1958 the young beat poet Gregory Corso made his way to the palazzo in the hopes of being shown Peggy's art collection, but once there he became beguiled by Peggy herself. 'Good news', he wrote to Allen Ginsberg, 'I had a wild alone ball, dancing thru Picassos and Arps and Ernsts with PG, she is a very sweet person...very strange and marvellous...and old with memories.' During the weeks that followed, an odd mutual infatuation sprang up between the two of them. Corso was captivated by Peggy's stories and by the idiosyncrasies of her patrician style, which seemed to him both very European and old New York. Once, when he arrived very late to see her, he was charmed by the 'wry sarcasm' with which Peggy took off her expensive wristwatch and handed it to him as a gift. She in turn was flattered by the poet's attentions, and pleasantly aroused by his

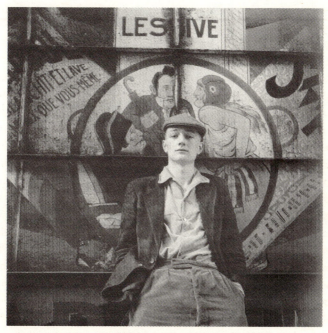

Ralph Rumney, hell-raiser and artist,
in Soho during the mid-1950s.

beatnik good looks. One evening, when she was reminiscing about her former love affairs and probing Corso about his own, it was very clear to the young man that she was in a mood for him to make a pass.

Corso refrained, although Peggy at sixty had become handsome, her nose looking less obviously out of proportion as her face and her body had broadened with age. Soon she would stop dying her hair, allowing it to revert to its much prettier natural grey ('Imagine,' she later commented, 'I was wearing the wrong colour hair for forty years'), and she made a point now of dressing herself well.[9] She always claimed it was a person's duty in Venice to look as theatrically stylish as the city itself: 'one can wear almost anything and not look ridiculous.'[10] And while some of her choices were outré – she now wore bat-shaped spectacles to match her extravagant sunglasses – others were extremely elegant, like the silvery-gold Fortuny dress that had become the most cherished item in her wardrobe. It was as shimmeringly sinuous in fabric and cut as the gowns Luisa had worn half a century earlier and it flattered Peggy, showing off her still-delicate ankles and wrists while smoothing over the thickening contours of her body.

Peggy had grown into her own style of *grande dame* eminence. She liked good manners, and now expected visitors to kiss her hand when they arrived at the palazzo. The writer William Burroughs fell out favour when, advised of Peggy's preference, he commented, 'I will gladly kiss her cunt if that is the custom.'[11] Peggy's friend Robert Brady passed the comment on to her, and she was so offended that she refused to allow Burroughs into her home. Despite her directness in matters of sex, certain forms of crudeness were abhorrent to Peggy: she greatly disapproved of a friend who was writing a pornographic novel, and she deplored the post-war tolerance of public kissing and petting.

A much more welcome guest to the palazzo was John Cage, who came to stay during the winter of 1959. It was nearly two decades since the composer had attended Peggy's New York parties and been awed by the stature of her guests. Now he was becoming eminent in his own right, his Duchamp-inspired experiments in found music and his signature silent score *4'33"* gaining recognition as milestone achievements of the international avant-garde. One of Cage's projects during his stay was gathering material for a new composition, *Sounds of Venice*, and

Peggy was greatly pleased when Cage's technician came to the palazzo to record the singing of her house painter and the barking of her dogs (she was correspondingly disappointed when the dogs simply yowled). But Cage had also come to Venice as a participant in the Italian TV quiz show, *Lose it or Double It*. He'd chosen mushrooms as his 'special topic' and as he revealed to the unsuspecting Italians, it was a subject on which he was exceptionally well informed. As he sailed through every round in the quiz he became something of a celebrity in Peggy's neighbourhood; people recognized Cage in the street and called out from their windows to wish him good luck. By the time he walked away with the $6,000 cash prize, he'd been adopted as a local hero.

Cage would use his prize to buy a Steinway piano for himself and a Volkswagen station wagon for his lover, the choreographer Merce Cunningham, who for years would use it as a tour bus for his dance company, with precious set designs by Jasper Johns and Robert Rauschenberg packed precariously onto its roof rack. Peggy herself became friendly with Cunningham (he came to stay when his company were dancing at the Fenice Opera House); and it was through Cage, three years later, that she also met a young Japanese performance artist, Yoko Ono, who would become one of her more intimate friends.

They were introduced to each other when Peggy was travelling with Cage in Japan, and he recommended Yoko to her as a translator, companion and guide.* Peggy liked Yoko immediately, finding her 'terribly efficient and nice', and Yoko was equally struck, impressed by Peggy's outlook, which she considered 'very open-minded and intelligent...she was in modern terms a very hip girl'.[12] Despite the difference in their ages, the two women formed an almost sisterly bond, and when they were touring the temples and art galleries together they had long conversations about art, sex and men. Yoko embraced the new feminism of the 1960s, and while Peggy disliked both the politics and the rhetoric of the women's movement, finding them too strident for her taste, she admired the clarity and confidence of Yoko's world view.

---

* Cage himself was oddly reluctant to see the sights; to Peggy, it seemed that his main interest in being in Tokyo was to find a tie to replace one he had bought in the city several years earlier.

The friendship continued beyond Japan. Yoko moved to England, where she became famous as the lover of John Lennon and reviled as the nemesis of The Beatles. She would visit Peggy in Venice several times, and when Peggy was travelling to London she would sometimes make a detour to see Yoko and Lennon at their home near Ascot. Peggy didn't actually like pop music, yet she enjoyed the frisson of Lennon's fame, and it was through him and Yoko that she formed a friendship with Kit Lambert, another prominent figure in the music industry.

Kit's principal claim to fame was managing the rock band The Who; it was he who'd persuaded the band to ramp up their sound to near-intolerable decibels, and to incorporate elements of showboating vandalism into their stage act. To Peggy, Kit's taste in music was anathema, yet they had one shared love in Venice. Kit's father, the composer Constant Lambert, had been a close friend of Lord Berners and had met both Luisa and Doris, Peggy's predecessors at the Venier palazzo. Intrigued by this connection, Peggy encouraged Kit to find a Venetian property of his own; and in 1971 he acquired the beautiful Ca' Dario, just a couple of hundred metres along the canal.

Whenever he was in residence, he and Peggy saw a great deal of one another. Kit was rich and troubled, addicted to drugs and attracted to the wrong kinds of men; but he was also gregarious, articulate and generous, and Peggy found him stimulating company. They were seen so often together that a rumour began to circulate that they were lovers. It was a ridiculous notion – Peggy was thirty-seven years older than Kit, and he was so obviously gay – but Venice thrived on small-town gossip and local myth. Ten years later, when Kit died from a drunken fall down a flight of stairs, those same Venetian gossips would insist he was the latest victim of the curse that lay over Ca' Dario, one of a long line of the palazzo's occupants to die in mysterious or violent circumstances.

In the company of these younger, curious and sympathetic friends Peggy was often at her confident best, less prone to the nervous mannerisms, the sliding, fearful glance, the pursing of her lips that had always betrayed her unease. To Mary McCarthy she seemed to acquire a new lightness of spirit as she got older, to become 'fresh and amusing like a naughty child'.[13] Gore Vidal, who'd first met Peggy in 1946, saw something else, a mature and wise woman settling into composure:

'there [is] something cool and impenetrable about her. She is capable of silence, a rare gift...She is master of the one-liner...it is the dry tone – the brevity with which she delivers her epithets – that one remembers with pleasure.'[14]

Peggy in her late sixties had established her true vintage as a hostess, yet for all the admiration she elicited, she was beginning to feel her age. Back in 1958 Gregory Corso had sensed there was a darkness shadowing her gregariousness. After one of their evenings together she'd accompanied him to the local vaporetto stop and had been nostalgically talkative on the way, telling him 'great things about...Beckett and her life'. Once they'd parted, however, Gregory had watched Peggy walk away and had a sudden piercing sense of her vulnerability: 'she put her hand to her head as though she were in pain. I suddenly realized the plight of the woman by that gesture. She is a liver of life and life is fading away.'[15]

That glimpse of mortality was only a premonition, and Peggy was still capable of extracting vigorous interest from her life. But in 1967 she suffered a tragedy from which her spirit never fully recovered. Pegeen's mental and physical health had continued to deteriorate over the years as even after marriage to Ralph, she'd slid deeper into the grooves of her depression and her addictions. Ralph saw the danger. He sought out the bottles of Scotch that she hid around the apartment and tried to wean her off the Valium, tearing up the prescriptions she managed to elicit from ignorant or careless doctors. Peggy attempted her own solutions, too, paying for a course of analysis at a Swiss sanitarium and trying to manage Pegeen by alternately cosseting her with presents or threatening to deprive her of money. Later she would claim that she'd tried every possible approach to fixing her daughter. But the solution at which she worked hardest – detaching Pegeen from her husband – would also prove to be the most destructive.

Peggy continued to hate Ralph, whose quick temper, extravagance with money and volatility all reminded her of Laurence at his worst; and she truly believed that the best way of saving Pegeen would be to remove her from Ralph's influence. However, even though the marriage was far from ideal, and Rumney's wildness was clearly having a destabilizing effect on Pegeen, Peggy had completely failed to perceive that her own hostility towards Ralph was making matters worse. Trapped between a warring mother and husband, Pegeen was being forced to relive the misery of her childhood, when she'd been caught between two antagonistic parents; and it may have been the pressure of divided loyalties that drove her towards the edge of suicidal despair.

The crisis came in February 1967 when Ralph had gone to Venice to complete a painting commission, a mural for a hotel. While there he had become involved in a police enquiry, and through some combination of official bungling and his own reflex insolence he'd ended up being thrown out of the city and escorted, handcuffed, to the French border. Peggy at this moment was thousands of miles away in Mexico, visiting Robert Brady, who had recently been ousted from Venice himself in one of the city's periodic raids on the gay community. But she somehow found out about the incident and informed Pegeen; and when Ralph got back to Paris, he immediately suspected that Peggy had engineered the whole thing. As he went over and over the situation with Pegeen, making wild accusations about her mother, she became progressively more upset and confused, to the point of believing that Ralph's expulsion from Venice extended to her as well. By the time Pegeen went to bed, drunk and exhausted, she felt she'd been betrayed by both her husband and her mother.

She told Ralph she would sleep in the maid's room that night, and asked him to take Nicholas and Sandro to school the next morning so that she could lie in. This in itself was not unusual; hangovers and insomnia often kept Pegeen in bed until late morning. By noon the next day, however, she still hadn't appeared; and when Ralph attempted to rouse her, he discovered that the door to her room was locked. His knocking and shouting met with no response, and when he eventually managed to retrieve the key he found Pegeen lying cold and immobile on the floor.

Sometime during the night she had taken a quantity of pills that had combined fatally with the alcohol she'd drunk, and as far as Ralph was concerned, she had done so intentionally. He claimed that Pegeen had been threatening suicide so often of late that it was only a matter of time before she succeeded; and he was supported by Hélion, who confirmed that during his own marriage to Pegeen he'd had to intervene more than once in her attempts at self-harm. Yet Pegeen had left no note and, as with Doris, it was impossible to know if the overdose was deliberate. Even the autopsy report was ambiguous, in so far as it concluded that the actual cause of death was Pegeen choking on her own vomit.

Peggy certainly refused to accept that it had been suicide. In her mind, the incident had been a tragic accident – a freak combination of alcohol and pills – and she continued to cling to that view, pointing to the fact that Pegeen had only recently assured her that she loved her sons too much ever to choose to abandon them. The alternative was simply too painful for her to contemplate: and not only did Peggy maintain that Pegeen's death had been accidental, she also blamed Ralph for allowing it to happen, arguing that he'd been culpably irresponsible in his failure to moderate her addictions.

If Peggy managed to remain dry-eyed in Mexico when Brady broke the news of Pegeen's death, if she was able to fly back to Paris without losing her composure, it was because she was channelling her grief into hatred of Ralph. She could not bring herself to attend the funeral because he would be there, and afterwards she fixated on making him pay for Pegeen's death. Her first, desperate ploy was to get Ralph charged with murder, which she then scaled back to the more plausible charge of 'non-assistance', a crime defined under French law as a failure to help someone in mortal danger. Lawyers were hired to extract damaging witness statements, and when it became clear that there were none to be had, Peggy focused on getting custody of Sandro transferred to Laurence and his daughter Kathe. She'd got her revenge, for Ralph would not see his son for another ten years.

While Peggy was deflecting her anguish into a crusade against Ralph, he was retaliating in kind, blaming Pegeen's death on Peggy's interference, her selfishness and manipulation. Nor was he alone. Although Laurence claimed it was Ralph who 'had finished off' their daughter, he'd always worried about Peggy's influence on Pegeen, fearing that her love had been too 'jealous', too 'possessive', and that she'd always done whatever she could to break up 'Pegeen's relationship with whoever she was living with'.[16] His daughter Kathe diagnosed the problem from a different angle, believing that Peggy had projected such a fantasy of perfection onto Pegeen that she had struggled miserably to live up to it.

There was no doubt that Peggy had demanded much of her daughter, and to some extent had lived vicariously through her beauty and talent. Yet even if Pegeen had been crushed by her mother's expectations and by her exacting version of love, the causes of her problems went wider and deeper. The combative family dynamic in which Pegeen had been raised had been as much Kay and Laurence's doing as Peggy's, and it had affected all the children – two of Kay's daughters had displayed suicidal impulses of their own. The fact that Pegeen seemed the most damaged of all, that she was so profoundly insecure about herself as a woman, a painter and a mother, may simply have been due to her exceptional fragility. One of her analysts had concluded that he could do nothing for her because her case 'went beyond Freud'; one of her

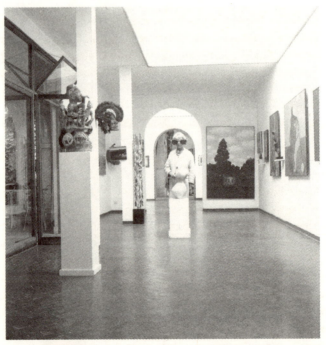

Peggy and her collection: the future of her legacy
became her overriding obsession.

friends believed that Pegeen had suffered from an innate and disabling 'lack of will, a fundamental weakness' in her emotional wiring.[17]

While others criticized Peggy's mothering, she walled herself up behind her own version of the truth. Forgetting the extent to which she and her daughter had argued, competed and disappointed each other, she came to speak of their relationship as 'a perpetual love affair'. In a final version of her memoir she would eulogize her 'darling Pegeen' as having been not only 'a daughter, but also a mother, a friend and a sister to me' – failing to recall that Pegeen had only, ever, wanted to be loved as a daughter.[18] In the palazzo, she turned one of the basement galleries into a memorial for Pegeen's art, putting twelve of her paintings on permanent display. Alongside them was her favourite photograph of Pegeen, sitting on the throne in the garden grounds, an ethereal princess, her golden beauty cast in mysterious shadow. One of Peggy's grandsons was caustically dismissive of her efforts: 'she's put up this shrine to our mother so I suppose she thinks that makes everything OK'.[19] But if the expressions of Peggy's grief appeared sentimental, her anguish was nonetheless genuine. 'I felt the light had gone out of my life', she wrote – and she never fully recovered it, commenting wistfully to an interviewer a few years later, 'I've had a very sad life I think.'

Peggy turned seventy in 1968, and in the midst of mourning her daughter, she was also conscious that many of her oldest friends and colleagues were starting to die. Jean Arp, André Breton and Marcel Duchamp had already gone, and Laurence too was failing. He had developed cancer, and although Peggy hadn't seen him for a long while, Djuna had met him when he'd made one last trip to see his daughters in New York. She had written to describe his gaunt, battered yet touchingly determined state; 'so old so ill so shattered yet holding together with incredible ferocity'. When Laurence died the following year, Peggy mourned him: 'He was gallant to the end.' But even as his death made her acutely conscious of her own mortality, Peggy's concern was not so much for herself but for her legacy; and during the last years of her life her principal preoccupation – her obsession, in fact – was all for the future security of her palazzo and her art.[20]

* * * * *

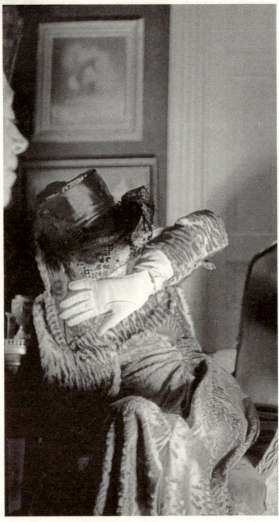

A startled, angry Luisa photographed
by Cecil Beaton in the early 1950s.

Many years earlier, Luisa Casati had been no less concerned with her material legacy, believing as she did that her image could be immortalized through the houses she decorated, the portraits for which she posed. Yet old age and poverty had induced in her a state of largely contented renunciation. Living in her one rented room in London, she was surrounded by only a derelict clutter of objects – a few antique books, a broken cuckoo clock, a crystal reliquary said to contain a fragment of St Peter's finger that had once been dramatically flung at her a during a séance. All that remained of the famously quixotic menagerie were her elderly Pekingese dog and a few stuffed birds; all that remained of her wardrobe were a few old gowns decorated with faded silk flowers and tatty lace.

Strangers who encountered Luisa on the street, occasionally rifling through a rubbish bin for an object that had caught her eye, would see her as a comically pathetic figure. Yet she continued to take careful pains with her appearance – masking her wrinkles with cheap cosmetics, and never going out in public without a veil. She was still eager to play the role of hostess – a friend in London recalled her telephoning to say, 'I have ten shillings. Shall we have a bottle of cheap wine or go for a taxi ride?' – and to Cecil Beaton at least, she retained some of her old charisma. Sometime in the early 1950s she asked Beaton to take some photographs of her dog, and during that session he tried discreetly to capture images of Luisa herself. She was furious when she realized what he was doing, both because he hadn't asked her permission and because he hadn't given her an opportunity to prepare her appearance. In fact these stolen photographs of Luisa are among the most spontaneously expressive that have survived. Her eyes glare hot and dark from behind her veil, her face a blur of angry angles as she jerks away from the intrusive lens and tries to conceal herself with a gloved hand. For Luisa herself, though, it was a transgression, and she never forgave Beaton for it.

She was far better prepared when she dressed for an Augustus John exhibition that was opening at the Royal Academy in 1954. It included the portrait he had painted of her back in Paris in 1919, and when Luisa was escorted through the crowd to look at it, people stood reverentially aside. Many of them had heard of La Casati, but it was widely assumed that she was dead, and she was already being spoken and written about as though she were a character from a fabulous past. A tattered reproduction of that same John portrait had inspired three poems in Jack Kerouac's *San Francisco Blues*; Maurice Druon had drawn on stories of Luisa's former decadent splendour in the writing of his 1954 novel *La Volupté d'être*; and when Tennessee Williams went on holiday to Venice, the stories he heard about Luisa's years at the palazzo inspired him to invent the character of Mrs Goforth, a woman obsessed by art and animals who became the heroine of his 1953 short story 'Man Bring This Up Road'.

But Luisa herself was living more and more in her memories. She spent hours compiling long, rambling lists of the men who had admired her, the guests who had attended her parties, the artists who had painted, sculpted or photographed her. She'd also returned to her childhood hobby of collage-art, cutting out photographs from newspapers and magazines and assembling them into fantastical versions of her past. One of them, which depicted a Venetian palazzo by the lagoon, also had the poet Byron floating in the sky, holding hands with a medieval angel.* And it was indicative, perhaps, of how much easier Luisa found it to manage the ghosts in her head than to deal with the people around her – especially the few remaining members of her family.

Relations with Cristina had not improved with Luisa's move to London. After her divorce from Jack, Cristina had remarried; but her second husband, Wogan Philipps, had taken a profound dislike to Luisa, unable to forgive her long history of maternal neglect or to tolerate the shamelessness with which she now approached them both for money. Wogan accepted that Cristina could hardly let her mother starve, but he banned Luisa from their house, and later even burned the audio diaries in which Cristina had recorded the details of her earlier life.

Cristina died of breast cancer in March 1953, and it's possible that Wogan even banned Luisa from attending her funeral. However, he had no jurisdiction over Cristina's daughter Moorea, who, having once been

---

* When the hapless Beaton suggested to Luisa that she might exhibit her collages and perhaps even make money from them, she took deep offence and refused to make any more. (Scot D. Ryersson and Michael Orlando Yaccarino, *Infinite Variety*, p. 179)

terrified of the weird and witchy grandmother she called 'Malu', had since learned to love her. Moorea was fascinated by Luisa's stories and by the unselfconscious entitlement of her manner, and the two of them fell into the habit of lunching together (Moorea paying). On these occasions, at least, Luisa felt that her family was paying their proper dues – Moorea was proud of her regally eccentric grandmother, and much entertained when she mimicked the comments of other diners in her heavily accented English.

Luisa was ageing fast, however. By early 1957, Moorea had to arrange for a nurse to check that she was eating properly; and as her memory started to slip, she withdrew even further into the world of her imaginings. She had continued to practise her supernatural rituals, resorting to Ouija boards and cheap incense now that she could no longer afford private consultations with fortune-tellers; and she had reached the point where she couldn't always distinguish the voices of her spirit companions from those of actual people. In some ways, Luisa was now protected by the very condition that had once been so socially disabling, retreating deeper into what Natalie Barney had called her 'inner strangeness'. She happily believed that she had developed powers of telepathic communication, and thus had no further need to write letters or use the telephone; she believed too that she was in contact with the ghost of her Pekingese dog, whose stiff little body had been preserved and stuffed by a taxidermist after his death.

When Luisa herself died of a cerebral haemorrhage on 1 June 1957 she was laid out in style, wearing her best black dress and leopardskin fur, with a new set of false eyelashes and her dog at her feet. There were few people to witness her final splendour, though. Both Beaton and John stayed away from the funeral, and Lord Berners and Naps Alington, Luisa's abidingly loyal friends, were no longer alive themselves. Among the small clutch of mourners who gathered around her grave, there were perhaps only two who grieved wholeheartedly: her granddaughter Moorea, and Emilio Basaldella, the gondolier who'd served her so loyally during her years in the Palazzo dei Leoni and who remained faithful to Luisa's memory still.

* * * * *

Peggy was incapable of surrendering control over her material life as Luisa had, and the question of what she should do with her palazzo and her art collection loomed fretfully large over her final years. She was juggling two options, the first of which was to bequeath both the building and its contents to the city of Venice to manage after her death; the other was to leave the palazzo to her family and give the collection to the Tate Gallery in London. Peggy received encouragement, for this last option, from Herbert Read, who had never quite got over his failure to secure Peggy's dollars and her artworks for London (he used to complain to his friend Ben Nicholson, 'Never trust a patron, especially if she is American and especially if she is a woman.')[21] For a couple of years this was the plan that Peggy favoured: Pegeen approved it, and the Tate was making gratifying attempts to court her, organizing an exhibition for the collection in London in 1964 and also paying to have some of the more damaged works restored. When the show opened in late December, Peggy wrote gloatingly to Djuna that it had all been a 'terrific success' and that her only rival in town had been the funeral of Winston Churchill.

That experience made her fondly disposed towards the idea of returning her collection to London, the city that had launched her career. And yet she dithered. Sentimentally, she was troubled to think of her artworks – her children – being separated from their Venetian home; and financially, she was bothered by the size of the export tax that would be levied if the collection were removed from Italy. Its value had soared to somewhere in the region of $250 million – a thousand times what she had paid for it – and if the tax came out of her own estate, there might be little money left for Sindbad and the grandchildren. Her indecision infuriated Read, who uttered harsh words about Peggy's 'schizophrenia' and claimed that her inclination to keep the collection in Venice was motivated by a purely selfish desire to create 'a memorial to herself'. Yet settling the future of her collection seemed to Peggy to be the defining decision of her life. She felt very keenly the lack of a trusted adviser, and it was perhaps a sense of isolation that drew her to a third option: that of keeping her legacy in the family. If the Guggenheim Foundation would agree to maintain the collection in Venice, then she would be willing to cede them entire control.

She and her cousin Harry had tentatively broached this possibility around the time of the Tate exhibition; five years later, in 1969, their discussions progressed to firmer ground when Harry invited Peggy to exhibit her collection at the Guggenheim's New York museum. It was a gesture of respect that went some way towards smoothing her historic antagonism towards her family, and even though she couldn't help a reflex instinct of criticism – complaining that her paintings hadn't been properly hung, that the smaller ones looked like postage stamps, out of proportion with the space – it was still a triumphal moment for her when she attended the opening. 'I never dreamt, after all the rows I had with my uncle Solomon, that I would one day see my collection descending the ramp of the Guggenheim Museum like Marcel Duchamp's nude descending the stairs.'[22] Peggy felt she was the famous Guggenheim now, and while she was in New York there were 'wonderful parties' in her honour and a welcoming fuss made by the press. Even though it would be another seven years before she could bring herself to sign a definitive agreement, this very public rapprochement convinced her that the Foundation was the best available option. Signing over her art to the family firm had felt as right, she said, as 'proposing to someone who wanted to marry me'.*[23]

* * * * *

Having more or less secured the future of her art, Peggy was free to enjoy the prestige it brought. There was an invitation to exhibit at the Louvre (a *volte-face* that greatly delighted her), and visitor numbers were rising so fast at the palazzo that Peggy could boast of being 'one of the most popular attractions in Venice'. The city itself had by now claimed her as one of its own; in 1962 she'd been granted honorary citizenship, and in 1967 she was made Commander of the Italian Republic (one of only three women, she believed, ever to receive that honour). Journalists came to interview her, an American writer called Jacqueline

---

*   Though Peggy made no binding provisos in her deed of gift, she did express her wish that the collection remain close to Venice, even if rising water levels made the city itself unsafe. (Anton Gill, *Peggy Guggenheim: The Life of an Art Addict*, p. 420)

Bograd Weld asked to write her biography and Peggy herself began to work on updating her own memoir.*

The 1970s could have been contented, mellow years. But Pegeen's death was always present to Peggy, and daily life was becoming more of a struggle. The upkeep of the palazzo was a constant worry and expense – the garden grew boggy in winter, the roof leaked, and mould was blooming in the basement. With wage bills rising, Peggy could now afford to keep only two of her servants: her butler Roberto, and Isia the housekeeper. Guests staying at the palazzo noticed that while the napkins at dinner might be beautifully folded, they were frequently grubby, and that the meals coming out of the kitchen were often little more than a tin of tomato soup and a simple pasta dish. Peggy's appetite had never been robust, and she was unwilling to spend money on food she didn't want, especially when there were so many other demands on her purse.

Peggy had always been careful with money, and these days she was irrationally frightened of it running out. As well as skimping on the maintenance of the palazzo, she depended on unpaid volunteers to help care for her collection. In 1973 she was introduced to the young British art historian Philip Rylands and his American wife Jane, and she became very dependent on their friendship, their generosity and their time. Peggy made a particular confidant of Jane; she would tell her stories about the past and used to enjoy sitting down with her after a party, chatting over the day's events. Her special favourite, however, was John Hohnsbeen, a dancer turned art dealer who used to come and stay with her every summer in return for doing administrative work and taking care of the paintings (a task that he claimed involved 'sweeping the maggots' off their backs every year).[24] Peggy called John her 'angel of kindness', but although he could be camply amusing and sweetly attentive when it suited him, his loyalties were superficial. He was often viciously gossipy about Peggy behind her back, and most evenings

---

* The growing fame of her collection had one negative side effect: it attracted thieves. After two burglaries, Peggy demanded that the Foundation install a security alarm – although it drove her mad, as she often set it off by accident and was faced with the exasperation of the local police, roaring up in their motorboats to investigate. (Anton Gill, *Peggy Guggenheim: The Life of an Art Addict*, p. 435)

he would leave her alone in her palazzo while he went out partying with friends.

'There was a slight feeling of the desert island castaway about her,' recalled one acquaintance who met Peggy during these last years. 'She was lost in time – the time she truly belonged in had passed.'[25] While she'd once been avid to explore the world and to embrace the new, Peggy's horizons were narrowing. The culture was changing too fast for her to keep up, and she didn't like much of what she saw – not the feminists or the hippies, and still not the art. In New York back in 1969, Peggy had encountered Andy Warhol at a party on Staten Island. The celebrated pop artist had been effusive – 'Oh, I am so honoured to be at the same party with Mrs Guggenheim!' – but Peggy had turned to their host and loudly enquired, 'Who is that man?' No one could decide whether her question was genuine or a snub.[26]

Peggy did try to keep pace with her grandchildren, who were starting to visit on their own. The older boys brought their girlfriends and she marvelled at their precocity, but she found it difficult to be natural with them. According to Sandro, Pegeen's youngest son, Peggy

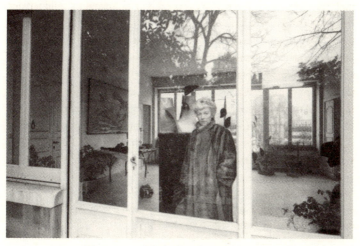

'There was a slight feeling of the desert island castaway about her': Peggy during her final years at the palazzo.

'wasn't nice, she didn't know how to do it'; she was either too invasive
in her manner, quizzing the children with mortifying bluntness about
their developing sex lives, or too hurtfully indifferent, behaving as if
their music, their jokes, their friendships were beneath her concern.[27]
Money also became an issue in her relationships with this generation,
for while Peggy handed out generous birthday cheques of between $50
and $100, as the grandchildren grew older, it seemed to her that they
grew less grateful and more demanding. One year she visited Sandro at
his boarding school in Switzerland and bought him the very expensive
stereo system he'd requested for his birthday. She expected him then to
have dinner with her, but when Sandro rebuffed her invitation, preferring to spend the evening with his friends and his new sound system,
Peggy was incensed at his bad manners and departed in high, huffy
dudgeon. She was overreacting to what was essentially a teenage lack
of consideration, yet it was symptomatic of what she felt to be a fundamental lack of appreciation – her grandchildren never quite ceding her
the love and respect that she believed were her due.

As well as feeling at odds with the young and their culture, Peggy
now had less energy for travel. She suffered from dizzy spells, a symp-
tom of high blood pressure; she'd been diagnosed with atherosclerosis;
and her joints hurt. Aside from the necessary journeys she took with
her collection, she now spent most of the year in Venice – and when the
winter damp percolated through the palazzo walls and the life of the
city retreated behind shutters, she took to hibernating in her bedroom,
listening to classical music and re-reading her favourite authors, James,
Dostoyevsky and Hardy. Eventually, though, even reading became hard
for her, as she developed cataracts in both her eyes; and her world
became narrower still after she had a bad fall in 1976, breaking eight of
her ribs and subsequently struggling to regain her balance and strength.

Having been for so long a dedicated walker of Venice, Peggy was
now unable to venture far beyond her palazzo walls. The uneven cobbles and steep bridges were no longer picturesque to her but obstacles,
treacherous to navigate with her brittle bones. She was no longer
allowed to drive, and had to get rid of the open-topped Fiat Ghia that for
years she'd kept parked near the station and taken out for 'exercise' on
long drives around the mainland. The motorboat *Cleopatra* she kept for

a while longer, and when Doris's youngest niece Caroline came to visit with her parents one summer, she was surprised by Peggy's insistence that they pile into the boat and motor out to the Lido for lunch. Caroline had imagined being given an intimate tour of the palazzo where her aunt had lived, and where her parents had summered so gloriously, but Peggy relished any opportunity now to experience wide horizons and open skies.

She had to give up the motorboat, however, when her driver Guido was offered more lucrative work with a water taxi, and the gondola became her only form of transport. Even that was limited: burly, taciturn Bruno, her one remaining gondolier, was now moonlighting with a funeral company and only available for two hours each day. His progress around the canals had also become less reliable owing to his own advancing years and fondness for drink. But still Peggy cherished what remained of her 'floating' afternoons: transported through the liquid maze of canals, entranced by the slow, regular splash of the oar, the darting of swifts, the sudden clamour of church bells, she felt the depredations of age fall away. She particularly loved the hour of sunset, when, as she wrote, the reflections of the palazzos in the water became 'like paintings more beautiful than any painted by the greatest masters'. Peggy had never lost her love for Venice, even when it had most irritated her with its slowness and insularity. When the city suffered catastrophic flooding in 1966 and alarms were sounded about rising sea levels and sinking foundations, she arranged for $15,000 to be paid each year from her estate to the Venice in Peril Fund. It was an expense on which she never reneged, even though she was becoming parsimonious in so many other ways.

All the things on which Peggy had most enjoyed spending her money – cars, travel, art – were now in the past; she had even stopped buying any new dogs, fearful that she would become too ill or too old to take proper care of them. Cellida, the last of them, would die in the autumn of 1979, her body buried in the garden alongside the other thirteen dogs, and Peggy had been right to be cautious, because the previous year she herself had suffered a heart attack so severe that the doctors had warned she might not recover. She had rallied in time for her 80th birthday, though, and had been celebrated with a party at the Gritti Palace hotel, which included a birthday cake baked in the shape of her own palazzo.

It was a distinguished as well as festive event, with a guest list that included the American film director Joseph Losey and the British consul. The Venetian press were on hand to photograph Peggy as she was handed out of her gondola in her Fortuny dress, and an Italian television crew was present to interview her. John Hohnsbeen thought she looked heartbreakingly fragile – her legs rickety, her eyes milky and half-blind – yet to Gore Vidal, her performance on screen was both witty and valiant: 'The camera came in for a very close shot of Peggy's handsome head. An off-camera voice asked her what she thought of today's Italian painters. The eyes shifted towards the unseen questioner; the half smile increased by a fraction. "Oh", she said, "they're very bad". And always the Jamesian heroine, she added, "Aren't they?"'[28]

Vidal's admiring snapshot featured in the introduction he wrote for the final version of Peggy's memoir, which was published the following year. She had begun updating it in 1978, planning to merge *Out of This Century* with the shorter, sanitized memoir *Confessions of an Art Addict*, which she'd published in 1960, and with a lyrical essay that she'd written on Venice two years later. In this definitive account of her life, Peggy had also restored the names of those lovers whose identities she had formerly concealed. But there was no hint of scandal when the book came out in New York and London, for these were now stories from another era, and most of the characters in Peggy's memoir were dead.

She felt herself to be one of the last survivors: 'life goes on too long', she'd written sadly to Djuna in the summer of 1978. When the jazz musician and art connoisseur George Melly came to the palazzo to film Peggy for a TV documentary, he was shocked by her decrepitude. She'd mustered some pugnacious semblance of gaiety for the interview and had been dressed carefully by her servants, yet to Melly she seemed tired and 'ever so frail'.[29] In the autumn of 1979 she had another fall, slipping as she stepped out of a boat that was taking her for supper at the Cipriani Hotel; and even though she only cracked a small bone in her foot, the injury would not heal. She eventually agreed to go to the hospital in Padua to get it operated on, yet she did so in a spirit of fatalism. Although she gamely insisted to Jane and Philip Rylands that she would be back in the palazzo by Christmas, she seems to have accepted that this trip to the hospital would be her last.

Peggy was resigning herself to death, and she had no interest in creating a fuss. At the hospital in Padua she refused to pay for the comfort of a private room, and when John Hohnsbeen offered to delay his winter departure from Venice she waved him away – there was no point hanging around to visit her in hospital, she joked, because he would only be visiting a corpse. To the Rylands, who did insist on coming to see her, she was adamant that none of her family were to be bothered, and that she particularly did not want Sindbad to be dragged all the way from Paris. They disregarded her wishes, though, when Peggy suffered a post-operative stroke that left her paralyzed down her right side. She was very, very frail when Sindbad arrived at her bedside, but she was still able to speak, and when he leaned towards her she whispered, 'Please kiss me.'

That moment of reconciliation was perhaps the simplest, most direct moment of communication between them in years. But when Peggy had a second massive stroke on 23 December, she was alone, and she died before Sindbad and the Rylands could get to her. Pragmatically, she would have approved of the fact that, rather than visiting her the day before, they and Sindbad's wife Peggy had all been occupied in shifting her paintings to safety after strong rain and high tides had flooded the basement. And she would equally have approved of the modesty of her funeral arrangements. There was no big family party accompanying her body when she was cremated on San Michele – Philip Rylands alone was in attendance – and when her ashes were buried in the garden in April alongside the graves of her dogs, it was only Philip and Jane, Sindbad and Peggy who marked the occasion, toasting her memory with a bottle of champagne. Peggy had craved love and affection all her life, but she was not sentimental about her death: a large family memorial would have seemed to her a waste of money, hypocritical even. She would have taken far more pleasure in the knowledge that just two days after her ashes were interred, the Peggy Guggenheim Collection was once again opened to the public.

Philip Rylands was now in charge. The day after Peggy's death, the Guggenheim Foundation had swung into action, appointing Rylands as temporary caretaker to the collection and later confirming him as its

official director. He spent his first weeks in the job doing frantic reme-
dial work, for the decades of Venetian damp and sunlight had done
their worst. Peggy had personally liked to see her paintings ageing and
flaking alongside her, but they were not up to the Foundation's standards; and in addition to getting the most serious damage attended to,
Rylands had to staunch further decay with the installation of correct
lighting and air conditioning.

As the artworks were cleaned and labelled, as the palazzo itself was
smartened up, the building was inexorably transformed from a private
house into a public museum. Over time, as every room was converted
into a gallery or office space and as the museum expanded to include a
café and a gift shop, Peggy's own presence was steadily erased. It was
a necessary operation, yet given the history of grudges within the family, it was inevitable that several of Peggy's heirs objected to the way in
which her legacy was handled. Financially, Sindbad and the grandchildren profited handsomely – Peggy had been richer than she realized,
and she had left them collectively two million dollars (before taxes).
But they minded that she had not bequeathed them a single item from
her art collection; and they minded too that she had sidelined them so
entirely from decisions about the collection's future.

Sindbad's grievance was the most personal. The speed with which
the Foundation had taken control of the palazzo made him feel as though
he'd been summarily evicted from his mother's home. He considered,
too, that he'd been crassly disregarded at the museum's relaunch party,
where he wasn't even invited to make a speech. But his animosity didn't
last. After he was diagnosed with cancer in the early 1980s he became
too ill to care; by then, he had also come round to accepting that the
family would have been less than ideal candidates to curate Peggy's
collection, and that some of them, almost certainly, would have wanted
to sell off its more valuable pieces. Sindbad was able to pass this spirit
of reconciliation on to his own children, all four of whom came to have
amicable working relationships with the Foundation. One of them, the
art historian Karole Vail, would end up working as a curator for the
Solomon R. Guggenheim Museum in New York.

But Pegeen's boys, having inherited more of their mother's angst,
perhaps, were angrier and more litigious. Nicolas, who had rather

hoped for the job of director himself, joined forces with Sandro in criticizing the style and philosophy of Rylands' management.* While Rylands remained faithful to the spirit of Peggy's wishes – that her collection should remain intact – both he and the Foundation believed that it could not remain static. Ever since the days of Guggenheim Jeune, Peggy had experimented with different strategies for bringing new audiences to art; now, in Venice, a programme of temporary exhibitions was established to complement the permanent collection. Later, in 2012, Rylands would agree to incorporate eighty-three new works that had been bequeathed to the collection from the estate of Hannelore and Rudolph Schulhof, friends and rival collectors whom Peggy had known since the 1950s. For Rylands, who'd known Peggy well, there was no inconsistency here, no betrayal of her wishes – but the surviving grandsons flatly opposed all interference and periodically attempted to sue the Foundation, demanding financial compensation for the offences against Peggy's legacy.

None these suits was successful, although the museum did accede to one request, that the gallery dedicated to Pegeen's art should remain (it was reconstituted upstairs, in Peggy's former bathroom). In death as in life, Peggy's art seemed to bring as much division to those close to her as it did pleasure. But it wasn't just her descendants who argued over the management of Peggy's collection; there were friends, acquaintances and casual visitors who'd come to the palazzo over the decades and who mourned its transition to a more conventional public museum. Among those who'd cherished the domestic intimacy of the collection – the paintings and sculptures muddled up with Peggy's personal belongings, her furniture, her jewelry and her dogs – there were many who felt some essential spirit had been lost.

And yet for over 400,000 new visitors who come to the palazzo each year, it is still possible to feel some traces of Peggy. Photographs of her and her friends are hung along the walls of the café and corridors. Some of her furniture remains in place – the Venetian antiques, the

---

* Before Peggy died, Nicolas had proposed changing his surname from Hélion to Guggenheim in preparation for taking up the post; however, he failed to address the fact that he had no formal training to equip him for it.

leatherette sofas, the Calder bedhead – and the stories of her collecting career can be read through the works on display: the early Tanguys she collected at Guggenheim Jeune; the Brancusi *Bird in Space*, rescued from the advancing Nazis; the unhappy traces of her marriage as depicted in Max Ernst's *The Antipope*; the Marini statue whose jaunty phallus became her wicked gift to the Venetian waterfront. The temporary exhibitions that now hang in a building across from the palazzo also bear witness to something essential in Peggy – the evangelic belief that helped to drive her career and her addiction to contemporary art.

To have preserved the palazzo exactly as Peggy left it would have displayed a form of nostalgia that she herself disdained. Life for her had always been about moving on to the next thing, even if she wasn't entirely clear what that might be. Such an approach would also have been inappropriate to the building itself, and to the long and chequered history through which it had evolved. Back in the late 18th century, the Veniers' proud plan to create a dynastic monument for themselves had been fundamentally thwarted – by recession, by Napoleon and by their failure to sustain a male line – yet it was out of the ruins of the family's ambition that Luisa had been able to create her own belle-époque fantasy, her gold-spun salon nestling within the palazzo's semi-derelict walls. It had been out of Luisa's dream of the aesthetic life that Doris had created her modern salon, as glossy and stylish as an advert in *Vogue*; and out of Doris's expensively remodelled building that Peggy in turn had created a living museum in whose unique muddle of genius and domesticity the cherished Lhasa terriers had scampered freely around a Brancusi bronze, and Gregory Corso had waltzed through roomfuls of Picasso and Ernst in a 'wild alone ball'.

EPILOGUE

The story of these women began to take shape when I discovered how interconnected their lives had been; not only by the palazzo they inhabited but by the aspirations and dissatisfactions that drove them, by the people that they knew and the culture they shared. The building itself, however, resisted my first attempts to visualize that layered past. When I walked around the bright white galleries of the Guggenheim Collection, among the museum guides and the visitors there seemed to be no spaces left for history to linger. Despite the physical evidence of Peggy's occupation; despite the decorative floors, the fireplaces and the marble that were left from Doris's short era; I was unable to see the place as anybody's former home. Even the layout of the rooms was frustrating – extensively remodelled and refurbished as they had been, I could only guess where Luisa's golden salon might once have been, or what palatial ballrooms, what airy loggias the Veniers and their architect had originally planned.

But just as Doris, in 1936, might have fancied that she'd caught the flicker of an albino blackbird within the palazzo's grounds, a fugitive glimpse of Luisa's past, I started to attune myself to the whispers and shadows of the palazzo's ghosts. A tour of the immediate neighbourhood made me appreciate how powerful a presence the Venier dynasty had been, with several of the district's tiny alleyways still boasting the family name, along with the *fondamenta* that borders one of its main canals. While those streets are now filled with pizza bars and souvenir shops, they would once have been busy with traders and artisans, supplying goods and services to the Veniers during the three centuries that they dominated the area. And in their geography at least, these same Dorsoduro streets would have looked much the same to the women who succeeded the Veniers, to Luisa as she set out from the palazzo with her cheetah and Garbi, to Doris as she clicked along the cobbles in

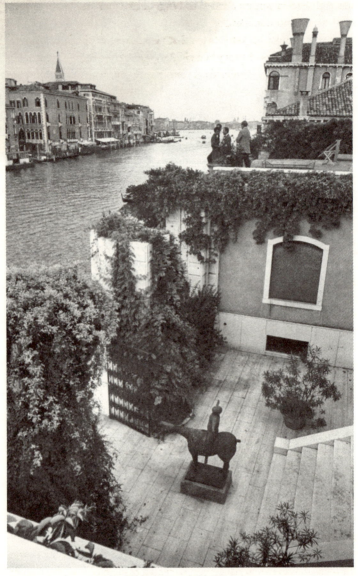

'Old stones and old views':
The waterfront terrace of the palazzo,
with Marini's *Angel of the Citadel*.

her high-heeled summer shoes, to Peggy as she took her Lhasa terriers on their constitutional walks.

It was in those backstreets too that I encountered one or two surviving local memories of Peggy herself. As I was taking photographs of the Sotoportego e Corte Venier dai Leoni, a dark alleyway just behind the palazzo, I fell into conversation with an elderly woman. She had assumed from the close attention I was paying to the street sign that I must be lost, but when I explained my interest in the place she became very animated, telling me about the small hotel she used to run nearby that was used by Peggy as a guest annex whenever the palazzo was full. She remembered Peggy clearly: 'We all knew Signora Guggenheim round here, she was very nice, very friendly.' And as we parted the woman gestured with a shrug to the visitors who were already converging on the museum gate, suggesting perhaps that she and Signora Guggenheim had inhabited different, more intimate times.

As I returned to the palazzo's grounds, other aspects of the past came into more vivid focus. The interior of the building may be implacably contemporary but the few limes and cypresses that remain in the garden hold an echo of the dark line of trees that has always been associated with this spot; pictured in early engravings, described by D'Annunzio and visible too in the first photograph that Doris sent to Churchill of her Venetian home. Even more resonant are the eight stone lions that jut regally out from the front façade; once standing guard over the flesh and blood lion that the Veniers were rumoured to keep tethered, they now stand sentinel over the palazzo's memories.

It is out on the waterfront terrace, however, that the ghosts of history become most clamorous. Tourists like to congregate here, stepping out of the museum to pose by the Marini statue or to gaze out towards the lagoon. But even now, as the waters of the Grand Canal slap against the steps and as the busy water traffic chugs by, it's in these old stones, these old Venetian views that the story of the Unfinished Palazzo feels most present. We can imagine Nicolò Venier first taking command of the property from this exact spot, triumphing in the expectation that his own palazzo would rise to far greater magnificence than the Corner residence opposite. Luisa posed here a century and a half later, flanked by her Nubian servants and with tuberoses heaped around her feet.

Doris stood here too, cool and blonde, as she prepared to motor off to the Lido or welcomed film stars and princes as her guests, and it was from the same terrace, in subsequent decades, that Peggy embarked on her sunset gondola rides. With her riotous jazzy sunglasses and her cherished lap dogs Peggy was the last 'female doge' of Venice. She was also the last, and most lastingly memorable, of the palazzo's extraordinary trio of châtelaines.

NOTES

CHAPTER 1

1 Hughes-Hallett, *The Pike*, p. 214.
2 Ryersson and Yaccarino, *Infinite Variety*, p. 6.
3 Ibid., p. 111.
4 Ibid., p. 14.
5 Letter from Gabriele D'Annunzio to Luisa Casati, 1922.
6 Jullian, *D'Annunzio*, p. 54.
7 Hughes-Hallett, *The Pike*, p. 323.
8 Jullian, *D'Annunzio*, p. 70.
9 D'Annunzio, *Forse che sì, forse che no*.
10 Letters from G.D'A. to L.C., 1908; see Castagnola, *Infiniti auguri alla nomade*, pp. 45–6.
11 Ryersson and Yaccarino, *Infinite Variety*, p. 15.
12 Hughes-Hallett, *The Pike*, p. 208.
13 Bates-Batcheller, *Glimpses*, p. 181.
14 Ryersson and Yaccarino, *Infinite Variety*, p. 20.
15 Philippe Jullian, 'Extravagant Casati', *Vogue* (New York), September 1970.
16 Ryersson and Yaccarino, *Infinite Variety*, p. 23.
17 Ibid., p. 21.
18 Marinetti, 'Against Venice, mired in the past', in Bohn, *The Other Futurism*, p. 8.
19 Acton, *Memoirs*, p. 37.
20 Benzi et al., *La Divina Marchesa*, p. 9.
21 Amory, *Lord Berners*, p. 48.
22 Quoted in Cecchi, *Giovanni Boldini*.
23 Cocteau, 'Le Coq et l'Arlequin', pamphlet (Paris, 1918).

CHAPTER 2

1 Roberto Montenegro, *Planos en el Tiempo*, quoted in Ryersson and Yaccarino, *Infinite Variety*, p. 54.
2 Ryersson and Yaccarino, *Infinite Variety*, p. 33.
3 Letter from G.D'A. to L.C., undated; see Castagnola, *Infiniti auguri alla nomade*, p. 172.
4 The procurator Andrea Tron, quoted in Mosto, *Francesco's Venice*, pp. 181, 227.
5 Ryersson and Yaccarino, *Infinite Variety*, p. 39.
6 'Ball in Paris Like Arabian Night Tale', *New York Times*, 31 May 1912 (http://query. nytimes.com/gst/ abstract.html?res=9F 0DE5D81F31E233A25 752C3A9639C94639 6D6CF&legacy=true, accessed 20 December 2016).
7 Cooper, *The Rainbow*, p. 94.
8 Ryersson and Yaccarino, *Infinite Variety*, p. 45.

CHAPTER 3

1 Ryersson and Yaccarino, *Infinite Variety*, p. 65; Jullian, *D'Annunzio*, p. 270.
2 Jullian, *D'Annunzio*, pp. 224, 289, 231; Hughes-Hallett, *The Pike*, p. 333.
3 D'Annunzio, *Cento e cento e cento*, p. 110 (author's translation).
4 Letter from G.D'A. to L.C., 26 July 1913.
5 Hughes-Hallett, *The Pike*, p. 288; Jullian, *D'Annunzio*, p. 147.
6 Jullian, *D'Annunzio*, p. 79.
7 Letter from G.D'A. to L.C., 9 July 1913.
8 Ryersson and Yaccarino, *Infinite Variety*, p. 75.
9 Ibid.
10 Letter from G.D'A. to L.C., 1913; Castagnola,

Infiniti auguri alla nomade, p. 55.

11 Letter from L.C. to G.D'A., 1913.

12 Letter from G.D'A. to L.C., 27 July 1913.

13 Letter from G.D'A. to L.C., 1913; Castagnola, *Infiniti auguri alla nomade*, p. 56–7.

14 Letter from G.D'A. to L.C., 9 August 1913.

15 Letter from G.D'A. to L.C., 1913.

16 Telegram from L.C. to G.D'A., 4 August 1913.

17 Ryersson and Yaccarino, *Infinite Variety*, p. 65.

18 Letter from G.D'A. to L.C., 1913.

19 Letter from L.C. to G.D'A., 14 August 1913.

20 Letter from L.C. to G.D'A., 14 August 1912.

21 Letter from G.D'A. to L.C., 16 August 1913.

22 Letter from L.C. to G.D'A., 23 August 1913 (author's translation).

23 Ryersson and Yaccarino, *Infinite Variety*, p. 65; Jullian, *D'Annunzio*, p. 27.

24 See Jullian, *D'Annunzio*, p. 183.

25 Ryersson and Yaccarino, *Infinite Variety*, p. 64.

26 Ryersson and Yaccarino, *Infinite Variety*, p. 65.

27 Letter from G.D'A. to L.C., 30 October 1913.

28 Letter from G.D'A. to L.C., 1915; Castagnola, *Infiniti auguri alla nomade*, p. 98–9.

29 Ryersson and Yaccarino, *Infinite Variety*, p. 20; Jullian, *D'Annunzio*, p. 271.

30 Letter from G.D'A. to L.C., July 1913.

31 Acton, *Memoirs*.

32 Ryersson and Yaccarino, *Infinite Variety*, p. 66.

33 Ibid., pp. 66–7.

34 Ibid., p. 55.

35 Rubinstein, *My Young Years*, p. 315.

36 Ryersson and Yaccarino, *Infinite Variety*, p. 47.

37 Rubinstein, *My Young Years*, p. 325.

38 Ryersson and Yaccarino, *Infinite Variety*, p. 51.

39 Ibid., p. 52.

40 Ibid., p. 67.

41 Ibid., p. 61.

42 Ibid.

43 Mazzeo, *Hotel*, p. 45.

CHAPTER 4

1 D'Annunzio, *Notturno*, pp. 410–11.

2 Hughes-Hallett, *The Pike*, p. 402.

3 Ibid., p. 68.

4 Ibid., p. 69.

5 Jullian, *D'Annunzio*, p. 258.

6 Letter from G.D'A. to L.C., 5 December 1917.

7 Letter from G.D'A. to L.C., 19 April 1918.

8 Ryersson and Yaccarino, *Infinite Variety*, p. 80.

9 Benzi et al., *La Divina Marchesa*.

10 Scheijen, *Diaghilev*, p. 312.

11 Amory, *Lord Berners*, p. 66.

12 Hastings, *The Red Earl*, p. 53.

13 Ibid., p. 64.

14 Ibid., p. 57.

15 Ibid., p. 20.

16 Ryersson and Yaccarino, *Infinite Variety*, p. 114.

17 Jullian, *D'Annunzio*, pp. 276, 306.

18 Epstein, *Let There Be Sculpture*, p. 87.

19 John, *Autobiography*, pp. 266–7.

20 Ibid., p. 116.

21 Ibid.

22 Holroyd, *Augustus John*, p. 455.

23 Ryersson and Yaccarino, *Infinite Variety*, p. 100.

24 Secrest, *Between Me and Life*, p. 297.

25 Ibid., p. 286.

26 Ibid., p. 297.

27 Hughes-Hallett, *The Pike*, p. 327.

28 Ryersson and Yaccarino, *Infinite Variety*, pp. 110–11.

29 Ibid., p. 67.

CHAPTER 5

1 Ryersson and Yaccarino, *Infinite Variety*, p. 121.

2 Ray, *Self-Portrait*, p. 124.

3 Ibid., p. 125.
4 Ibid.
5 Benzi et al., *La Divina Marchesa*, p. 7.
6 Ryersson and Yaccarino, *Infinite Variety*, p. 128.
7 Letter from L.C. to G.D'A., 11 February 1925.
8 Ryersson and Yaccarino, *Infinite Variety*, p. 130.
9 L. Brimberg et al., 'Brain-reactive IgG correlates with autoimmunity in mothers of a child with an autism spectrum disorder', *Molecular Psychiatry* 18 (11), November 2013.
10 Ryersson and Yaccarino, *Infinite Variety*, p. 116.
11 De Meyer, 'Paris Gossip by a Mere Man', *Harper's Bazaar*, September 1922.
12 Schiaparelli, *Shocking Life*, p. 75.
13 Ryersson and Yaccarino, *Infinite Variety*, pp. 136–7.
14 Ibid., p. 139.
15 Ibid., p. 115.
16 Ibid., pp. 42–3.
17 Ibid., p. 141.
18 'Italy's Famous Beauty Who Lives Like a Fairy Princess', *San Francisco Chronicle*, 18 April 1926.
19 Ryersson and Yaccarino, *Infinite Variety*, p. 143.

20 'Italy's Famous Beauty', *San Francisco Chronicle*.
21 Letter from G.D'A. to L.C., 23 February 1922.
22 Letter from L.C. to G.D'A., 10 March 1922.
23 Letter from L.C. to G.D'A., 1923.
24 Letter from G.D'A. to L.C., 5 December 1923.
25 Letter from G.D'A. to L.C., 19 December 1923.
26 Letter from G.D'A. to L.C., 14 August 1924.
27 Letter from G.D'A. to L.C., 15 August 1924.
28 Letter from G.D'A. to L.C., 5 February 1925.
29 Letter from L.C. to G.D'A., 31 July 1924.
30 *Vogue* (Paris), September 1927.
31 Ryersson and Yaccarino, *Infinite Variety*, pp. 157–8.
32 Ibid., pp. 153, 155; letters from G.D'A. to L.C., 25 September 1929 and 27 March 1930.
33 Faulks, *The Fatal Englishman*, p. 80.
34 Ryersson and Yaccarino, *Infinite Variety*, p. 160.
35 Ibid., p. 162.
36 Ibid.
37 Hastings, *The Red Earl*, p. 177.
38 Ryersson and Yaccarino, *Infinite Variety*, p. 165.

CHAPTER 6

1 Nancy Mitford, *The Pursuit of Love*, in Amory, *Lord Berners*, p. 138.
2 Gordon, *Nancy Cunard*, p. 84.
3 Mosley, *Castlerosse*, p. 81.
4 Ibid., pp. 79–80.
5 Young, *Try Anything Twice*, p. 185.
6 Thomson, *Lord Castlerosse*, p. 97.
7 Masters, *Rosa Lewis*, p. 160.
8 Mosley, *Castlerosse*, pp. 79–80.
9 Nichols, *A Case of Human Bondage*; see also Delevingne archive.
10 Thomson, *Lord Castlerosse*, p. 96.
11 Mosley, *Castlerosse*, p. 80.
12 Thomson, *Lord Castlerosse*, p. 80.
13 Ibid., pp. 78, 79.
14 Mosley, *Castlerosse*, p. 82.
15 Ibid., p. 81.
16 Ibid., p. 86.
17 Souhami, *Greta & Cecil*, p. 132.
18 Chisholm and Davie, *Beaverbrook*, p. 251.
19 Mosley, *Castlerosse*, pp. 90–2.
20 Ibid., p. 89.
21 Thomson, *Lord Castlerosse*, p. 104.
22 Mosley, *Castlerosse*, p. 100.
23 Ibid., p. 93.

24 Ibid., p. 94.
25 Chisholm and Davie, *Beaverbrook*, p. 273.
26 Caroline Delevingne, personal interview.
27 Chisholm and Davie, *Beaverbrook*, p. 267.
28 Thomson, *Lord Castlerosse*, p. 107.
29 Ibid., p. 110.
30 Mosley, *Castlerosse*, p. 103.
31 Thomson, *Lord Castlerosse*, p. 111.
32 Mosley, *Castlerosse*, p. 103.
33 Thomson, *Lord Castlerosse*, p. 166.
34 Ibid., p. 113.
35 Mosley, *Castlerosse*, p. 108.
36 Thomson, *Lord Castlerosse*, p. 98.

CHAPTER 7

1 Mosley, *Castlerosse*, p. 103.
2 Wishart, *High Diver*, p. 92.
3 Mosley, *Castlerosse*, p. 113.
4 Vickers, *Cecil Beaton*, p. 73.
5 Ibid.
6 Thomasson, *A Curious Friendship*, p. 181.
7 Vickers, *Cecil Beaton*, p. 40.
8 Thomasson, *A Curious Friendship*, p. 240.
9 Vickers, *Cecil Beaton*, p. 162.
10 Ibid.
11 Ibid., p. 163.

12 Zinovieff, *The Mad Boy*, pp. 111, 166; Vickers, *Cecil Beaton*, p. 163.
13 Vickers, *Cecil Beaton*, pp. 161, 167.
14 Ibid., p. 166.
15 Ibid., p. 167.
16 Ibid., p. 204.
17 Ibid., p. 217.
18 Zinovieff, *The Mad Boy*, p. 109.
19 Ibid.
20 Amory, *Lord Berners*, p. 144.
21 Zinovieff, *The Mad Boy*, p. 131.
22 Ibid., p. 110.
23 Amory, *Lord Berners*, p. 210.
24 Thomasson, *A Curious Friendship*, p. 265.
25 Thomson, *Lord Castlerosse*, p. 161.
26 Chisholm and Davie, *Beaverbrook*, p. 255.
27 Letter from Doris Castlerosse to Winston Churchill, CHAR 1/285/178, Winston Churchill archive.
28 Caroline Delevingne, personal interview.
29 Letter from D.C. to W.C., CHAR 1/299/77, Winston Churchill archive.
30 'Miss Margot Flick Will Be Wed Today', *New York Times*, 14 February 1936 (http://query.nytimes.com/gst/abstract.html?res=980CEEDA1630E13BBC4C52DFB466838D629EDE&legacy=true,

accessed 20 December 2016).
31 'Cholly Chats of Mayfair Divorces', *Syracuse American*, 20 December 1936.
32 Caroline Delevingne, personal interview.
33 Cooper, *Light of Common Day*, p. 103.
34 Letter from D.C. to W.C., CHAR 1/298/49-51, Winston Churchill archive.
35 Vickers, *Cecil Beaton*, p. 217.
36 Mosley, *Castlerosse*, p. 146.
37 Caroline Mellor, personal interview.
38 Vickers, *Cecil Beaton*, p. 217.
39 Caroline Mellor, personal interview.
40 Thomson, *Lord Castlerosse*, p. 163.
41 Ibid., p. 165.
42 Mosley, *Castlerosse*, p. 183.
43 Ibid., p. 167.
44 Ibid., p. 165.

CHAPTER 8

1 Guggenheim, *Out of This Century*, pp. 379–80.
2 Ibid., p. 380.
3 Ibid., p. 381.
4 Ibid., p. 6.
5 Ibid.
6 Ibid., p. 10.
7 Ibid., p. 5.
8 Ibid., p. 14.
9 Ibid.

10 Dearborn, *Mistress of Modernism*, p. 27.
11 From interview in *Peggy Guggenheim: Art Addict*.
12 Guggenheim, *Out of This Century*, p. 24.
13 Ibid.
14 Ibid., p. 26.
15 Ibid., p. 27.
16 Ibid., p. 29.
17 Ibid., p. 33.
18 Ibid.
19 Ibid., p. 36.
20 Dearborn, *Mistress of Modernism*, p. 52.
21 Ibid., p. 95.
22 Gill, *Peggy Guggenheim*, p. 95.
23 Guggenheim, *Out of This Century*, p. 73.
24 Prose, *Peggy Guggenheim*, p. 105.
25 Guggenheim, *Out of This Century*, p. 83.
26 Prose, *Peggy Guggenheim*, p. 69.

CHAPTER 9

1 Guggenheim, *Out of This Century*, p. 154.
2 Ibid., pp. 79–80.
3 Dearborn, *Mistress of Modernism*, p. 87.
4 Guggenheim, *Out of This Century*, p. 90.
5 Ibid.
6 Dearborn, *Mistress of Modernism*, p. 96.
7 Guggenheim, *Out of This Century*, p. 122.
8 Guggenheim, *Out of This Century*, p. 109.
9 Prose, *Peggy Guggenheim*, p. 79.
10 Dearborn, *Mistress of Modernism*, p. 101.
11 Ibid., p. 112.
12 Guggenheim, *Out of This Century*, p. 123.
13 Prose, *Peggy Guggenheim*, pp. 80–81.
14 Guggenheim, *Out of This Century*, p. 124.
15 Prose, *Peggy Guggenheim*, p. 83.
16 Guggenheim, *Out of This Century*, p. 128.
17 Ibid.
18 Dearborn, *Mistress of Modernism*, pp. 130, 135.
19 Guggenheim, *Out of This Century*, p. 159.

CHAPTER 10

1 Letter from Peggy Guggenheim to Peggy Waldman, May 1937, in Guggenheim Collection archive.
2 Guggenheim, *Out of This Century*, p. 157.
3 Guggenheim, *Out of This Century*, p. 159.
4 Ibid., p. 162.
5 Dearborn, *Mistress of Modernism*, p. 158.
6 Ibid., p. 152.
7 Guggenheim, *Out of This Century*, p. 175.
8 Dearborn, *Mistress of Modernism*, pp. 156–9.
9 Guggenheim, *Out of This Century*, p. 188.
10 Dearborn, *Mistress of Modernism*, p. 186.
11 Guggenheim, *Out of This Century*, p. 198.
12 Dearborn, *Mistress of Modernism*, p. 189.
13 Guggenheim, *Out of This Century*, p. 205.
14 Ibid., p. 210.
15 Ibid., p. 218.
16 Ibid., p. 228.
17 Ibid., p. 231.
18 Ibid., p. 244.

CHAPTER 11

1 Guggenheim, *Out of This Century*, p. 246.
2 Prose, *Peggy Guggenheim*, p. 126.
3 Guggenheim, *Out of This Century*, p. 248.
4 Dearborn, *Mistress of Modernism*, p. 211.
5 Prose, *Peggy Guggenheim*, p. 175.
6 Dearborn, *Mistress of Modernism*, p. 182.
7 Guggenheim, *Out of This Century*, p. 245.
8 Dearborn, *Mistress of Modernism*, p. 221.
9 Guggenheim, *Out of This Century*, p. 256.
10 Ibid., p. 265.
11 Dearborn, *Mistress of Modernism*, p. 227.
12 Ibid., p. 219.
13 Ibid., p. 238.
14 Guggenheim, *Out of This Century*, p. 276.
15 From interview in *Peggy Guggenheim: Art Addict*.
16 Charles Seliger quoted in Dearborn, *Mistress*

of Modernism, p. 282;
Motherwell quoted
in ibid., p. 239; letter
from Joseph Levy,
in Guggenheim
Collection archive.

17 Guggenheim, Out
of This Century, p. 279.

18 Ibid., p. 277.

19 Ibid., p. 288.

20 Dearborn, Mistress
of Modernism, p. 253.

21 Ibid., p. 273.

22 Ibid., p. 283.

23 Ibid., p. 259.

24 Ibid., p. 260.

25 Ibid.

26 Ibid., p. 279.

27 Gill, Peggy Guggenheim,
pp. 348–9.

28 Letters from Peggy
Guggenheim to
Emily Coleman,
October 1944, and
to Laurence Vail,
n.d., in Guggenheim
Collection archive.

29 Dearborn, Mistress
of Modernism, p. 291.

30 Letter from P.G.
to L.V., n.d., in
Guggenheim
Collection archive.

31 Dearborn, Mistress
of Modernism, p. 291.

32 Gill, Peggy Guggenheim,
p. 365.

33 Ibid.

CHAPTER 12

1 Letter from P.G. to
Clement Greenberg,
in Dearborn, Mistress
of Modernism, p. 309.

2 Dearborn, Mistress
of Modernism, p. 297.

3 Ibid., p. 262.

4 Guggenheim, Out
of This Century,
p. 329.

5 Dearborn, Mistress
of Modernism, p. 315.

6 Guggenheim, Out
of This Century, p. 336.

7 Ibid., p. 341.

8 Ibid., p. 354.

9 Ibid., p. 334.

10 Gill, Peggy Guggenheim,
p. 380.

11 Dearborn, Mistress
of Modernism, p. 317.

12 Guggenheim, Out
of this Century, p. 340.

13 Dearborn, Mistress
of Modernism, p. 319.

14 Gill, Peggy Guggenheim,
p. 443.

15 Ibid., p. 377.

16 Guggenheim, Out
of This Century, p. 368.

17 Gill, Peggy Guggenheim,
p. 382.

18 Dearborn, Mistress
of Modernism, p. 326.

19 Ibid., p. 325.

20 Gill, Peggy Guggenheim,
p. 388.

CHAPTER 13

1 Guggenheim, Out
of This Century, p. 350.

2 Ibid., p. 353.

3 Ibid., p. 359.

4 Ibid., p. 361.

5 Ibid., p. 347.

6 Dearborn, Mistress
of Modernism, p. 331.

7 Ibid., p. 329.

8 Gill, Peggy Guggenheim,
p. 428.

9 Dearborn, Mistress
of Modernism, p. 323.

10 Guggenheim, Out
of This Century, p. 381.

11 Prose, Peggy
Guggenheim, p. 169.

12 Dearborn, Mistress
of Modernism, p. 341.

13 Ibid., p. 364.

14 Guggenheim, Out
of This Century, p. xii.

15 Dearborn, Mistress
of Modernism, p. 339.

16 Ibid., p. 359.

17 Ibid., p. 330.

18 Guggenheim, Out
of This Century, p. 370.

19 Gill, Peggy Guggenheim,
p. 429.

20 Dearborn, Mistress
of Modernism, p. 360.

21 Ibid., p. 190.

22 Guggenheim, Out
of This Century, p. 372.

23 From interview in
Peggy Guggenheim: Art
Addict.

24 Gill, Peggy Guggenheim,
p. 443.

25 Ibid., p. 439.

26 Ibid., p. 433.

27 Ibid., p. 441.

28 Gore Vidal, in
Guggenheim, Out
of This Century, p. xiv.

29 Gill, Peggy Guggenheim,
p. 448.

BIBLIOGRAPHY

The correspondence between Luisa Casati and Gabriele D'Annunzio has been collected in Raffaella Castagnola (ed.), *Infiniti auguri alla nomade*. Most of the excerpts quoted have been translated from the Italian by Eliza Apperly.

The letters between Doris Castlerosse and Winston Churchill are held in the Churchill Papers collection at the Churchill Archives Centre, Churchill College, Cambridge.

Papers relating to Peggy Guggenheim and the history of the Palazzo Venier dei Leoni can be found in the archives of the Peggy Guggenheim Collection, Venice.

Ackroyd, Peter, *Venice, Pure City* (London, 2009).

Acton, Harold, *Memoirs of an Aesthete* (London, [1948] 1984).

Amory, Mark, *Lord Berners: The Last Eccentric* (London, [1998] 1999).

Attwood, Tony, *The Complete Guide to Asperger's Syndrome* (London, 2008).

Bates-Batcheller, Tryphosa, *Glimpses of Italian Court Life* (New York, 1906).

Beaton, Cecil, *The Glass of Fashion* (London, 1954).

Beaton, Cecil, *The Unexpurgated Beaton Diaries*, ed. Hugo Vickers (London, 2002).

Benzi, Fabio, Gioia Mori, and Daniela Ferretti, *La Divina Marchesa. Arte e vita di Luisa Casati dalla Belle Époque agli anni folli* (The Art and Life of Luisa Casati, from the Belle Epoque to the Roaring Twenties), exhibition catalogue (Milan, 2014).

Bohn, Willard, *The Other Futurism: Futurist Activity in Venice, Padua and Verona* (Ontario, 2004).

Bosworth, R. J. B., *Italian Venice: A History* (London, 2014).

Buckle, Richard, *Diaghilev* (London, 1979).

Castagnola, Raffaella (ed.), *Infiniti auguri alla nomade: Carteggio con Luisa Casati Stampa* (Milan, 2000).

Cecchi, Dario, *Giovanni Boldini* (Turin, 1962).

Cecchi, Dario, *Coré: Vita e dannazione della marchesa Casati* (Bologna, 1986).

Chisolm, Ann, and Michael Davie, *Beaverbrook: A Life* (London, 1992).

Coleman, Emily, *Rough Draft: The Modernist Diaries of Emily Holmes Coleman, 1929–37*, ed. Elizabeth Podnieks (Newark, DE, 2012).

Cooper, Diana, *The Rainbow Comes and Goes* (London, [1958] 1984).

Cooper, Diana, *The Light of Common Day* (London, [1959] 1984).

Crowley, Roger, *City of Fortune: How Venice Won and Lost a Naval Empire* (London, 2012).

D'Annunzio, Gabriele, *Pleasure*, trans. Alexander Stille (London, 2013); Italian original, *Il Piacere* (1898).

D'Annunzio, Gabriele, *Fire* (London, 1900); Italian original, *Il fuoco* (1900).

D'Annunzio, Gabriele, *Forse che sì, forse che no* (Milan, [1910] 1952).

D'Annunzio, Gabriele, *Notturno*, trans. Stephen Sartarelli (New Haven, CT, 2012); Italian original, *Notturno* (1921).

D'Annunzio, Gabriele, *Cento e cento e cento e cento pagine del Libro segreto di Gabriele d'Annunzio tentato di morire* (Milan, 1935).

Davidson, Susan, and Philip Rylands (eds), *Peggy Guggenheim & Frederick Kiesler: The Story of Art of This Century* (Venice, 2005).

Dearborn, Mary, *Mistress of Modernism: The Life of Peggy Guggenheim* (New York, 2004; London, 2006).

Epstein, Jacob, *Let There Be Sculpture* (New York, 1940).

Faulks, Sebastian, *The Fatal Englishman: Three Short Lives* (London, 1996).

Flanner, Janet, *Paris Was Yesterday* (London, 2003).

Gilbert, Martin, *Churchill: A Life* (London, 2000).

Gill, Anton, *Peggy Guggenheim: The Life of an Art Addict* (London, 2002).

Gold, Arthur, and Robert Fizdale, *Misia: The Life of Misia Sert* (New York, 1980).

Gordon, Lois, *Nancy Cunard: Heiress, Muse, Political Idealist* (New York, 2007).

Guggenheim, Peggy, *Out of This Century* (London, 1979).

Hastings, Selina, *The Red Earl: The Extraordinary Life of the 16th Earl of Huntingdon* (London, 2014).

Herring, Phillip, *Djuna: The Life and Work of Djuna Barnes* (New York, 1995).

Holroyd, Michael, *Augustus John* (London, [1976] 1997).

Hughes-Hallett, Lucy, *The Pike: Gabriele D'Annunzio, Poet, Seducer and Preacher of War* (London, 2013).

John, Augustus, *Autobiography* (London, 1975).

Jullian, Philippe, *D'Annunzio* (London, [1971] 1972).

Leslie, Anita, *Cousin Clare: The Tempestuous Career of Clare Sheridan* (London, 1976).

Mackenzie, Compton, *Extraordinary Women: Theme and Variations* (London, [1928] 1987).

Mackrell, Judith, *Flappers: Six Women of a Dangerous Generation* (London, 2013).

Massine, Léonide, *My Life in Ballet* (London, 1968).

Masters, Anthony, *Rosa Lewis: An Exceptional Edwardian* (London, 1978).

Mazzeo, Tiler J., *The Hotel on Place Vendôme* (New York, 2014).

Morley, Sheridan, *Gertrude Lawrence* (New York, 1981).

Morris, James, *Venice* (London, 1960).

Mosley, Leonard, *Castlerosse* (London, 1956).

Mosto, Francesco da, *Francesco's Venice* (London, 2004).

Motion, Andrew, *The Lamberts: George, Constant and Kit* (London, 1986).

Nichols, Beverley, *A Case of Human Bondage* (London, 1966).

Peggy Guggenheim: Art Addict, film, dir. Lisa Immordino Vreeland (UK, 2015).

Prose, Francine, *Peggy Guggenheim: The Shock of the Modern* (New Haven, CT, 2015).

Purnell, Sonia, *Clementine: The Life of Mrs. Winston Churchill* (New York, 2015).

Ray, Man, *Self-Portrait* (Boston, 1963).

Richardson, John, *A Life of Picasso, Vol. 3* (London, 2007).

Rosenthal, Margaret F., *The Honest Courtesan: Veronica Franco, Citizen and Writer in 16th-Century Venice* (Chicago, 1992).

Rubinstein, Arthur, *My Young Years* (London, 1973).

Ryersson, Scot D., and Michael Orlando Yaccarino, *Infinite Variety: The Life and Legend of the Marchesa Casati* (Minneapolis, [1999] 2004).

Ryersson, Scot D., and Michael Orlando Yaccarino, *The Marchesa Casati: Portraits of a Muse* (New York, 2009).

Scarlini, Luca, *Memorie di un'opera d'arte: La Marchesa casati* (Florence, 2014).

Schanke, Robert A., *That Furious Lesbian: The Story of Mercedes De Acosta*, (Carbondale, IL, 2003).

Schiaparelli, Elsa, *Shocking Life* (London, [1954] 2007).

Searle, Ruth, *Asperger Syndrome in Adults* (London, 2010).

Secrest, Meryle, *Between Me and Life: A Biography of Romaine Brooks* (London, 1976).

Sjeng, Scheijen, *Diaghilev: A Life* (London, 2009).

Souhami, Diana, *Cecil & Greta* (London, 1994).

Souhami, Diana, *Wild Girls: Paris, Sappho and Art: The Lives and Loves of Natalie Barney and Romaine Brooks* (London, 2004).

Thomasson, Anna, *A Curious Friendship: The Story of a Bluestocking and a Bright Young Thing* (London, 2015).

Thomson, George Malcolm, *Lord Castlerosse: His Life and Times* (London, 1973).

Vickers, Hugo, *Cecil Beaton* (New York, 1985).

Weld, Jacqueline Bograd, *Peggy: The Wayward Guggenheim* (New York, 1986).

West, Rebecca, *Selected Letters*, ed. Bonnie Kime Scott (New Haven, CT, 2000).

Wishart, Michael, *High Diver: An Autobiography* (London, 1978).

Young, Desmond, *Try Anything Twice* (London, 1963).

Zinovieff, Sofka, *The Mad Boy, Lord Berners, My Grandmother and Me* (London, 2014).

ACKNOWLEDGMENTS

When Peggy Guggenheim wrote about Venice in 1960, she described her relationship with the city in the language of a love affair. 'After your first visit you are destined to return at every possible chance or with every possible excuse. There is no staying away for long.' In researching this book I have been very fortunate in having my own love affair with Venice subsidized by a Society of Authors' K. Blundell Trust award. I also owe a debt of gratitude to Emanuela Caldirola and Maria Stefanoni, the press team for the Venice Biennale Dance and Theatre Festival, whose invitations to cover the Dance Festival over the years have allowed me to deepen my knowledge of Venice and its unique cultural life.

Special thanks must also go to Maria Stefanoni for putting me in touch with Claudia Zini, to whom I'm indebted for helping me with research into property deeds held in the State Archives of Venice.

For the chapters on Luisa Casati I want to thank Daniela Feretti, curator at the Fortuny Museum, and Gioia Mori for their help and insights, and especially Eliza Apperly for her wonderfully elegant and perceptive translations of the Casati-D'Annunzio correspondence. Special thanks also to Scot Ryersson and Michael Orlando Yaccarino. Their painstaking research into Luisa's history and their two biographical works have been an invaluable resource to me, and they have themselves been very generous in their personal support and assistance.

For the Doris Castlerosse chapters I owe an enormous debt of gratitude to the Delevingne family for supporting the project and in particular to Caroline Delevingne and her daughter Edwina Gieve, who provided vivid and detailed accounts of Doris's history and allowed me to make use of family papers and photographs. Hugo Vickers was extremely generous with his time and with his immense fund of knowledge, and thanks to him also for permission to quote from the unpublished diaries of Cecil Beaton (© The Literary Executors of the late Sir Cecil Beaton). Richard Toye gave me the benefit of his own scholarly research into the life of Winston Churchill, and I also want to thank Louise Watling, archivist of the Churchill Archive in Cambridge.

The Peggy Guggenheim chapters were written with the benefit of several distinguished biographies, notably those of Mary Dearborn and Francine Prose. Philip Rylands, director of the Peggy Guggenheim Collection, was very generous with his time, as were members of his team, including Alexia Boro and Silvio Ruffert Veronese, Head Librarian in the PGC Archives. Costandiz Kizis, Evgenios Matthiopoulos and JoAnn Locktov were very helpful to me when I was looking into Carolo Scarpa's work on the Biennale pavilions in 1948.

Permission from Carlton Books to quote from Peggy's memoir *Out of This Century* is gratefully acknowledged.

I want to thank my agent, Clare Alexander, and my commissioning editor, Jamie Camplin, for seeing the possibilities in this book so early on, and the rest of the editorial teams at both Thames & Hudson and Regan Arts, including Sophy Thompson and Amanda Vinnicombe. Camilla Rockwood's close reading and lucid commentary on the late stages of the book went very far beyond the call of duty; Jen Moore has been a kind and patient proof reader; and Sally Nicholls found beautiful and unexpected images of Venice.

During the writing of this book Paul and Kate Bogan offered me fantastic hospitality, as did Gillian Darley and Michael Horovitz. Many friends, among them Debra Craine, were patient sounding boards.

And as always, my best love and thanks to my family.

AUTHOR'S NOTE

Given the close intersection of private and public lives in this book, it has been difficult to maintain a consistent line on the use of surnames and first names. In the case of major historical figures, like Winston Churchill, I have tended to use the latter only at key moments of intimacy, or familiarity in the narrative; however, there are other eminent figures, such as Max Ernst, whose first names I have used more freely – Ernst always featured as Max in Peggy's own writing, and so it felt natural to take my cue from her.

In the matter of money, it has been too unwieldy to translate all sums to modern values, especially given the extreme fluctuations in exchange rates at certain periods. However the following table, using the Retail Price Index (RPI), gives a rough guide to the sums that were inherited, spent and owed by Luisa, Doris and Peggy at different points in their lives.

1910s £1 = $4.70; 25 Fr. francs; 25 lire
1920s £1 = $3.50; 50 Fr. francs; 140 lire
1930s £1 = $3.50; 95 Fr. francs; 90 lire
1940s £1 = $4.00; 183 Fr. francs; 100–500 lire
1950s £1 = $2.80; 116 Fr. francs; 1650 lire
1970s £1 = $2.50; 973 Fr. francs; 1500–3000 lire

SOURCES OF ILLUSTRATIONS

INDEX